T0380707

1000 Novelty & Fad Dances

A Guide to How These are Danced

First Edition - 1 January 2009

COMPILED By *CoupleDanceWorld* Under the Direction of THOMAS L. NELSON

1000 Novelty & Fad Dances

A Guide to How These are Danced

First Edition - 1 January 2009

COMPILED By *CoupleDanceWorld* Under the Direction of THOMAS L. NELSON

AuthorHouse™
1663 Liberty Drive, Suite 200
Bloomington, IN 47403
www.authorhouse.com
Phone: 1-800-839-8640

International Standard Book Number 978-1-4389-2638-4 (sc)

Library of Congress Catalog Card Number *2008910146*

Copyright @ 2009 by Thomas L. Nelson

Thomas L. Nelson
CoupleDanceWorld
8581 Owensmouth Ave., Canoga Park, CA 91304

First Edition
First published by AuthorHouse 1/27/2009

Printed in the United States of America
Bloomington, Indiana

This book is printed on acid-free paper.

    With the hope that this book provides the world with something useful, these pages and data may be copied for any purpose, except for those purposes that could be in direct **financial** competition with this book. Otherwise, except as permitted under the Copyright Act of 1976, this book may not be reproduced in whole or in part in any manner. Tom Nelson has asserted his right under the Copyright, Designs and Patents Act, 1988, to be identified as the author of this work.

PREFACE and OVERVIEW

This *Novelty & Fad Dances* Encyclopedia has been derived by extracting all of these **1000 Novelty and Fad Dances** data out of our massive *Dancing and Related Skills* Encyclopedia, which covers all types of **C**oupledancing and the like. Both books have been written by Tom Nelson, Director of *CoupleDanceWorld*. If one cannot find the particular description referring to a certain item one might be seeking that clarifies some dance listed herein, one can be certain to find it by consulting this later, volumnous, above-named Encyclopedia.

This book begins with an alphabetical listing index entitled "Novelty-and-Fad Genre," and is followed alphabetically by those listed **Novelty-and-Fad** Dances, Routines, Patterns, Figures, Maneuvers, and Movements, which are usually described in great detail, and have been invented by creative people.

Fad-Dances and **Novelty-Dances** have similar characteristics. **Fad-Dances** are those which are characterized by a short-time burst of popularity, while **Novelty-Dances** are typically longer lasting in popularity. This is because **Novelty-Dances** seem to be more unique and more humorous or more humor-invoking than are **Fad-Dances**.

Novelty Dances are sometimes called **Party Dances** or **Dance-Party Dances**, which are terms for Coupledances characterized by humor. Meant to be funny, **Novelty Dances** are laughable, comical, and/or capricious, and probably verge upon silliness on the part of participants. The name might be unusual. Perhaps quirky and containing unusual Steps, they may carry a special sense of newness or uniqueness, but might not necessarily have ever been in fashion or popular. A **Novelty Dance** may or may not be associated with a specific time period. But if it is perhaps "*timeless*," that certain **Novelty Dance** may also have been a **Fad Dance** that has simply remained popular for a longer time period.

Dancing Style **Fads** have always been a part of Social Dancing. **Fad Dances** are sometimes called a **Dance-Craze** or **Dance-Mania**. These are terms for Coupledances which are characterized by a limited time period of popularity or of at least being in vogue. **Fad Dances** have sometimes glided smoothly into tradition after their newness has faded, or they have simply faded away into oblivion. In general, **Fad Dance**s have been non-traditional, non-standard and/or non-classic dances. **Fad Dances** are in fashion only at the time of their popularity. Since a particular **Fad Dance** is in vogue associated with a definite popularity time period, that dance generally evokes nostalgia when encountered or danced at some later time. Some sample dances that were once only a **Fad** but have since become dance tradition are the Waltz, Charleston, and Jitterbug. **Fad Dances** have often been choreographed to an eponymous and/or current song. Certain movies and music videos would often be their source of exposure to their public, and dance magazines would sometimes print the proposed dance steps. Some particular **Fad Dances** are meant to be danced only with a partner, but some are danced solo, and then there are some meant to be danced in groups. Some **Fad Dances** are danced only Freestyle, and some could only be distinguished by their Style-of-Movement, (Twist, Shake, Swim, Pony, Hitchhike, etc.) Only a few **Fad Dances** have survived into the present; perhaps in name only within some recognized dance, such as a current Step, e.g., *Suzie-Q* or *Shimmy*, or as the name of a Style, e.g., *Mashed-Potato*, or the like.

(See Timeless-Dances, Dance-Craze, Dance-Mania, Dance-Party, and Bash.)

Timeless-Dances: *Traditional, Standard* and/or *Classic*, **Timeless-Dances** is a Term for Coupledances that have weathered the course of years and have survived until now. These are dances that have remained popular, or simply in vogue, such as the Genres of the *Waltz, Foxtrot, Tango, Rumba,* and *Swing.* Possibly a certain **Timeless-Dance** has survived only as the name of a current Step, e.g., *Suzie-Q* or *Shimmy*, or as that of a Style, e.g., *Mashed-Potato*, or the like.

Dance-Craze: A General Coupledance Term for some brief, short-lived dance fad, fashion or rage; or, a dance that is popular or in demand; or, an extravagant liking or enthusiasm for the dance.

   "A day I don't dance is a day I don't live." -- Anonymous
   "To be on the dancefloor is life; the rest is waiting." -- Anonymous
   Same as **Fad Dances**. Similar to or same as **Dance-Mania**.

Dance-Mania: (*MAY-nee-ah*) A General Coupledance Term for an inordinately intense and extraordinary enthusiasm for the dance; or, an exaggerated or irrational craving for, or an infatuation with a particular dance.

   "Dancing is the loftiest, the most moving, the most beautiful of the arts, because it is no mere translation or abstraction from life; it is life itself." -- Havelock Ellis
   "Dance like there's nobody watching, love like you'll never get hurt.
    Sing like there's nobody listening, live like there's heaven on earth." -- Anonymous
   "Dancing is the only art of which we ourselves are the stuff." -- Anonymous
   "Every day I count wasted in which there has been no dancing." -- Nietzche
   "If you're going to walk on thin ice, you might as well dance!" -- Anonymous
   "Those who dance are thought mad by those who hear not the music." -- Anonymous
   "To dance is to live!" -- Anonymous
   Similar to or the same as **Dance-Craze**, and **Fad Dances**.

Dance-Party: A General Coupledance Term for a Social Dancing Party. A **Dance-Party** refers to a social interaction gathering for pleasure, usually involving a certain particular type of Coupledancing; an occasion in which people assemble for their own entertainment.
   Same as a **Bash**.

Bash: A slang Term for a kind of **Dance-Party**. The following is from the *"Encyclopedia of Word and Phrase Origins"* by Robert Hendrickson:

   *"**bash**. Meaning a blow or even a wild party, bash seems to have originated in the world of boxing, the first use of the word recorded in the 19th century, when a basher was a prizefighter. No one is sure whether the word is a blendof 'bang' and 'smash,' or simply of echoic origin."*

   "Common sense and a sense of humor are the same thing, moving at different speeds. A sense of humor is just common sense, dancing." -- Clive James
   Same as a **Dance-Party**.

ABOUT THE AUTHOR

To begin with, about the Dance Specialist and compiler in charge of this book, Tom Nelson wishes to thank his contributors and helpers. He wishes to thank his many teachers, both for private and for group Coupledance lessons he has had through the years. These include: Phil Adams, Neale Allen, Lee Atkinson, Art Balloy, Skippy Blair, George and Sharri Blume, Ron and Lois Cassard, Felix Chavez, Opal and Joe Cohen, Dean and Mary Collins, Steve and Elizabeth Cullip, Lisa Fay, Alice Ferris, Ray Fox, Ed and Diane Gaines, Hi and Cookie Gibson, Silky Griffith and Betty, Laure Haile, Ray and Kitty Harrison, Frank Hermann, Finn and Berthe Hoffler, Tom Hyatt, Jonathan and Sylvia, Michael and Mari Kiehm, Lori Llamas, John March, Mickey and Clara Marshall, Bill Martin, Roger and Shirley McAndrews, Margaret Michael, John Michaelson, Fred and Keiko Migliorini, Carol Montez, John Morton, Sherry Novak, Eddie and Audrey Palmquist, Dan Rand and Kendy, Ricky and Kay Sexton, Ken and Shiela Sloan, Sonny Watson, Jill Weston, Ron and Nancy Yanke, Glenn and Lezlie Yata, and numerous others.

Tom says,"About me? I'm a `Dance Specialist'. My trade is Coupledancing." The Author, with more than seventy years of constant, multiple and diverse kinds of Coupledancing under his belt, is a learned authority about the contents of this text. He is uniquely qualified with more than 26 years of teaching Coupledancing, mostly in his own `CoupleDanceWorld' studio. Much herein was learned through his own practice and discipline.

At the age of six, in 1931, Tom was formally taught Coupledance routines with his sister in a dance school run by his aunt. By the age of 14, Tom was already proficient and experienced on the dancefloor at many dances. He was an accomplished Coupledancer when he went in the service at 17 for World War II. He was fortunate to dance to many of the "big bands". Tom swore to himself "to become the best dancer in the world." A Cadet then Pilot in the Army Air Force, he Coupledanced at every chance, at USO's, hotels, dance halls, even in a Navy-only wharf dive and at the Hollywood Paladium. He loved to dance the Lindy. He was sometimes able to accurately guess where in the U.S. a lady was from, by her style of dancing. Tom could perceive different dance trends in various parts of the country, especially in how different Swings were danced. On occupation duty, Tom danced much with Tokyo ladies, Seoul ladies and with Manila ladies.

Back to college in 1947, Tom picked up the Balboa and the Samba. Later, Tom learned the Mambo, ChaCha, the Twist, the Pony, Watusi, Mashed Potato, and many other dances. By 1970, Tom had become the proverbial "Studio-Hopper," with formal lessons in West-Coast-Swing, different Hustles, International and Latin, and in most all Coupledances. Tom has logged many thousands of hours on the dancefloor. Tom began teaching Coupledancing in 1977, and began Roundancing in 1980, which he has continued with a relish to date.

KEY DEFINITIONS and TERMINOLOGY

Description of Dances: That known by the author are in sufficient detail herein to completely describe the subject term, position, action, movement, figure, or pattern, and the like.

Defining Elsewhere: Capitalized words or terms are further defined elsewhere, by alphabetized paragraphs of their own. This "defined elsewhere" is within the "parent" *Dancing and Related Skills Encyclopedia.*

Footwork: Unless otherwise noted, partners always Coupledance the Pattern, Figure or subject-item upon opposing feet, in mirror-image, rather than upon their identical feet.

Defining Left and Right Footwork: Always in *Italics*, **Right Feet** words begin Capitalized while **left feet** begin in lower-case letters, throughout this book.

Turning Right and Left: "Clockwise" and "Counter-Clockwise" are viewed as if the clock face is on the Dancefloor, not on the ceiling.

Defining Rotations: With noted exceptions, rotation amounts notated herein, for turns, swivels, spirals, etc., refer to foot-rotation, and not necessarily to the amount of body-rotation.

Items with Multiple Names: All the various item names known at time of printing are listed. The name selected for listing first in the writeup herein is not necessarily the name preferred by some, but is the name the writer considers the most commonly used.

Item Names with Multiple Meanings: Certain names have multiple listings or definitions herein for clarity.

Copyrights: Every effort has been taken to locate, inform and receive approval from owners of copyrighted material reproduced within these pages.

Index
for at least 1000
Novelty & Fad Dances

Novelty-and-Fad Genre or **Fad Genre:**   The following is the listing of miscellaneous Coupledances, Singular-Dances, and Patterns. **Fad-Dances** and **Novelty-Dances** have similar characteristics. **Fad-Dances** are those which are characterized by a short-time burst of popularity, while **Novelty-Dances** are typically longer lasting in popularity. This is because **Novelty-Dances** seem to be more unique and more humorous or more humor-invoking than are **Fad-Dances**. (See Dance-Party, and Bash.)

Looking under **Amalgamation-of-Dances**, the following **Novelty-and-Fad** Dances, Routines, Patterns, Figures, Maneuvers, and Movements are listed below as an index, and all are described in detail elsewhere, alphabetically in this encyclopedia. What follows is a total of **1,029** different entries, of which the preponderance are 673 entries for the 1960s, and 96 entries for the 1980s:

Aardvark-Walk - 1960s | Aba-Dabba-Doo - 1960s | Abe-Kabbible - date? | Adler-Sock - 1960s | African-Anteater-Ritual - 1980s | African-Strut - 1960s | Afro-Shingaling - 1960s | Afro-Twist - 1960s | Agent-007 - 1960s | Air-Guitar - 1990s | Alabama-Shake - 1960s | Alexander - 1913 | Alf - 1980s | Algorithm-March - date? | Ali-Shuffle - 1967 | Alley-Cat - 1962 | Alley-Oop - 1960s | Alligator(1) - 1963 | Alligator(2) - 1980s | Alligator-Stomp - ~1994 | American-Hustle - late 1970s | A-Minor-Drag - 1910s-20s | And-Away-We-Go! - 1960s | And-Change-And-Change-And - date? | Animal-Dances - 1912 & 1960s | Ant - 1980s | Ants - 1960s | Ape - 1960s | AppleJack - 1948 | Apple-Jacks - date? | Armstrong - 1990s | Arthur - 1960s | Aunt-Jemima-Slide - 1914 | Axel-Rose - 1980s |

Baboon - 1960s | Baby-Baby - 1960s | Baby-Beatle-Walk - 1960s | Baby-Walk - 1960s | Baby-Workout - 1963 | Back-the-Bus-Up - 1980s | Bacon-Fat - 1952 | Bad-Baboon - 1960s | Ballin'-The-Jack - 1914 | Bal-Trot - 2000s | Bamba (A Murray) - date? | Bambuco - 1950s | Banana-Split - 1960s | Bang - 1960s | Barefootin' - 1966 | Barracuda - 1966 | Basketball - 1960s | Bastella - 1960s | Batman - 1960s | Bat-Tusi - 1960s | Beatle-Boogie - 1960s | Beatle-Bounce - 1960s | Beatle-Stomp - 1960s | Bedrock - 1980s | Beetle-Squash - 1960s | Beetle-Walk - 1960s | Behemoth - 1960s | Belinda - 1980s | Belly-Dance - 1890s | Belly-Roll - date? | Bend-Down-Low - 1967 | Bend-It! - 1960s | Big-Apple - 1937 | Big-City-Stomp - 1960s | Big-Egg - 1960s | Big-'M' - 1960s | Big-Willie - 1969 | Billy-Jo - 1960s | Bingo-Boy - 1980s | Bin-Laden - 2000s | Bird - 1960s | Bird-Dog - 1966 | Birdland - 1960s | Black-Bottom - 1927 | Blackout-Stroll - 1939 | Black-Stomp - 1960s | Blakes-Beat - 1960s | Block - 1960s | BlueBeat - 1964 | Blue-Chip - 1960s | Body-Popping - 2000s | Bomba - 1996 | Bombay - 1960s | Bombie - 1960s | Boney-Maronie - 1959 | Bongo-Hop - 1960s | Boogaloo - 1960s | Boogaloo-Popeye - 1960s | Boogie-Back - 1920s | Boogie-Back-and-Forward-Shorty - 1920s | Boogie-Down - 1980s | Boogler - 1960s | Boomerang - 1965 | Boomps-A-Daisy - 1939 or 1940 | Booty-Green - 1960s | Bop - 1956 | Boss-Walk - 1960s | Boston-Dip - 1912 | Boston-Hop - 1960s | Boston-Monkey - 1960s | Boston-Waltz - 1840s | Bounce - 1965 | Box - 1960s | Boxer - 1960s | Brain - 1960s | Break-A-Way - 1926 | Break-Dancing - 1980s | Breakdown - 1960s | Break-Endings - 1930s | Bristol-Stomp - 1961-62 | Broadway-Freeze - 1968 | Broadway-Hustle - 1970s | Broadway-Sissy - 1960s | Broadway-Walk - 1967 | Broken-Hip - 1960s | Buckingham - 1966 | Bug - 1960s | Bugg - 1970s-80s | Bull-Frog-Hop - 1912-14 | Bull-Nose-Stomp - 1960s | Bump - 1975 | Bumpsi - 1960s | Bunny-Hop - 1950s | Bunny-Hug - 1910 or 1912 | Burn - 1960s | Bush-Dance - date? | Bushman - 1969 | Bus-Stop - 1970s | Butterfly - 1990s | Buzzard-Lope - 1910s |

(Continued)

                    (Continued)

Novelty-and-Fad Index: (Continued)

Fairy-Dance - 1980s | Fall-Off-the-Log - 1920s | Fancy-Feet - 1980s | Fanny-Bump - 1900s-1910s | Fatman - 1965 | Fila - 1980s | Fine-Twine - 1960s | Finger-Poppin' - 1960 | Fink - 1966 | Finnjenica - 1964 | Fish - 1966 | Fishin'-Pole - 1960s | Fishing-Pole - 1980s | Fish-Tail - 1960s | Fishtail-Shag - 1930s | Fish-Walk - 1913 | Fishy - 1980s | Flake - 1960s | Flamingo - date? | Flapper-Flip - 1960s | Flea - 1960s | Flea-Hop - 1950s | Flick - 1960s | Flintstone-Flop - 1960s | Flip - 1960s | Flip-Flop - 1960s | Float - 1960s | Florida-Twist - 1960s | Fly - 1965 | Fly-Back - date? | Foot-Boogie - date? | Footsee - 1960s | Foot-Stomping - 1960 | Forty-Five(1) - 1966 | Forty-Five(2) - date? | Four-Corners - 1970s | Four-Count - date? | Fox - 1960s | Frankenstein-Walk - 1960s | Freak(1) - 1965 | Freak(2) - 1977 or 1978 | Freaking - 1980s | Freddy - 1965 | Freeze - 1950s-60s | French Tango - date? | Fridge - 1960s | Frog - 1963 | Frug - 1962 | Fumigate-Funky-Broadway - 1960s | Funky-Alien - 1980s | Funky-Broadway - 1966-69 | Funky-Bull - 1960s | Funky-Butt - 1900s-1910s | Funky-Buzzard - 1960s | Funky-Chicken - 1960s | Funky-Disposition - 1969 | Funky-Donkey - 1960s | Funky-Fat-Man - 1960s | Funky-Horse - 1960s | Funky-Hump - 1960s | Funky-Jerk - 1960s | Funky-Line - 1960s | Funky-Mississippi - 1960s | Funky-Penguin - 1968 | Funky-Soul-Shake - 1960s | Funky-Strut - 1960s | Funky-Twist - 1980s | Funky-Walk - 1969 |

Gaby-Glide - 1915 | Gallop - 1960s | Gamma-Goochie - 1960s | Garrett - 1980s | Gator(1) - 1960s | Gator(2) - 1980s | Gawk-'n'-Stroll - 1960s | Gene-Chandler - 1960s | Georgia-Grind - 1930s | Georgia-Slop - 1962 | Get-Down - 1965 | Get-E-Up - 1960s | Get-It - 1968 | Gigolo - 1980s | Ginza - 1960s | Girls-Just-Wanna-Have-Fun - 1980s | Glide - 1960s | Glue - 1960s | Goat - 1960s | Goblin-Trot - 1960s | Go-Go - 1960s | GoGo-Dancer - 1960s | Go-Go-Wine - 1990s | Goodfoot - 1960s | Good-Times-Stomp - 1960s | Goose - 1960s | Gorilla - 1963 | Go-Song - 1980s | Gotham-Gobble - 1912-1914 | Granny - 1960s | Graple - 1980s | Graveyard-Cha-Cha - 1960s | Greasy-Chicken - 1957 | Gremmie - 1960s | Grind(1) - 1900s-1910s | Grind(2) - 1970 | Grind-Snake - 1930s | Grizzly-Bear - 1889 | Grunt - 1960s | Guapacha - 1950s | Guess - 1980s | Guitar-Boogie-Stomp - 1960s | Gully - 1960s |

Hammer - 1960s | Hammer-Dance - 1980s | Hand-Jive - 1959 | Hand-Jive Routine - date? | Hand-Jive-Workout - 1960s | Hangin'-Tough - 1980s | Hangman - date? | Hang-the-Meringue - 1959 | Hanky-Panky - 1960s | Happy-Feet - 1980s | Harlem-Shuffle - 1964 | Harlem-Tango - 1960s | Harvest-Moon Tango - date? | Headache - 1980s | Heatwave - 1964 | Heel-and-Toe - 2000s | Hello-Kitty - 1980s | Hip - 1960s | Hip-Drop - 1969 or 1970 | HipHop-Lindy - 2005 | Hip-Huggin' - 1960s | Hippies Waltz - 1960s | Hippy-Hippy-Shake - 1959 | Hitch-Hiker - 1960s | Hitch-It-To-Horse - 1960s | Hit-It! - 1960s | Hitler - 1960s | Hoe-Down - date? | Hog - 1964 | Hokey-Cokey - 1944 | Hokey-Pokey - 1950s | Honey-Dipper - 1960s | Hoochi-Coochi-Coo - 1960s | Hoochy-Koochy - 1899 | Hook - 1965 | Hook-and-Boogit - 1972 | Hook-and-Slink - 1969 | Hook-Unwind - date? | Hook-Wind - date? | Hoopy-Doo - 1960s | Hootch - 1960s | Hootier - 1980s | Hop - 1967 | Hopple-Popple - 1966 | Hop-Scotch - 1960s | Hornet - 1960s | Horse - 1960s | Horse-Trot - 1913 | Hot-Pastrami - 1960s | Huckee-Buck - 1965 | Hucklebuck - 1940s-1950s | Huddle - 1960s | Hug-Me-Close - 1912 | Hula-Dance - date? | Hullabaloo - 1960s | Hullaballoon - 1960s | Hullie-Gullie - 1963-1964 | Hully-Gully-Bongo -1960s | Hully-Gully-Rock - 1960s | Hump - 1960s | Hump-Back - 1966 | Humphrey-Stomp - 1960s | Humpty-Dance - date? | Hunch - 1965 | Hustle - late 1970s | Ickey-Shuffle - 1980s | Itch - 1900s-1910s | Itchy-Koo - 1960s |

(Continued)

<u>**Novelty-and-Fad Index:**</u> (Continued)

Jackie-Gleason - 1960s | Jamaican-Twist - date? | James-Brown - 1960s | James-Brown-Bougelou - 1960s | Jazz-Box - date? | Jed - 1960s | Jelly-Belly - 1960s | Jerk - 1969 | Jerry-Springer - 2000s | Jersey-Bounce - 1960s | Jesse-James - 1967 | Jig-Hop - 1930 | Jingle-Bob - date? | Jivin'-Around - 1960s | Joogie-Boogie - 1960s | Jordan-Stomp - 1960s | Joropo - date? | Jump - 1960s | Jump-and-Hump - 1960s | Jumpen - date? | Junkernoo - 1960s | Junk-Man-Rag - 1912 |

Kangaroo - 1964 | Kangaroo-Dip - 1912-1914 | Kangaroo-Hop - 1914 | Kangaroo-Tail-Twist - 1961 | Kangaroo-Twist - 1965 | Karate - 1960s | Karate-Boogaloo - 1967 | Karate-Monkey - 1960s | Ketchup-Song - date? | Kickapoo(1) - 1904 | Kickapoo(2) - 1960s | Kid-and-Play - 1980s | Kiddie-A-Go-Go - 1965 | King-Kong's-Monkey - 1960s | Klak-Stick-Kick - 1960s | Knees-Up-Mother-Brown - 1956 | Koo-Koo - 1960s | Kosher-Twist - 1960s | Krunch - 1960s | Kwella-Stroll - 1966 |

Lambada - 1990s | Lambda-Nu - date? | Lambeth-Walk - 1938 | Lame-Duck - 1915 | Lanciers - 1870s | L.A.-Stomp - 1968 | Last-Waltz - 1912-1918 | Latin-Boogaloo - 1960s | Latin-Hustle - late 1970s | Latin-Hustle Basic-Step - late 1970s | Latin-Hustle Basic-Walk-In - late 1970s | Lawn-Mower - 1980s | Leg-Kick-Line - 1980s | LeRoc - 1980s-2000s | Letkajenkka - 1960s | Letkiss - 1960s | Letkiss-Trot - 1960s | Letkiss-Walk - 1960s | Limbo - 1962 | Limbo-Rock - 1962 | Little-Apple - 1920s | Little-Peach - 1920s | Locking - 1972 & 1990s | Loco-Motion - 1960s | Loddy-Lo - 1962 | Log - 1964 | Lone-Star-Stomp - 1960s | Lookey-Dookey - 1962 | Loop-De-Loop - 1964 | Love-Bird - 1980s | Louie-Louie - date? | Lowdown-Popcorn - 1960s | Luau - 1960s | Lurch - 1960s |

Mac - 1960s | Macarena - 1996 | Madison - 1960 | Magoo - 1960s | Majestic - 1960s | Malibu - 1960s | Mambo-Boogie - 1960s | Manhattan-Stomp - 1960s | Marathon-Dancing - 1930s | Marchessi - date? | March-of-the-Mods - 1960s | Martian-Hop - 1960s | Marvel - 1960s | Mash - 1960s | Mashi - 1960s | Mashed-Potato - Early 1960s | Mashed-Potatoes - 1960s | Mashed-Taters - 1960s | Massacre-Stomp - 1960s | Matador - 1962 | Matrix - 2000s | Maxixe - 1916 | Melbourne-Shuffle - date? | Mess-Around(1) - 1930s | Mess-Around(2) - 1960s | Mexican-Hat-Dance - date? | Mexican-Stretch - 1960s | Michael-Jackson-Circles - 1980s | Milking-the-Cow - 1980s | Millie - 1960s | Mint - 1960s | Miserloo - date? | Mississippi-Cutback - 1963 | Mod - 1965 | Mojo-Workout - 1960s | Molecule-A-GoGo - 1960s | Money-Musk - 1840s | Monkey - 1964 | Monkey-Bird - 1960s | Monkey-Dog - 1960s | Monkey-Donkey - 1960s | Monkey-Glide - 1912-14 | Monkey-Hop - 1960s | Monkey-Jerk - 1960s | Monkey-Jump - 1960s | Monkey-Shine - 1960s | Monkey-Ska - 1963 | Monkey-Stroll - 1960s | Monkey-Walk - 1960s | Monkey-Wobble - 1960s | Monster-Mash - 1960s | Moochie - 1930 to 1933 | Moon-Step-Twist - 1965 | Moonstomp - 1968 | Moon-Walk - 1980s | Mope - 1960s | Moppety-Stomp - 1960s | Mother-Goose - 1960s | Mother-Popcorn - 1960s | Mountain-Stomp - 1960s | Mouse - 1962 | Mozart-Stomp - 1960s | Mule - 1960s | Mumble-Shing-A-Ling - 1960s | Munch - 1960s | Muppet - 1980s | My-Dog - 1960s |

Na!Na!Na! - 2000s | Nanigo - date? | Napoleon - 1960s | Neo-Tango - 2005 | New-Kids-Move - 1980s | New-Low-Down - 1970 | Nick-Nack-Hully-Gully - 1960s | NightClub Tango - date? | NightLife - 1920s | Night-Stomp - 1960s | Nitty-Gritty - 1965 |

Okey-Cokey - 1944 | Olympic-Shuffle - 1960s | Oobie-Doobie - 1960s | Ooh-Poo-Pah-Doo - 1960s | Op - 1960s | Ops-and-Ops - 1960s | Ostrich - 1960s |

(Continued)

(Continued)

Novelty-and-Fad Index: (Continued)

Skanking - 1980s-2000s | Ska-Punk - date? | Ska-Ride - 1960s | Skate - 1960s | Skate-Boogaloo - 1960s | Skaters'-Sways - late 1970s | Skaters-Waltz - 1930 | Skip - 1960s | Slam-Dancing - 1980s | Slaussen - 1960s | Slauson-Shuffle - 1964 | Slide - 1960s | Slime - 1964 | Slip-and-Slide - 1960s | Slop - 1960s | Slop-and-Slide - 1960s | Sloppy-Twist-A-Fish - 1960s | Slosh - 1972 | Slow-Dance - 1966 | Slow-Drag - 1910s-1920s | Slow-Fizz - 1960s | Slow-Jerk - 1960s | Slow-Locomotion - 1960s | Slurp - 1960s | Smashed-Potato - 1960s | Smock - 1960s | Smurf - Early 1980s | Snacky-Poo - 1960s | Snake(1)&(2) | Snake(3) - 1912-1914 | Snake(4)&(5) - 1970s-1980s | Snake(6) - 1960s | Snake-Hips - 1960s | Snake-Walk - 1960s | Snatch(1) - 1929?-1932? | Snatch(2) - 1965 | Sno-Cone - 1960s | Snoopy - 1960s | Soca - 1980s | Soch - 1960s | Sookie - 1960s | Soul-Clap - 1960s | Soulful-Jerk - 1960s | Soulful-Stomp - 1960s | Soulja-Boy - date? | Soul-Stomp - 1960s | Soul-Struttin' - 1960s | Soul-Train - 1969 | Soul-Twine - 1960s | Soupy-Shuffle-Stomp - 1962 | Spanish-Strut - 1960s | Spanish-Twist - 1960s | Spank-the-Baby - 1920s | Spanns-Stomp - 1960s | Speed-Lindy - 2005 | Spider-Walk - 1960s | Spin - 1960s | Split - 1960s | Spongebob - date? | Sprinkler - 1970s-1980s | Spunky-Onions - 1960s | Squat(1) - 1900s-1910s | Squat(2) - 1960 | Squat-Charleston - 1920s | Stereo-Freeze - 1963 | Steve-Martin - date? | Stewardess - 1980s | Stomp - 1960s | Stomp-Off - 1930s | Stop - 1960s | Stop-Touch - 1960s | Strand - 1962? | Stretch - 1960s | Strobing - date? | Stroke - 1966 | Strokin' - 1980s | Stroll - 1956-1957 | Strut - 1960s | Struttin' - 1960s | Stupidity - 1960s | Stutter-Step - date? | SugarFoot - 1920s | Sugartime-Twist - 1961 | Super-Robot - 1980s | Surf - 1960s | Surfer-Boogie - 1960s | Surfers - 1960s | Surfer-Stomp - 1960s | Surfin'-Bird - 1960s | Surfing-Monkey - 1960s | Surfink - 1960s | Suzie - 1960s | Suzy-Q - 1930s | Swalsa - 2005 | Swango - 2005 | Sway - 1960s | Swim - 1963 | Swing - 1960s | Swing-Out - 1968 | Swing-Rueda - 2005 | Swish-Fish - 1960s | Switch - 1960s | Switch-A-Roo - 1960s | Switchy-Walk - 1960s | Syncopated-Splits - date? |

Tack-Annie - 1920s | Tango-Hustle - late 1970s | Tango-Twist - 1963 | Tantrum - 1960s | Tarzan's-Monkey - 1960s | Tate - 1990s | Teenagers-Waltz - 1960s | Teen-Dancing - 1990s | Teen-Wolf - 1980s | Temtation-Walk - 1960s | Ten-Step - date? | Texas-Hop - 1966 | Texas-Rag - 1900s-1910s | Texas-Tommy - 1913 | Thang - 1900s | Thaxton - 1960s | Thing - 1960s | Thriller - date? | Tiffany - 1980s | Tiger - 1960s | Tiger-Rag - 1906 | Tiger-Walk - 1960s | Tighten-Up - 1968 | Time-Warp - 1980s | Tip-Toe - 1960s | Toe/Heel-Walk - date? | Toe-Splits - 1920s | Toe-Stands - 1980s | Tootsie-Roll - 1960 | Train - 1960s | Train-Stomp - 1960s | Trance - 1960s | Traveling-SugarFoot - 1920s | Trot - 1960s | Truck - 1930s | 'T'-Time - 1960s | Tumba-Cha - 1950s | Turkey-Neck-Stretch - 1960s | Turkey-Trot(1) - 1912 | Turkey-Trot(2) - 1963 | Twine - 1960s | Twirl - 1960s | Twist - 1959 | Twist-and-Freeze - 1960s | Twist-and-Limbo - 1960s | Twist-and-Shout - 1960 | Twister - 1950s | Twitch - 1963 | Twostep - 1970 | Typewriter(1) - 1960s | Typewriter(2) - 1980s |

Ubangi-Stomp - 1960s | Uncle-Willie - 1960s | Underdog-Back-Street - 1968 | Underwater - 1960s | Unwind-Twine - 1960s | Urban-Dance - 1967 | Urkel - 1990s | U.T. - 1962 |

Valentino Tango - date? | Valse-Classique - 1914 | Varsity-Drag - 1920s | Valeta - 1900 to 1912 | Viper's-Drag - 1910s-20s | Voodoo-Mash - 1960s |

(Continued)

Novelty-and-Fad Index: (Continued)

Waddle - 1960s | Wah-Watusi - 1960s | Wak-A-Cha - 1960s | Walk - 1958 | Walkin'-the-Dog - 1964 | Wallop - 1962 | Wamboo - 1962 | War-Canoe - 1960s | Warm-Up - 1960s | Washboard-Rub - 1990s | Washing-Machine - 1960s | Washington-Post-Twostep - 1894 | Wash-Wash - 1963 | Watusi - 1960s | Watusi-Boogaloo - 1960s | Watusi-Wussi'-'Wo - 1960s | Wa-Wabble - 1960s | Weasel - 1960s | Wedge - 1960s | Werewolf-Watusi - 1960s | Whammy - 1960s | Whatchama-Call-It - 1960s | Wheel - 1960s | Whip - 1964 | Whiplash - 1964 | Whirl - 1960s | Whirlwind-Waltz - 1907 | Whisk - 1960s | Whoopee - 1960s | Wibble - 1960s | Wiggle - 1962 | Wiggle-Wobble - 1960s | Wiggle-Worm - 1910s | Wild-Stomp - 1960s | Wild-Weekend - 1960s | Willy-Nilly - 1965 | Wobble - 1964 | Wobble-Cha - 1960s | Wobble-Drum - 1960s | Wobble-Lou - 1960s | Wombat-Twist - 1960s | Woodpecker - date? | World-Dance - 1990s | Worm - 1970s-1980s | Wrangler-Stretch - 1960s |

Yak-A-Poo - 1960s | Yale-Blues-SugarStep - 1929 | Yankee-Doodle - date? | Yankee-Tangle - 1900s-1910s | YMCA - 1978 | Yolk - 1960s | Yo-Yo - 1960s | Yuletide-Jerk - 1960s |

Zig-Zag - 1960s | Zip-It-Up - 2000s | Zizzle - 1960s | Zombie-Stomp - 1960s | Zonk - 1960s | Zorba's-Dance - 1965 |

Novelty-&-Fad Dances-of-the-1960s: The 1960s nurtured hundreds of these dances, as shown listed below, (673 of them found here.) This Craze for Novelty-Dances was due in large part to '*American Bandstand*,' a popular televised dance party that began in 1954. Initially, the show's regulars created the popular dance called the '*Bunny-Hop*.' This Craze was also due to '*The Twist*;' starting in 1960, *The Twist* fostered many similar Novelties, both in the U.S. and abroad, thanks to *Chubby Checker* and *Joey Dee*.

Following these successes, the kids began churning out new dances for every new danceable tune, and vice-versa, creating matching tunes for their Steps. In addition, nation-wide in the U.S. throughout the 1960s, the television pop show '*Ready Steady Go!*' broadcasted its (almost) weekly '*new moves*' section to a huge audience. Resident dancers on the show were *Theresa Confrey* and *Patrick Kerr* who both invented and demonstrated new dances alongside '*members of the public.*'

[The above is from *www.jitterbuzz.com/dance50*; and *www.sixtiescity.com/Culture/dance.*]

The following alphabetized listing lists **673** dances and Patterns. These were all, if not a **Novelty** they were at least a **Fad**, in vogue **in the 1960s**. All are included within this encyclopedia:

See the Aardvark-Walk, Aba-Dabba-Doo, Adler-Sock, African-Strut, Afro-Shingaling, Afro-Twist, Agent 007, Alabama-Shake, Ali-Shuffle, Alley-Cat, Alley-Oop, Alligator, And-Away-We-Go!, Ants, Ape, Arthur,   Baboon, Baby-Baby, Baby-Beatle-Walk, Baby-Walk, Baby-Workout, Bad-Baboon, Banana-Split, Bang, Barefootin', Barracuda, Basketball, Bastella, Batman, Bat-Tusi, Beatle-Boogie, Beatle-Bounce, Beatle-Stonp, Beetle-Squash, Beetle-Walk, Behemoth, Bend-Down-Low, Bend-It!, Big-City-Stomp, Big-Egg, Big-'M', Big-Willy, Billy-Jo, Bird, Bird-Dog, Birdland, Black-Stomp, Blakes-Beat, Block, Blue-Beat, Blue-Chip, Bombay, Bombie, Boney-Maronie, Bongo-Hop, Boogaloo, Boogaloo-Popeye, Boogler, Boomerang, Booty-Green, Boss-Walk, Boston-Hop, Boston-Monkey, Bounce, Box, Boxer, Brain, Breakdown, Bristol-Stomp, Broadway-Freeze, Broadway-Sissy, Broadway-Walk, Broken-Hip, Buckingham, Bug, Bull-Nose-Stomp, Bumpsi, Burn, Bushman,   Cage-Dancer, Calypso, Camel-Walk(1), Camel-Walk-Stroll, Capri, Carnaby, Caterpillar, Cat-Walk, CeeCee, Cha-Jerk, Charge, Charleston-Fish, Chatanooga-Walk, Cheater-Stomp, Chicago-Bird, Chicago-City, Chicken(1), Chicken-Back-Twist, Chichen-Scratch, Chicky-Goo, Chill, Chiller, Chiller-Limbo, Chin-A-Ling, Choo-Choo, Cinnamon-Cinder, Cissy-Popcorn, Clam, Clap-Boogaloo, Claw, Cleopatra-ChaCha, Cleopatra-Stroll, Cleveland-Box, Click, Climb, Cling, Clyde, Coco-Cherry-Mash, Coffee-Grind, Cold-Sweat, Conga-Twist, Congo, Continental, Continental-Mash, Continental-Walk, ContinentalWhip, Cool-Broadway, Cool-Jerk, Cool-Off, Cool-Shake, Corrido-Twist, Cotton, Count, Cow, Crack-Up, Crawl, Craze, Crazy-Chicken, Creamy-Mashed-Potato, Crossfire, Crown, Cruise, Crumble, Crusher, Cum-A-La-Be-Stay,   Danceannette, Dartell-Stomp, Debby's, Del-Viking, Dip, Dipsey-Dooble, Dirt, Dirty-Boogie, Dirty-Dog, Discophonic-Walk, Dish-Rag, Dive, Do, Doctors-Boogie, Dog, Dogin, Donkey-Step, Donkey-Stroke, Donkey-Trot, Donkey-Twine, Donkey-Walk, Doodle-Pickle, Doolang, Doublemint, Double-Rock, Drag, Drum-Stomp, Drunkard, Duck(2), Duck-Walk,   Earthquake, Earthworm, Ebb-'n'-Flow, Egyptian, Egyptian-Shumba, Eighty-One, El-Cable, El-Matador, El-Watusi, Elephant-Walk, Everything,   Fatman, Fine-Twine, Finger-Poppin', Fink, Finnjenica, Fish, Fishin'-Pole, Fish-Tail, Flake, Flapper-Flip, Flea, Flea-Hop(1), Flick, Flintstone-Flop, Flip, Flip-Flop, Float, Florida-Twist, Fly, Footsee, Foot-Stomping, Forty-Five(1), Fox, Frankenstein-Walk, Freak(1), Freddy, Freeze, Fridge, Frog, Frug, Fumigate-Funky-Broadway, Funky-Broadway, Funky-Bull,

(Continued)

Novelty-and-Fad Index: (Continued)

Novelty-&-Fad Dances-of-the-1960s: (Concluded)

Skate-Boogaloo, Skip, Slauson-Shuffle, Slaussen, Slide, Slime, Slip-and-Slide, Slop, Slop-and-Slide, Sloppy-Twist-A-Fish, Slow-Dance, Slow-Fizz, Slow-Jerk, Slow-Locomotion, Slurp, Smashed-Potato, Smock, Snacky-Poo, Snake, Snake-Hips, Snake-Walk, Snatch(2), Sno-Cone, Snoopy, Soch, Sookie, Soul-Clap, Soulful-Jerk, Soulful-Stomp, Soul-Stomp, Soul-Struttin', Soul-Train, Soul-Twine, Soupy-Shuffle-Stomp, Spanish-Strut, Spanish-Twist, Spanns-Stomp, Spider-Walk, Spin, Split, Spunky-Onions, Squat(2), Stereo-Freeze, Stomp, Stop, Stop-Touch, Strand, Stretch, Stroke, Stroll, Strut, Struttin', Stupidity, Sugartime-Twist, Surf, Surfer-Boogie, Surfers, Surfer-Stomp, Surfin'-Bird, Surfing-Monkey, Surfink, Suzie, Sway, Swim, Swing, Swing-Out, Swish-Fish, Switch, Switch-A-Roo, Switchy-Walk,   Tango-Twist, Tantrum, Tarzan's-Monkey, Teenager's-Waltz, Temptation-Walk, Texas-Hop, Thaxton, Thing, Tiger, Tiger-Walk, Tighten-Up, Tip-Toe, Train, Train-Stomp, Trance, Trot, 'T'-Time, Turkey-Neck-Stretch, Turkey-Trot, Twine, Twirl, Twist, Twist-and-Freeze, Twist-and-Limbo, Twist-and-Shout, Twitch, Typewriter,   Ubangi-Stomp, Uncle-Willie, Underdog-Back-Street, Underwater, Unwind-Twine, Urban-Dance, U.T.,   Voodoo-Mash, Waddle, Wah-Watusi, Wak-A-Cha, Walkin'-the-Dog(2), Wallop, Wamboo, War-Canoe, Warm-Up, Washing-Machine, Wash-Wash, Watusi, Watusi-Boogaloo, Watusi-Wussi'-'Wo, Wa-Wabble, Weasel, Wedge, Werewolf-Watusi, Whammy, Whatchama-Call-It, Wheel, Whip, Whiplash, Whirl, Whisk, Whoopee, Wibble, Wiggle, Wiggle-Wobble, Wild-Stomp, Wild-Weekend, Willy-Nilly, Wobble, Wobble-Cha, Wobble-Drum, Wobble-Lou, Wombat-Twist, Wrangler-Stretch,   Yak-A-Poo, Yolk, Yo-Yo, Yuletide-Jerk,   Zig-Zag, Zizzle, Zombie-Stomp, Zonk, and Zorba's-Dance;   which were all **Novelt**ies or **Fad**s in vogue **in the 1960s.**

Novelty-&-Fad Dances-of-the-1980s: Although fewer than those in the 1960s, **the 1980s** still nurtured perhaps a hundred of these dances, as shown listed below, (96 of them found here.) This Craze for Novelty-Dances was due in large part to popular televised MTV dance videos. Many of these **1980s Novelt**ies or **Fad**s predominately happen to be individuals Solo-Dancing in Pantomime, Mimicking everyday Motions and often in Comedy.

The following alphabetized listing lists 96 dances and Patterns. These were all, if not a **Novelty** they were at least a **Fad**, in vogue **in the 1980s.** All included within this encyclopedia:

See the African-Anteater-Ritual, Alf, Alligator(2), Ant, Axel-Rose,   Back-the-Bus-Up, Bedrock, Belinda, Bingo-Boy, Boogie-Down, Break-Dancing, Bugg,   Cabbage-Patch, Caustic-Potash, Centipede, Chicken-Dance, Chinese-Typewriter, Churnin'-Butter, Cotton-Eyed Joe, Curly-Shuffle,   Dancin'-in-the-Dark, Dancin'-in-the-Dark-Improved, Deathrocker, Debbie-Gibson, Dinosaur-Groove, Dolphin,   Ed-Lover-Dance, E.T.,   Fairy-Dance, Fancy-Feet, Fila, Fishing-Pole, Fishy, Freaking, Funky-Alien, Funky-Twist,   Garrett, Gator(2), Gigolo, Girls-Just-Wanna-Have-Fun, Go-Song, Graple, Guess,   Hammer-Dance, Hangin'-Tough, Happy-Feet, Headache, Hello-Kitty, Hootier, Ickey-Shuffle,   Kid-and-Play,   Lambada, Lawn-Mower, Leg-Kick-Line, Love-Bird,   Michael-Jackson-Circles, Milking-the-Cow, Moon-Walk, Muppet,   New-Kids-Move,   Pac-Man, Palm-Tree, ParaPara, Pee-Wee-Herman, Pencil, Pogo, Popcorn(3), Pop'n-Loc, Prep(1), Push-It,   Q-Tip,   Red-Indian-Dance, Robocop, Roger-Rabbit, Rubber-Knees, Running-Man,   Shopping-Cart, Shout-Dance, SideSlide, Skanking, Slam-Dancing, Smurf, Snake(4)&(5), Soca, Sprinkler, Stewardess, Strokin', Super-Robot,   Teen-Wolf, Tiffany, Time-Warp, Toe-Stands, Typewriter,   Worm,   and YMCA, which were all **Novelt**ies or **Fad**s in vogue **in the 1980s.**

Novelty & Fad Dances

Aardvark-Walk: A **Novelty Fad C**oupledance of the 1960s. This had its own Eponymous record, "*The Aardvark Walk*" by *The High Rollers*.
      (See Novelty-&-Fad Dances-of-the-1960s.) [From www.bluejuice.org.au]

Aba-Dabba-Doo: A **Novelty Fad C**oupledance of the 1960s. It's Eponymous Music was "*AbaDabbaDoo Dance*" by *The Tradewinds*.
      (See Novelty-&-Fad Dances-of-the-1960s.) [From www.bluejuice.org.au]

Abe-Kabbible: The following is a **Novelty Fad Tap-Dancing** Pattern consisting of three 4/4 Time Measures, with a total of twenty sounds or Actions.
      In 1917 Comedy, there was `*Abe Kabibble Does His Bit*,' and `*Abe Kabibble at The Ball Game*.' Also, **Abe Kabbible** was in an early newspaper comic strip.
      The following is taken from *Vance's Fantastic Tap Dance Dictionary*:
      "*Abe Kabbible: A commonly used movement in jazz dancing:*
            "*1:   Step L (to L side)*   First Measure
            "*2:   Step R (XF of L)*
            "*3:   Step L (to L side)*
            "*4:   Heel tap R (to R side)*
            "*and: Step L (to L side)*   Second Measure
            "*1:   Step R (XF of L)*
            "*and: Step L (to L side)*
            "*2:   Heel tap R fwd (to R side)*
            "*and: Step R (to R side)*
            "*3:   Step L (XF of R)*
            "*and: Step R (to R side)*
            "*4:   Heel tap L fwd (to L side)*
            "*and: Leap fwd to L ft (to L side)*   Third Measure
            "*1:   Step R (XFof L)*
            "*and: Leap fwd to L ft (to L side)*
            "*2:   Heel tap R fwd (to R side)*
            "*and: Leap fwd to R ft (to R side)*
            "*3:   Step L (XFof R)*
            "*and: Leap fwd to R ft (to R side)*
            "*4:   Heel tap L fwd (to L side).*"
      (See Jazz, Jazz-Box, Jazz-Dance, Jazz-Dances, and Jazz-Tap.)

Adler-Sock: Only this name for an American **Novelty** or **Fad** of the 1960s is listed simply as a Dance, Pattern, or Figure in the "*Dance Crazes of the Sixties*."
      (See Novelty-&-Fad Dances-of-the-1960s.) [From *www.sixtiescity.com/Culture/dance*]

African-Anteater-Ritual: An American **Novelty Fad** Solo-Dance of the 1980s in Cadence with the Music.

   The following is an excerpt from "*Eighties Dances*" - [www.inthe80s.com]:

   "*From* [the song] *'Can't Buy Me Love' ... You step back then step forward, then do it again with the opposite foot. Next, you hold your arms up at 90 degree angles and shake your entire torso.*"

   (See Novelty-&-Fad Dances-of-the-1980s. Also see Animal-Dances.)

African-Strut: A **Novelty Fad** Coupledance of the 1960s. This had its own Eponymous record, the "*African Strut* " by *Lynn Westbrook*.

   (See Novelty-&-Fad Dances-of-the-1960s.) [From www.bluejuice.org.au]

Afro-Shingaling: A **Novelty Fad** Coupledance of the 1960s. It's Eponymous Music was "*Afro-Shingaling* " by *Latinaires*.

   (See Novelty-&-Fad Dances-of-the-1960s. Especially see Latin-Boogaloo.)
   [From www.bluejuice.org.au]

Afro-Twist: An Unstructured, American **Novelty Fad** Singular dance Pattern or Routine. In 4/4 Tempo, this Six-Count **Afro-Twist** Routine that splits its Measures, was in vogue in the 1960s at the Brigham Young University, in Provo, Utah. This may have been one of the dances that was later banned in 1966 at the same University.

In 1968, particular records to which the **Afro-Twist** was danced, were "*Lickin' Stick*" by *James Brown*, and "*Heard It Through The Grapevine*" by *Gladys Knight & The Pips*. [From *Soul, www.trinity.unimelb.edu.au*]

   Slowly Forward-Curving Left then Right then dancing Backward three mostly Quick Steps, the Pattern did not Progress. It is assumed that the Forward Curves were danced with Softened-Knees and arms Spread High with Hands twitching, and the Rearward Steps were danced Bent over with a **Puppet** Pose. Rhythm Timing for three Measures probably was *Slow Slow Slow Slow; Quick Quick Slow Slow Slow; Slow Slow Quick Quick Slow.*

   Danced as follows: *forcurveleft ForCurveLeftSwivel1/4CW forcurveright ForCurveRightSwivel1/4CCW; back Back back ForCurveRight forcurverightswivel1/4CCW; ForCurveLeft forcurveleftswivel1/4CW Back back Back.* Then Start over.

   (See Novelty-&-Fad Dances-of-the-1960s.)   [Data mostly from "Rhythm and Dance" by Alma Heaton.]

Agent-007:   Only this name for an American **Novelty** or **Fad** of the 1960s is listed simply as a Dance, Pattern, or Figure in the "*Dance Crazes of the Sixties.*"

   (See Novelty-&-Fad Dances-of-the-1960s.) [From *www.sixtiescity.com/Culture/dance*]

Air-Guitar: A **Novelty Fad**; a pretended dance object. This *"Air-Guitar"* is a non-existent guitar.   The dancer holds and *"plays"* this *"Air-Guitar"* as he dances around.

The following excerpts are from *air guitar*; [www.answers.com]:

*"**Air guitar** is the act of pretending to play guitar, consisting of an exaggerated strumming motion and often coupled with loud singing or lip-synching. Air guitar is generally used in the imaginary simulation of loud electric guitar music, especially rock, heavy metal, and so on. Although it is acceptable to play air guitar to acoustic songs, it is an act traditionally left to rock. Headbanging is often used in conjunction with an air guitar. Real guitar players also often play air guitar quite accurately while listening to their favorite artists.*

"Musical artists often instinctively follow the rhythm and mood of their music with their body while they play which is also a means of identifying metre and keeping time. In rock music, many guitarists exaggerate these movements to make them a part of their performance; some even add acrobatic stunts, the choreography becoming their distinctive characteristic. Their fans often mimic their idol's movements in adoration, and can become swept away by the music. Playing air guitar can be considered a specialised form of dance.

"For some, playing air guitar has become a hobby in itself, and they pride their ability to mimic the style of countless artists. In fact, organised air guitar competitions are regularly held in many countries, and since 1996 The Annual Air Guitar World Championship contest has been a part of the Oulu Music Video Festival in Oulu, Finland. The first organised air guitar competition in the UK was held in 1994, in Australia in 2002, and in the United States in 2003."

(See Jazz-Hands-Air-Guitar-Style, and Praise-You.)

Alabama-Shake: Only this name for an American **Novelty** or **Fad** of the 1960s is listed simply as a Dance, Pattern, or Figure in the *"Dance Crazes of the Sixties."*

(See Novelty-&-Fad Dances-of-the-1960s.) [From *www.sixtiescity.com/Culture/dance*]

Alexander or **The Alexander**:   A British **Novelty Fad** Coupledance popular in England in 1913; a Twostep. Some say more than a hundred new Coupledances were invented between 1912 and 1914; the **Alexander** was then one of them.

(Also see the Lame-Duck, Boston-Dip, Bunny-Hug, Gaby-Glide, Hug-Me-Close, Shiver-Dance, and Turkey-Trot; which were all Novelty Fad dances in vogue in the 1910s.)

Alf: An American **Novelty Fad** comical Solo-Dance or Maneuver of the 1980s. Named after the little alien "**Alf**" who was a monstrous but comical and witty 1980s TV character.

One version was as follows: Bent-Over In-Place, each "**Alf**" was Performed in four even Beats (one Measure in 4/4 Time). One Knee was Bent, then the Opposite Toe was Pointed Straight Forward, then both Fisted Hands were Thrust Downward straddling the Bent Knee and held one Beat. The Maneuver was repeated Mirror-Image, in Time.

Another version is as follows, from *"Eighties Dances"* - [www.inthe80s.com]:

"The Alf is very simple. You just bend at the knee but with your toe pointed, and then thrust both arms downward while in a fist, toward the bent knee. Then do the opposite leg. Repeat over and over and stay with the beat!"

(See Novelty-&-Fad Dances-of-the-1980s.)

Algorithm-March: A **Novelty** or **Fad** dance of an unknown time, listed in "*Novelty and fad dances*" under [http://en.wikipedia.org/wiki].

Ali-Shuffle: A **Novelty Fad** dance of 1967. The **Ali-Shuffle** had its own Eponymous record, "*Ali Shuffle*" by *Alvin Cash*. [From *Soul*, www.trinity.unimelb.edu.au]

Alley-Cat: A **Novelty Fad C**oupledance of 1962. It's Eponymous Music was "*Alley Cat* " by *Bent Fanbric*.
(See Novelty-&-Fad Dances-of-the-1960s.) [From www.bluejuice.org.au]

Alley-Oop: Only this name for an American **Novelty** or **Fad** of the 1960s is listed simply as a Dance, Pattern, or Figure in the "*Dance Crazes of the Sixties*."
(See Novelty-&-Fad Dances-of-the-1960s.) [From *www.sixtiescity.com/Culture/dance*]

Alligator(1): A **Novelty Fad** dance of 1963. The **Alligator** had its own Eponymous record, "*Alligator Boogaloo*" by *Lou Donaldson*. [From *Soul*, www.trinity.unimelb.edu.au]

Alligator(2): An American **Fad** comical Solo Maneuver of the 1980s in Cadence with the Music.
The following is from "*Eighties Dances*" - [www.inthe80s.com]:
"***The Alligator:*** *You lay down on the floor, bend your knees to your stomach, then kick your legs (alternating) from your knees down. (Popular on ABC's 'Full House.')*"
(See Novelty-&-Fad Dances-of-the-1980s. Also see Pantomime, Mime, and Mimicry-En-Masse. Also see Animal-Dances.)

Alligator-Stomp: A **Novelty Fad** dance of about 1994.
The following is from *Alligator*; [www.answers.com]:
"*The 'Alligator Stomp' is a dance that was introduced in a most effective way by 'The Cramps' in a song of the same name on their album 'Look Mom No Head'. There's quite a bit of jumping about and rolling on the floor with lots of chomping, staggering the line between human fun and morbid acts of homicide.*"

American-Hustle: A **Novelty Fad** Hustle Coupledance of the 1970s in the United States, especially in Los Angeles. A Hustle with a softness.
(See Disco-Era.)

A-Minor-Drag: An American **Novelty Fad** Coupledance (or possibly just a tune) in vogue in the 1910s or `20s. Other *"drag dances"* of the time were the Dizzy-Drag, Saratoga-Drag, Shoe-Shiner's-Drag, Slow-Drag, Viper's-Drag, and the most famous **Varsity-Drag**.

And-Away-We-Go!: A slang phrase and joking expression. This jargon is the famous saying by the comic **Jackie Gleason** as he gleefully danced his Forward Triples with Bent Elbows.
(See **Jackie Gleason**, Happy-Feet, Humorous, Laughing, and With-Abandon.)

Animal-Dances: Free and individualistic, there have been extensive series of dances and Patterns Mimicking the Actions of various animals. There were actually two different definite waves of **Novelty Fad Animal-Dances** that became very popular in the United States during the twentieth century. Many or most had their own Eponymous song:

Animal-Dances of 1912-1914: Over one hundred of these American **Novelty Fad** Coupledances were created during this period. These particular dances were derided at the time by newspapers, magazines, church officials, and even by Pope Pius X of the Catholic Church, as "such foolish and decadent behavior."

See the Bull-Frog-Hop, Bunny-Hug, Buzzard-Lope, Camel-Walk(2), Chicken-Reel, Chicken-Scratch(2), Crab-Step, Fish-Walk, Gotham-Gobble, Grizzly-Bear, Horse-Trot, Kangaroo-Dip, Kangaroo-Hop, Lame-Duck, Monkey-Glide, Possum-Trot, Snake(3), Turkey-Trot, and Viper's-Drag; which were all **Animal-Dances** of 1910-1914.

Animal-Dances of the 1960s: The second wave of **Animal-Dances** were created and became popularized in the 1960s. These were created perhaps mostly by the **Hullie-Gullie** dance game played at the time. But this Craze for Novelty-Dances was also due in large part to *'American Bandstand,'* a popular televised dance party that began in 1954. Initially, the show's regulars created the popular dance called the *'Bunny-Hop.'* Following this success, the kids began churning out new Animal-Dances for every new danceable tune, and vice-versa, creating matching tunes for their Steps. In addition, nation-wide in the U.S. throughout the 1960s, the television pop show *'Ready Steady Go!'* broadcasted its (almost) weekly *'new moves'* section to a huge audience. Resident dancers on the show were *Theresa Confrey* and *Patrick Kerr* who both invented and demonstrated new Animal-Dances alongside *'members of the public.'*

All of these 1960s dances were American **Novelty Fad** Singles and Coupledances as were those 1912-1914 dances above. People enmasse, mostly teens with long hair, were dancing by themselves and inventing as they danced. These particular Fad-Dances were banned by the Mormon Church at Brigham Young University in 1966 as being too silly.

See the Aardvark-Walk, Alley-Cat, Ants, Ape, Baboon, Batman, Beatle-Walk, Bad-Baboon, Barracuda, Bird, Bird-Dog, Boston-Monkey, Bug, Bull-Nose-Stomp, Camel-Walk(1), Camel-Walk-Stroll, Caterpillar, Cat-Walk, Charleston-Fish, Chicago-Bird, Chicken(1), Chicken-Back-Twist, Chicky-Goo, Clam, Cow, Crazy-Chicken, Dirty-Dog, Dog, Dogin, Donkey-Step, Donkey-Stroke, Donkey-Trot, Donkey-Twine, Donkey-Walk, Duck(2), Duck-Walk, Earthworm, Elephant-Walk, Fish, Fish-Tail, Flea, Flea-Hop(1), Fly, Fox, Funky-Bull, Funky-Buzzard, Funky-Chicken, Funky-Horse, Funky-Penguin, Gator, Goat, Goose, Gorilla, Hog, Hornet, Horse, Kangaroo, Kangaroo-Tail-Twist, Karate-Monkey, King-Kong's-Monkey, Monkey, Monkey-Bird, Monkey-Dog, Monkey-Donkey, Monkey-Hop, Monkey-Jerk, Monkey-Jump, Monkey-Shine, Monkey-Ska, Monkey-Stroll, Monkey-Walk, Monkey-Wobble, Monster-Mash, Mother-Goose, Mouse, Mule, My-Dog, Ostrich, Peanut-Duck, Penguin, Philly-Dog, Philly-Horse, Pig, Pony(2), Pony-Horse, Pony-Tail, Rat-Fink, Roach, Rooster-Walk, Shaggy-Dog, Shake-a-Tail-Feather, Shake-Rattle-Snake, Shakey-Bird, Shout-and-Do-the-Duck, Sloppy-Twist-a-Fish, Snake, Snake-Hips, Snake-Walk, Snoopy, Spider-Walk, Surfin'-Bird, Surfing-Monkey, Swish-Fish, Tarzan's-Monkey, Tiger, Tiger-Walk, Turkey-Neck-Stretch, Underdog-Backstreet, Walkin'-the-Dog, Weasel, Worm, and the Wombat-Twist; which were all Novelty Fad **Animal-Dances** in vogue in the 1960s.

All of the above **Animal-Dances**, from both periods, can be found more or less extensively enumerated and described herein.

And-Change-And-Change-And: An Unleadable, In-Place-Coupledance Movement, mostly for **West-Coast-Swing**. An alternate Ending replacing Anchor-Step, or suitable for a two-Beat add-on. **And-Change-And-Change-And** shifts Weight from one Foot to the other then back, etc. Man's Rhythm Timing is *A'quick a'Quick Slow*. Partners are always upon Opposing Feet. Twice, one Foot is Drawn to Home, Weighted, as the other Foot is Moved to Touching. All is followed by a Weighted Foot.

Starting with his Right Foot Slightly Forward, Man's Movements are *Andchange andChange And*; Lady's Movements are *andChange Andchange and*.

Similar to **Change-and-Change, Switch**(3), **Side-Switches, Heel-Switches, Hangman, Quick-Points**, and **California-Shuffle**. (See Change-Feet-Multiplicity, and Change-Feet. Also see The-Change, and Change-of-Weight.)

Ant: An American **Novelty Fad** Solo-Dance or Maneuver of the 1980s.
The following is an excerpt from "*Eighties Dances*" - [www.inthe80s.com]:
         "*Adam Ant often swung his arms (left then right) and bopped up and down to the beat at the same time. ...*"
(See Novelty-&-Fad Dances-of-the-1980s. Also see Ants.)

Ants: Only this name for an American **Novelty** or **Fad** of the 1960s is listed simply as a Dance, Pattern, or Figure in the "*Dance Crazes of the Sixties.*"
(See Novelty-&-Fad Dances-of-the-1960s.) [From *www.sixtiescity.com/Culture/dance*]

Ape: A **Novelty Fad** Coupledance of the 1960s. This had its own Eponymous record, "*Do The Ape* " by *Reggie Powell.*
(See Novelty-&-Fad Dances-of-the-1960s.) [From www.bluejuice.org.au]

AppleJack: A **Novelty Fad** Coupledance of 1948. It's Eponymous Music was "*The Appeljack* " by *Joe Morris.*
(See Novelty-&-Fad Dances-of-the-1960s.) [From www.bluejuice.org.au]

Apple-Jacks: An Unleadable 1930s **Break-A-Way Novelty Fad** Pattern, usually Performed while dancing the **Big-Apple** or the **Carolina-Shag**. Also suitable for **Line-Dancing**, and for the many **Swing** dances.

  Walk Forward Pigeon-Toed with Hands Pointed Down. Opposite shoulders Lift Up and Down. Continue for eight Counts but Hop Step on *&8*.

  The following is from ***Glossary of Dance Terminology***, (www.arjjazedance.free-online.co.uk):

   "APPLEJACKS - A foot traveling movement in place as follows:

 1 With weight on left heel and ball of right foot, swivel Left toe to the left and Right heel to the left (feet are in a "V" position, toes pointed outward.

 & Swivel Left toe and Right heel back to centre.

 2 With weight on Right heel and ball of left foot, swivel Right toe to the right and Left heel to the right (feet = in a "V" position, toes pointed outward.

 & Bring feet together

   "Move can be done with opposite weight changes. Also see Traveling Applejacks."

   "TRAVELING APPLEJACK - A pattern traveling sideways bringing the toes together leaving the heels apart, Then bringing the heels together leaving the toes apart. Weight is on one toe and the opposite heel, then reversed to result in sideways travel - See Applejacks." [Same as Ramble(2), and Toe/Heel-Walk.]

  As a novelty **Fad**, how to dance the **Apple-Jacks** to the Music's Beat is further described as follows: (From http://ourworld.compuserve.com.)

   "APPLEJACK -- (R) With the weight on the heel of your left foot and ball of your right foot, twist right heel to left instep while turning both toes out and return to centre position

   "(L) With weight on heel of right foot and ball of left foot, twist left heel to right instep while turning both toes out and return to centre position."

  For the **Big-Apple**, the **Apple-Jacks** was one of the **Break-A-Way** Genre. Wiggling their hips, certain **Break-A-Way** Patterns were danced. The original **Suzie-Q, Boogie-Back, Tack-Annie, Georgia-Grind, Praise-Allah!, Truckin', Peckin', Charleston, Shorty-George**, and other Break-A-Ways, were probably originated early by blacks; while **Spank-the-Baby, Rusty-Dusty, Pose-and-a-Peck**, the **Little-Apple**, the **Little-Peach, Mess-Around, Stomp-Off, Apple-Jacks**, and **Fall-Off-the-Log**, and other Break-A-Ways, were probably originated later by whites. Most all of these Patterns seem to have been influenced or derived from the classic **Lindy-Hop** and/or **Big-Apple** dances.

  Traveling-Applejacks are the same as **Ramble**(2), and **Toe/Heel-Walk**. (For the Carolina-Shag, see Flamingo, Belly-Roll, Duck-Walk, Fly-Back, Lean, Stutter-Step, and the SugarFoot. See **Break-A-Way Glossary** for a more complete listing.)

Armstrong: From Kingston, Jamaica, an Underground **Novelty Fad**, Singular- or Group-Dance Movement, associated with dancing **Dancehall/Ragga**, which, in turn, are outgrowths of **Ska/Reggae**. **Armstrong** was and is danced mainly by youths of color.

   The following is from *Ragga Fashions*: [www.bbc.co.uk]

      "*Armstrong - This dance was the successor to the Bogle.*

      "*Stand with feet slightly apart. Raise your arms and hold them straight out in front of you. Bend your elbows as if doing bicep curls. On the ball of one foot twist the heel inwards and lift the corresponding elbow, allow the opposite elbow to drop. Twist the heel back into the original position and straighten-up. Repeat with other foot.*"

   See **Dancehall**(2) for further explanation. (Also see Bogle, Butterfly, Go-Go-Wine, Body-Basic-and-Exercise, Tate, and World-Dance. Also see Jerry-Springer, Prang, Heel-and-Toe, Na!Na!Na!, Screechie, Zip-It-Up, Drive-By, Shizzle-Ma-Nizzle, Matrix, and Bin-Laden. Also see Underground Step-Listing.)

Arthur: Only this name for an American **Novelty** or **Fad** of the 1960s is listed simply as a Dance, Pattern, or Figure in the "*Dance Crazes of the Sixties*."

   (See Novelty-&-Fad Dances-of-the-1960s.) [From *www.sixtiescity.com/Culture/dance*]

Aunt-Jemima-Slide: A **Novelty Fad** Coupledance of 1914.

Axel-Rose: An American **Novelty Fad** comical Solo-Dance or Maneuver of the 1980s in Cadence with the Music. These shinanigans were seen on "*Sweet Child Of Mine*" and other "*Guns & Roses*" late-eighties videos.

   The following is an excerpt from "*Eighties Dances*" - [www.inthe80s.com]:

      "**The Axel Rose:** *Hold on to a fake microphone stand and, with head lowered, move one leg out to the side, only about a foot off of the ground. As soon as your foot hits the ground, immediately repeat move with other leg. Repeat at least 10 times. ...*"

   (See Novelty-&-Fad Dances-of-the-1980s. Also see Pantomime, Mime, and Mimicry-En-Masse.)

Baboon: A **Novelty Fad** Coupledance of the 1960s. It's Eponymous Music was "*Bad Baboon*" by *Madisons*.

   (See Novelty-&-Fad Dances-of-the-1960s.) [From www.bluejuice.org.au]

Baby-Baby: An Unstructured, American **Novelty Fad** Singular or Coupledance in vogue in the 1960s. In 1964, from whence **The Baby-Baby** dance came, *The Supremes* sang and recorded *Where Did Our Love Go*, with its *Baby-Baby* chorus.

   (See Novelty-&-Fad Dances-of-the-1960s.)

Baby-Beatle-Walk: Only this name for an American **Novelty** or **Fad** of the 1960s is listed simply as a Dance, Pattern, or Figure in the "*Dance Crazes of the Sixties*."

   (See Novelty-&-Fad Dances-of-the-1960s.) [From *www.sixtiescity.com/Culture/dance*]

Baby-Walk: Only this name for an American **Novelty** or **Fad** of the 1960s is listed simply as a Dance, Pattern, or Figure in the "*Dance Crazes of the Sixties.*"
    (See Novelty-&-Fad Dances-of-the-1960s.) [From *www.sixtiescity.com/Culture/dance*]

Baby-Workout: A **Novelty Fad** Coupledance of 1963. This had its own Eponymous record, the "*Baby Workout* " by *Jackie Wilson.*
    (See Novelty-&-Fad Dances-of-the-1960s.) [From www.bluejuice.org.au]

Back-the-Bus-Up: An American **Novelty Fad** comical Solo-Dance or Maneuver of the 1980s in Cadence with the Music.
    The following is from "*Eighties Dances*" - [www.inthe80s.com]:
      "***Back The Bus Up:*** *Hands out with arms slightly bent, fists closed as if your hands are on a steering wheel. Then slowly walk backwards with small steps. Keep your head looking back both ways and turn your hands like you're moving a steering wheel.*"
    (See Novelty-&-Fad Dances-of-the-1980s. Also see Pantomime, Mime, and Mimicry-En-Masse.)

Bacon-Fat: A **Novelty Fad** dance of 1952. The **Bacon-Fat** had its own Eponymous records, "*Bacon Fat*" by *Andre Williams,* and "*Bacon Fat*" by *Sir Douglas Quintet.*
    [From *Soul*, www.trinity.unimelb.edu.au]

Bad-Baboon: Only this name for an American **Novelty** or **Fad** of the 1960s is listed simply as a Dance, Pattern, or Figure in the "*Dance Crazes of the Sixties.*"
    (See Novelty-&-Fad Dances-of-the-1960s.) [From *www.sixtiescity.com/Culture/dance*]

Ballin'-The-Jack: An American **Novelty Fad** Singular dance that was introduced in Harlem in 1913 in a musical named *The Darktown Follies.* The song became very popular. Many composers of that day would write sheet music with directions by the words of its song to its particular dance; **Ballin'-The-Jack** was one of these: (Words by Jim Burris.)
    "*First you put your two knees close up tight,*
      Then you sway `em to the left, then you sway `em to the right,
    Step a-round the floor kind of nice and light,
      Then you twis' a-round and twis' a-round with all - your might,
    Stretch your lov-in' arms straight out in space,
      Then you do the **Ea-gle Rock** *with sty-le and grace -*
    Swing your foot way `round then bring it back, -
      Now that's what I call Ball-in' the Jack. - "
    (See Texas-Tommy, Maxixe, Bunny-Hug, Grizzly-Bear, and Turkey-Trot, for dances of that time where dance directions were in their verses. The Texas-Tommy dance was introduced in the same musical. Also see the Boston-Dip, Gaby-Glide, Hug-Me-Close, Shiver-Dance, Last-Waltz, and Lame-Duck; which were all Novelty Fad dances in vogue in the 1910s.)

Bal-Trot: A Leadable, **Novelty Fad** Traveling-Coupledance of the 2000s. A **Pure-Balboa** Variation, this **Bal-Trot** is one of the several **Balboa** dance versions as listed under the **Balboa-Genre**, which, in turn, is of the Foxtrot Amalgamation.

The following are excerpts from "*Class Details - Here's What We Do*"; [www.2plyswing.com]:

"*go go pivot step, go go pivot step*"

"*The birth came from an event we attended on the Queen Mary for a Vintage Dance.   Our other Balboa mentor, Willie Desatoff, was in attendance. The crowd was dancing along the floor doing One Step and Fox Trot and we were scared to join in and get run over doing Lindy or Balboa...   We asked Willie what to do and of course he said 'aaaah, just do Balboa...' so we danced into the swirling crowd and the BAL-TROT was born. Willie always said the Balboa was a versatile dance - how true!*"

This Traveling **Bal-Trot** is Coupledanced entirely in a Closed Position (not just Mush Position). The **Bal-Trot** Starts with the Man's Facing Reverse-Line-of-Dance, but the dance Travels Line-of-Dance. Pivoting on Counts 3 and 7, with his Lady Following, the Man dances this **Bal-Trot** Basic-Step as follows:

back Back Swivel1/2 fwd, Fwd fwd spiral1/2 Back; etc.

[See Balboa, and Basic-Balboa(1)(2)(3).]

Bamba: An old Mexican air from the province of Vera Cruz, Mexico, to which [this] charming folk dance depicts two lovers who [by] throwing a narrow sash on the floor manage to tie it into a knot with their dancing feet.

From *Dictionary of Dance* (Arthur Murray), [http://arthurmurraydayton.com].

Bambuca: See Bambuco.

Bambuco or **Bambuca:** A Latin **Novelty Fad** Coupledance of the 1950-60s. The **Bambuco** is a romantic pursuit dance. It's music has cross accents.

Also a **Folkdance, Bambuca** is the Columbian national dance, originating with the native Columbians. **Bambuca** later became the dance of Columbian society when it was added to their favorite, the Gentle **Pasillo** dance. The **Bambuco** is presently popular in Cuba, in other West Indies, and in Central American countries.

Similar to **Fimeza, Escondido**, and **Jarabe**. (Also see the Bop, Bunny-Hop, Calypso, Creep, Fish, Flea-Hop, Frug, Guapacha, Hand-Jive, Hitch-Hiker, Hokey-Pokey, Hullie-Gullie, Jerk, Limbo-Rock, Mashed-Potato, Monkey, Pachanga, Plena, Pony, Rock-and-Around, Scooter, Slide, Strole, Surfers, Swim, Tumba-Cha, Twist, Twister, and the Watusi; which were all Novelty Fads in vogue in the 1950-60s. Also see Novelty-&-Fad Dances-of-the-1960s.)

Banana-Split: Only this name for an American **Novelty** or **Fad** of the 1960s is listed simply as a Dance, Pattern, or Figure in the "*Dance Crazes of the Sixties*."

(See Novelty-&-Fad Dances-of-the-1960s.) [From *www.sixtiescity.com/Culture/dance*]

Bang: Only this name for an American **Novelty** or **Fad** of the 1960s is listed simply as a Dance, Pattern, or Figure in the "*Dance Crazes of the Sixties*."

(See Novelty-&-Fad Dances-of-the-1960s.) [From *www.sixtiescity.com/Culture/dance*]

Barefootin': An American **Fad** dance of 1966. This **Barefootin'** Dance had its own Eponymous record, *"Barefootin'"* by *Robert Parker*.
    (See Novelty-&-Fad Dances-of-the-1960s.) [From "*Soul*," *www.trinity.unimelb.edu.au*, and from "*Dance Crazes of the Sixties*," *www.sixtiescity.com/Culture/dance*]

Barracuda: An American **Fad** dance of 1966. This **Barracuda** Dance had its own Eponymous record, *"The Barracuda"* by *Alvin Cash*.
    (See Novelty-&-Fad Dances-of-the-1960s.) [From "*Soul*," *www.trinity.unimelb.edu.au*, and from "*Dance Crazes of the Sixties*," *www.sixtiescity.com/Culture/dance*]

Basketball: A Structured but Unleadable, **Novelty** Pattern for a Singular-Dancer, three-Measures long, Mimicking playing **Basketball**. This **Basketball** Pattern is one of the Qued Steps often Called for while dancing the **Madison** Audience-Participation-Dance's Basic-Step.
    While Stepping Forward, beginning first upon the Left Foot, and with the extended Right Hand "*dribbling*" four Quick Beats Up-and-Down, this **Basketball** Step includes the "*Wilt-Chamberlain-Hook*," wherein-which the Right Hand extended High, Sweeps once, Down and Backwards as in a hook.
    The following are excerpts from *Madison Figures* -- [www.sixtiescity.com/Culture/]:
    "*Chasse to the left dribbling the ball. Jump to shoot the hoop turning anticlockwise (2 beats). Jump back clockwise to front (2 beats).*
    "*Chasse back to the right, calling out the score. ('Two points').*"
    The following are excerpts from *The Madison* -- [www.albertj.btinternet.co.uk/]:
    "*Facing slightly to right, take two steps forward whilst bouncing ball with right hand.*
    "*Turn on spot jump and 'slam' ball down.*
    "*Turn back and whilst stepping back facing right two steps, show and shout 'Two Points!*'"
    [See Double-Cross, Cleveland-Box, Big-'M', 'T'-Time, Jackie-Gleason, Birdland, and Rifleman. Also see the Novelty-&-Fad Dances-of-the-1960s.]

Bastella: Only this name for an American **Novelty** or **Fad** of the 1960s is listed simply as a Dance, Pattern, or Figure in the "*Dance Crazes of the Sixties*."
    (See Novelty-&-Fad Dances-of-the-1960s.) [From *www.sixtiescity.com/Culture/dance*]

Batman: The **Batman** was an Unstructured and Unleadable, **Novelty Fad** Singles Dance or **Coupledance** of the 1960s, with Swinging arms. The dance Mimicked a **Bat**, and was one of a whole series of 1960s Mimicking dance Patterns, (see Hullie-Gullie.) This silly **Batman**, along with other silly Fad-Dances, was banned at Brigham Young University in 1966.
    In 1967, The Eponymous record to which the **Batman** was danced was *"Do The Batman"* by *Gate Wesley & Band*. [From *Soul*, www.trinity.unimelb.edu.au]
    (See Novelty-&-Fad Dances-of-the-1960s.)

Bat-Tusi: Only this name for an American **Novelty** or **Fad** of the 1960s is listed simply as a Dance, Pattern, or Figure in the "*Dance Crazes of the Sixties*."
    (See Novelty-&-Fad Dances-of-the-1960s.) [From *www.sixtiescity.com/Culture/dance*]

      Beatle-Boogie: Only this name for an American **Novelty** or **Fad** of the 1960s is listed simply as a Dance, Pattern, or Figure in the "*Dance Crazes of the Sixties*."
      (See Novelty-&-Fad Dances-of-the-1960s.) [From *www.sixtiescity.com/Culture/dance*]

      Beatle-Bounce: Only this name for an American **Novelty** or **Fad** of the 1960s is listed simply as a Dance, Pattern, or Figure in the "*Dance Crazes of the Sixties*."
      (See Novelty-&-Fad Dances-of-the-1960s.) [From *www.sixtiescity.com/Culture/dance*]

      Beatle-Stomp: Only this name for an American **Novelty** or **Fad** of the 1960s is listed simply as a Dance, Pattern, or Figure in the "*Dance Crazes of the Sixties*."
      (See Novelty-&-Fad Dances-of-the-1960s.) [From *www.sixtiescity.com/Culture/dance*]

      Bedrock: An American **Fad** Solo Maneuver of the 1980s.
      The following is from "*Eighties Dances*" - [www.inthe80s.com]:
          "***The Bedrock:*** *Named for a popular song that was out at the time. Swing your arms back and forth, while stepping side to side in sync with the music.*"
      (See Novelty-&-Fad Dances-of-the-1980s.)

      Beetle-Squash: A **Novelty Fad** Coupledance of the 1960s. It's Eponymous Music was the "*Beetle Squash* " by *Sonny Bloch's Elephants*.
      (See Novelty-&-Fad Dances-of-the-1960s.) [From www.bluejuice.org.au]

      Beetle-Walk: A **Novelty Fad** Coupledance of the 1960s. This had its own Eponymous record, "*The Beetle Walk* " by *Phaetons*. [From www.bluejuice.org.au]
      (See Novelty-Dances, Fad-Dances, Novelty-and-Fad Genre, and the Novelty-&-Fad Dances-of-the-1960s. Also see Beetle-Squash, Baby-Beetle-Walk, Beatle-Boogie, Beatle-Bounce, and Beatle-Stomp.)

      Behemoth: Only this name for an American **Novelty** or **Fad** of the 1960s is listed simply as a Dance, Pattern, or Figure in the "*Dance Crazes of the Sixties*."
      (See Novelty-&-Fad Dances-of-the-1960s.) [From *www.sixtiescity.com/Culture/dance*]

      Belinda: A 1980s **Novelty Fad** Singular-Dance Movement. How to dance the **Belinda** to the Beat is described as follows in the "*Eighties Dances*," [www.inthe80s.com]:
          "***The Belinda*** *- The dance is done by bending your arms at the elbows and moving them side to side while kind of snapping your fingers. Your lower body should be twisting slightly.*"
      Similar to the (a) portion of **Hand-Jive-Routine**. Also to the **Palm-Circles**(1), **Churnin'-Butter, Sprinkler, Teen-Wolf , Hand-Jive, Hitch-Hiker,** and **Tiffany**. [See Chair-Dancing, Finger-Snaps, Finger-Flourishes, Arms-and-Hands, Free-Hand-Fashioning, and Gestures-Free-Hand. Also see Twist(1)&(2).]

Belly-Dance or **Hootchie-Kootchie** or **Danse-Du-Ventre** or **Middle-Eastern Dance:** Danced Solo to Arabic music and by the Lady only, this Traditional yet ever-popular **Belly-Dance** is a mildly lascivious dance in which the feminine navel is normally covered by a jewel.

"The truest expression of a people is in its dances and its music." -- Agnes deMille

All of the Sensuous Lady's Body-parts are Moved independently, especially the erotic stomach.

"Belly dancing is like a plate of jelatin with a vibrator under it." -- Anonymous

The following is from the *"Encyclopedia of Word and Phrase Origins"* by Robert Hendrickson:

*"**hootchie-kootchie**. The Turkish belly dance that many of us `have no stomach for,' as Beatrice Lillie once said. This name for the `mildly lascivious' dance -- `not as sensuous as actual bumps and grinds since the hips are swayed rather than the pelvis rotated,' we're told -- has no source in an oriental name unless it possibly comes from the Bengal state of Coach Behar. The best guess is that **hootchie-kootchie** derives from the English dialect words `hotch,' (`to shake') and `couch,' (pronounced `cooch,' `to protrude.') But this fails to explain why the dance was first recorded as the `cootchie-coot' in the 1890s. Dancer Little Egypt (Catherine Deviene) made a fortune and got herself arrested several times by dancing the **hootchie-kootchie** in the nude at the 1893 Chicago World's Fair and a number of private parties. A lowdown **hootchie-kootcher**, like Danny Kaye's `Minnie the Moocher,' is a **hootchie-kootchie** dancer."*

The three most common modern styles of isolated abdominal, hips, and chest **Belly-Dance** Movements are (1) the *Egyptian Raqs-Sharqi (`dance-of-the-East)*, (2) the *American-Niteclub*, and (3) the *American-Tribal*. She Performs in a `Bedleh,' which is a beaded bra/belt/skirt costume. The *Turn, Turn, Turn* of the **Belly-Dance**r's Repertoire includes *belly rolls, hip bumps, squeezing glutes, shoulder-shimmies, walking shimmies, forward and backward shimmies, back bends, poly-rhythmic clapping, figure eights,* and *camel walks*. With their Movement centered in the hips, arms are loose and casual with heavy elbows. Feet are flat and heavily grounded.

Same as the **Ghaziya-Dancer**. This dance may have been the same as the 1899s **Hoochy-Koochy**, and/or the **Hoochi-Coochi-Coo** of the 1960s.

[See Exotic-Dancer(1), Zills, Ankle-Bells, and Tambourine. Also see Veil-Dancing, Dance-of-the-Seven-Veils, Rai, Jeel, Al-Aghanni-Wataniyeh, and Whirling-Dervish. Also see Strip-Tease, Snake-Hips, Hip-Motion, Grinds, Hip-Bumps, and Fan-Dance.] [Some data from www.shira.net, & www.desertmoondance.com, & *www.sixtiescity.com/Culture/dance.*]

Belly-Roll: The **Belly-Roll** can be an Unleadable **Break-A-Way Novelty Fad** Pattern. This **Belly-Roll** is usually Performed while dancing the **Carolina-Shag**, the Faster **Arthur-Murray-Shag**, or the **Balboa**, among other dances. Timing for two Measures is usually *Slow Slow Quick Quick, Slow Slow Quick Quick*; but could be all eight *Slows*. If the Couple is Stepping the **Pure-Balboa**, the Lady is then Held Close in **Mush Position** with Upper-Body Couple-Rotational Movements Rolled Horizontally in Unison, either CW or CCW. This **Belly-Roll** can also be Performed Standing In-Place with Ad-Lib Timing.

[See Shorty-George, Boogie-Back, Ramble(2), Flamingo, Duck-Walk, Fly-Back, Lean, Stutter-Step, and the SugarFoot, for like Patterns. Also see **Break-A-Way Glossary**, and Balboa Step-Listing..]

Bend-Down-Low: A **Novelty Fad** dance of 1967. **Bend-Down-Low** had its own Eponymous record, *"Bend Down Low"* by *The Wailers.* [From *Soul,* www.trinity.unimelb.edu.au]

Bend-It!: This name for an Unleadable American **Novelty** or **Fad** dance of the 1960s is listed in the *"Dance Crazes of the Sixties"*, along with sketches showing this as a Singular-Dance, Pattern, or Figure.

Referred to as Patrick Kerr's dance, it shows six figures of a Lady Moving within one Spot. She Starts almost Squatting with her Feet Spread. She Slowly Rises until she Stands Straight with Feet Together, then she Lowers to almost Squatting again and again with her Feet Spread.

(See Novelty-&-Fad Dances-of-the-1960s.) [From *www.sixtiescity.com/Culture/dance*]

Big-Apple: A popular American **Novelty Fad** Group-Dance of the 1930s; began with a March and was Swing-oriented in 4/4 Time. The **Big-Apple** originated as a **Break-A-Way** about 1936 in a Columbia, South Carolina abandoned church, turned into a black *"Big Apple NightClub."* The **Big-Apple** was also an offshoot of the **Shag.** It was later influenced by Arthur Murray.

The following is a 12/03/02 letter from *Judy Pritchett*, friend of *Frankie Manning*, (www.swingshiftontap.com):

"I agree-- the Big Apple is a ball!! That version is from 1938. There is a plan for a Big Apple instructional video but it keeps changing so I can't tell you when it will come out. I think Frankie wants to do a different version for the video. He wants people to realize how variable the Big Apple was. It was a called dance, like in square dancing, and always different. You can hear Frankie calling it on Keep Punchin'."

The **Big-Apple** incorporated early Swing Steps, and had a **Caller** directing and requesting the following particular Steps. It started when the Caller yelled *"Cut the Apple!"* or sometimes *"Shine!"*, the dancers, wiggling their hips and without Clasping Hands, would then form circles of some eight or ten people each, facing mostly inwards. Then, at intervals in eight-Count increments, the Caller would yell, *"Come on and Swing!", "Charleston!", "Shorty-George!", "Suzie-Q!", or "Boogie-Back!", "Tack-Annie!", "Georgia-Grind!", "Praise-Allah!", "Truck to the Left! (or Right)", or "Peck to the Left! (or Right)", "Spank-the-Baby!", "Rusty-Dusty!", "Pose-and-a-Peck!", "Little-Apple!", "Little-Peach!", "Mess-Around!", "Stomp-Off!", "Apple-Jacks!", or "Fall-Off-the-Log!"*, etc. Only one Couple, or one Solo, was supposed to volunteer and Perform, in the circle center, that particular Step requested for the crowd, with the rest of the dancers clapping, shouting, dancing and circling around them. But by 1937, the **Big-Apple** allowed for improvisation by the whole group. See **Break-A-Way Glossary** for a more complete listing.

New York City was nicknamed **The Big Apple** due to this dance.

The **Big-Apple** Dance was similar to the **Casino-Rueda, Roundance**(1), and **Sequence-Dancing**, in that all four were/are Cued or Called.

(See Carioca, Conga-Line, Boomps-A-Daisy, and Lambeth-Walk; which were all Fads in vogue in the 1930s. Also see Lindy-Hop.) [Much data from Sonny Watson's StreetSwing.com]

Big-City-Stomp: Only this name for an American **Novelty** or **Fad** of the 1960s is listed simply as a Dance, Pattern, or Figure in the *"Dance Crazes of the Sixties."*

(See Novelty-&-Fad Dances-of-the-1960s.) [From *www.sixtiescity.com/Culture/dance*]

Big-Egg: Only this name for an American **Novelty** or **Fad** of the 1960s is listed simply as a Dance, Pattern, or Figure in the "*Dance Crazes of the Sixties*."
(See Novelty-&-Fad Dances-of-the-1960s.) [From *www.sixtiescity.com/Culture/dance*]

Big-'M': A Structured but Unleadable, **Novelty** Pattern for a Singular-Dancer; an eight-Measure Pattern, tracing the letter "M" upon the Dancefloor and then erasing it. This **Big-'M'** Pattern is one of the Qued Steps often Called for while dancing the **Madison** Audience-Participation-Dance's Basic-Step.
The following is an excerpt from *Madison Figures* -- [www.sixtiescity.com/Culture/]:
"*Trace the letter M on the floor with chasses to the left and right. There are 4 chasses to draw the M and another 4 to erase it.*"
The following are excerpts from *The Madison* -- [www.albertj.btinternet.co.uk/]:
"*LS, LS, RS, RS, LS, LS, RS, RS - Tracing line of a letter M in front of you.*
"*RS, RS, LS, LS, RS, RS, LS, LS - Reversing line of an M to erase it.*"
(See Double-Cross, Cleveland-Box, Basketball, 'T'-Time, Jackie-Gleason, Birdland, and Rifleman. Also see the Novelty-&-Fad Dances-of-the-1960s.)

Big-Willie: A **Novelty Fad** dance of 1969. **Big-Willie** was danced to the record, "*Runaway Child*" by *The Temptations*. [From *Soul*, www.trinity.unimelb.edu.au]

Billy-Jo: Only this name for an American **Novelty** or **Fad** of the 1960s is listed simply as a Dance, Pattern, or Figure in the "*Dance Crazes of the Sixties*."
(See Novelty-&-Fad Dances-of-the-1960s.) [From *www.sixtiescity.com/Culture/dance*]

Bingo-Boy: An American **Novelty Fad** Solo-Dance or Maneuver of the 1980s in Cadence with the Music.
The following is from "*Eighties Dances*" - [www.inthe80s.com]:
"***The Bingo Boy:*** *Made famous in the song by the Bingo Boys 'How To Dance'. Step left, around, together with the right, stand straight, bend knees, thrust hips. Was huge in the clubs.*"
(See Novelty-&-Fad Dances-of-the-1980s.)

Bin-Laden: From Kingston, Jamaica, an Underground **Novelty Fad**, Singular- or Group-Dance Movement, associated with dancing **Dancehall/Ragga**, which, in turn, are outgrowths of the **Ska/Reggae**. **Bin-Laden** was and is danced mainly by youths of color.
The following is from *Ragga Fashions*: [www.bbc.co.uk]
"*Bin-Laden - Glide across the floor from side to side in a skating motion. At the same time use your hands to stroke your imaginary beard.*"
See **Dancehall**(2) for further explanation. (Also see Bogle, Armstrong, Butterfly, Go-Go-Wine, Body-Basic-and-Exercise, Tate, and World-Dance. Also see Jerry-Springer, Prang, Heel-and-Toe, Na!Na!Na!, Screechie, Zip-It-Up, Drive-By, Shizzle-Ma-Nizzle, and Matrix. Also see Underground Step-Listing.) [Also see Skate(1)&(2).]

Bird or **Birdie**: An Unstructured, American **Novelty Fad** Singular or Apart-Coupledance Pattern in vogue in the 1960s. In 1962, there were the following two records to which the **Bird** was danced: *"Grandma Bird"* by *The Four Hollidays*, and *"The Bird's The Word"* by *The Rivingtons*. [From *Soul*, www.trinity.unimelb.edu.au] There is also *"The Bird"* by *The Time*. There also is mention of a 1963 Eponymous music with *DeeDee Sharp* singing for this dance. **Bird** attempted to imitate a Bird's actions through Pantomime, as follows:

To 4/4 Tempo music, **Birdie**'s Comical Basic-Step by the dancer was to constantly High Step In- Place, by Raising Heels onto Balls or off the floor, while simultaneously Slightly Bowing the Upper-Body with each Step. The dancer's upper arms protruded Outward parallel with the Dancefloor, with both forearms Forward and with wrists Flexing Slightly Up and Down with each Step or Faster. Fingers remained Spread like feathers and the dancer's protruding lips Quivered at times, **Bird**-like.

[See Novelty-Dances, Fad-Dances, Novelty-and-Fad Genre, and the Novelty-&-Fad Dances-of-the-1960s. Also see Bird-Dog, Birdland, Buzzard-Lope, Chicago-Bird, Chicken(1), Chicken-Back-Twist, Chicken-Dance, Chicken-Reel, Chicken-Scratch(2)&(3), Chicky-Goo, Claw, Crazy-Chicken, Eagle-Rock, Funky-Buzzard, Funky-Chicken, Greasy-Chicken, Monkey-Bird, Ostrich, Peck, Rooster-Walk, Scratch, Scratchin', Shake-a-Tail-Feather, Shakey-Bird, Surfin'-Bird, Turkey-Neck-Stretch, and Turkey-Trot(1)&(2).]

Bird-Dog: A **Novelty Fad** Coupledance of 1966. It's Eponymous Music was *"Bird Dog "* by the *Del Counts*.

(See Novelty-&-Fad Dances-of-the-1960s.) [From www.bluejuice.org.au]

Birdie: See Bird.

Birdland: The **Birdland** was a 1960s **Novelty Fad** Coupledance. It was both Unstructured and Unleadable. At that time, Chubby Checker sang the Eponymous words to its record, *"Birdland"*. The following are a few excerpted lines from his words to it:

"It's got rhythm and the rock and roll, a little chacha gonna move my soul
Yeah come on baby and we're gonna swing
Come on and show me how you shake that thing
Look at Susie who lives next door, she can shake it but she shake it more"

A portion of this **Birdland** was also a Novelty, Qued Step incorporated into the **Madison** Audience-Participation-Dance. The two Qued *Slow Slow QuickQuick Slow* Measures of this *"Birdland"* could be danced *forward Backward shake Shake shake...; backward Forward Shake shake Shake....*

The following is an excerpt from *Madison Figures* -- [www.sixtiescity.com/Culture/]:

*"**Birdland**, [6 1/2 Measures]: Totally freeform. Walk around doing various bird impressions as you wish."*

The following is an excerpt from *The Madison* -- [www.albertj.btinternet.co.uk/]:

"Strut around, acting like a demented chicken."

[See Double-Cross, Cleveland-Box, Basketball, Big-'M', 'T'-Time, Jackie-Gleason, and Rifleman. Also see the Novelty-&-Fad Dances-of-the-1960s.]

Black-Bottom: An American wild Novelty **Fad**, danced to a 4/4 Beat at 140 to 160 BPM, Singularly at first as a Black Solo-Dance and later as a Coupledance.

Some say the **Black-Bottom** was originally from New Orleans or Georgia in the 1910s, and that it may have been influenced by an earlier dance named the **Echo**. In 1919, "_The Original Black Bottom Dance_" sheet Music by Perry Bradford gave the dance instructions as well as giving its song. Bradford had first seen the dance done in Jacksonville and had first started writing about it in 1907. In 1924, the "_Dinah_" Stage Play gave the New York White public a view of the **Black-Bottom**, and a famous rendition of the **Black-Bottom** was in "_The George White Scandals of 1926_" at the Apollo Theater in Harlem.

A song was written about this time named "_Black Bottom Stomp_" by Jelly Roll Morton. Also, sheet Music for the song, "_Don't-Take-That-Black-Bottom-Away_" was copyrighted in 1926 and published by _Henry Waterson, Inc._, with _Barbelle_ illustrating its cover. Composers and lyricists were _Sam Coslow, Addy Britt_, and _Harry Link_. Principal Performer was _John E. Frenkel_.

In 1927, the Roseland in New York City hosted a **Black-Bottom** Marathon. By 1928, the **Black-Bottom** had become so popular that it had replaced the **Charleston** altogether as a dance, with the exceptions of the **Charleston**'s inclusion in dances such as the **Lindy-Hop** and the **Big-Apple**.

The Solo **Black-Bottom** was one of at least two dances inspired by the **Charleston** and was difficult to dance. It emphasized the Up-Beat(1) or [Off-Beat(1)] and was the beginning for modern Tap-Dancing Phrasing, [see Pickup(2).] The dance involved Swaying the Torso, Bending the Knees, and had short Kicks. One often slapped one's own backside while Hopping Forward and Back. It's Stomping Steps, Torso Gyrations, Knee Sway and Shuffling were of Afro-American influence. Arms Moved in Time to the Music and there was an occasional Back-Flick or Mulekick. Some of the original Solo **Black-Bottom** Figures or Patterns were named the **Flick**, the **Side-Shuffle**, and the **Walk**.

Its Basic Step in 1927, off the Music's regular Beat, was a mixture of Jazz Steps. Both index fingers Pointed Up and eyes rolled while doing two long Stomps, Right then Left, followed by four short Stomps.

Some of the **Black-Bottom** Lyrics from "_The George White Scandals of 1927_":
> **Hop Down** _front and then you doodle_ (**Slide**) _back,_
> **Mooch** _to your left and then you_ **Mooch** _to your right,_
> _Hands on your hips and do the_ **Mess-Around**,
> _Break-a-Leg_ (**Wobble**) _until you're near the ground,_
> _Now that's the old Black-Bottom Dance ......(more)_

The **Black-Bottom** was refined by 1927 or 1928 for Ballroom Coupledance suitability. This naughty-and-nice dance suited the time.

(See Mess-Around, and Mooch. Also see Varsity-Drag, and the Shimmy; both Fads in vogue in the 1920s.) [Much data from Sonny Watson's StreetSwing.com]

Blackout-Stroll: A **Novelty Fad** Coupledance in vogue after 1939. Its Music by Joe Loss was heard for the first time in November 1939. Others say its Music was by Tommie Connor, and that this was a "_War Novelty Sequence Dance_."

(See Sequence-Dance, and Chestnut-Tree.) [Some from _Novelty Dances Through the Years_ by Pony Moore.]

Black-Stomp: Only this name for an American **Novelty** or **Fad** of the 1960s is listed simply as a Dance, Pattern, or Figure in the "*Dance Crazes of the Sixties.*"
     (See Novelty-&-Fad Dances-of-the-1960s.) [From *www.sixtiescity.com/Culture/dance*]

Blakes-Beat: Only this name for an American **Novelty** or **Fad** of the 1960s is listed simply as a Dance, Pattern, or Figure in the "*Dance Crazes of the Sixties.*"
     (See Novelty-&-Fad Dances-of-the-1960s.) [From *www.sixtiescity.com/Culture/dance*]

Block: This name for an Unleadable American **Novelty** or **Fad** of the 1960s is listed in the "*Dance Crazes of the Sixties,*" along with a 12-pictures Sequence (showing Patrick Kerr?) and the following writeup describing this as a Singular-Dance, Pattern, or Figure:
     "*Crouch down with arms slightly bent, palms facing down. Quickly place one foot in front of the other and twist your heel as it lands. Spin around on your heels and improvise a bit of fancy footwork.*"
     (See Novelty-&-Fad Dances-of-the-1960s.) [From *www.sixtiescity.com/Culture/dance*]

BlueBeat: This Unleadable **Novelty** or **Fad** American **Group-Dance** of **1964** had its own Eponymous record, "*Do The Bluebeat* " by *Dinah Lee*. This **BlueBeat** Dance is listed in the "*Dance Crazes of the Sixties,*" along with writeups on its *Basic-Swing* and on its *Fly-Away*, written as follows, plus it shows three pictures: (Group consists of several Couples.)
     "***The Blue-Beat:-*** *BasicBlue-BeatSwing (same steps for boy and girl)* *Stand with feet apart, hands held at side of body two or three inches from side.*
     "*1. Swing weight over onto left foot, both knees bending over to the left, swinging arms across each other at the same time.*
     "*2. Swing weight over to the right foot, both knees bending over to the right, uncrossing arms and swinging them wide open away from body.*
     "*Continue this swinging movement left and right, keeping time to the very definite background beat that you can hear in all 'blue-beat' music. Keep arm swing sharp and defined.*"
     "*Blue-Beat Fly-Away (can be danced before or after the basic swing)*
     "*1. Straighten right knee, raising left foot in sharp, small kick in front of right foot.*
     "*2. Step onto left foot, lowering it in front of right foot.*
     "*3-4. Transfer weight onto right foot, then left foot, in a rocking action.*
     "*5. Straighten left knee, raising right foot in sharp, small kick in front of left foot.*
     "*6. Step onto right foot, lowering it in front of left foot.*
     "*7-8. Transfer weight onto left foot, then right foot, in a rocking action.*"
     Titled "*Fly-away step1,*" the first picture shows one Couple alone, unattached, each small Kicking.
     Titled "*Swing step 1,*" the second picture shows four people In-Line, each Bent Forward upon Left Foot and with Crossed Arms.
     Titled "*Fly-away (group),*" the third picture shows four people facing each other in a Circle, unattached, each small Kicking their left foot.
     (See Novelty-&-Fad Dances-of-the-1960s.) [From *www.sixtiescity.com/Culture/dance*, and from *www.bluejuice.org.au*]

Blue-Chip: Only this name for an American **Novelty** or **Fad** of the 1960s is listed simply as a Dance, Pattern, or Figure in the "*Dance Crazes of the Sixties*."
    (See Novelty-&-Fad Dances-of-the-1960s.) [From *www.sixtiescity.com/Culture/dance*]

Body-Popping: Teen-Age underground Singular-Dance **Novelty Fad** Movements, that includes Flicking one's Head in Time with the Stepping. See **Pop** for detailed instructions.
    Head Flicking is similar to Na!Na!Na! (See Electric-Boogie.)

Bomba or **LaBomba:** (Spanish for *pump*.) A simple, **Novelty Fad** Coupledance, at times danced Singularly. **Bomba** is a variation of the **Merengue**. Popular with Spanish-speaking young Latins in Southern California in 1996. With medium 4/4 Timing, dancers Bob, One-Stepping, rarely Doubling, Lifting Feet with Slight contortions.
    Bomba was originally a distinctly Puerto Rican Folkloric Rhythm and Folkdance featuring a big drum, with African influence predominating. **Bomba** Rhythm is commonly associated with **Salsa** music.
    (See Clave-Beat, Bamba, Soca, Calypso, Conga-Line, and the Plena. Also see Chicken-Dance, Dirty-Dancing, Lambada, Macarena, Punta y Soka, Quebradita, Teen-Dancing, and Urban-Dance; which were all Novelty Fads in vogue in the 1980s and 1990s.)

Bombay: Only this name for an American **Novelty** or **Fad** of the 1960s is listed simply as a Dance, Pattern, or Figure in the "*Dance Crazes of the Sixties*."
    (See Novelty-&-Fad Dances-of-the-1960s.) [From *www.sixtiescity.com/Culture/dance*]

Bombie: A **Novelty Fad** Coupledance of the 1960s. This had its own Eponymous record, the "*Bombie* " by *Johnny Sharp & The Yellow Jackets.*
    (See Novelty-&-Fad Dances-of-the-1960s.) [From www.bluejuice.org.au]

Boney-Maronie: A **Novelty Fad** Coupledance of 1959. It's Eponymous Music was "*Boney Maronie* " by *Larry Williams.*
    (See Novelty-&-Fad Dances-of-the-1960s.) [From www.bluejuice.org.au]

Bongo-Hop: Only this name for an American **Novelty** or **Fad** of the 1960s is listed simply as a Dance, Pattern, or Figure in the "*Dance Crazes of the Sixties*."
    (See Novelty-&-Fad Dances-of-the-1960s.) [From *www.sixtiescity.com/Culture/dance*]

   Boogaloo or **Electric-Boogaloo** or **Boog-Style**: An Unstructured, American **Novelty Fad** Singular or Coupledance in vogue in the 1960s. Believed beginning in 1965, there were the following records to which the **Boogaloo** was danced: "*Boogaloo*" by *Les Mccann,* "*Boogaloo #3*" by *Roy Lee Johnson,* "*My Baby Likes To Boogaloo*" by *Don Gardner,* "*Do The Boogaloo*" by *King Coleman,* and "*Sock Boogaloo*" by *Bobby Rush.* [From *Soul,* www.trinity.unimelb.edu.au]
In 1967, *Fantastic Johnny C* recorded "*Boogaloo Down Broadway.*" There were probably Eponymous dance Movements named The Boogaloo. At the time, Chubby Checker came out with the song, *Hey You! Boo-Ga-Loo,* (but it carried no dance instruction.) It is known that **The Boogaloo** had (or has) some Moves Illusionary in nature, (see **Electric-Boogie.**) **Boogaloo** combines Mime and Theatrics, and involves contorting the dancer's Body and face. Compared to Breakin' which is down upon the Dancefloor, **Boogaloo** is Up and off the floor.
   With new dances every week, not all caught on nationally, As songs came out in 1967, so did a corresponding dance, and few of either lasted more than a few weeks. But **The Boogaloo** dancing has since stayed and is current with the **Underground** urban youth pop culture.
   Boogaloo dancing has stayed current with that culture since the late 1970s, especially as part of the **Funk-Style** that has been danced mainly in California. Not truly **Break-Dancing**, yet the **Boogaloo** is often currently incorporated into it. **Boogaloo** is the dance version of **Popping**. The **Boogaloo,** along with **Popping** and **Locking,** is (or was) actually part of the 1990s **Funk-Style** of dancing, mainly of California.
   The following is from "*Funk Styles,*" [www.electricboogaloos.com]:
   "*In a town called Fresno, California, there lived a shy boy named Sam. Inspired to create his own style of dance after seeing the original Lockers perform on TV, in 1975 Sam started putting together movements which later became known as boogaloo or boog style.*
   "*The name came from the old James Brown song `Do the Boogaloo'.  One day when Sam was dancing around the house, his uncle said `Boy, do that boogaloo!' A puzzled Sam asked his uncle, `What's boogaloo?'.  `That means you're gettin down' his uncle replied. From that day on he was known as Boogaloo Sam.*
   "*Not many people know what boogaloo style is or how to do it. Boogaloo is a fluid style that uses every part of the body. It involves using angles and incorporating fluid movements to make everything flow together, often using rolls of the hips, knees, head. Making your legs do wierd things, and covering a lot of space on stage using `walkouts' or other transitions to get from one spot to the next spot. Although it is described as fluid, please note that boogaloo is different from the style known as waving.*"
   The following is an exerpt from *DanceCulture.com*:
   "*Electric Boogaloo-* --- *The term was used especially by the B-Boys who used these moves in their battles. But there are other cases where it's been described as a style all its own. Who better to describe electric boogaloo than the Electric Boogaloos dance crew? Though some say that, like popping, the style is based on isolation, the Boogaloos make sure to note that boogaloo is distinct from popping and waving: `Boogaloo is a fluid style that uses every part of the body.  It involves using angles and incorporating fluid movements to make everything flow together, often using rolls of the hips, knees, head.  Making your legs do weird things, and covering a lot of space on stage using `walkouts' or other transitions to get from one spot to the next spot.' (electricboogaloos.com) It seems that Boogaloo involves more fluid movements and popping involves flexing the muscles.*"

(Continued)

Boogaloo: (Continued)

The following _BOOGALOO_ is extracted from _HOT SALSA: The Dictionary_:

"_In the middle of the 60ties, in the USA, Latin music is in crisis. Pachanga, that shakes dancers from few years, begins to run out of steam from 1965. With its big bands, pachanga is not adapted to the brand new times, ..._

"_From this [the swing of the Latin big bands] fusion - Latin music, twist, rhythm`n'blues - the boogaloo rises. The new fashion, generally using English for the lyrics, looks for commercial success. Sometimes it succeeds, with hits like `I like it like that' by Pete Rodriguez, who is sacred `king of boogaloo'. Affected by the virus, all the Latin musicians are converted to the new fashion, and try to take advantage of the commercial effects._

"_The silly but effective boogaloo (and its few variants like `shing a ling' and `afroloo') reach its highest point in 1967; it regns on Latin music till the early `70ties, before to be dethroned by `salsa', for which it prepared the ground. ..._"

Boogaloo Moves are similar to those for **Animation**(3), incorporating Moves such as **Waving, Strobing, Ticking, Roboting, Tutting,** and **Floating-and-Gliding.** [Data from www.glowsticking.com]

Boogaloo is the same as **Electric-Boogie,** and **Electric-Boogaloo,** (see Electric-Boogie). Being an American folk artform, see "**Mime,**" and "**Robot,**" for some slices of history of this **Boogaloo**.

Some of the California `Funk' brand of this **Boogaloo** Genre of Mime "Moves" are as follows: (From "_Funk Styles,_" [www.electricboogaloos.com])

"_Air posing, Animation, Boogaloo, Bopping, Centipede, Crazy Legs, Cobra, Dime Stopping, Filmore, Floating/Gliding, Hitting, Popping, Puppet, Robot, Saccin, Scarecrow, Snaking, Spiderman, Sticking, Strobing, Strutting, Ticking, Tutting, and Waving._"

See **Underground Step-Listing.** (Also see Novelty-&-Fad Dance-of-the-1960s.)

Boogaloo-Popeye: Only this name for an American **Novelty** or **Fad** of the 1960s is listed simply as a Dance, Pattern, or Figure in the "_Dance Crazes of the Sixties._"

(See Novelty-&-Fad Dances-of-the-1960s.) [From _www.sixtiescity.com/Culture/dance_]

Boogie-Back or **Kick-Backs:** An Unleadable 1930s **Separated-Break-A-Way Novelty Fad** Shine-Step Pattern, usually Performed while dancing the **Big-Apple,** or the **Carolina-Shag,** or a **Swing-Bal** Break from the **Pure-Balboa.** Also suitable for the many **Swing** dances.

Kick-Ball-Change 4 times for 8 Counts, drifting Rearward. Clap Hands on Counts 2,4,6,8. Usually followed by a **Shorty-George.** [See **Boogie**(1), and **Boogie-Back-And-Forward-Shorty.**)

For the **Big-Apple, Boogie-Back** was one of the **Break-A-Way** Genre. Wiggling their hips, certain **Break-A-Way** Patterns were danced. The original **Suzie-Q, Boogie-Back, Tack-Annie, Georgia-Grind, Praise-Allah!, Truckin', Peckin', Charleston, Shorty-George,** and other Break-A-Ways, were probably originated early by blacks; while **Spank-the-Baby, Rusty-Dusty, Pose-and-a-Peck,** the **Little-Apple,** the **Little-Peach, Mess-Around, Stomp-Off, Apple-Jacks,** and **Fall-Off-the-Log,** and other Break-A-Ways, were probably originated later by whites. Most all of these Patterns seem to have been influenced or derived from the classic **Lindy-Hop** and/or **Big-Apple** dances. See **Break-A-Way Glossary** for a more complete listing.

[See Shim-Sham(2), and Shuffling-to-OffStage.]

Boogie-Back-and-Forward-Shorty: An Unleadable 1930s **Separated-Break-A-Way** Novelty **Fad** Shine-Step Pattern, originating with the **Cake-Walk**, and usually Performed while dancing the **Lindy-Hop**, **Big-Apple**, or the **Carolina-Shag**, or a **Swing-Bal** Break from the **Pure-Balboa**. Also suitable for the many **Swing** dances, and for dances of the **Tap-Dance Genre**.

To Start the **Boogie-Back-and-Forward-Shorty**, the dancer would separate from one's Partner (on a Primary-DownBeat) by Executing a **Kick-Ball-Change 4 times for 8 Counts, drifting Rearward, Clapping Hands on Counts 2,4,6,8.** The dancer would then Perform a **Shorty-George** to return back Together:

The separated Partner `**Boogie**s' from four to six *Slow*, short Steps Forward, with index fingers Pointed Down, as Walks slope Downward. The Free Hip is Raised DiagForward in a Circular Motion and Moved out from one's Supporting-Leg before Free-Foot is Stepped Forward, i.e., one's free Hip-Lifts to Move Circularly in the direction of the Supporting-Foot. Swiveling on Balls, with Knees Together and Well Bent, Hips are Swayed Side-to-Side. One's Right Step rolls from Inner-Edge onto the Outer-Edge of Right Ball-of Foot, as one's Right Hip protrudes Outward and Up. One's Left Step is Opposite.

See **Break-A-Way Glossary** for more listing. Also see **Break-Endings** for many additional Break-A-Ways that were derived or influenced by **West-Coast-Swing**. [Also see Shim-Sham(2), Boogie(1), and Boogie-Woogie(3).]

Boogie-Down: An American **Novelty Fad** comical Solo-Dance or Maneuver of the 1980s in Cadence with the Music.

The following is from "*Eighties Dances*" - [www.inthe80s.com]:

"*Boogie Down: This dance was in the hit song 'Wake Me Up Before You Go-Go' by Wham!. It works best if you have long hair. You sway your head in a circle and twist your arms around. Keep your legs in place but sway them around. You will be a hit on the dance floor.*"

(See Novelty-&-Fad Dances-of-the-1980s.)

Boogler: Only this name for an American **Novelty** or **Fad** of the 1960s is listed simply as a Dance, Pattern, or Figure in the "*Dance Crazes of the Sixties.*"

(See Novelty-&-Fad Dances-of-the-1960s.) [From *www.sixtiescity.com/Culture/dance*]

Boomerang: A **Novelty Fad** dance of 1965. The **Boomerang** had its own Eponymous record, "*The Boomerang*" by *Jr. Walker & The Allstars*. [From *Soul*, www.trinity.unimelb.edu.au]

Boomps-A-Daisy: A **Novelty Fad** Coupledance in vogue in the U.S. in 1940, similar to the Lambeth-Walk. Partners would **Bump** hips at regular intervals while dancing to its own special Waltz Music.

Similar to the later **Bump**(2) Novelty **Fad** Coupledance of the 1970s. (Also see Big-Apple, Carioca, Conga-Line, and Lambeth-Walk; which were all Novelty Fads in vogue in the 1930s.)

Booty-Green: Only this name for an American **Novelty** or **Fad** of the 1960s is listed simply as a Dance, Pattern, or Figure in the "*Dance Crazes of the Sixties.*"
    (See Novelty-&-Fad Dances-of-the-1960s.) [From *www.sixtiescity.com/Culture/dance*]

Bop: An American **Novelty** Spot-dance, in vogue from 1967 to about 1973. There were "**Bop**" records as early as 1955. These were "*Do The Bop*" by *Arthur Lee Maye & The Crowns*, and "*Bop With Me*" by *Rosco Gordon*. [From *Soul*, www.trinity.unimelb.edu.au]
    Bop was danced Singularly or with the Couple Apart but mostly Facing each other. These 1960s dances were (and are) free and individualistic. People enmasse, mostly teens with long hair, were dancing by themselves and inventing as they danced. This same **Bop** has continued to be danced clear into the 2000s, as a Move of the California `Funk' brand of the **Boogaloo** Genre of Mime "Moves," which seems to be part of the **Electric-Boogie** Style of **Break-Dancing**, which, in turn, is part of **Hip-Hop**.
    To dance the **Bop**, Feet are extremely Swiveled to and fro, with one Foot often Crossing Behind the other. Sometimes Spastic, other times soft and gentle to Slow music. As a Couple, Partners would Turn or Spin Singularly, sometimes upon the Man's hand signal.
    Six-Count, ten-Weight-Changes, *Quickand Quickand Quickand Slow, quickAnd slow,* Basic-Step, danced on Partner's Same-Feet, was *ForCrossBallinplace   Homeinplace ForCrossBallinplace Home, backlockballInPlace home.*
    The following is from "*Rewind the Fifties*" - [www.loti.com/fifties]:
    "***The Bop:*** *When you dance the bop,you usually dance separately from your partner. It's a lot like jive or swing, but there's a lot of toe tapping involved, and you don't hold hands. Usually you alternately tap the heel and toe of either foot as you dance. The Bop is still popular in many dance clubs and events, and is especially popular in many areas of England.*"
    [See the Bambuco, Bunny-Hop, Calypso, Creep, Fish, Flea-Hop, Frug, Guapacha, Hand-Jive, Hitch-Hiker, Hokey-Pokey, Hullie-Gullie, Jerk, Limbo-Rock, Mashed-Potato, Monkey, Pachanga, Plena, Pony, Rock-and-Around, Scooter, Slide, Strole, Surfers, Swim, Tumba-Cha, Twist, Twister, and the Watusi; which were all Novelty Fads in vogue in the 1950-60s. Also see Air-Posing, Animation(3), Centipede, Cobra, Crazy-Legs, Dime-Stopping, Filmore, Floating(2), Glides, Hitting, King-Tut, Pop(3), Puppet, Robot, Saccin, Scarecrow, Snake(4), Spiderman, Sticking, Strobing, Strut, Tick, and Wave(1); for other related Moves. Also see Underground Step-Listing. Also see Novelty-&-Fad Dance-of-the-1960s.]

Boss-Walk: Only this name for an American **Novelty** or **Fad** of the 1960s is listed simply as a Dance, Pattern, or Figure in the "*Dance Crazes of the Sixties.*"
    (See Novelty-&-Fad Dances-of-the-1960s.) [From *www.sixtiescity.com/Culture/dance*]

Boston-Dip: See Boston-Waltz.

Boston-Hop: Only this name for an American **Novelty** or **Fad** of the 1960s is listed simply as a Dance, Pattern, or Figure in the "*Dance Crazes of the Sixties.*"
    (See Novelty-&-Fad Dances-of-the-1960s.) [From *www.sixtiescity.com/Culture/dance*]

Boston-Monkey: This name for an Unleadable American **Novelty** or **Fad** of the 1960s is listed in the "_Dance Crazes of the Sixties_," as a Dance or Pattern, along with the following writeup:

"_**The Boston Monkey:** Feet together, knees bent. Body bent from the waist. Hands in front of you, palms down, at waist level. Movement: Hips to the left, hips to the right. You push your right hip out and slightly back, at the same time moving your hands to the left. You push your left hip out and slightly back, at the same time moving yuor hands to the right. All done bobbing monkey-like._"

(See Novelty-&-Fad Dances-of-the-1960s.) [From _www.sixtiescity.com/Culture/dance_]

Boston-Waltz or **Boston** or **Boston-Dip** or **Slow-Waltz:** A Coupledance that was danced with an "Accent" in an informal Loose-Closed Position. In Boston, Massachusetts in 1834, the more difficult **Waltz**es that were in vogue were modified by a Lorenzo Papatino into the creation of this easier **Boston-Waltz**, which soon became popular internationally in the 1840s.

Danced at a leisurely 90 BPM, the **Boston** was different and was generally danced much Slower and Smoother than the Viennese and other Waltzes of the early 1800s, (_Step -- Rise_, instead of such as _Leap -- Hop_.) Evenly danced with two Steps per Measure, the Floating "Accent" was a _Slow Quick_ per a three-Beat Measure. This new **Boston-Waltz** retained the early Waltze's characteristic Turning Figures, and added other Movements such as Dips. Also, it was danced with Partners Holding with their Hands on each other's hips. This new **Boston** had the distinction of being the first Coupledance to be danced with Feet Parallel, rather than with Feet Turned-Out as in Ballet. Social Dancers had had their **Boston** in 3/4 Time; then, popular in America in 1912, came both their **Onestep** and **Twostep** in 4/4 Time. With these three dances, there developed the Forward Traveling Step with the Heel-Lead.

Allen Dodworth's manual, published in 1885, explains how to dance the **Boston** thusly:

"_The **Motion Step** ---- when Stepping with the Right Foot, the Left Knee is Slightly Bent, producing the Dip, from which the name **Boston-Dip** was derived. In Stepping with the Left Foot, Bend the Right Knee._

[This also necessitates a Slight Softening of the Stepping-Foot Knee.]

"_The **Motion Rise** is simply Raising the Heel of the Foot upon which the Step is made, marking the third Beat by the descent._

"_The Turn is made by changing the angles of the Steps, and twisting upon the Foot at the Rise, while the Heel is Up. Right Turn, Right Forward, Left Backward. Left Turn (Reverse), Left Forward, Right Backward._"

Several different versions of the **Boston** developed: There was the **American-Boston** (Slower), the **French-Boston** (more rapid), and (probably) the **Valse-L'Americaine**, first composed in 1866 by the Societe' Academique des Profeseurs de danse de Paris.

Minor versions also developed: The _Five Step Boston, One Step Waltz, Herring Bone Boston, Seven Step Boston, Double Triple Boston, Philadelphia Boston, Long Boston, New York Boston, Double Boston, Russian Boston, Drop Step, English Berceuse, Boston Point, Cross Boston, Cradle Boston, Boston Spanish (stairs), English or Three Step Boston_, and the _Triple Boston_.

Later, as this **Boston-Waltz** waned in popularity in the early 1900s, (but still from 1910 to 1914, many danced the **Boston-Waltz** at the Bostonclub in the Savoy Hotel in central London,) it stimulated the Floating Styling for the coming **American** (Medium) **Waltz**, and for the coming **International Slow-Waltz**.

(See Slow-Waltz, American Medium Waltz, and Redowa. Also see The-Leap, and The-Hop.) [Much from streetswing.com, geocities.com, and memory.loc.gov]

Bounce: A **Novelty Fad** Coupledance of 1965. This had its own Eponymous record, *"The Bounce"* by *The Olympics*.
   (See Novelty-&-Fad Dances-of-the-1960s.) [From www.bluejuice.org.au]

Box: An American **Novelty Fad** Singular or Coupledance in vogue in the 1960s. The dance, itself, attempted to imitate a **Box** through Pantomime. This length by width by height **Box** was probably one of the subjects mimicked in the **Hullie-Gullie** dance game of 1963. Although having had its own Eponymous song, the **Box** proved to be not very popular and faded soon with its song.
   (See the Novelty-&-Fad Dances-of-the-1960s.)

Boxer: An Unstructured and Unleadable, **Novelty Fad** Spot-Coupledance, popular in the Eastern U.S. in the early 1960s. The dance Mimicked a **Boxer** Shadow-Boxing, and was one of a whole series of 1960s Mimicking dance Patterns, (see Hullie-Gullie.) This silly **Boxer**, along with other silly Fad-Dances, was banned at Brigham Young University in 1966.
   This **Boxer** had constant Knee-Bounce and prominent Shoulder-Lead with Spot-Movement. Firstly, two jabs were by the Leading Clenched-Fist then two were by the Trailing Clenched-Fist. These jabs were profusely included and were danced in Time to the Music. Footwork is constant Cadence while Armwork might be *and Slow   and Slow, and Slow   and Slow.*
   Similar to the **Cleveland-Box**. (See the Novelty-&-Fad Dances-of-the-1960s. Also see Boxing, Punch, Battling, Dance-Battle, Martial-Arts, Uprock, Krumping, Capoeira, Frevo, and Batucado. Also see Antigravity-Sign, HighStand-Display, and Broadside-Display.)

Brain: A **Novelty Fad** Coupledance of the 1960s. This had its own Eponymous record, *"The Brain"* by *Jimmy Troy*.
   (See Novelty-&-Fad Dances-of-the-1960s.) [From www.bluejuice.org.au]

Break-A-Way or **Shine-Step:**   American Coupledance **Break-Endings** that were in vogue from 1926 and into the early 1930s; related, some say, to the early **Lindy-Hop, Texas-Tommy, Charleston**, and to the **Apache Dance. Break-A-Ways** are **Shine-Step**s. There are **Butterfly-Break-A-Ways**, that are normally Coupledanced in Butterfly Position, and there are completely **Separated-Break-A-Ways**, that are normally Coupledanced **Solo**, without Partner contact.
   The first known form of Swing, first seen in 1909, was the **Texas-Tommy**, which had changed names by some to the **Mooch-and-Sugar** in 1916. By 1919, this dance was called by some the **Break-A-Way**. The **Break-A-Way** was mixing with the Charleston by the middle and late 1920s, forming a new dance style, perhaps called **The-Hop**. (See Lindy-Hop.)
   After dancing a sort of **Twostep**, or the **Swing-Bal** portion of the **Balboa**, Partners would **Break-A-Way**, dance a few Measures Solo, and then Close Together again. Wiggling their hips, certain **Break-A-Way** Patterns danced were the **Boogie-Back, Suzie-Q, Tack-Annie, Georgia-Grind, Praise-Allah!, Truckin', Peckin', Charleston, Shorty-George, Spank-the-Baby, Rusty-Dusty, Pose-and-a-Peck**, the **Little-Apple**, the **Little-Peach, Mess-Around, Stomp-Off, Apple-Jacks**, and **Fall-Off-the-Log**, and other **Break-A-Ways**. See **Break-A-Way Glossary** for a more complete listing. Some of this supposedly was as seen in the *Fox Movietone Follies* Movie of about 1929.

(Continued)

Break-A-Way: (Continued)
See **Break-Endings**, and **ChaCha-Break-Endings-for-Man**. (Also see Flash-Step. Also see Swing-Out, and Apache-Spin. Also see Big-Apple, and Speed-Lindy. Also see Syncopations-in-the-Dance, Light-and-Shade, Freeze-and-Melt, Smartly, and Ooze.) [Much data from Sonny Watson's StreetSwing.com]

Break-A-Way Glossary: The following is a Spot-Coupledance alphabetized listing of many of the possible **Break-A-Way** Open or Butterfly Position Pattern names:
Apple-Jacks, And-Change-And-Change-And, Belly-Roll, Boogie-Back, Boogie-Back-and-Forward-Shorty, Charleston, Circle-Pivot, Corta-Jaca, Curls, Double-Foot-Boogie, Duck-Walk, Fall-Off-the-Log, Flamingo, Fly-Back, Foot-Boogie, Georgia-Grind, Heel-Splits, Heel-Switches, Jazz-Boxes**, Leans, Little-Apple, Little-Peach, Marchessi, Mess-Around, NightLife, Peckin'** [Peck to the Left (or Right)]**, Pose-and-a-Peck, Praise-Allah, Ramble, Rusty-Dusty, Sailor-Shuffle, Sailor-Shuffle-InFront, Sand-Step, Shorty-George, Spank-the-Baby, Stomp-Off, Stutter-Step, SugarFoot, Suzie-Q, Tack-Annie, Toe-Splits, Traveling-SugarFoot**, and **Truckin'** [Truck to the Left (or **Right**)].
The above **Break-A-Ways** can be Performed while dancing the **Lindy, Lindy-Hop, West-Coast-Swing, Carolina-Shag, Big-Apple**, the **Swing-Bal** portion of the **Balboa**, and the **Texas-Tommy**, among other dances. Many of these are Coupledanced as Mirror-Patterns.
See **Break-Endings** for many additional Break-A-Ways. [Also see Challenge(2). Also see Speed-Lindy, Funk-Swing, Shine, Hijacking, SugarPush-Fancy, Break-Pattern, Challenge-Step, and Dummying.]

Break-Dancing or **Breaking** or **Break** or **Rocking** or **Good-Foot** or **B-Boy'n** or **Break-Boy** or **Breakin'** or **Gangsta-HipHop**: Terms for **Urban-Street-Dancing** of about 1981 and before. A Genre, a Style of very Fast **Acrobatic-Dancing**, usually Performed to rap music in the streets, and characterized by improvised and intricate Footwork, Tumbling, and Spinning headstands. **Break-Dancing** is so different from all other kinds of dancing! Overall, **Break-Dancing**, being a part of **Hip-Hop**, is roughly made up of three dance forms, **Electric-Boogie, Breaking**, and **Uprock**.
Breakin' has become more difficult to dance as it has aged. **Old-Style-Breakin'** was popular from 1969 until about 1977, then came **New-Style-Breakin'**. **Old-Style-Breakin'** involved mostly complicated leg Moves that included the **Moon-Walk**, while **New-Style-Breakin'** also incorporated fancy **Acrobatic-Dancing** additions such as the **Head-Spin**, the **Back-Spin, Hand-Glides**, the **Windmill**(3), and the **Jack-Hammer**.
In the late 1970s, there were innocent and fun `battles' in youth clubs, Competing against other dancers, in which teen-age males could **Head-Spin** for what seemed hours.
The following are exerpts from "*A Brief History of Breakdancing*," [www.angelfire.com]:
"Breakdancing started in 1969 [in South Bronx]. That was the year that James Brown recorded `Get on the Good Foot,' a song that inspired an acrobatic dance based on the high energy moves that Brown performed on stage.  Soon, kids in New York were doing the Good Foot - better known as `B Boy' (short for Break Boy) - which was the direct precursor to the sort of breakdancing we know today.
"--- breakdancing (a term by Afrika Bambaataa) became an integral part of hip-hop.

(Continued)

Break-Dancing: (Continued)

"--- *evolved into a highly stylized form of mock combat called `Uprock'* [upon one's feet]. *In an uprock battle, a dancer would lose if he actually touched his opponent. A BBoy named Rubberband is credited with developing Uprock.*

"*Breakin' was originally known as `Rocking'. `Old Style' breakin' and B Boy'n consisted only of floor work (`Floor Rock' or `down rock') and `top rock' (dancing on two feet, like the Moonwalk). Acrobatic moves such as the headspin had yet to emerge. Floor Rock* [Old-Style-Breakin'] *involved complicated leg moves.*

[Old-Style-]"*Breakin' remained popular until 1977, when a dance called the Freak took over.*"

The following is an exerpt from "*The History of Break Dancing,*" [www.jam2dis.com]:

"*But the new-style Breaking was different from the old. Rock Steady added a lot of acrobatic moves. Breaking now included not only Floor Rock but Headspins, Backspins, Handglides, and Windmills. In 1981, ----.*"

The following is from "*Electric Boogie,*" [www.actor.force9.co.uk/]:

"*Electric Boogie is linked as a part of `Breakdancing', which includes `Breaking' and `Uprock'. `Breaking' is an acrobatic dance style performed with moves like `Backspins', `Headspins' and `The Windmill'. `Uprock' is a dancing fighting style, in which the dancers get very close but do not touch. It is very fast and looks like a Kung-Fu battle. The winner is the one with the best and fastest moves.*

"*At the end of 1983 and early 1984, for reasons no one really knows, Breakdancing suddenly became a dance craze, and spread to every major city. Now it is very popular and can be seen in Films, Pop Videos, Commercials and Kids Dancing on street corners, and shopping precincts.*"

The following are exerpts from "*History of Breakdance,*" [www.jahsonic.com]:

[In the 1980s,] "*to popularize* [Break-Dancing,] *Broadway choreographers were sanding the raw edges and trying to format moves into a style which would not be out of place in `Come Dancing'. Mainstream pop artists were blatantly stealing the B-Boy moves, claiming props for originality, and offering themselves to the suburban middle-classes as the ultimate in street cred. Sanitized and safe, of course.*

"*There is no quicker way to kill an exciting street movement than to have the Establishment join.*"

There is a more aggressive New York style of **Break-Dancing** or **Rocking**, which involves **Locking-and-Popping**, in vogue in 1997. In the 1990s, while **Uprock** was a favorite of the New York gangs, **Locking** was a favorite of gangs in Los Angeles. Some say **Locking** had been started by *Lockatron* and *Shabba-Doo*. West Coast *Shabba* was also responsible for introducing New Yorkers to **Popping**, all of which, some say, resulted in the first genuine **Hip-Hop** Dance. In New York, local Break-Dancers then added **Waves**(1) and Smoother Moves to their **Popping**, resulting Generally in the style that exists in the early 2000s.

See **Underground Step-Listing.** (Also see Teen-Dancing, and Open-Step. Also see Ska, Punk-Rock, Grunge, and New-Wave. Also see Hip-Hop, MTV-Style Dancing, Street-Dancer, Lyrical-Dancer, Jazz-Dance, and Urban-Dance. Also see Rock, Hard-Rock, Pop, Rhythm-and-Blues, Motown-Sound, Rap, and Heavy-Metal. Also see Cumbia-Villera.)

Break-Endings: (Continued)

3) In addition, there are **Break-Endings** called **Break-A-Way** Patterns. These are as follows and are also delineated within this encyclopedia:

Apple-Jacks, And-Change-And-Change-And, Belly-Roll, Boogie-Back, Boogie-Back-and-Forward-Shorty, Charleston, Circle-Pivot, Corta-Jaca, Curls, Double-Foot-Boogie, Duck-Walk, Fall-Off-the-Log, Flamingo, Fly-Back, Foot-Boogie, Georgia-Grind, Heel-Splits, Heel-Switches, Leans, Little-Apple, Little-Peach, Marchessi, Mess-Around, NightLife, Peckin' [Peck to the Left (or Right)], Pose-and-a-Peck, Praise-Allah, Ramble, Rusty-Dusty, Sailor-Shuffle, Sailor-Shuffle-InFront, Sand-Step, Shorty-George, Side-Breaks, Spank-the-Baby, Stomp-Off, Stutter-Step, SugarFoot, Suzie-Q, Tack-Annie, Toe-Splits, Traveling-SugarFoot, and Truckin' [Truck to the Left (or Right)].

4) In addition, there are **Break-Endings** called **Time-Step**(2) Patterns. These are as follows and are also delineated within this encyclopedia:

Standard Time-Step, Standard Toe-Tap Time-Step, Standard Double-Time-Step, Standard Triple-Time-Step, Standard Double-Triple Time-Step, Vaudeville-Time-Step, Traveling-Time-Step, Stomp-Time-Step, Five, and Waltz-Clogging Time-Step.

"There are as many time steps as sweat drops to learn them!" -- Anonymous

For **Funk-Swing**, the Lady often **"Hijacks,"** (to do her own thing, extending the Pattern at her will,) during a **SugarPush**, **PullThru**, **HugMe**, or **Side-Pass**; as the Man is Dummying, or is **on Hold** in some Figure, perhaps in his Press-Line offering to Trigger her past him on his Left side. Her **"Hijacks"** are called various names; these **"Shines"** are mainly called **Break-Endings** but are also called **Break-Pattern**s or **Challenge-Step**s.

In addition to the many above-listed **Break-Endings**, there seems to be hundreds more that are not listed, and mostly are for the Lady. Either the Man or the Lady, usually it is the Man, who must **Dummy** while the Partner **Shine**s with their Fancy-Footwork **Break-Ending**. Normally, both cannot **Shine** successfully with their own **Break-Ending** at the same time. **Dummying** often requires sensitive and Skillful **Marking-Time**, so as to not interfere with their Partner's **Break-Ending** Steps.

[See West-Coast-Swing Step-Listing, Balboa Step-Listing, Syncopations-in-the-Dance, Push-Break(1)&(2), SugarPush-Fancy, PullThru-Fancy, Break-A-Way(3), Time-Step(2), and Light-and-Shade.]

Bristol-Stomp: An Unleadable American **Novelty** or **Fad** Coupledance, named for Bristol, a small town in either Texas or Pennsylvania. This was a 1961-62 dance hit that had its own Eponymous song by *The Dovells*, also named *"The Bristol Stomp."* Apparently it was danced as a Couple but Apart. From the words, its song mentions kids Stomping, Jumping, Twisting, Spinning, Ponying, Rocking, and whistling. Its name is also listed in *"Dance Crazes of the Sixties."*

(See Novelty-&-Fad Dances-of-the-1960s.) [Some from *www.sixtiescity.com/Culture/dance*]

Broadway-Freeze: A **Novelty Fad** dance of 1968. The **Broadway-Freeze** had its own Eponymous record, *"Broadway Freeze"* by *Harvey Scales*. [From *Soul*, www.trinity.unimelb.edu.au]

Broadway-Hustle: See Couple-Hustle.

Broadway-Sissy: A **Novelty Fad** Coupledance of the 1960s. It's Eponymous Music was "_Broadway Sissy_" by _Roscoe & Friends_.
   (See Novelty-&-Fad Dances-of-the-1960s.) [From www.bluejuice.org.au]

Broadway-Walk: An American **Fad** Coupledance of 1967. This dance had its own Eponymous record, the "_Broadway Walk_" by _Bobby Womack_.
   (See Novelty-&-Fad Dances-of-the-1960s.) [From _www.bluejuice.org.au_, and from "_Dance Crazes of the Sixties_," _www.sixtiescity.com/Culture/dance_]

Broken-Hip: Only this name for an American **Novelty** or **Fad** of the 1960s is listed simply as a Dance, Pattern, or Figure in the "_Dance Crazes of the Sixties_."
   (See Novelty-&-Fad Dances-of-the-1960s.) [From _www.sixtiescity.com/Culture/dance_]

Buckingham: A **Novelty Fad** dance of 1966. The **Buckingham** was danced to the record, "_Can't Hurry Love_" by _The Supremes_. [From _Soul_, www.trinity.unimelb.edu.au]

Bug: An Unleadable, American **Novelty** or **Fad** Group-Dance in vogue in the 1960s. **The Bug** is believed to have been Choreographed and danced in the movie, _Hairspray_. **The Bug** Routine attempted to imitate a **Bug** being passed around to each other through Pantomime.
   This **Bug** name is listed in the "_Dance Crazes of the Sixties_," as a Dance, along with the following writeup: (This writeup sounds British.)
   "**_The Bug:_** _The dance begins by forming a circle. Everyone in the circle dances in place. One person gets into the centre of the circle and begins dancing, swatting and scratching like having caught a bug in their clothes. The centre dancer with the bug finally 'throws' it onto someone else in the circle. This person then moves into the centre and starts scratching as the first dancer moves back into the circle._"
   There is an Eponymous record, "_The Bug_," for this game, but it's very short - only 2 1/4 minutes long. Therefore the record needs to be played several times.
   (See Novelty-&-Fad Dances-of-the-1960s.) [Partly from _www.sixtiescity.com/Culture/dance_]

Bugg or **Swedish-Bug:** A **Novelty fad**, Circular Pattern Coupledance, the **Bugg** is currently popular in Sweden. It originated in Sweden in the 1970s or 80s from the **Lindy-Hop**, but the **Bugg** is a more upright dance with simpler Basic-Steps, and without the Triples, Kicks, Swinging and Twisting. Instead, the **Bugg** is Walked more-or-less as a One-Step.
   Similar to the **Double-Bug** when One-Stepped. (See American Onestep, Onestep, Four-Count, Peabody, March, and Charleston.)

Bull-Frog-Hop: An American *"animal dance"*, a **Novelty Fad** Coupledance in vogue about 1912 to 1914. Derided by newspapers, magazines, church officials, and even by Pope Pius X, as "such foolish and decadent behavior," over one hundred of these dances were created during this period.

(See Animal-Dances, Bunny-Hug, Buzzard-Lope, Camel-Walk, Chicken-Reel, Chicken-Scratch, Crab-Step, Fish-Walk, Gotham-Gobble, Horse-Trot, Kangaroo-Dip, Kangaroo-Hop, Lame-Duck, Monkey-Glide, Possum-Trot, Snake, and Turkey-Trot; which were all Animal-Dances of 1910-1914.)

Bull-Nose-Stomp: Only this name for an American **Novelty** or **Fad** of the 1960s is listed simply as a Dance, Pattern, or Figure in the "*Dance Crazes of the Sixties.*"
(See Novelty-&-Fad Dances-of-the-1960s.) [From *www.sixtiescity.com/Culture/dance*]

Bump: A **Novelty Fad** Coupledance popular in the U.S. about 1975. The Couple would at regular intervals, momentarily Sweep Up against each other's hip and/or buttocks, **"Bump"**; otherwise, they danced to **Rock**, Apart.

The following is from *bump (dance)*; [www.answers.com]:
*"The **bump** was a primarily 1970's fad dance wherein the main move of the dance is to lightly 'bump' hips on every other main beat of the music. As the dance (and the evening) progressed, the bumping could become more intimate, bumping hip to backside, low bending, etc."*

The **Bump** had a related dance, "*Ain't Gonna Bump (With No Big Fat Woman)*" by *Joe Tex.*

Similar to the earlier "**Boomps-A-Daisy**" novelty Fad **Coupledance** of 1940. (See American-Hustle, Bugg, Bus-Stop, Four-Corners, Locking, Snake, Sprinkler, Tango-Hustle, and the Worm; which were all Novelty Fads in vogue in the 1970s.)

Bumpsi: Only this name for an American **Novelty** or **Fad** of the 1960s is listed simply as a Dance, Pattern, or Figure in the "*Dance Crazes of the Sixties.*"
(See Novelty-&-Fad Dances-of-the-1960s.) [From *www.sixtiescity.com/Culture/dance*]

Bunny-Hop; Classified herein as in the **Audience-Participation-Dance** Category, and as both a **Novelty** Dance and **Fad** Dance. This is a Leadable American **Group-Dance** of from 1953, with its own Eponymous "*The Bunny Hop*" **Foxtrot** Music by *Ray Anthony*. This dance was still much in vogue in the 1960s.

The **Bunny-Hop** is one of the **Follow-the-Leader Dances** that include the **Conga-Line, Madison**, and the **Letkajenkka**. The **Bunny-Hop** is danced in a Traveling chain resembling the **Conga-Line**. Each person Forward-Jumps three times, "*Hop Hop Hop*" in Cadence at the Ending of each Phrase of Music, which went "*bop bop bop*".

(Continued)

Bunny-Hop; (Continued)

Following from the "_Dance Crazes of the Sixties,_" [_www.sixtiescity.com/Culture/dance_]:

  "_**The Bunny Hop:** The participants dance in a line, holding on to the hips of the person in front of them. They tap the floor two times with their right foot, then with their left foot, then they hop forwards, backwards, and finally three hops forward to finish the sequence, which continues throughout the song. The first person in the line leads the group around the floor, much like a conga._"

In addition, this **Bunny-Hop** is a common inclusion for an April, Easter Coupledance party.

(Also see the Bambuco, Bop, Calypso, Creep, Fish, Flea-Hop, Frug, Guapacha, Hand-Jive, Hitch-Hiker, Hokey-Pokey, Hullie-Gullie, Jerk, Limbo-Rock, Mashed-Potato, Monkey, Pachanga, Plena, Pony, Rock-and-Around, Scooter, Slide, Strole, Surfers, Swim, Tumba-Cha, Twist, Twister, and the Watusi; which were all Novelty Fads in vogue in the 1950-60s. Also see Novelty-&-Fad Dances-of-the-1960s.)

Bunny-Hug: A grotesque, **Novelty Fad** Coupledance popular in America from 1901 through 1910. Some say it was danced Fast but others say Slow, to a 4/4 Beat. There was sheet music to its particular song, which had directions by its words for Steps for this dance.

(See Animal-Dances, the Boston-Dip, Gaby-Glide, Hug-Me-Close, Lame-Duck, and Shiver-Dance; which were all novelty Fads in vogue in the 1910s. Also see Texas-Tommy, Maxixe, Grizzly-Bear, Turkey-Trot, and Ballin'-The-Jack, for dances of that time, where dance directions were given in their verses. Also see Grizzly-Bear, and Turkey-Trot, for Coupledances of that time with some type of animal's name.)

Burn: Only this name for an American **Novelty** or **Fad** of the 1960s is listed simply as a Dance, Pattern, or Figure in the "_Dance Crazes of the Sixties._"

(See Novelty-&-Fad Dances-of-the-1960s.) [From _www.sixtiescity.com/Culture/dance_]

Bush-Dance: A simple Australian version of the Old English Traditional Square Dance, popular in the Outback in the 1990s; four Couples squared up as usual, and with calls familiar to American Square Dancers, but with a nineth person (Man or Lady) standing in the square center. Similar to Musical Chairs, the odd one tries for a Partner as they are called to scatter. The left out one then becomes the odd one.

(See Eightsome-Reel.)

Bushman: An American **Fad** dance of 1969. This **Bushman** had its own Eponymous record, "_The Bushman_" by _Tenth Dimension._

(See Novelty-&-Fad Dances-of-the-1960s.) [From _Soul, www.trinity.unimelb.edu.au,_ and from "_Dance Crazes of the Sixties,_" from _www.sixtiescity.com/Culture/dance_]

Bus-Stop: A **Novelty Fad** dance of the early 1970s. How to dance the **Bus-Stop** should be found on a VHS Video by Christy Lane (www.centralhome.com). There may be Eponymous music: Tina Turner – 1972, "*Bus Stop*" by Hollies, or "*Waiting at the Bus Stop*" by Bobby Sherman.

(See American-Hustle, Bugg, Bump, Four-Corners, Locking, Snake, Sprinkler, Tango-Hustle, and the Worm; which were all Novelty Fads in vogue in the 1970s.)

Butterfly: From Kingston, Jamaica, an Underground **Novelty Fad**, Singular- or Group-Dance Movement, associated with dancing **Dancehall/Ragga**, which, in turn, are outgrowths of **Ska/Reggae**. **Butterfly** was and is danced mainly by youths of color.

The following is from *Ragga Fashions*: [www.bbc.co.uk]

"*Butterfly* - *Stand with feet quite wide apart and knees bent. Keeping feet in the same position bring knees together and then move them forward and out to original position, creating a circular wave type motion. Move waist in a forward and back gyration with each wave motion of the legs. What you do with the top half of your body is up to you, although hands are often just placed on the legs.*"

See **Dancehall**(2) for further explanation. (Also see Bogle, Armstrong, Go-Go-Wine, Body-Basic-and-Exercise, Tate, and World-Dance. Also see Jerry-Springer, Prang, Heel-and-Toe, Na!Na!Na!, Screechie, Zip-It-Up, Drive-By, Shizzle-Ma-Nizzle, Matrix, and Bin-Laden. Also see Underground Step-Listing.)

Buzzard-Lope: A **Novelty Fad** Coupledance in vogue in the United States, probably in the 1910s, and probably danced to Ragtime music.

(See Animal-Dances, Lame-Duck, Horse-Trot, Grizzly-Bear, Crab-Step, Turkey-Trot, Kangaroo-Hop, Fish-Walk, and Bunny-Hug.)

Cabbage-Patch: A **Novelty Fad** dance of the 1980s. How to dance the **Cabbage-Patch** should be found on a VHS Video by Christy Lane (www.centralhome.com).

The following is from "*Eighties Dances*" (www.inthe80s.com):

"**Cabbage Patch** - Hold your fists closed, bend your elbows, push out and rotate your arms in a circle from your chest out and around!!!"

(See Break-Dancing, Bugg, Chicken-Dance, Funky-Twist, Moonwalk, New-Kids-Move, Pac-Man, Popping, Robocop, Roger-Rabbit, Running-Man, Snake, Tickin', Wavin', and the Worm; which were all Novelty Fads in vogue in the 1980s.)

  Cafe Tango or **NightClub Tango** or **French Tango:** A **Continental Tango** Free-Style of Coupledance, preferred by the more advanced dancer, and related to the **American Tango** Free-Style.

  "The Cafe and Night Club styles features closed position, sharp progressive movements and intricate footwork. Here the music is more dramatic in character and the interpretation more intimate. The man is more dominant in this interpretation and here you are always conscious of his lead and styling, rather than a series of framed Picture poses characteristic of the Harvest Moon version. Each version has its uses and its adherents.

  "---- and the sharp Cafe, or so-called French style, is preferred by the advanced dancer." -- [From www.geocities.com/danceinfosa.]

  Same as **Milonguero-Tango**, and **Tango-Apilado**. (See Petroleo-Tango, Valentino Tango, and Contest Tango.)

  Cage-Dancer: A Singular-Dance of 1960s and 1970s vintage that was popularized on TV. **Cage-Dancer** refers to a scantily-clad feminine dancer, perhaps wearing a mini-skirt or hot-pants, and (supposedly) trapped **inside of a hanging bird cage.** She probably would be Stationary-Dancing the **Pony** or the like with her long hair flying. The idea is said to have begun in a West Hollywood Nightclub named *Whisky A Go-Go.*

  The following are excerpts from *cage dancing*; [wwww.answers.com]:

  *"A **cage dance** is a specific type of erotic dance, performed inside a cage, usually at a night club or dance hall. The activity originated in the 1960s and rose in popularity with the advent of disco music. In particular, the practice began at a Los Angeles music venue called Whisky A Go-Go.*

  "Though the club was billed as a discotheque, meaning only recordings with no bands, the Whisky A Go-Go opened with a live band led by Johnny Rivers and a short skirted DJ spinning records between sets from a suspended cage at the right of the stage. When the female DJ danced during Rivers' set, the audience thought it was part of the act and the concept of Go-Go dancers in cages was born. ...

  "Cage dancing is referenced in Gordon Lightfoot's 1967 song, 'Go Go Round'."

  Similar to the **GoGo-Dancer**. (See Disco, and Jacking. Also see Sexercise-Dance, PassaPassa, and Juking.)

  Cake-Walk or **Parading** or **Take-the-Cake:** An American Traditional Performance, either Singular or **Parading** arm-in-arm with Partner, to Ragtime Rhythms. It was one that had become very popular socially as a novelty Fad by December of 1900, after theatrical showings to whites in 1889, 1892 and 93. It was the first American dance to cross over from black to white society as well as from stage shows to Ballroom. The **Cake-Walk** eventually died in the 1920s, although its Steps such as the **Shorty-George** live on.

(Continued)

Cake-Walk: (Continued)   The following is an exert from *Encyclopedia of Word and Phrase Origins* by R. Hendrickson:

"take the cake; cakewalk. Cakes have been awarded as prizes clear back to classical times, so when slaves on Southern plantations held dance contests to help a needy neighbor, or just for the fun of it, giving a cake to the winning couple was no innovation. But the `cakewalk' inspired by these contests was definitely another black contribution to American culture.  Dancers tried to outdo each other with fancy steps, struts, and ways of walking while the fiddler played and chanted, `Make your steps, and show your style!' By 1840 `cakewalk' was recorded as the name of these steps, which became the basis of many top dance routines still seen today.  Whether the expression `that takes the cake,' [meaning] `that wins the highest prize,' comes from the cakewalk is another matter. Though the phrase is recorded a century earlier elsewhere, it almost certainly originated with the cakewalk in America. ..."

The following are excerpts from *Tin Pan Alley - Part 1* [http://www.wrkf.org/tinpan1]:

"Egbert Austin Williams (known as Bert Williams) and George Walker, both of whom were black, formed a duo in 1896 and did their act in the middle of a show called `The Gold Bug.' It was enormously successful and they went on to popularize their highly distinctive version of the Cake Walk.

"Several types of songs were popular in the 1880's and 90's... songs of love and romance (which inspire the majority of popular music), tear-jerkers, cakewalks, coon songs, topical songs, and, in 1899, with the publication of Scott Joplin's `Maple Leaf Rag,' Ragtime.

"Cakewalks were songs written to accompany dances on a stage. The most famous, which we still hear today, was `Golliwog's Cake Walk' by French classical music composer, Claude Debussy.

"The most famous American composer of Cake Walks was Frederick A. Mills, who wrote under the name of Kerry Mills. ... Cake Walks were popularized nationally on stage by the duo of Williams and Walker, two black performers, and in vaudeville by Genaro and Bailey. Mill's first Cake Walk was `Rastus on Parade' which he published in 1896.  He also published `At a Georgia Camp Meeting' in 1897 and it became the standard by which other Cake Walks were judged."

The following are excerpts from "*The Word Detective* " [www.word-detective.com]:

"One kind of contest popular in the African-American community in the 19th century was the 'cakewalk,' in which couples competed strolling arm in arm, with the prize, a cake, being awarded to the most graceful and stylish team.

"Cake is so popular, in fact, that it has long served as a prize awarded to the winner of all sorts of competitions, giving rise to the 19th century expression 'take the cake.' Originally simply meaning 'to win,' 'take the cake' now is usually used sarcastically to mean 'to be an outrageous example of something bad' ... .

"Since 'cakewalking' demanded both skill and grace, victory in the contest was rarely a 'cakewalk' in our modern 'easy' sense.

"By 1877, 'cakewalk' had ... acquired its general meaning of 'an effortless victory.'

"... 'cakewalk' is an American invention, meaning 'a very easy victory against little or no real opposition.'"

Some say the **Cake-Walk** originated with the 1850s **Chalk-Line-Walk**. Others say that the **Cake-Walk** had its beginnings in Florida about 1889, where, as a form of entertainment, the black's Walking Style was Practiced to an art. The Man voted best in Promenading with the most accomplished Steps was awarded with a cake as the prize, hence the term, *"That takes the cake!"*

(Continued)

Cake-Walk: (Concluded)
The **Cake-Walk** is very happily danced with a Forward Walk with Weight back on Heels, and at times with stiff, straight arms and with legs swung Back-and-Forth. There were other special Movements, such as the bending far back of the body, and the drooping of the hands at the wrists.

Later, Stage-Dancing developed from these **Cake-Walks**, where blacks, mimicking high society, would parody whites' mannerisms with dignified Walking, Bowing low, waving canes, doffing hats, ending perhaps with a High-Kicking Promenade. Minstrel show grand finales were often times the **Cake-Walk**. White _"Walkers"_ would compete in very big contests such as in the _"National Cakewalk Jubilee"_ in New York City.

[See Dance-for-Baton, Majorette-Strutting-with-Baton, High-Stepping, Moon-Walk, SideSlide, Boogie, Sissy-Walk, Walkin'-the-Dog, Trench, Camel-Walk(3), Running-Man, Side-Touches, Step-Scoot, Stationary-Copas, and Syncopated-Splits. Also see the Hoochy-Koochy, Kickapoo, Rag-Time, and Tiger-Rag; these were all Novelty Fads in Vogue in the 1900 to 1910 era.] [Some from streetswing.com]

California-Shuffle or **Heel-and-Toe-Touches:** A Leadable In-Place-Coupledance Pattern of multiple Changes of the Feet in Sequence; used in **West-Coast-Swing** and in other similar dances.

With no Traveling, Pattern is two Measures long in 4/4 Time. Rhythm Timing is _&1&2&3&4,&5&6&7&8_. Pattern Starts with one Heel then the other Heel Touching Slightly Forward, Followed by one Toe then the other Toe Touching Slightly Sidewards. This is all then repeated. Steps _&1&2_ and _&5&6_ are Forward Heel Touches. _&3&4_ and _&7&8_ are Sidewards Toe Touches.

These eight Counts can be either **Danced Flat** or Executed **with a Slight Hop**, while almost simultaneously Touching the other Foot Forward or Pointing Sideward; i.e., one Foot is Drawn to Home, Weighted, as the other Foot is Moved to Touching.

Similar to **Change-And-Change, And-Change-And-Change-And, Switch**(3), **Side-Switches, Heel-Switches,** and **Quick-Points**. (See Change-Feet-Multiplicity, and Change-Feet.)

Calypso: Probably initially derived from a similar West African Musical Style called _"kaiso,"_ **Calypso** is a tropical ballad type Latin-American and Caribbean Music and **Folk** Coupledance, that became a **Novelty Fad** Singular and Coupledance, popular in the U.S. in the late 1950s and early 1960s. Unstructured and Unleadable, it is danced to **Calypso** songs. The Caribbean state of **Trinidad-and-Tobago** is the homeland of **Calypso** Music. These **Calypso** songs were sung originally by Trinidad natives, often to their version of English ballads. Dancing Steps were created later, after the Music had been popularized.

Calypso is a variation of the **Merengue** and the **Danzon**, with predominant **Hip-Waves**. **Calypso** has influenced diverse Music Styles, including **Reggae, Soca,** and **Rapso. Calypso** was made famous in the U.S. in 1956 by Harry Bellafonte.

Similar to **Corrido,** and **Zandunga.** (See Caribbean Dance-Music Amalgamation Listing. Also see Clave-Beat, Beguine, Soca, Conga-Line, Bomba, and the Plena. Also see the Bambuco, Bop, Bunny-Hop, Creep, Fish, Flea-Hop, Frug, Guapacha, Hand-Jive, Hitch-Hiker, Hokey-Pokey, Hullie-Gullie, Jerk, Limbo-Rock, Mashed-Potato, Monkey, Pachanga, Pony, Rock-and-Around, Scooter, Slide, Strole, Surfers, Swim, Tumba-Cha, Twist, Twister, and the Watusi; which were all Novelty Fads in vogue in the 1950-60s. Also see Novelty-&-Fad Dances-of-the-1960s.) [Some from _http://en.wikipedia.org/wiki,_ and from "_Dance Crazes of the Sixties,_" from _www.sixtiescity.com/Culture/dance_]

Camel-Walk(1): Two Unleadable, General Coupledance Movements or Figures, Left or Right, Mirror-Image Opposite. Suitable for most **Country-Western, Swing**s and other dances. Danced in two or three Counts total, Timing varies.

It is also an Unstructured, American **Novelty Fad** Singular or Coupledance Mimicking Movements in vogue in the 1960s. The dance's Movements attempted to imitate through Pantomime, a **Camel-Walk**ing, and was one of a whole series of 1960s Mimicking dance Patterns, (see Hullie-Gullie.) In 1967, _James Brown_ sang and recorded _"The Camel Walk"_ for its Eponymous dance. But earlier, _James Brown_ had recorded " _There Was A Time,_" and _Magic Sam_ had recorded "_Do The Camel Walk,_" to which the **Camel-Walk** also was danced. [From _Soul_, www.trinity.unimelb.edu.au]

Usually danced in multiples, but Singularly and Apart from Partner. After Stepping _Forward_ on the DownBeat, that newly Supporting-Leg Knee-Pops in one or two Counts, then the Free-Leg is Stepped _Forward_ Straight-Kneed. The Trailing-Foot Slides under the UpRaised Heel of the Forward Foot.

(See Horse. Also see Novelty-&-Fad Dances-of-the-1960s.)

Camel-Walk(2): An American "_animal dance_", a **Novelty Fad** Coupledance in vogue about 1912 to 1914. Derided by newspapers, magazines, church officials, and even by Pope Pius X, as "such foolish and decadent behavior," over one hundred of these dances were created during this period.

See the later 1960s **Camel-Walk**(1), which could have been the same or similar Movements. (Also see Animal-Dances, Bull-Frog-Hop, Bunny-Hug, Buzzard-Lope, Chicken-Reel, Chicken-Scratch, Crab-Step, Fish-Walk, Gotham-Gobble, Horse-Trot, Kangaroo-Dip, Kangaroo-Hop, Lame-Duck, Monkey-Glide, Possum-Trot, Snake, and Turkey-Trot; which were all Animal-Dances of 1910-1914.)

Camel-Walk(3): An Australian **Novelty Fad** Solo or Coupledance Movement, used at times in **Country-Western Line-Dances**. The following description of this Movement is from http://ourworld.compuserve.com:

"_CAMEL WALK - Australian Variation:_

"_Step forward at 45 degrees onto right foot thrusting right hip forward, drag left foot together with hand clap straightening body._"

Note: Dancer may continue Traveling by next dancing the above as Mirror-Image Opposite.

Similar to **Sissy-Walk**. [See Cake-Walk, Boogie(1), Walkin'-the-Dog, Moon-Walk, SideSlide, Running-Man, and Step-Scoot.]

Camel-Walk-Stroll: Only this name for an American **Novelty** or **Fad** of the 1960s is listed simply as a Dance, Pattern, or Figure in the "_Dance Crazes of the Sixties._"

(See Novelty-&-Fad Dances-of-the-1960s.) [From _www.sixtiescity.com/Culture/dance_]

Capri: Only this name for an American **Novelty** or **Fad** of the 1960s is listed simply as a Dance, Pattern, or Figure in the "_Dance Crazes of the Sixties._"

(See Novelty-&-Fad Dances-of-the-1960s.) [From _www.sixtiescity.com/Culture/dance_]

Carioca or **Samba-Carioca:** A Variation of the **Samba** and native to Rio de Janeiro and Bahia, Brazil. A Latin Rhythm **Folkdance**, that became a Leadable **Novelty Fad** Coupledance popular in the 1930s, and is still popular at the Carioca Carnival. People dance together in cordoes (chains or cues) of holding hands to Cole Porter's song, "_The Carioca_," which plays at a moderately lively Tempo. **Carioca** dance Steps are very similar to those of the **Samba**, but the Tempo is Faster. They dance Forward then Rearward with Bounce, and sing and Sway their Bodies. They alternately dance this way to Marchas.

The following is from _Carioca_ [www.webref.org/]:

A **Carioca** is "_a native of Rio de Janeiro. Also the abbreviation of the Brazilian dance, the Samba-Carioca. At the Carioca Carnival, from the moment the music starts until it dies off, people get together in cordoes (chains or cues). Holding hands in this fashion they sing and sway their bodies to the Samba-Carioca and the Marchas._"

The following is from _Carioca_ [www.streetswing.com/]:

"_The Carioca was first a song in the 1933 movie "Flying Down To Rio" with Fred Astaire. Astaire did a version of the Carioca which has been modified over time. It was hailed as the new ballroom dance, however it really never took off. The Carioca music is basically a Rumba or Samba (Carioca Samba) rhythm and is patterned after another Brazilian dance called the Machichi [basically a modified Rumba]. When dancing the Ballroom Carioca, Rumba movements and Fox-trot variations are executed._"

The following is from _Flying Down to Rio_ [www.brightlightsfilm.com/]:

"_The Carioca is a `passionate' ballroom dance, one in which the dancers must keep their foreheads touching while they dance. [This requires a good deal of dexterity when, for example, both partners perform a spin.] `What's the deal with the foreheads?' asks Ginger. `Mental telepathy,' Fred explains. `I can tell what they're about from here,' Ginger scoffs. `Let's try it,' Fred says, and Ginger, in a line no critic can resist quoting, replies, `We'll show `em a thing or three._'"

The following is an excerpt from "_Cole Porter: a Biography_":

"_Though 'Night and Day' was already a popular classic when 'The Gay Divorcee' was released, the number became even better known because of the film and the dance built around it. The song that got the lion's share of attention in 'The Gay Divorcee,' however, was not Cole's 'Night and Day' but Con Conrad's 'The Continental' (with lyrics by Herb Magidson). Conrad's tune had the benefit of a long dance sequence in the film -- some seventeen minutes' worth -- in which a large group dressed in black and white sashayed about doing 'The Continental,' a follow-up dance to the Carioca, which had become enormously popular as a result of its exposure in 'Flying Down to Rio.' RKO also did its part to build up the tie-in between the 'Continental' and the 'Carioca' by advertising Astaire and Rogers in 'The Gay Divorcee' as 'The King and Queen of Carioca' ...._"

Note that the **Machichi** name is similar to the **Machich** name, which is mentioned in the **Maxixe** writeup herein.

(See the Samba-Carioca, Bahia-Carioca, and Marcha. Also see Samba, and Samba-in-Rio. Also see the Pagode, LaBamba, Street-Samba, BossaNova, and Lambada. Also see the Big-Apple, Conga-Line, Boomps-A-Daisy, and Lambeth-Walk; which were all Novelty Fads in vogue in the 1930s. Also see Folkdance Genre - Brazilian.)

Carnaby: Only this name for an American **Novelty** or **Fad** of the 1960s is listed simply as a Dance, Pattern, or Figure in the "_Dance Crazes of the Sixties_."

(See Novelty-&-Fad Dances-of-the-1960s.) [From _www.sixtiescity.com/Culture/dance_]

Castle-Combination: An American **Novelty Fad** Coupledance in vogue from about 1912 to about 1918. Some say more than a hundred new Coupledances were invented between 1912 and 1914. **Vernon and Irene Castle** invented many of these, and one was this **Castle-Combination.**

(See Castle-Valse-Classique, Hesitation-Waltz, Castle-Tango, Castle-Last-Waltz, Castle-Walk, Castle-Lame-Duck, Castle-Grizzly-Bear, Castle-Texas-Tommy, and the Maxixe; all of which were other dances presented by the Castles. Also see the Boston-Dip, Bunny-Hug, Gaby-Glide, Hug-Me-Close, Shiver-Dance, and Turkey-Trot; which were all Novelty Fad dances in vogue in the 1910s.)

Castle-Lame-Duck: See Lame-Duck.

Castle-Last-Waltz: See Last-Waltz.

Castle-Tango: An American **Novelty Fad** Coupledance in vogue from about 1912 to about 1918. Some say more than a hundred new Coupledances were invented between 1912 and 1914. **Vernon and Irene Castle** invented many of these, and one was this **Castle-Tango.**

Tango-Dreams was a tune written by a J. Rosamond Johnson, and could possibly have been the music for this **Castle-Tango** Dance. [Tune data from http://nfo.net/usa/dance]

(See Castle-Valse-Classique, Hesitation-Waltz, Castle-Walk, Castle-Last-Waltz, Castle-Combination, Castle-Lame-Duck, Castle-Grizzly-Bear, Castle-Texas-Tommy, and the Maxixe; all of which were other dances presented by the Castles. Also see the Boston-Dip, Bunny-Hug, Gaby-Glide, Hug-Me-Close, Shiver-Dance, and Turkey-Trot; which were all Novelty Fad dances in vogue in the 1910s.)

Caterpillar: An Unleadable American **Novelty Fad** Singular dance Pattern or Routine of 1967. The **Caterpillar** had its own Eponymous record, *"The Caterpillar"* by *Lou Donaldson.* [From *Soul*, www.trinity.unimelb.edu.au]

Laying Down flat upon one's back, the dancer manipulates their Body length Slightly Up then Down, in Wave-like Motions to the Beat, proceeding Forward in small increments.

Similar to the **Worm**, and the **Centipede.** [See Six-Step, Layout(1) face-Up and arms Closed-Forward, Ripple, and Body-Wave. Also see Novelty-&-Fad Dances-of-the-1960s. Also mentioned in "*Dance Crazes of the Sixties*," from *www.sixtiescity.com/Culture/dance*]

Cat-Walk: Only this name for an American **Novelty** or **Fad** of the 1960s is listed simply as a Dance, Pattern, or Figure in the "*Dance Crazes of the Sixties.*"

(See Novelty-&-Fad Dances-of-the-1960s.) [From *www.sixtiescity.com/Culture/dance*]

Caustic-Potash: An American **Novelty Fad** comical Solo-Dance or Maneuver of the 1980s in Cadence with the Music.

The following is from "*Eighties Dances*" - [www.inthe80s.com]:

"*Let your arms fall in a rhythmic wave-ish motion and then lower your head and swing it the way a fish swings his head when he/she swims. Then repeat.*"

(See Novelty-&-Fad Dances-of-the-1980s.)

CeeCee: A **Novelty Fad** Coupledance of the 1960s. It's Eponymous Music was "*Mister C.C.*" by *Jim Pipkins & Boss Five*.
     (See Novelty-&-Fad Dances-of-the-1960s.) [From www.bluejuice.org.au]

Centipede: A **Novelty Fad** Movement, **Centipede** is one small Move of the California `Funk' brand of the **Boogaloo** Genre of Mime "Moves," which seems to be part of the **Electric-Boogie** Style of **Break-Dancing**, which, in turn, is part of **Hip-Hop**.
     The following is from "*Eighties Dances*," [www.inthe80s.com]:
     "*The Centipede - You lay down flat on your stomach and kind of push your body up and down* [to the Beat] *as you go forward. It was big with break dancers.*"
Similar to **Worm**, and **Caterpillar**. [See Six-Step, and Layout(1) face Down and with arms Forward. Also see Air-Posing, Animation(3), Bop(2), Cobra, Crazy-Legs, Dime-Stopping, Filmore, Floating(2), Glides, Hitting, King-Tut, Lean(4), Pop(3), Puppet, Robot, Saccin, Scarecrow, Snake(4), Spiderman, Sticking, Strobing, Strut, Tick, and Wave(1); for other related Moves. Also see Underground Step-Listing.]

Cha-Cha-Cherry: A **Novelty Fad** dance of 1958. The **Cha-Cha-Cherry** was danced to the records, "*The Cha Cha Cherry*" by the Five *Royales*, and "*Willie Did The Cha-Cha*" by *Johnny Otis*. [From *Soul*, www.trinity.unimelb.edu.au]

Cha-Cha-Slide or **Casper-Slide:**   An American and European **Novelty Fad** Singular **Line-Dance**(1) and song. It's 2000 Eponymous song, the "*Cha-Cha Slide*," in "*The Original Slide Album*,"is often played at Dance Clubs, Dance-Parties, and particularly at midwestern U.S. and Canadian weddings.
     The **Cha-Cha-Slide** was developed in 1996 for a fitness gym's use, where it became a hit with its gym members. This **Cha-Cha-Slide**, with its **called-out instructions**, is an update of the **Electric-Slide** Novelty **Fad** Singular Line-Dance. This dance became very popular in the U.S. in 2001, then the song was played often in European Night-Clubs and Discos, especially around the Mediterranean and in the U.K.
     See the extensive listing of **Line-Dance Terms**. [Also see **Line-Dances**(1).]

Cha-Jerk: Only this name for an American **Novelty** or **Fad** of the 1960s is listed simply as a Dance, Pattern, or Figure in the "*Dance Crazes of the Sixties.*"
     (See Novelty-&-Fad Dances-of-the-1960s.) [From *www.sixtiescity.com/Culture/dance*]

Charge: An American **Fad** dance of 1966. This **Charge** was danced to the record, "*Love Is Like An Itching In The Heart*" by *The Supremes*.
     (See Novelty-&-Fad Dances-of-the-1960s.) [From *www.sixtiescity.com/Culture/dance*, and from *Soul, www.trinity.unimelb.edu.au*]

Charleston(1): Mostly Unleadable 1930s Patterns. See the various **Charleston** entries herein for the multitude of Steps that were often danced during the **Break-A-Way** for the **Big-Apple**.

For the **Big-Apple**, the various **Charleston** Steps for eight Counts were items of the **Break-A-Way** Genre. Wiggling their hips, certain **Break-A-Way** Patterns were danced. The original **Suzie-Q, Boogie-Back, Tack-Annie, Georgia-Grind, Praise-Allah!, Truckin', Peckin', Charleston, Shorty-George**, and other Break-A-Ways, were probably originated early by blacks; while **Spank-the-Baby, Rusty-Dusty, Pose-and-a-Peck**, the **Little-Apple**, the **Little-Peach, Mess-Around, Stomp-Off, Apple-Jacks**, and **Fall-Off-the-Log, Squat-Charleston**, and other Break-A-Ways, were probably originated later by whites. Most all of these Patterns seem to have been influenced or derived from the classic **Lindy-Hop** and/or **Big-Apple** dances. See **Break-A-Way Glossary** for a more complete listing.

Charleston(2) or **Common-Charleston**: A **Break-A-Way**(3) Shine-Step, Coupledanced either in Butterfly Position or without Partner-contact. Suitable for the **Lindy-Hop**, all **Swings**, and for a **Swing-Bal** Break from the **Pure-Balboa**,, and for many other Coupledances. These are the names for the General Step-Pattern in which the Singular dancer, or Coupledancer (Side-by-Side), Swivels their Feet In-and-Out. Taken in 8 even Counts, Rhythm with 4/4 Timing is *1&2&3&4&*:

forwardheelin swivelheelout ForKickswivelheelin swivelheelout BackwardHeelOut SwivelHeelIn touchtoebackSwivelHeelOut SwivelHeelIn.

If Partners are Facing, the Man dances as above, while the Lady dances the Opposite of Man:

BackwardHeelOut SwivelHeelIn touchtoebackSwivelHeelOut SwivelHeelIn forwardheelin swivelheelout ForKickswivelheelin swivelheelout.

[See Charleston-Kick, and Charleston(1). Also see Balboa Step-Listing.]

Charleston-Fish: Only this name for an American **Novelty** or **Fad** of the 1960s is listed simply as a Dance, Pattern, or Figure in the "*Dance Crazes of the Sixties.*"
(See Novelty-&-Fad Dances-of-the-1960s.) [From *www.sixtiescity.com/Culture/dance*]

Chatanooga-Walk: A **Novelty Fad** Coupledance of 1966. This had its own Eponymous record, the "*Chatanooga Walk*" by *Roy Grant & The Arabian Knights.*
(See Novelty-&-Fad Dances-of-the-1960s.) [From www.bluejuice.org.au]

Cheater-Stomp: Only this name for an American **Novelty** or **Fad** of the 1960s is listed simply as a Dance, Pattern, or Figure in the "*Dance Crazes of the Sixties.*"
(See Novelty-&-Fad Dances-of-the-1960s.) [From *www.sixtiescity.com/Culture/dance*]

Cherokee: A **Novelty Fad** dance of 1956. The **Cherokee** had its own Eponymous record, "*Cherokee Dance*" by *Bob Landers*. [From *Soul*, www.trinity.unimelb.edu.au]

Chestnut-Tree: A **Novelty Fad** Coupledance in vogue in 1938-39.

A 1938 vintage sheet music copy states the following upon its cover: "*The Chestnut Tree*" *(neath the Spreading Chestnut Tree) Novelty Singing Dance*. The copy states that it contains "*the full instructions and illustrations for this dance, including many arm movements.*" It also states, "*A ballroom routine devised by Miss Adele England.*" "*By Jimmy Kennedy, Tommie Connor and Hamilton Kennedy.*"

Following are the first and last verses of "*The Village Blacksmith*":
"*Under a spreading chestnut-tree the village smithy stands;*
"*The smith, a mighty man is he, with large and sinewy hands;*
"*And the muscles of his brawny arms are strong as iron bands.*

"*Thanks, thanks to thee, my worthy friend, for the lesson thou hast taught!*
"*Thus at the flaming forge of life our fortunes must be wrought;*
"*Thus on its sounding anvil shaped each burning deed and thought.*"
By Henry Wadsworth Longfellow (1807-1882)
(See Blackout-Stroll.) [Some from *Novelty Dances Through the Years* by Pony Moore.]

Chicago-Bird: A **Novelty Fad** Coupledance of 1962. It's Eponymous Music was "*Chicago Bird*" by the *Dial Tones*.

(See Novelty-&-Fad Dances-of-the-1960s.) [From www.bluejuice.org.au]

Chicago-City: An Unleadable, American **Novelty Fad**, Choreographed Singular or Coupledance Routine, to medium-Cadence 4/4 Tempo music with a heavy Beat. The Routine had its own Eponymous song, *Chicago City*. The dance Routine, itself, was not very popular and faded with its song. The following four-Measures long Pattern was in vogue in the 1960s at the Brigham Young University, in Provo, Utah.

There is a picture from Brigham Young University, labeled and showing a young couple dancing **Chicago-City**. They are Apart in a Shine Position, shown facing the same direction, and dancing the **Sissy-Walk** upon same, identical Feet.

The Routine was danced with two **Kick-Ball-Change**s, then four **Sissy-Walk** Steps, then finally a **Grapevine**. Rhythm Timing was *Quick And Slow Quick And Slow; Slow Slow Slow Slow; Slow Slow Slow Slow; Slow Slow Slow Hold*. **Chicago-City** was danced *Flick Ball flat Flick Ball flat; DiagSideSwivel1/4CCW diagsideswivel1/4CW DiagSideSwivel1/4CCW diagsiderise; SideSwivel1/2CW sideward CrossBehind sideward; swivel3/4 StepInPlace stepinplace rise*. Start over in new direction.

(See Novelty-&-Fad Dances-of-the-1960s.) [Much data from "Rhythm and Dance" by Alma Heaton.]

Chicken(1): An Unstructured and Unleadable, circa 1960 **Novelty Fad** American Singles dance, and a derivative of the **Twist**. *Rosco Gordon* sang the record *"The Chicken"* in 1957. Subsequently, the **Frug** was derived from the **Chicken**. The **Chicken** was danced with **a lateral Body Movement**, and was another primary Movement as a change when dancing the **Twist**. This silly **Chicken**, along with other silly Fad-Dances, was banned at Brigham Young University in 1966.

The **Chicken** Strutted almost In-Place, Deep-Into-Knees with Angular-Elbows Flailing. There were Pecking chin Movements. Weight was upon Balls-of-Feet with Turning and reversing Movements Forward and Rearward. With Thumbs under armpits, elbows Flapped Up and Down.

This dance is listed in the *"Dance Crazes of the Sixties,"* along with the following writeup:

"*The Chicken*

"*1. Stand with feet together and put right heel out.*

"*2. Jump back into place with right foot, landing on left toe on ground, left heel raised.*

"*3. Put heel of left foot out to left side.*

"*4. Jump back in place with left foot, landing with right toe on ground, right heel raised. Repeat over and over in place. The body moves easily from side to side by dropping the opposite shoulder each time the foot goes out.*

"*The counts are 1-2-3-4. Repeatit over and over.*

"*Note: The hands are raised, the fingers snapping on the beat.*"

Almost the same as The **Funky-Chicken**. [See **Chicken-Dance**. Also see Novelty-Dances, Fad-Dances, Novelty-and-Fad Genre, and the Novelty-&-Fad Dances-of-the-1960s. Also see Bird, Bird-Dog, Birdland, Buzzard-Lope, Chicago-Bird, Chicken-Back-Twist, Chicken-Dance, Chicken-Reel, Chicken-Scratch(2)&(3), Chicky-Goo, Claw, Crazy-Chicken, Eagle-Rock, Funky-Buzzard, Funky-Chicken, Greasy-Chicken, Monkey-Bird, Ostrich, Peck, Rooster-Walk, Scratch, Scratchin', Shake-a-Tail-Feather, Shakey-Bird, Surfin'-Bird, Turkey-Neck-Stretch, and Turkey-Trot(1)&(2). Also see Tate.]

Chicken(2): See Peck.

Chicken-Back-Twist: An American **Fad** Dance of the 1960s. This had its own Eponymous record, the *"Chicken Back Twist"* by the *Cellos*.

(See Novelty-&-Fad Dances-of-the-1960s.)

[From *www.bluejuice.org.au,* and *www.sixtiescity.com/Culture/dance*]

Chicken-Dance: A funny **Novelty Fad**, partially Choreographed, Spot-Coupledance from Germany, popular in 1980-90s. Patterned after the successful 1960s American Pantomime dance Movements, the **Chicken-Dance** has its own Eponymous song in 4/4 Time. The British dance it as a custom at their Social Dances. This is a dance they do to get non-dancers on to the floor.

The entire **Chicken-Dance** is done in a Circle; Man-Lady, Man-Lady. Partners part and gesture In-Place, with Thumbs under armpits, **Flapping their elbows** like a chicken, along with Pecking chin Movements, in Cadence at the Ending of certain Phrases of the music.

Similar to The **Chicken**(1). [See Peck, Hullie-Gullie, Frug, and Funky-Chicken. Also see the Bunny-Hop, Hokey-Pokey, and Limbo-Rock. Also see the Bomba, Cabbage-Patch, Dirty-Dancing, Funky-Twist, Lambada, Macarena, New-Kids-Move, Pac-Man, Punta y Soka, Quebradita, Teen-Dancing, and Urban-Dance; which were all Novelty Fads in vogue in the 1980-90s. Also see Tate. Also see Flap(3).]

Chicken-Noodle-Soup: A **Novelty** or **Fad** dance of an unknown time, listed in "*Novelty and fad dances*" under [http://en.wikipedia.org/wiki].

Chicken-Reel: An American "*animal dance*", a **Novelty Fad** Coupledance in vogue about 1914 to 1918. It was to a tune written by a Joseph Daly. Derided by newspapers, magazines, church officials, and even by Pope Pius X, as "such foolish and decadent behavior," over one hundred of these dances were created from 1912 to 1914.

(See Animal-Dances, Bull-Frog-Hop, Bunny-Hug, Buzzard-Lope, Camel-Walk, Chicken-Scratch, Crab-Step, Fish-Walk, Gotham-Gobble, Horse-Trot, Kangaroo-Dip, Kangaroo-Hop, Lame-Duck, Monkey-Glide, Possum-Trot, Snake, and Turkey-Trot; which were all Animal-Dances of 1910-1914.)

Chicken-Scratch(1): An Unleadable Spot-Coupledance two-Measure Pattern, suitable for both **ChaChas**, played *Slow*. The **Chicken-Scratch** one-Measure Figure dances Mirror-Image, Left and Right Foot, Singularly danced Apart in Shine Position. Rhythm with 4/4 Timing is *Quick Quick, Quick Quick, Quick Quick, Quick And Quick; Quick Quick, Quick Quick, Quick Quick, Quick And Quick.*

The dancer dances *sidestepBackFlick SideStepbackflick sidestepBackFlick SidecloseSide; SideStepbackflick sidestepBackFlick SideStepbackflick sideCloseside.*

May Start instead with its second (Mirror-Image) Figure. Back-Flicks are Slight.

(See ChaCha Step-Listing, and Break-A-Ways.) [From www.geocities.com/danceinfosa/]

Chicken-Scratch(2): An American "*animal dance*", a **Novelty Fad** Coupledance in vogue about 1912 to 1914. Derided by newspapers, magazines, church officials, and even by Pope Pius X, as "such foolish and decadent behavior," over one hundred of these dances were created during this period.

See **Chicken-Scratch**(1)&(3), which could be the same or similar Movements. (Also see Animal-Dances, Bull-Frog-Hop, Bunny-Hug, Buzzard-Lope, Camel-Walk, Chicken-Reel, Crab-Step, Fish-Walk, Gotham-Gobble, Horse-Trot, Kangaroo-Dip, Kangaroo-Hop, Lame-Duck, Monkey-Glide, Possum-Trot, Snake, and Turkey-Trot; which were all Animal-Dances of 1910-1914.)

Chicken-Scratch(3): There were two Eponymous versions of this **Novelty Fad** dance. One was danced in 1964 to the *"Chicken Scratch"* U.S.A. Record by *J.C. Davis*. The other was danced in 1969 to the *"Chicken Scratch"* Jamaican Record by *Count Suckle*.
          (See Novelty-&-Fad Dances-of-the-1960s.) [From *Soul*, www.trinity.unimelb.edu.au]

Chicky-Goo: A **Novelty Fad** Coupledance of the 1960s. This had its own Eponymous record, *"Chicky Goo"* by the *Metronomes*.
          (See Novelty-&-Fad Dances-of-the-1960s.) [From www.bluejuice.org.au]

Chill: Only this name for an American **Novelty** or **Fad** of the 1960s is listed simply as a Dance, Pattern, or Figure in the *"Dance Crazes of the Sixties*."
          (See Novelty-&-Fad Dances-of-the-1960s.) [From *www.sixtiescity.com/Culture/dance*]

Chiller: Only this name for an American **Novelty** or **Fad** of the 1960s is listed simply as a Dance, Pattern, or Figure in the *"Dance Crazes of the Sixties*."
          (See Novelty-&-Fad Dances-of-the-1960s.) [From *www.sixtiescity.com/Culture/dance*]

Chiller-Limbo: Only this name for an American **Novelty** or **Fad** of the 1960s is listed simply as a Dance, Pattern, or Figure in the *"Dance Crazes of the Sixties*."
          (See Novelty-&-Fad Dances-of-the-1960s.) [From *www.sixtiescity.com/Culture/dance*]

Chin-A-Ling: Only this name for an American **Novelty** or **Fad** of the 1960s is listed simply as a Dance, Pattern, or Figure in the *"Dance Crazes of the Sixties*."
          (See Novelty-&-Fad Dances-of-the-1960s.) [From *www.sixtiescity.com/Culture/dance*]

Chinese-Typewriter: In comical Pantomime, a **Novelty Fad** Singular dance Pattern or Routine of the 1980s. The **Chinese-Typewriter** was danced to the Beat by **Jump**ing Side-to-Side reversing **Heels-Out** then **Toes-Out**. [From the *"Eighties Dances*," www.inthe80s.com]
          The **Chinese-Typewriter** might be danced in conjunction with the Routines described under
"Typewriter," including the "Ripple."
          Similar to **Ramble**(2). (See Mime, Jump, Heel-Splits, Toe-Splits, Kid-and-Play, and Foot-Boogie.)

Choo-Choo: An American **Fad** dance of 1968. The **Choo-Choo** had its own Eponymous record, *"Do The Choo Choo"* by *Archie Bell & The Drells*.
          (See Novelty-&-Fad Dances-of-the-1960s.) [From *Soul*, *www.trinity.unimelb.edu.au*. Mentioned in *Dance Crazes of the Sixties*, *www.sixtiescity.com/Culture/dance*]

Churnin'-Butter: A 1980s Pantomime **Novelty Fad** Singular-Dance simulating Hand Movement. How to dance the **Churnin'-Butter** to the Beat is described as follows in the _"**Eighties Dances**,"_ [www.inthe80s.com]:

> _"With your arms slightly bent out in front of you, make one fist on top of the other and move them around in circles like you are churning butter..."_

Similar to **Sprinkler**, **Teen-Wolf**, **Belinda**, **Palm-Circles**(1), **Hand-Jive**, **Hitch-Hiker**, and **Tiffany**. [See Chair-Dancing, Arms-and-Hands, Finger-Flourishes, Free-Hand-Fashioning, and Gestures-Free-Hand.]

Cinnamon-Cinder: An Unleadable, American **Novelty Fad**, Choreographed Coupledance Routine, to medium-Cadence 4/4 Tempo music with a heavy Beat. The following four-Measures long Pattern was in vogue in the 1960s at the Brigham Young University, in Provo, Utah.

There is a picture from Brigham Young University, labeled and showing a young couple dancing the **Cinnamon-Cinder**. They are Apart in a Shine Position, but dancing upon Opposite Footwork. Their Bodies are ninety degrees from Facing with Trailing sides closest, but they are looking at each other. Both hips Sway Slightly Left. All arms are Slightly Spread, all with loose fists and bent elbows. The Lady, with Weight upon her straight Left leg, is Kicking Forward Straight-Legged and Slightly Crossed with her Pointed Right Toe, in the direction of her Man. The Man has his Right leg Crossed In-Front and Away from his Lady, with his Weight appearing to be upon both Balls.

Positions in the dance were in Butterfly, in full Open, and Back-to-Back. Lady danced Mirror-Image Opposite to her Man. Rhythm Timing was all _Slow_s.

In Butterfly and with Feet in Second-Position, the Man danced _sidesway SideSway sidesway SideSway_; _swaysidestep CrossKick SwaySideStep crosskick_; in full Open Position, he danced _sidestep CrossKick StepCrossed backstep_; _SideStep crosskick stepcrossed BackStepSwivel1/4CW_; Back-to-Back and retaking Hands, he repeated his dance Routine.

(See the Novelty-&-Fad Dances-of-the-1960s.) [Data mostly from "Rhythm and Dance" by Alma Heaton. Mentioned in _Dance Crazes of the Sixties_, _www.sixtiescity.com/Culture/dance_]

Circle-Pivot: An Unleadable **Break-A-Way Novelty Fad** Pattern, usually Performed while dancing the **Carolina-Shag**.

(See Shorty-George, Belly-Roll, Boogie-Back, Apple-Jacks, Flamingo, Duck-Walk, Fly-Back, Lean, Stutter-Step, and the SugarFoot, for like Patterns. See **Break-A-Way Glossary** for a more complete listing.)

[Note: Mechanics of Circle-Pivot's Steps are unknown.]

Cissy-Popcorn: A **Novelty Fad** Coupledance of 1969. This had its own Eponymous record, "Cissy Popcorn" by _Preston Love_.

(See Novelty-&-Fad Dances-of-the-1960s.) [From www.bluejuice.org.au]

Clam: Only this name for an American **Novelty** or **Fad** of the 1960s is listed simply as a Dance, Pattern, or Figure in the "_Dance Crazes of the Sixties_."

(See Novelty-&-Fad Dances-of-the-1960s.) [From _www.sixtiescity.com/Culture/dance_]

Clap-Boogaloo: Only this name for an American **Novelty** or **Fad** of the 1960s is listed simply as a Dance, Pattern, or Figure in the "*Dance Crazes of the Sixties*."
(See Novelty-&-Fad Dances-of-the-1960s.) [From *www.sixtiescity.com/Culture/dance*]

Claw: Only this name for an American **Novelty** or **Fad** of the 1960s is listed simply as a Dance, Pattern, or Figure in the "*Dance Crazes of the Sixties*."
(See Novelty-&-Fad Dances-of-the-1960s.) [From *www.sixtiescity.com/Culture/dance*]

Cleopatra-ChaCha: Only this name for an American **Novelty** or **Fad** of the 1960s is listed simply as a Dance, Pattern, or Figure in the "*Dance Crazes of the Sixties*."
(See Novelty-&-Fad Dances-of-the-1960s.) [From *www.sixtiescity.com/Culture/dance*]

Cleopatra-Stroll: Only this name for an American **Novelty** or **Fad** of the 1960s is listed simply as a Dance, Pattern, or Figure in the "*Dance Crazes of the Sixties*."
(See Novelty-&-Fad Dances-of-the-1960s.) [From *www.sixtiescity.com/Culture/dance*]

Cleveland-Box: A Structured but Unleadable, Novelty Pattern for a Singular-Dancer, two-Measures long, Mimicking a **Boxer** Boxing through Pantomime. While dancing its Basic-Step, this **Cleveland-Box** Pattern is one of the Qued Steps often Called for while dancing the **Madison** Audience-Participation-Dance.
The following are excerpts from *The Madison* -- [www.albertj.btinternet.co.uk/]:
"*Bring hands together and roll them forwards as if hitting a boxers practice ball.*
"*Step forward on left, lean back, lean forward, step to right, lean back, step back whilst leaning forward, step to left, lean back, lean forward.*"
With constant Knee-Bounce and prominent Shoulder-Lead with Spot-Movement. Firstly, two jabs by the Leading Clenched-Fist then two by the Trailing Clenched-Fist in Time to the Music. Footwork is constant Cadence while Armwork might be *and Slow   and Slow, and Slow and Slow*.
Similar to the **Boxer**. [See Double-Cross, Basketball, Big-'M', 'T'-Time, Jackie-Gleason, Birdland, and Rifleman. Also see the Novelty-&-Fad Dances-of-the-1960s.]

Click: Only this name for an American **Novelty** or **Fad** of the 1960s is listed simply as a Dance, Pattern, or Figure in the "*Dance Crazes of the Sixties*."
(See Novelty-&-Fad Dances-of-the-1960s.) [From *www.sixtiescity.com/Culture/dance*]

Climb: Only this name for an American **Novelty** or **Fad** of the 1960s is listed simply as a Dance, Pattern, or Figure in the "*Dance Crazes of the Sixties*."
(See Novelty-&-Fad Dances-of-the-1960s.) [From *www.sixtiescity.com/Culture/dance*]

Cling: Only this name for aa American **Novelty** or **Fad** of the 1960s is listed simply as a Dance, Pattern, or Figure in the "*Dance Crazes of the Sixties*."
(See Novelty-&-Fad Dances-of-the-1960s.) [From *www.sixtiescity.com/Culture/dance*]

Clown-Walk: A **Novelty** or **Fad** dance of an unknown time, listed in *"Novelty and fad dances"* under [http://en.wikipedia.org/wiki].

Clyde: Only this name for an American **Novelty** or **Fad** of the 1960s is listed simply as a Dance, Pattern, or Figure in the *"Dance Crazes of the Sixties."*
    (See Novelty-&-Fad Dances-of-the-1960s.) [From *www.sixtiescity.com/Culture/dance*]

Coco-Cherry-Mash: An American **Fad** dance of 1967. It's Eponymous Music was *"Coco Cherry Mash"* by the *Catalinas.*
    (See Novelty-&-Fad Dances-of-the-1960s.)
    [From *www.bluejuice.org.au*; and from *www.sixtiescity.com/Culture/dance*]

Coffee-Grind: Only this name for an American **Novelty** or **Fad** of the 1960s is listed simply as a Dance, Pattern, or Figure in the *"Dance Crazes of the Sixties."*
    (See Novelty-&-Fad Dances-of-the-1960s.) [From *www.sixtiescity.com/Culture/dance*]

Cold-Sweat: An Unleadable, American **Novelty Fad**, Choreographed Singular or Coupledance, sort of Line-Dance Routine. With a medium-Cadence 4/4 Tempo, the following four-Measures long Pattern was in vogue in the 1960s at the Brigham Young University, in Provo, Utah.
    There is a picture from Brigham Young University, labeled and showing a young couple dancing the **Cold-Sweat.** They are Apart Side-by-Side in Shine Position, upon the Same-Feet, Facing the same direction and looking Forward. Their Straight-Legged Left Feet are Pointed Forward and Slightly Crossed. Their Right arms are straight and Forward with hands at Waist-Level. Their Left arms are straight and Sideways with hands at Waist-Level; the Man's arm is behind the Lady. All fingers are fairly straight.
    The first Measure was all *Quick*s, while all other Steps were *Slows: flick ball Flat flat CrossFlick Ball flat Flat; sidepoint forcrossstep BackStepSpiral1/4CCW backstepspiral1/4CW; BackStepSpiral1/4CCW forstamp close ForStamp; Close forstamp close InPlaceStepSwivel1/4CW.* Start over.
    (See Novelty-&-Fad Dances-of-the-1960s.) [Data mostly from "Rhythm and Dance" by Alma Heaton.]

Come-To-Me-Tommy: A **Novelty Fad** Coupledance of about 1912 that allowed Partners to dance very Close. "Tommy" at that time meant a harlot.

Conga-Line or **Conga**(1) or **Conga-Chain**: Classified herein as in the **Audience-Participation-Dance** Category, and as both a **Novelty** Dance and **Fad** Dance. This **Conga-Line** is a Brazilian lighthearted dance for street parades during the Carnival; and is a Latin Rhythm **Group-Dance**, or possibly a Coupledance or Singular dance; a variation of the **Merengue** but definitely not a Ballroom-Dance. As a Novelty Fad, the **Conga** came into vogue in the U.S. about 1938, was very popular in the early 1940s and is still currently danced. Very repetitive.

The **Conga-Line** is one of the **Follow-the-Leader Dances** that include the **Bunny-Hop, Madison**, and the **Letkajenkka**. Danced in a chain or long line of many people, each holding another's waist from the rear. At times, it has its own accompanying music, named *"The Conga."*

Music, played in rather Fast 2/4 Time with heavy Accents, has a Rhythmic anticipation of the second Beat in every other Measure. Music's Rhythm Timing is *Quick And Quick And, Slow Slow; Quick And Quick And, Slow Slow.* The four-Measure Basic-Step is danced *slow Slow, andhop Touch; Slow slow, AndHop touch.* Basic Pattern is three Forward Steps then a Hop with a Side-Touch, repeated on Opposing Feet. A Kick might substitute at times for the Side-Touch.

Still currently danced for hours in Brazil, drums drumming for hours without stopping, the Conga-Beat is at times traded off for the Samba-Beat. Brazilians, en-masse, tend to Single-Dance **"The Conga."**

(See Clave-Beat, Soca, Calypso, Bomba, and the Plena. Also see the Big-Apple, Carioca, Boomps-A-Daisy, and Lambeth-Walk; which were all Novelty Fads in vogue in the 1930s. Also see Comparsa.)

Conga-Twist: A **Novelty Fad** Coupledance of 1964. This had its own Eponymous record, the *"Conga Twist"* by the *Revels.*
(See Novelty-&-Fad Dances-of-the-1960s.) [From www.bluejuice.org.au]

Congo: Only this name for an American **Novelty** or **Fad** of the 1960s is listed simply as a Dance, Pattern, or Figure in the "*Dance Crazes of the Sixties.*"
(See Novelty-&-Fad Dances-of-the-1960s.) [From *www.sixtiescity.com/Culture/dance*]

Contest Tango or **Harvest-Moon Tango:** An **American Tango** Style of Coupledance, often danced in **American Tango** Free-Style Competitions.
"Contest Tango is a more wide open Tango, with many steps originating from Promenade Position. Here, kicks by the lady, Rondes and Oversways are extensively used, and the whole dance concentrating on picture-type figure that features the lady in a variety of framed postures." -- [From www.geocities.com/danceinfosa.]
(See Valentino Tango.)

Continental: An American **Novelty** Choreographed and perhaps Cued **Coupledance Routine**, in vogue in the 1960s at Brigham Young University, in Provo, Utah. There was "*The Continental Walk*" which had been sung on a record by *The Midnighters* in 1968.

But this dance might have been fashioned after, or at least influenced by the song, ***The Continental***, which had a grand and lengthy *Busby Berkeley* massive Team-Coupledance scene in the 1934 movie, "*The Gay Divorcee.*"

The following is an excerpt from "*Cole Porter: a Biography*":

"*Though 'Night and Day' was already a popular classic when 'The Gay Divorcee' was released, the number became even better known because of the film and the dance built around it. The song that got the lion's share of attention in 'The Gay Divorcee,' however, was not Cole's 'Night and Day' but Con Conrad's 'The Continental' (with lyrics by Herb Magidson). Conrad's tune had the benefit of a long dance sequence in the film -- some seventeen minutes' worth -- in which a large group dressed in black and white sashayed about doing 'The Continental,' a follow-up dance to the Carioca, which had become enormously popular as a result of its exposure in 'Flying Down to Rio.' RKO also did its part to build up the tie-in between the 'Continental' and the 'Carioca' by advertising Astaire and Rogers in 'The Gay Divorcee' as 'The King and Queen of Carioca' ....*"

Success as a dance of *Con Conrad's* ***The Continental*** is unknown but was probably nil.

There is a picture from Brigham Young University, labeled and showing a young couple dancing ***The Continental***. They are Apart but closely Side-By-Side, Facing the same direction, dancing upon identical Feet and Kicking High their Kick-Turn while Clapping their own Hands. Their Right Free-Toes are Pointed. With medium 4/4 Timing, from a Facing Shine Position, both commence upon Left Foot. Starting with 4 Step-Swings with Finger-Snaps, then Vine-Three Left, both Partners Swiveling 1/2 CCW upon the last Left Step and Kicking their Right Foot Forward. Each then Steps *Back back Back swingacross*, and then Starts over. Danced twice, Partners end their dance Facing again.

Perhaps the same as the **Continental-Walk**. (See Novelty-&-Fad Dances-of-the-1960s.)
[Data mostly from "Rhythm and Dance" by Alma Heaton.]

Continental-Mash: Only this name for an American **Novelty** or **Fad** of the 1960s is listed simply as a Dance, Pattern, or Figure in the "*Dance Crazes of the Sixties.*"
(See Novelty-&-Fad Dances-of-the-1960s.) [From *www.sixtiescity.com/Culture/dance*]

Continental-Walk: An American **Fad** Coupledance of 1968. This had its own Eponymous record, "*The Continental Walk*" by the *Midnighters*.
Might be the same as the **Continental**. (See Novelty-&-Fad Dances-of-the-1960s.)
[From *www.bluejuice.org.au*. Mentioned in *www.sixtiescity.com/Culture/dance*]

Continental-Whip: Only this name for an American **Novelty** or **Fad** of the 1960s is listed simply as a Dance, Pattern, or Figure in the "*Dance Crazes of the Sixties.*"
(See Novelty-&-Fad Dances-of-the-1960s.) [From *www.sixtiescity.com/Culture/dance*]

Cool-Broadway: Only this name for an American **Novelty** or **Fad** of the 1960s is listed simply as a Dance, Pattern, or Figure in the "*Dance Crazes of the Sixties.*"
(See Novelty-&-Fad Dances-of-the-1960s.) [From *www.sixtiescity.com/Culture/dance*]

Cool-Jerk: Only this name for an American **Novelty** or **Fad** of the 1960s is listed simply as a Dance, Pattern, or Figure in the "*Dance Crazes of the Sixties*."
(See Novelty-&-Fad Dances-of-the-1960s.) [From *www.sixtiescity.com/Culture/dance*]

Cool-Off: Only this name for an American **Novelty** or **Fad** of the 1960s is listed simply as a Dance, Pattern, or Figure in the "*Dance Crazes of the Sixties*."
(See Novelty-&-Fad Dances-of-the-1960s.) [From *www.sixtiescity.com/Culture/dance*]

Cool-Shake: Only this name for an American **Novelty** or **Fad** of the 1960s is listed simply as a Dance, Pattern, or Figure in the "*Dance Crazes of the Sixties*."
(See Novelty-&-Fad Dances-of-the-1960s.) [From *www.sixtiescity.com/Culture/dance*]

Corrido-Twist: A **Novelty Fad** Coupledance of 1962. This had its own Eponymous record, the "*Corrido Twist*" by the *Venturas.*
(See Novelty-&-Fad Dances-of-the-1960s.) [From www.bluejuice.org.au]

Corta-Jaca: (Spanish for *Cutting Pony*) A **Break-A-Way**(3) Shine-Step, this **Corta-Jaca** is a partially Leadable, two-Measures (minimum) Advanced Coupledance Figure, primarily suitable for both **Samba**s, and for the **Cumbia**. It is also suitable for when in Butterfly or close-Coupledancing the **Pure-Balboa,** and for other dances.
Travel is gradual and toward Man's Left, with no Float or Rocking. Danced in Loose-Closed Position, or in Mush Position if for Balboa, with seven Steps per Measure. Rhythm for 4/4 Timing is *Slow, Quick Quick; Quick Quick, Quick Quick; 1 2&3&4&.*
The Man's Right Foot and the Lady's Left Foot remain as the Sliding center (Home) point, as Partners *Heel* Forward and *Toe* Rearward.
On Man's *Forward* (Right) Flat first Step, he Lowers her Hand below Waist-Level to Lead her Left foot *rearward*. Then the Man dances *heel SlideLeft toe SlideLeft heel SlideLeft*; his Right Foot Moves Sideward only.
Lady dances the corresponding Opposing Steps.
If *2&3&4&* is continued, end with Steps *2&.*
Similar to **Marchessi**, and **Rocking-Chair**. (See SugarFoot, Sand-Step, Electric-Kicks, Rock, and Rocking-Steps.)

Cotton: Only this name for an American **Novelty** or **Fad** of the 1960s is listed simply as a Dance, Pattern, or Figure in the "*Dance Crazes of the Sixties*."
(See Novelty-&-Fad Dances-of-the-1960s.) [From *www.sixtiescity.com/Culture/dance*]

Cotton-Eyed Joe: A series of Choreographed **Country-Western** Folkdances, eight or more Measures long, Coupledanced in 2/4 Time, either as a Texas-Twostep or Polka-American. Some are still current today. Several original versions from Texas contained Clog Steps requiring much Skill.

Cotton-Eyed Joe Traditional words sung while dancing were as follows:

> *"I hold my fiddle and I hold my bow*
> > *"Whilst I knock ol' Cotton-Eyed Joe!*
> *"Don't you remember, don't you know?*
> *"Don't you remember, Cotton-Eyed Joe?*
> *"Cotton-Eyed Joe, he was some guy!*
> *"He was handsome and he wasn't shy.*
> *"I hold my fiddle and I hold my bow*
> > *"Whilst I knock ol' Cotton-Eyed Joe!*
> *"He stole my money and my gal so fair;*
> *"I should be mad but I don't care.*
> *"Made some more money, hid it in a log,*
> *"Got another honey, went fishin' with my dog."*

A modern version was introduced in Las Vegas about 1980 as follows:

Danced on Same-Feet as if an American Twostep in Varsouvienne Position. Danced first as a Standing-Step Pattern then with Shuffles, repeated and repeated. The Shuffle portion is Leadable.

For the **Kicks** portion, Rhythm Timing is *Slow Slow, Quick Quick Slow*, four times. Both dance *crossinfrontheel kick, backward Backward backward; CrossInFrontHeel Kick, Backward backward Backward,* all repeated again before the **Shuffle.**

Then comes the Polka-American **Shuffle** portion, Forward Traveling or the Couple might Turn and dance In-Place. Timing is *quick Quick slow, Quick quick Slow;* for from four to sixteen times, after which the **Kicks** are repeated.

Note: Sometimes, even four of more people will dance this Together; the Head-Couple reaches Behind and Leads the second Couple Forward for the **Shuffle.**

The CWDI (Country-Western-Dance-International) calls this an entire CompetitiveCoupledance and names it the "**Cotton-Eyed Joe** ". The following is from their "*97-98 Standard Competition Rules*" "Dance Divisions":

> "***Cotton-Eyed Joe:*** *A step pattern that consists of 16 counts of standing step patterns (four, 4 count patterns), followed by 16 counts of shuffle steps (8 shuffle steps total), done in a progressive counterclockwise direction around the dance floor. Dancers may start with either the left or right foot. Dancers are expected to show the proper floor coverage. Any move which temporarily slows forward progression, must be performed toward the center of the dance floor."*

(See Ten-Step, Salty-Dog-Rag, and Rocky-Top.)

Count: Only this name for an American **Novelty** or **Fad** of the 1960s is listed simply as a Dance, Pattern, or Figure in the "*Dance Crazes of the Sixties.*"

(See Novelty-&-Fad Dances-of-the-1960s.) [From *www.sixtiescity.com/Culture/dance*]

Couple-Hustle or **Broadway-Hustle** or **Hollywood-Hustle:** A Leadable, Six-Count **Disco** Spot-Coupledance, popular in the U.S. in the 1970s. The heavy-beat music Tempo ranges from 27 to 36 MPM in 4/4 Time, and is played at 108 to 144 BPM.

Danced on Opposing-Feet, (Feet Mirror-Image Opposite.) Rhythm Timing is *Slow Quick And Slow Slow, Slow Slow*, or *1 2& 3 4, 5 Tap*, with this Footwork kept throughout their dance. Partners *Tap* DiagForward on the last of six Beats with Opposing Toes. See **Couple-Hustle Basic-Step** for more details.

See **Hustles-Latin-Same-Foot-and-Couple Step-Listing.** Similar to the **Latin-Hustle**. (See Hustle, Hustles-of-Tap-Genre, Same-Foot-Hustle, and NewYork-Hustle.)

Couple-Hustle Basic-Step: A Leadable, Six-Count, Spot-Coupledance Pattern, unique to the **Couple-Hustle**, 1 1/2-Measures long if in 4/4 Time, (music could also be in 2/4 Time.)

1 2& 3 4, 5 Tap Rhythm Timing for both Partners for the **Couple-Hustle**, is *slow Quick and Slow slow, Slow tap* for the Man; and, *Slow quick And slow Slow, slow Tap* for the Lady.

Coupledanced with repetition in Butterfly Position. Pattern does not Travel but Accordions. Ladys' Steps are Mirror-Image Opposite the Mans'. **Basic-Step** may be danced with no Turn or may be Couple-Rotated in either direction.

The lengthy Backward Step is on the One-Beat, reaching Rearward with a Long-Stride for both, while all Forward Steps are short. The second Step *Backward* and Recover is a **Back-Step**.

Partners *Tap* Sideward or DiagForward with Opposing Toes; Toes Slightly Pass upon *Tap*ping with Man's Toe Outside. Upon their *Tap*, Man Spreads Lady's Hands Apart, at Chest-Level with Man's Thumbs Up, as Lady often Touches Inside of Man's Left Foot with her Right Toe.

Man Steps *stridewaybackward *Backward inplace TinyForward tinyforward, TinyForward fortap.*

Lady Steps *StrideWayBackward *backward InPlace tinyforward TinyForward, tinyforward ForTap.*

Backward = On Ball with only half one's Weight applied.

Almost identical to the **Latin-Hustle Basic-Walk-In** except *Tap* is on the last Beat instead of on the first. (See Couple-Hustle, NewYork-Hustle Basic-Step, and Same-Foot-Hustle Basic-Step.)

Cow: A **Fad** dance of 1960. There were two records to which the **Cow** was danced. One was "*The Cow*" by *Bill Robinson*. The other was "*Milk That Cow*" by the *Essau/Group*.

(See Novelty-&-Fad Dances-of-the-1960s.)

[From *Soul, www.trinity.unimelb.edu.au.* Also some from *www.sixtiescity.com/Culture/dance*]

Cowboy-ChaCha Routine: A **ChaCha** Coupledance Routine popular in the early 2000s. In five Sequences, 20 Measures long, it is danced continually upon Same-Feet, and Basically in Varsouvian Position. Each Sequence is four Measures long and consists of Coupledancing a particular Pattern twice. All Couples present dance in Unison Counter-Clockwise around the Dancefloor.

The Routine Sequence is: 1) Basic ChaCha Forward and Back; 2) While retaining all Hands, Turning Lady Out to Face Man then returning her; 3) ChaCha-SwitchWalks, Right then Left while retaining all Hands; 4) ChaChas with both Traveling Forward as Man Spins Lady CW then CCW; and 5) While remaining Facing LOD, Lady dances CCW around Man as he continues to Travel Forward.

This memorized Routine is repeated and repeated, usually without Cues.

(See ChaCha Step-Listing.)

Crab-Step: A **Novelty Fad** Coupledance in vogue in the United States, probably in the 1910s, and probably danced to Ragtime music.

(See Animal-Dances, Lame-Duck, Horse-Trot, Grizzley-Bear, Buzzard-Lope, Turkey-Trot, Kangaroo-Hop, Fish-Walk, and Bunny-Hug.)

Crack-Up: Only this name for an American **Novelty** or **Fad** of the 1960s is listed simply as a Dance, Pattern, or Figure in the "*Dance Crazes of the Sixties.*"

(See Novelty-&-Fad Dances-of-the-1960s.) [From *www.sixtiescity.com/Culture/dance*]

Crank-Dat: A **Novelty** or **Fad** dance of an unknown time, listed in "*Novelty and fad dances*" under [http://en.wikipedia.org/wiki].

Crawl: A **Fad** dance of 1963. The **Crawl** had its own Eponymous record, "*The Crawl*" by *Guitar Junior*.

(See Novelty-&-Fad Dances-of-the-1960s.)

[From *Soul, www.trinity.unimelb.edu.au*. Also some from *www.sixtiescity.com/Culture/dance*]

Craze: A **Novelty Fad** Coupledance of the 1960s. This had its own Eponymous record, "*The Craze*" by *Sherman Evans*.

(See Novelty-&-Fad Dances-of-the-1960s.) [From www.bluejuice.org.au]

Crazy-Chicken: Only this name for an American **Novelty** or **Fad** of the 1960s is listed simply as a Dance, Pattern, or Figure in the "*Dance Crazes of the Sixties.*"

(See Novelty-&-Fad Dances-of-the-1960s.) [From *www.sixtiescity.com/Culture/dance*]

Crazy-Legs: A **Novelty Fad** Movement, **Crazy-Legs** is one small Move of the California `Funk' brand of the **Boogaloo** Genre of Mime "Moves," which seems to be part of the **Electric-Boogie** Style of **Break-Dancing**, which, in turn, is part of **Hip-Hop**. (Description of **Crazy-Legs** Movement is unknown by author.)

[See Air-Posing, Animation(3), Bop(2), Centipede, Cobra, Dime-Stopping, Filmore, Floating(2), Glides, Hitting, King-Tut, Lean(4), Pop(3), Puppet, Robot, Saccin, Scarecrow, Snake(4), Spiderman, Sticking, Strobing, Strut, Tick, and Wave(1); for other related Moves. Also see Underground Step-Listing.]

Creamy-Mashed-Potato: Only this name for an American **Novelty** or **Fad** of the 1960s is listed simply as a Dance, Pattern, or Figure in the "*Dance Crazes of the Sixties*."

(See Novelty-&-Fad Dances-of-the-1960s.) [From *www.sixtiescity.com/Culture/dance*]

Creep or **The Creep**: A **Novelty Fad** Group-Dance, where they **Creep** to Change-Partners. Imported from England into the U.S. in 1954. **The Creep** had its own music, (no words,) which was a medium-Tempo Swing in Syncopated 4/4 Time. Couples first dance In-Place, then upon a signal, each individual **Creep**s around the room.

(Also see the Bambuco, Bop, Bunny-Hop, Calypso, Fish, Flea-Hop, Frug, Guapacha, Hitch-Hiker, Hokey-Pokey, Hullie-Gullie, Jerk, Limbo-Rock, Mashed-Potato, Monkey, Pachanga, Plena, Pony, Rock-and-Around, Scooter, Slide, Strole, Surfers, Swim, Tumba-Cha, Twist, Twister, and the Watusi; which were all Novelty Fads in vogue in the 1950-60s. Also see Novelty-&-Fad Dances-of-the-1960s.)

Crossfire: An American **Fad** dance of 1959. The **Crossfire** had its own Eponymous record, "*Crossfire*" by *The Orlons*.

(See Novelty-&-Fad Dances-of-the-1960s.)

[From *Soul*, www.trinity.unimelb.edu.au. Also some from *www.sixtiescity.com/Culture/dance*]

Cross-Unwind or **CrossTurn-Counter-Clockwise** or **CrossSwivel-Left** or **CrossSpin-Left** or **Left-Cross-Turn** or **Half-Twist-Turn** or **Full-Twist-Turn**: An Unleadable, General, Counter-Clockwise Coupledance Figure, suitable for many different dances. Danced Apart, by either or both Partners. Can be danced to any *Slow Slow Slow* or *Slow Slow* or *Slow Quick Quick* or *Quick Quick Slow* Rhythm. Rhythm Timing is *Slow slow*. **Cross-Unwind** Rotates a **Half-** to **Full-Turn** in one Spot.

One's Right Ball is Crossed In-Front of the Supporting Left Foot and beyond in CBMP, then by Pressing both Feet, the Body is Rotated Counter-Clockwise. In other words, one's Right **Outer-Ball** Crosses over, parallel to and past the Left Foot Instep, then one Swivels on both Balls-of-Feet. Feet re-Cross Opposite with CBM, if upon Full-Turn completion.

Optional: One's Right **Outer-Heel** Crosses over, parallel to and past the Left Foot Instep, then one Swivels on the Left Ball then also on the Right Heel to Flat-of-Foot.

Cross-Unwind is a more explicit version of **Corkscrew**. Similar to the General **Unwind** Figure, which Rotates a **Half-Turn maximum**. Similar to **Hook-Overspin-Left**, **Hook-Overspin-Right**, **Cross-Overspin-Left**, **Cross-Overspin-Right**, **Toe-Spin-Clockwise**, and **Toe-Spin-Counter-Clockwise**, which Rotate a **Full-Turn minimum**. [See Cross-Wind, Hook-Unwind, Hook-Wind, Twist-Turn(1), Promenade-RunAround, Cross, and Hook. Also see Voltatonda, and Giro.]

    Cross-Wind or **CrossTurn-Clockwise** or **CrossSwivel-Right** or **CrossSpin-Right** or **Right-Cross-Turn** or **Half-Twist-Turn** or **Full-Twist-Turn:** An Unleadable, General, Clockwise Coupledance Figure, suitable for many different dances. Danced Apart, by either or both Partners. Can be danced to any *Slow Slow Slow*, or *Slow Slow*, or *Slow Quick Quick*, or *Quick Quick Slow* Rhythm. Rhythm Timing is usually *slow Slow*. **Cross-Wind** Rotates a **Half- to Full-Turn** in one Spot.

    One's Left Ball is Crossed In-Front of the Supporting Right Foot and beyond in CBMP, then by Pressing both Feet, the Body is Rotated Clockwise. In other words, one's Left Outer-Ball Crosses over, parallel to and past the Right Foot Instep, then one Swivels on both Balls-of-Feet. Feet re-Cross Opposite with CBM, if upon Full-Turn completion.

    Cross-Wind is a more explicit version of **Corkscrew.** Similar to the General **Unwind** Figure, which Rotates a **Half-Turn maximum.** Similar to **Hook-Overspin-Left, Hook-Overspin-Right, Cross-Overspin-Left, Cross-Overspin-Right, Toe-Spin-Clockwise,** and **Toe-Spin-Counter-Clockwise,** which Rotate a **Full-Turn minimum.** [See Cross-Unwind, Hook-Wind, Hook-Unwind, Twist-Turn(1), Cross, and Hook. Also see Voltatonda, Giro, and Chekessia.]

    Crown: Only this name for an American **Novelty** or **Fad** of the **1960s** is listed simply as a Dance, Pattern, or Figure in the "*Dance Crazes of the Sixties.*"
    (See Novelty-&-Fad Dances-of-the-1960s.) [From *www.sixtiescity.com/Culture/dance*]

    Crubbing or **Lovers-Rock** or **Dip-and-Grind:** An underground Coupledance, Movements, Pattern or form, associated with **Ska/Reggae.**
    The following is from *Reggae - Fashion and Dance - Lovers Rock*: [www.bbc.co.uk]
    "*The main reggae musical force to have emerged from the UK was Lovers Rock. The music was picked up by black, working-class, teenage girls --- .*
    "*The Lovers Rock era was not one for being on your own, this was definitely music for two. As ladies such as Janet Kay and Carroll Thompson sang couples onto the dance floors, the slow melodic music created a perfect environment for a new kind of intimate dancing known as crubbing. Crubbing can only be done with a partner, preferably someone you are involved with or attracted to. We think the title dip and grind better explains the dance move.*
    "*Crubbing / or Dip and Grind - Find a partner and both stand with feet shoulder width apart and knees slightly bent. Draw closer to one another and place one leg in-between your partners legs and the other on the outside of their legs (taking up a straddling motion) your partner does the same. The lady usually places both arms around her partners neck, whilst he in turn puts his hands around her waist. Both of you gently move your waists in time with the music, try to synchronise your movements together. Dip and then grind.*"
    Same as **Dirty-Dancing(1),** and the **Lambada.** Similar to **Freaking, Grind-Train, Perreo, Frottage,** and **Lap-Dance.** (See Underground Step-Listing, especially RockSteady. Also see Slow-Dancing, Swaying-to-the-Music, and Body-Contact.)

    Cruise: Only this name for an American **Novelty** or **Fad** of the **1960s** is listed simply as a Dance, Pattern, or Figure in the "*Dance Crazes of the Sixties.*"
    (See Novelty-&-Fad Dances-of-the-1960s.) [From *www.sixtiescity.com/Culture/dance*]

Crumble: Only this name for an American **Novelty** or **Fad** of the **1960s** is listed simply as a Dance, Pattern, or Figure in the "*Dance Crazes of the Sixties.*"
   (See Novelty-&-Fad Dances-of-the-1960s.) [From *www.sixtiescity.com/Culture/dance*]

Crusher: An American **Fad** dance of 1964. It's Eponymous Music was "*The Crusher*" by the *Novas.*
   (See Novelty-&-Fad Dances-of-the-1960s.)
   [From www.bluejuice.org.au. Also some from *www.sixtiescity.com/Culture/dance*]

Cum-A-La-Be-Stay: Only this name for a **Novelty** or **Fad** of the **1960s** is listed simply as a Dance, Pattern, or Figure in the "*Dance Crazes of the Sixties.*"
   (See Novelty-&-Fad Dances-of-the-1960s.) [From *www.sixtiescity.com/Culture/dance*]

Cupid-Shuffle: A **Novelty** or **Fad** dance of an unknown time, listed in "*Novelty and fad dances*" under [http://en.wikipedia.org/wiki].

Curls: Two two-Measure, partially Leadable, Left and Right Coupledance Shine-Step Patterns, primarily suitable for all **Swing**s and **ChaCha**s. **Curls** can be Coupledanced in the **Balboa Swing-Bal** as a Break-A-Way to Butterfly Position. **Curls** can also be cooperatively Coupledanced the Eight-Counts of **Pure-Balboa** entirely in Mush Position, but using the noted Timing.
   Curls begin and end in Butterfly Position with all Hands Grasped and with Leaning-Into-EachOther throughout. **Curls** Start in Butterfly Position, except begins with all four Feet Pointing in one Twisted-Waist direction, (CBMP,) and end with all four Feet Pointing in the Opposite Twisted-Waist direction. Feet change direction three times.
   Quarter-Turn and Brush then Swivel a Half-Turn on the Weighted-Foot, until the Free-Foot forms a Figure-Four Outside the Weighted-Foot, then Brush the Outside of the Weighted-Foot. Ends with four Half-Turn Swivels.
   (a) Begins by **Swivel**ing a Quarter-Turn Outward, Away from one's Free-Foot, with both Feet Pointing in one Twisted-Waist direction.
   (b) The Free-Leg is Swinging Forward as a pendulum, with the Free-Toe **Brush**ing then Passing the Supporting-Foot Instep, to a Slight Knee-Up.
   (c) The Supporting-Foot is **Swivel**ed a Half-Turn, so that both Feet are now Pointed in the Opposite Twisted-Waist direction, forming the **Figure-Four**.
   (d) The same Free-Foot is then again Swung Forward as a pendulum, with its Outer-Edge **Brush**ing then Passing the Supporting-Foot Outer-Edge.
   (e) **Swivel** a Half-Turn on both Feet, with both Feet Pointing same direction, four times.
   (f) (a) through (e) are repeated Mirror-Image Opposite.
   Timing for Left-Curl is *slow slow, Quick quick Quick quick*; and danced *swivelBrush swivelBrush, Swivel swivel Swivel swivelRecover.*
   Timing for Right-Curl is *Slow Slow, quick Quick quick Quick*; and danced *Swivelbrush Swivelbrush, swivel Swivel swivel Swivelrecover.*
   Lady Follows by dancing Mirror-Image Opposite Man. A Left-Curl Pattern is usually followed by a Right-Curl Pattern.
   (See Figure-Fore, Figure-Four Position, Sand-Step, and Sailor-Shuffle. Also see Balboa Step-Listing.)

Curly-Shuffle: An American **Novelty Fad** comical Solo-Dance or Maneuver of the 1980s.
> The following is from "_Eighties Dances_" - [www.inthe80s.com]:
> > "**_The Curly Shuffle:_** _Named after the Stooge, himself. There was a song by that name, too._"
> (See Novelty-&-Fad Dances-of-the-1980s. Also see Pantomime, Mime, and Mimicry-En-Masse.)

Danceannette: Only this name for a **Novelty** or **Fad** of the **1960s** is listed simply as a Dance, Pattern, or Figure in the "_Dance Crazes of the Sixties_."
> (See Novelty-&-Fad Dances-of-the-1960s.) [From _www.sixtiescity.com/Culture/dance_]

Dancin'-in-the-Dark: American **Novelty Fad** Solo-Dance or Maneuver of the 1980s.
> The following is from "_Eighties Dances_" - [www.inthe80s.com]:
> > "**_Dancin' In The Dark:_** _As a man in the 80's, I learned only one dance that carried me through the decade. It was from Courtney Cox and Bruce Springsteen and the Dancin' In The Dark video. You just swing your arms back and forth to the rhythm of the music and maybe put in a hip wiggle or something. The best thing about it is that you can do it to any song from the eighties. From the Beastie Boys to Boy George. This dance was resurrected in the 90's by the Carlton character on the Fresh Prince of Bel-Air._"
> (See Novelty-&-Fad Dances-of-the-1980s.)

Dancin'-in-the-Dark-Improved: An embellishment of the "**Dancin'-in-the-Dark**" **Novelty Fad** Solo-Dance or Maneuver of the 1980s, in Cadence with the Music.
> The following is from "_Eighties Dances_" - [www.inthe80s.com]:
> > "**_Dancin' In The Dark Improved:_** _Hang arms by side, and lock elbows (bent) onto hip. Looks like you're doing yoga. Swing arms back and forward pivoted at the hips, up in front of body, then back behind you outstretched._"
> (See Novelty-&-Fad Dances-of-the-1980s.)

Darktown-Strutters'-Ball: A **Novelty Fad** Coupledance that was written by _Sheldon Brooks_. Sheet Music for this, "_The Darktown Strutters' Ball_" was copyrighted in 1917 and published by _Leo. Feist, New York_. Principal Performer was _Mabel Burke_.
> "_I'll be down to get you in a taxi, Honey; better be ready 'bout half past eight._
> "_Now, Honey, don't be late; I wanna be there when the band starts playing._
> "_Remember when we get there, Honey, the two-steps, I'm gonna have them all._
> "_I'm gonna dance off both my shoes when they play those 'Jelly Rose Blues,'_
> "_Tomorrow night at the **Darktown Strutters' Ball**._"
> (Continued)

Darktown-Strutters'-Ball: (Continued)
The following is from *www.cstone.net/*:
        "*Sheldon Brooks was one of the African Americans born in the late 19th century in Canada which was the northern end of the Underground Railroad. He was born in 1886 in Amesburg, Ontario, but his family moved to Detroit when Sheldon was 15, and the remainder of his life was spent in the United States. He began his career playing ragtime piano in cafes in Cleveland and also began writing songs. In 1910 one of them, called 'Some of These Days' became a great favorite of Sophie Tucker, a star of American musical theater. She popularized the song, which was then published by an African American-owned firm in Chicago.*
        "*Brooks began performing in all-black musical shows, in Chicago and New York, and he toured Europe with a vaudville group known as Lew Leslie's Blackbirds that gave a command performance in England for King George V. In additional to songs that became immensely popular as they were sung in various big-city nightclubs in America, Brooks wrote some instrumental numbers and sometimes performed as a trap drummer. His 1916 instrumental number, which he named 'Walkin' the Dog' inspired a dance of the same name in Manhattan that soon spread to the rest of the country.*
        "*Brooks's most famous song is 'Darktown Strutters' Ball,' written in 1917. It was eventually recorded as a 'race record,' which--like the many musicals Brooks appeared in--was a euphemistic way of referring to all-black music and music companies. Nevertheless, 'Darktown Strutters' Ball' was an enthusiastic recounting of the fun that was to be had at fancy dress balls in 'Darktown' when people got dressed in their very best clothes and participated in fancy dances like 'Walkin' the Dog' and listened to lively renditions of the 'Jelly Roll Blues.' Brooks's song crossed racial lines to become an enormous hit in both black and white communities and has remained a classic from that era.*"
        [See Walkin'-the-Dog(1)&(2).]

Dartell-Stomp: Only this name for a **Novelty** or **Fad** of the **1960s** is listed simply as a Dance, Pattern, or Figure in the "*Dance Crazes of the Sixties.*"
        (See Novelty-&-Fad Dances-of-the-1960s.) [From *www.sixtiescity.com/Culture/dance*]

Deathrocker: An American **Novelty Fad** Solo-Dance or Maneuver of the 1980s.
        The following is from "*Eighties Dances*" - [www.inthe80s.com]:
        "***The Deathrocker:*** *This dance was mostly seen within the 'deathrocker community.' Music that this was danced to was 'Depeche Mode,' by Siouxie and the Banshees, New Order, and The Cure. Basically the dance was much like belly dancing with the hand movements, minus the grinding.*"
        (See Novelty-&-Fad Dances-of-the-1980s. Also see Belly-Dance.)

Debbie or **Back-Clap:** An Unleadable, American **Novelty Fad**, Choreographed Singular or Coupledance, sort of Line-Dance Routine. With a medium-to-fast Cadence 4/4 Tempo, the following eight-Measures long Pattern was in vogue in the 1960s at the Brigham Young University, in Provo, Utah.

The **Debbie** was danced Apart Side-by-Side in Shine Position, upon the Same-Feet, Facing the same direction and looking Forward. Although written up by BYU as a Singular Line-Dance, there is a picture from Brigham Young University, showing a young couple **Back-Clapping** while dancing the **Debbie**. Facing-Away in a Back-to-Back Vee-Line Position without Holding Hands, her Left and his Right hips are Pressed Together. Their own Hands are **Clap**ped Closed at Chest-Level. They Slightly Bend Forward with their Inside Supporting-Legs Softened. Their Outside **Opposing** Free-Legs are Extended Away Straight with both Heels Touching the Dancefloor.

Danced entirely with One-Step, even Rhythm Timing, the **Debbie** was danced with Side-Touches, Vines, **Back-Claps**, and Forward Swivels, thusly: (1) *sidestep CloseTouch SideStep closetouch*; (2) *sidestep CloseTouch SideStep closetouch*; (3) *sidestep CrossBehindStep sidestep CloseTouch*; (4) *SideStep crossbehindstep swivel1/4CWHeelTouch Clap*; (5) *CrossBehindStep Swivel1/4CCWheeltouch Clap crossbehindstep*; (6) *swivel1/4CWHeelTouch Clap CrossBehindStep Swivel1/4CCWheeltouch Clap*; (7) *forstepswivel1/4CW ForStepSwivel1/8CCW forstepswivel1/8CW CrossInFrontStep*; (8) *forstepswivel1/4CW ForStepSwivel1/8CCW forstepswivel1/8CW CrossInFrontStep*. Start over.

(See Novelty-&-Fad Dances-of-the-1960s.) [Data mostly from "Rhythm and Dance" by Alma Heaton.]

Debbie-Gibson: An American **Novelty Fad** comical Solo-Dance or Maneuver of the 1980s in Cadence with the Music.

The following is from "*Eighties Dances*" - [www.inthe80s.com]:

"*The Debby Gibson: Girls did this... It basically involved standing sideways, tilting back the head, spinning both hands in a short circle, and 'pushing' one's face back with the palm of the hand. (From her 'Foolish Beat' video).*"

(See Novelty-&-Fad Dances-of-the-1980s.)

Del-Viking: Only this name for a **Novelty** or **Fad** of the **1960s** is listed simply as a Dance, Pattern, or Figure in the "*Dance Crazes of the Sixties*."

(See Novelty-&-Fad Dances-of-the-1960s.) [From *www.sixtiescity.com/Culture/dance*]

Dinosaur-Groove: An American **Novelty Fad** comical Solo-Dance or Maneuver of the 1980s in Cadence with the Music.

The following is from "*Eighties Dances*" - [www.inthe80s.com]:

"*The Dinosaur Groove: Performed during .. 'Walk The Dinosaur' video. The prehistoric gals in the video showed you each step. Favorite part of the groove at dances was the 'Boom boom I can like-a like-a boom' shake.*"

(See Novelty-&-Fad Dances-of-the-1980s. Also see Animal-Dances.)

Dip: An American **Fad** dance of the 1960s. It's Eponymous Music was "*Dip Baby Dip*" by the *Cymbols.*
    (See Novelty-&-Fad Dances-of-the-1960s.)
    [From www.bluejuice.org.au. Also some from *www.sixtiescity.com/Culture/dance*]

Dipsey-Dooble: Only this name for an American **Novelty** or **Fad** of the **1960s** is listed simply as a Dance, Pattern, or Figure in the "*Dance Crazes of the Sixties.*"
    (See Novelty-&-Fad Dances-of-the-1960s.) [From *www.sixtiescity.com/Culture/dance*]

Dirt: Only this name for an American **Novelty** or **Fad** of the **1960s** is listed simply as a Dance, Pattern, or Figure in the "*Dance Crazes of the Sixties.*"
    (See Novelty-&-Fad Dances-of-the-1960s.) [From *www.sixtiescity.com/Culture/dance*]

Dirty-Boogie: Only this name for an American **Novelty** or **Fad** of the **1960s** is listed simply as a Dance, Pattern, or Figure in the "*Dance Crazes of the Sixties.*"
    (See Novelty-&-Fad Dances-of-the-1960s.) [From *www.sixtiescity.com/Culture/dance*]

Dirty-Dancing(1): A **Novelty Fad**, sensuous, intimate Coupledance in vogue in the U.S. in 1988 and 1989. While Slow-Dancing to a 4/4 Beat in Closed Position, the severely Backward Bending Lady would ride her Man's leg with her crotch, as the Man Supported her waist and swept her Upper-Body To-and-Fro in Time with the music. This medium-slow and seductive dance was popularized by the movie, *Dirty Dancin'.*
    Same as the **Lambada,** and **Crubbing.** Similar to **Freaking, Frottage, Perreo, Grind-Train,** and **Lap-Dance.** (See Slow-Dancing., Swaying-to-the-Music, and Body-Contact. Also see the Bomba, RockSteady, Chicken-Dance, Macarena, Punta y Soka, Quebradita, Teen-Dancing, and Urban-Dance; which were all Novelty Fads in vogue in the 1980-90s.)

Dirty-Dancing(2): See Freaking.

Dirty-Dog: Only this name for an American **Novelty** or **Fad** of the **1960s** is listed simply as a Dance, Pattern, or Figure in the "*Dance Crazes of the Sixties.*"
    (See Novelty-&-Fad Dances-of-the-1960s.) [From *www.sixtiescity.com/Culture/dance*]

Discophonic-Walk: Only this name for an American **Novelty** or **Fad** of the **1960s** is listed simply as a Dance, Pattern, or Figure in the "*Dance Crazes of the Sixties.*"
    (See Novelty-&-Fad Dances-of-the-1960s.) [From *www.sixtiescity.com/Culture/dance*]

Dish-Rag: Only this name for an American **Novelty** or **Fad** of the **1960s** is listed simply as a Dance, Pattern, or Figure in the "*Dance Crazes of the Sixties.*"
    (See Novelty-&-Fad Dances-of-the-1960s.) [From *www.sixtiescity.com/Culture/dance*]

Dive: A **Novelty Fad** Coupledance of the 1960s. This had its own Eponymous record, _"Do The Dive"_ by _Ronnie Fuller._
    (See Novelty-&-Fad Dances-of-the-1960s.) [From www.bluejuice.org.au]

Dizzy-Drag: An American **Novelty Fad** Coupledance (or possibly just a tune) in vogue in the 1910s or `20s. (Description of any **Dizzy-Drag** Movements are unknown by author.)
    Other _"drag dances"_ of the time were the A-Minor-Drag, Saratoga-Drag, Shoe-Shiner's-Drag, Slow-Drag, Viper's-Drag, and the most famous **Varsity-Drag.**

Do: A **Novelty Fad** Coupledance of the 1960s. It's Eponymous Music was _"Do The Dog"_ by _Howlin' Wolf._
    (See Novelty-&-Fad Dances-of-the-1960s.) [From www.bluejuice.org.au]

Doctors-Boogie: Only this name for an American **Novelty** or **Fad** of the **1960s** is listed simply as a Dance, Pattern, or Figure in the _"Dance Crazes of the Sixties."_
    (See Novelty-&-Fad Dances-of-the-1960s.) [From _www.sixtiescity.com/Culture/dance_]

Dog: An Unstructured and Unleadable, 1960s **Novelty Fad** American Singles dance. In 1963, _Rufus Thomas_ recorded _Walking The Dog._ Its Eponymous dance was The **Dog.**   Also, in 1962, there was _"The Dog"_ played and sung by _Junior and the Classics._
    Having been derived from The **Frug,** The **Dog** was related to The **Swim,** The **Monkey,** The **Watusi,** The **Waddle,** and The **Jerk** dances. The dance Mimicked a **Dog,** and was one of a whole series of 1960s Mimicking dance Patterns, (see Hullie-Gullie.) Danced In-Place, dancers Swung hips Side-to-Side, with certain added arm Movements. This silly **Dog,** along with other silly Fad-Dances, was banned at Brigham Young University in 1966.
    The following Basic-Step is from _Crazy Dance Moves!_ by Yana:
        "-- dancing plays a large role in the Ska subculture. Why? Ska was originally played at clubs and dancehalls in Jamaica. These spaces provided Jamaicans with the opportunity to dance the night away --
        "The Dog - 1. Feet apart, with slightly bent knees. Arms a bit bent and extended in front of you. 2. Jump so you are facing front (in same position) with your arms which remain bent with clenched fists. Move them up and down to the beat of the music. Do the same with your body. 3. Continue motions while going lower until your arms are below your arse. 4. Continue motions upwards until your fists reach past your shoulders. 5. Jump to the side and repeat."
    The following is from _www.sixtiescity.com/Culture/dance_:
        Listed in the _"Dance Crazes of the Sixties,"_ along with a 12-pictures Sequence (showing Patrick Kerr?) and the following writeup describing this as a Singular-Dance, Pattern, or Figure:
        The Dog: _"With feet slightly apart, crouch down with arms bent and fists clenched. Move body and arms backwards and forwards with the beat. Jerk clenched fists over shoulders alternately similar to Hitch Hike movement and jump to the left or right."_
    Note: While **Skanking** to the **Ska,** the **Dog** is a Variation.
    (See Novelty-&-Fad Dances-of-the-1960s. Also see Underground Step-Listing.)

Dogin: Only this name for an American **Novelty** or **Fad** of the **1960s** is listed simply as a Dance, Pattern, or Figure in the "*Dance Crazes of the Sixties.*"
(See Novelty-&-Fad Dances-of-the-1960s.) [From *www.sixtiescity.com/Culture/dance*]

Dolphin: A 1980s Pantomime **Novelty Fad** Singular-Dance Movement. How to dance the **Dolphin** to the Beat is described as follows in the *"Eighties Dances,"* [www.inthe80s.com]:
"Similar to the `snake', but moving forward. The chin dips down, head lifts up and the body follows: ribs, stomach, hips, knees and then two steps back with the feet."
[This `**Snake**'(5) is described as *"Pretend you're having to duck under a bar that is next to you. Then let that motion travel all the way down to your foot."*]
(See Body-Ripple, and Body-Wave.)

Donkey-Step: Only this name for an American **Novelty** or **Fad** of the **1960s** is listed simply as a Dance, Pattern, or Figure in the "*Dance Crazes of the Sixties.*"
(See Novelty-&-Fad Dances-of-the-1960s.) [From *www.sixtiescity.com/Culture/dance*]

Donkey-Stroke: Only this name for an American **Novelty** or **Fad** of the **1960s** is listed simply as a Dance, Pattern, or Figure in the "*Dance Crazes of the Sixties.*"
(See Novelty-&-Fad Dances-of-the-1960s.) [From *www.sixtiescity.com/Culture/dance*]

Donkey-Trot: Only this name for an American **Novelty** or **Fad** of the **1960s** is listed simply as a Dance, Pattern, or Figure in the "*Dance Crazes of the Sixties.*"
(See Novelty-&-Fad Dances-of-the-1960s.) [From *www.sixtiescity.com/Culture/dance*]

Donkey-Twine: Only this name for an American **Novelty** or **Fad** of the **1960s** is listed simply as a Dance, Pattern, or Figure in the "*Dance Crazes of the Sixties.*"
(See Novelty-&-Fad Dances-of-the-1960s.) [From *www.sixtiescity.com/Culture/dance*]

Donkey-Walk: Only this name for an American **Novelty** or **Fad** of the **1960s** is listed simply as a Dance, Pattern, or Figure in the "*Dance Crazes of the Sixties.*"
(See Novelty-&-Fad Dances-of-the-1960s.) [From *www.sixtiescity.com/Culture/dance*]

Doodle-Pickle: A **Novelty Fad** Coupledance of the 1960s. This had its own Eponymous record, the "*Doodle Pickle*" by *Joe Cook.*
(See Novelty-&-Fad Dances-of-the-1960s.) [From www.bluejuice.org.au]

Doolang: Only this name for an American **Novelty** or **Fad** of the **1960s** is listed simply as a Dance, Pattern, or Figure in the "*Dance Crazes of the Sixties.*"
(See Novelty-&-Fad Dances-of-the-1960s.) [From *www.sixtiescity.com/Culture/dance*]

Double-Cross: A Novelty, Singular-Dance one-Measure Figure; four even Counts. *Forward* is the Starting Position. This **Double-Cross** Figure is one of the Qued Steps often Called for while dancing the **Madison** Audience-Participation-Dance's Basic-Step.

The following is an excerpt from *The Madison* -- [www.albertj.btinternet.co.uk/]:

"Double Cross = Facing forward, step onto left foot, cross right foot over in front, cross left over right, right over left. Start [with] *knees together slightly bent, swing sideways keeping body straight, whilst swinging arms together in a forward arc like a skier until ... "*

(See Madison.)

Double-Foot-Boogie: Two Unleadable Spot-Dance Steps, suitable for **Line-Dances**, **Country-Western** Fixed-Pattern-Partner-Dances, and for other dances. Performed either Singular or as a Couple in Open Position. One-Measure long, Rhythm Timing is *Slow Slow Slow Slow*.

Both Toes or Heels are Swiveled simultaneously. Weight is on Heels to Swivel Toes, and on Toes to Swivel Heels.

For **Toes-Double-Foot-Boogie**, Man (or person) dances *SwivelToesDiagOut SwivelHeelsDiagOut SwivelHeelsDiagIn SwivelToesParallel.*

For **Heels-Double-Foot-Boogie**, Man (or person) dances *SwivelHeelsDiagOut SwivelToesDiagOut SwivelToesDiagIn SwivelHeelsParallel.*

If as a Couple, Lady dances Same-Feet as Man.

(See Foot-Boogie, Ramble, SugarFoot, Sand-Step, Toe-In, Toe-Out, Toes-Out, Toe-Splits, Toe-Fan, Heel-Fan, Heels-Out, Heel-Splits, Swivet, Marchessi, Corta-Jaca, and Celtic-Storm.)

Doublemint: Only this name for an American **Novelty** or **Fad** of the **1960s** is listed simply as a Dance, Pattern, or Figure in the "*Dance Crazes of the Sixties.*"

(See Novelty-&-Fad Dances-of-the-1960s.) [From *www.sixtiescity.com/Culture/dance*]

Double-Rock: A **Novelty Fad** Coupledance of the 1960s. This had its own Eponymous record, the "*Double Rock*" by *Bobby & the Bengals.*

(See Novelty-&-Fad Dances-of-the-1960s.) [From www.bluejuice.org.au]

Drag: A Leadable but Unstructured, American **Novelty Fad**, four-Measure, Singular or Coupledance Pattern or Routine. In a 4/4 One-Step Tempo, this **Drag** Routine was in vogue in the 1960s at the Brigham Young University, in Provo, Utah.

The-Drag is a halting, Forward Traveling Routine that Progressed by dancing as follows: *forstep DigSideward ForStep digclosed; forstep DigClosed ForStep forstep.* Repeat Mirror-Image Opposite, e.g., *ForStep digsideward,* etc. Dig with Ball-of-Foot. Couples may have danced In-Step Side-by-Side.

(See Novelty-Dances, Fad-Dances, Novelty-and-Fad Genre, and Novelty-&-Fad Dances-of-the-1960s. Also see A-Minor-Drag, Saratoga-Drag, Slow-Drag, and Varsity-Drag.)

[Mostly from "Rhythm and Dance" by Alma Heaton. See *www.sixtiescity.com/Culture/dance*]

Drive-By: From Kingston, Jamaica, an Underground **Novelty Fad**, Singular- or Group-Dance Movement, associated with dancing **Dancehall/Ragga**, which, in turn, are outgrowths of **Ska/Reggae**. **Drive-By** was and is danced mainly by youths of color.

The following is from *Ragga Fashions*:   [www.bbc.co.uk]

"*Drive-By - Stand with feet apart. Take two steps to the left and forward. At the same time lift your arm and hold an imaginary car steering wheel, turning slightly from left to right in a driving motion. Swap feet and repeat steps, you can travel with this movement, your driving arm remains the same.*"

See **Dancehall**(2) for further explanation. (Also see Bogle, Armstrong, Butterfly, Go-Go-Wine, Body-Basic-and-Exercise, Tate, and World-Dance. Also see Jerry-Springer, Prang, Heel-and-Toe, Na!Na!Na!, Screechie, Zip-It-Up, Shizzle-Ma-Nizzle, Matrix, and Bin-Laden. Also see Underground Step-Listing.)

Drum-Stomp: Only this name for an American **Novelty** or **Fad** of the **1960s** is listed simply as a Dance, Pattern, or Figure in the "*Dance Crazes of the Sixties.*"

(See Novelty-&-Fad Dances-of-the-1960s.) [From *www.sixtiescity.com/Culture/dance*]

Drunkard: Only this name for an American **Novelty** or **Fad** of the **1960s** is listed simply as a Dance, Pattern, or Figure in the "*Dance Crazes of the Sixties.*"

(See Novelty-&-Fad Dances-of-the-1960s.) [From *www.sixtiescity.com/Culture/dance*]

Duck: A fun, American **Novelty Fad** Singular or Coupledance that was Unstructured and Unleadable, and that Traveled. In 1965, particular singing records to which the **Duck** was danced, were "*The Duck*" by *Jackie Lee*, "*The Duck*" by *Cookie & The Cupcakes*, and "*Shotgun*" by *Jr. Walker & The Allstars*. [From *Soul*, www.trinity.unimelb.edu.au]

One of a whole series of 1960s Mimicking dance Patterns, (see Hullie-Gullie,) its Eponymous dance Steps attempted to imitate a **Duck** through Pantomime by Waddling. This silly **Duck**, along with other silly Fad-Dances, was banned at Brigham Young University in 1966.

Waddles are Charlie-Chaplin Tilting Steps, wery short and Flat with Toes pointed Outward. Arms and Hands are Held at sides with Palms-Down. Swaying, the hip Opposite the Stepped Foot protrudes (Side-Stretch) as the Lower-Body Torques with CBM.

Same as or similar to **Waddle**, and **Penguin**. (See Novelty-&-Fad Dances-of-the-1960s.) [Also see *www.sixtiescity.com/Culture/dance*]

Duck-Walk(1): An Unleadable **Break-A-Way** novelty **Fad** Pattern, usually Performed while dancing the **Carolina-Shag**.

(See Shorty-George, Boogie-Back, Apple-Jacks, Belly-Roll, Flamingo, Belly-Roll, Fly-Back, Lean, Stutter-Step, and the SugarFoot, for like Patterns. See **Break-A-Way Glossary** for a more complete listing.) [Note: Mechanics of its Steps are unknown.]

Duck-Walk(2): Only this name for an American **Novelty** or **Fad** of the **1960s** is listed simply as a Dance, Pattern, or Figure in the "*Dance Crazes of the Sixties.*"

(See Duck, Waddle, and Penguin. Also see Novelty-&-Fad Dances-of-the-1960s.) [From *www.sixtiescity.com/Culture/dance*]

Eagle-Rock: See Ballin'-The-Jack.

Earthquake: A **Novelty Fad** Coupledance of the 1960s. This had its own Eponymous record, *"The Earthquake"* by *Troy Dodds.*
    (See Novelty-&-Fad Dances-of-the-1960s.) [From www.bluejuice.org.au]

Earthworm: A **Novelty Fad** Coupledance of the 1960s. This had its own Eponymous record, *"The Earthworm"* by *Maurice Dollison.*
    (See Novelty-&-Fad Dances-of-the-1960s.) [From www.bluejuice.org.au]

Ebb-'n'-Flow: Only this name for an American **Novelty** or **Fad** of the **1960s** is listed simply as a Dance, Pattern, or Figure in the *"Dance Crazes of the Sixties."*
    (See Novelty-&-Fad Dances-of-the-1960s.) [From *www.sixtiescity.com/Culture/dance*]

Ed-Lover-Dance: An American **Novelty Fad** Solo-Dance or Maneuver of the 1980s in Cadence with the Music.
    The following is from *"Eighties Dances"* - [www.inthe80s.com]:
       *"**Ed Lover Dance:** From 'Yo MTV Raps.' With both arms out to the sides, step with your right and pop your right hip forward, then to the left with the left hip, then back to the right twice, left, right, left, left."*
    (See Novelty-&-Fad Dances-of-the-1980s.)

Egyptian: An Unleadable, American **Novelty Fad** dance of the 1960s. How to dance the **Egyptian** should be found on a VHS Video by Christy Lane (www.centralhome.com).
    The following is from *"Eighties Dances"* (www.inthe80s.com):
       *"**The 'Egyptian' dance** - Performed during the Bangles classic 'Walk Like an Egyptian', basically the intent is to mimic walking like the old illustrations in Egyptian art, moving your head back and forth. It is done by walking with your head bobbing forward and backward while having one arm bent 90 degrees and facing backwards and the other arm bent 90 degrees and facing forward, both moving forward and back. Front arm bent upwards back arm bent downwards."*
    (See King-Tut, and Egyptian-Pose. Also see Novelty-&-Fad Dances-of-the-1960s.)
    [Mentioned in *www.sixtiescity.com/Culture/dance*]

Egyptian-Shumba: A **Novelty Fad** Coupledance of the 1960s. It's Eponymous Music was *"Egyptian Shumba"* by the *Tammys.*
    (See Novelty-&-Fad Dances-of-the-1960s. Also see Egyptian, Egyptian-Pose, and King-Tut.)
    [From www.bluejuice.org.au. Also mentioned in *www.sixtiescity.com/Culture/dance*]

Eighty-One: A **Novelty Fad** Coupledance of 1964. The **Eighty-One** had its own Eponymous record, *"The 81"* by *Candy & The Kisses*.

[See Novelty-&-Fad Dances-of-the-1960s. Also see Forty-Five(1).]

[From *Soul*, www.trinity.unimelb.edu.au, and from www.bluejuice.org.au. Also mentioned in *www.sixtiescity.com/Culture/dance*]

El-Cable: Only this name for an American **Novelty** or **Fad** of the **1960s** is listed simply as a Dance, Pattern, or Figure in the "*Dance Crazes of the Sixties.*"

(See Novelty-&-Fad Dances-of-the-1960s.) [From *www.sixtiescity.com/Culture/dance*]

Electric-Slide: A **Novelty** or **Fad** dance of an unknown time, listed in "*Novelty and fad dances*" under [http://en.wikipedia.org/wiki].

Elephant-Walk: An Unleadable, fun, American **Novelty Fad** Coupledance Choreographed Routine, perhaps Cued, in vogue in the 1960s. It may have been named after the movie starring Elizabeth Taylor, titled *Elephant-Walk*. The dance Mimicked an **Elephant-Walk**ing, and was one of a whole series of 1960s Mimicking dance Patterns, (see Hullie-Gullie.)

The Elephant-Walk Dance in vogue at Brigham Young University, Provo, Utah, had medium 4/4 Timing. Each Measure was immediately repeated Mirror-Image Opposite. Danced in Shine or in Butterfly Position, both Partners commenced upon Right Foot. *Side-Touch Close-Touch Side-Touch Close*; *side-touch close-touch side-touch close*; *Back-Touch Close-Touch Back-Touch Close*; *back-touch close-touch back-touch close*; *Knee-Touch-elbow Side-Touch Knee-Touch-elbow Close*; *knee-touch-Elbow side-touch knee-touch-Elbow close*; *Cross-Kick Close, cross-kick close*; Slide Right and Clap. Start over.

There is a picture labeled and showing a young BYU couple Touching Knee to elbow, dancing **The Elephant-Walk**. They are Apart, Facing upon identical Feet with their Right Knees Raised High and Crossed. Also, they have four Angular-Elbows with all fists Raised.

(See Novelty-&-Fad Dances-of-the-1960s.)

[Much data from "Rhythm and Dance" by Alma Heaton. See *www.sixtiescity.com/Culture/dance*]

El-Matador: Only this name for an American **Novelty** or **Fad** of the **1960s** is listed simply as a Dance, Pattern, or Figure in the "*Dance Crazes of the Sixties.*"

(See Novelty-&-Fad Dances-of-the-1960s.) [From *www.sixtiescity.com/Culture/dance*]

El-Watusi: Only this name for an American **Novelty** or **Fad** of the **1960s** is listed simply as a Dance, Pattern, or Figure in the "*Dance Crazes of the Sixties.*"

(See Novelty-&-Fad Dances-of-the-1960s.) [From *www.sixtiescity.com/Culture/dance*]

Everybody's-Doin'-It: A **Novelty Fad** Coupledance with words and Music by *Irving Berlin*. Its Eponymous sheet Music called "*Everybody's Doin' It Now*" was copyrighted in 1911and published by *Ted Snyder Co.* Principal Performer was *Lydia Barry*.

Related to **Grizzly-Bear**. Words in its chorus says, "It's a bear, it's a bear, it's a bear."

Everything: Only this name for an American **Novelty** or **Fad** of the **1960s** is listed simply as a Dance, Pattern, or Figure in the "*Dance Crazes of the Sixties.*" (See Novelty-&-Fad Dances-of-the-1960s.) [From *www.sixtiescity.com/Culture/dance*]

E.T.: An American **Fad** comical Solo Maneuver of the 1980s in Cadence with the Music.

The following is from "*Eighties Dances*" - [www.inthe80s.com]:

"*The E.T.: Hold your arms straight down, hands fisted and shuffle side to side. Slightly lift your leg as you shift your body weight from side to side.*"

(See Novelty-&-Fad Dances-of-the-1980s. Also see Pantomime, Mime, and Mimicry-En-Masse.)

Fairy-Dance: An American **Novelty Fad** Solo-Dance or Maneuver of the 1980s. The following is from "*Eighties Dances*" - [www.inthe80s.com]:

" *Fairy-Dance: Okay, not politically correct but that's what it was called. You hold your hands and lower arms out in front of you loosely, waving them about, while the rest of your body sways to the music. Usually a dance done to the Smiths or similar depressing music.*"

(See Novelty-&-Fad Dances-of-the-1980s.)

Fall-Off-the-Log or **Falling-Off-a-Log** or **Rolling-Off-the-Log:** A General Shine-Step. A Singular and Coupledance Figure or Pattern, often of the **Tap-Dance Genre** since it is a take-off from the **Buffalo.** Also a possibly Leadable 1930s **Break-A-Way** Novelty **Fad** Pattern, usually Performed while dancing the **Big-Apple.** Also suitable for the many **Swing** dances, and as a Swing-Bal Variation for the **Balboa.**

Fall-Off-the-Log normally is a Twisting, Sideward Movement in a Vine fashion while the dancer's Weight Falls Forward: **Kick-Step to one side, Hook Behind, Step Step. Repeat in the other direction. Eight Counts total.**

For the **Big-Apple,** the **Fall-Off-the-Log** was one of the **Break-A-Way** Genre. Wiggling their hips, certain **Break-A-Way** Patterns were danced. The original **Suzie-Q, Boogie-Back, Tack-Annie, Georgia-Grind, Praise-Allah!, Truckin', Peckin', Charleston, Shorty-George**, and other **Break-A-Ways**, were probably originated early by blacks; while **Spank-the-Baby, Rusty-Dusty, Pose-and-a-Peck,** the **Little-Apple,** the **Little-Peach, Mess-Around, Stomp-Off, Apple-Jacks**, and **Fall-Off-the-Log**, and other **Break-A-Ways**, were probably originated later by whites. Most all of these Patterns seem to have been influenced or derived from the classic **Lindy-Hop** and/or **Big-Apple** dances. See **Break-A-Way Glossary** for a more complete listing.

A Variation of the "*Hook Behind*" is to **Cross In-Front.**

Similar in feeling to **Sailor-Shuffle.** (Also see Flash-Step, Balboa Step-Listing, and Balboa-CrossOvers.)

Fancy-Feet: An American **Novelty Fad** comical Solo-Dance or Maneuver of the 1980s in Cadence with the Music.

The following is from "_Eighties Dances_" - [www.inthe80s.com]:

"_Fancy Feet: This dance is a simple move that travels a short distance from side to side. Start with your toes turned inwards and then lift up your right toe and your left heel and kind of twist them separately to the right so they turn outwards._ _Keep repeating._ _This move is seen frequently in Michael Jackson's 'Black or White' video._"

Same as the **Toe/Heel-Walk, Ramble**(2), and **Traveling-Applejacks**. (See Novelty-&-Fad Dances-of-the-1980s.)

Fanny-Bump: The **Fanny-Bump** was a **Novelty Fad** Coupledance in vogue in the United States, somewhere in the 1900s-1910s.

(See Yankee-Tangle, Texas-Rag, Funky-Butt, Squat, Itch, Grind, and Mooch.)

Fatman: An American **Novelty Fad** dance of 1965. The **Fatman** was danced to the record, "_Hole In The Wall_" by _The Packers_.

(See Novelty-&-Fad Dances-of-the-1960s.)

[From _Soul_, www.trinity.unimelb.edu.au. Also see _www.sixtiescity.com/Culture/dance_]

Fila: A 1980s Pantomime **Novelty Fad Singular-Dance** Maneuver. How to dance the **Fila** to the Beat is described as follows in the "_Eighties Dances_," [www.inthe80s.com]:

"_Very big with the Rap music fans._ _Basically like doing the moonwalk but in place._ _Stepping one foot in front of the other, then spelling out the word `FILA'._  _Taking your right toes and touching your left toes with heel away from the other forming an `F'._ _Then returning your right heel back to its place to form the `I' and turning your right toes away to form an `L'._ _Finally touching once again your two right toes to form an `A'._"

(See YMCA. Also see Macarena, and Time-Warp .)

Finger-Poppin': An American **Novelty Fad** dance of 1960. **Finger-Poppin'** had its own Eponymous record, "_Finger Poppin' Time_" by _Hank Ballard & the Midnighters_.

(See Novelty-&-Fad Dances-of-the-1960s.)

[From _Soul_, www.trinity.unimelb.edu.au. Also see _www.sixtiescity.com/Culture/dance_]

Fine-Twine: Only this name for an American **Novelty** or **Fad** of the **1960s** is listed simply as a Dance, Pattern, or Figure in the "_Dance Crazes of the Sixties._"

(See Novelty-&-Fad Dances-of-the-1960s.) [From _www.sixtiescity.com/Culture/dance_]

Fink: A **Novelty Fad** Coupledance of 1966. It's Eponymous Music was "_Let's Do The Fink_" by _Alf Newman_.

(See Novelty-&-Fad Dances-of-the-1960s.) [From www.bluejuice.org.au]

Finnjenica: A **Novelty Fad** Coupledance in vogue in 1964.

[From _Novelty Dances Through the Years_ by Pony Moore.]

Fish: A fun American **Novelty Fad** Singular or Coupledance that was Unstructured and Unleadable. The **Fish** appeared in the U.S. about 1966-68. Some say The **Fish** originated about 1963 with The **Hullie-Gullie.** A Spot-dance, danced in 4/4 Time to Jazz type Foxtrot music. The **Fish** was usually danced Apart but Facing Partner, and was often danced in conjunction with the **Swim.** The **Fish** and these 1960s dances were free and individualistic. People enmasse, mostly teens with long hair, were dancing by themselves and inventing as they danced. The dance Mimicked a **Fish Swim**ming, and was one of a whole series of 1960s Mimicking dance Patterns, (see Hullie-Gullie.) This silly **Fish**, along with other silly Fad-Dances, was banned at Brigham Young University in 1966.

One of the **Fish**'s primary, Unleadable Movements was to sink **Down and Up** while Swiveling to the Music Beat. The dancer danced while **holding one's nose** with one Hand, and while having Raised the other Hand Straight Up, **wobbling it Down**, simulating bubbles. Another primary Movement was to rock one's **pelvis Forward and Rearward**, while Balancing first on one Foot and then the other, in a Slow and Gyrating manner.

(See Novelty-&-Fad Dances-of-the-1960s. Also see Bend-It!)
[See *www.sixtiescity.com/Culture/dance*]

Fishin'-Pole: Only this name for an American **Novelty** or **Fad** of the **1960s** is listed simply as a Dance, Pattern, or Figure in the "*Dance Crazes of the Sixties.*"
(See Novelty-&-Fad Dances-of-the-1960s.) [From *www.sixtiescity.com/Culture/dance*]

Fishing-Pole: An American **Fad** comical Solo Maneuver of the 1980s.
The following is from "*Eighties Dances*" - [www.inthe80s.com]:
   "*TheFishing Pole: You cast your line out and reel it in. Pretty simple but all done to the beat of the music.*"
(See Fishy. Also see Novelty-&-Fad Dances-of-the-1980s. Also see Pantomime, Mime, and Mimicry-En-Masse.)

Fish-Tail: Only this name for an American **Novelty** or **Fad** of the **1960s** is listed simply as a Dance, Pattern, or Figure in the "*Dance Crazes of the Sixties.*"
(See Novelty-&-Fad Dances-of-the-1960s.) [From *www.sixtiescity.com/Culture/dance*]

Fishtail-Shag -Novelty-Dance: This is a Coupledance that was a **Fad** in vogue in the 1930s.
[See Fishtail, Extended-Fishtail, and Whaletail. Also see Shag(1)&(2).]

Fish-Walk: A **Novelty Fad** Coupledance in vogue in the United States, probably in the 1910s, and probably danced to Ragtime music.
(See Animal-Dances, Lame-Duck, Horse-Trot, Grizzley-Bear, Crab-Step, Buzzard-Lope, Turkey-Trot, Kangaroo-Hop, and Bunny-Hug.)

    Fishy: An American **Novelty Fad** comical Coupledance or Maneuvers of the 1980s in Cadence with the Music.

    The following is from "*Eighties Dances*" - [www.inthe80s.com]:

       "*Fishy: Have your hands on each side of your head* [like gills] *and have someone pretend they are reeling a fish in* [facing, see 'Fishing-Pole']. *Keep your hands on each side of your head as they are doing that, and move forward towards the person and move your arms* [but with hands still at your head]."

    (See Novelty-&-Fad Dances-of-the-1980s. Also see Pantomime, Mime, and Mimicry-En-Masse.)

    Flake: Only this name for an American **Novelty** or **Fad** of the **1960s** is listed simply as a Dance, Pattern, or Figure in the "*Dance Crazes of the Sixties*."

    (See Novelty-&-Fad Dances-of-the-1960s.) [From *www.sixtiescity.com/Culture/dance*]

    Flamingo: An Unleadable **Break-A-Way** novelty **Fad** Pattern, usually Performed while dancing the **Carolina-Shag**.

    (See Shorty-George, Boogie-Back, Apple-Jacks, Belly-Roll, Duck-Walk, Fly-Back, Lean, Stutter-Step, and the SugarFoot, for like Patterns. See **Break-A-Way Glossary** for a more complete listing.)

    [Note: Mechanics of its Steps are unknown.]

    Flapper-Flip: Only this name for an American **Novelty** or **Fad** of the **1960s** is listed simply as a Dance, Pattern, or Figure in the "*Dance Crazes of the Sixties*."

    (See Novelty-&-Fad Dances-of-the-1960s.) [From *www.sixtiescity.com/Culture/dance*]

    Flea: An American **Fad** dance of the1960s. This had its own Eponymous record, "*The Flea*" by the *Stratacats.*

    (See Novelty-&-Fad Dances-of-the-1960s.)

    [From www.bluejuice.org.au. Also see *www.sixtiescity.com/Culture/dance*]

    Flea-Hop(1) or **The Flea-Hop** or **Inside-Slide:** A **Novelty Fad** Singular or Coupledance Step that appeared in the U.S. in the 1950s. Believed to have originally been a **Shag** Step, this same **Flea-Hop** is also presently danced as Left and Right Coupledance Movements, suitable for both **Swings**, Jive, **Balboa**, both **ChaCha**s, both **Quicksteps**, the **Tap-Dance Genre**, and for **Country-Western**, among other dances.

    Most often Performed Apart but Facing Partner, the **Flea-Hop** is almost always repeated on one's Opposite Foot. Its primary, almost Unleadable Movements, Left and Right Mirror-Image, are as follows:

    A Skip or Hop or Scoot Sideways Toward the Free-Foot, Raising one's Free-Foot, the hip Raises, then Lowering same to Tap the Dancefloor.

Flea-Hop(1):   (Continued)
The following is "*Flea Hop*" from *Vance's Fantastic Tap Dance Dictionary*:
          "*A sliding movement on one foot while the other foot is in the air; executed from side to side or front to back: Raise R leg up to waist level with the knee flexed and parallel to the body; swing R leg straight to R side while sliding to the R side on the left foot; follow with a Step R. This movement may also be executed with the knee in a flexed position.*"
          Doing **Swing-Bal** Movements for the **Balboa**, some Couples are capable of dancing this **Flea-Hop**(1) coordinated Together as a Variation, while locked in their **Mush Position**.
          Same as **Entretaille**. (Also see the Bambuco, Bop, Bunny-Hop, Calypso, Creep, Fish, Frug, Guapacha, Hand-Jive, Hitch-Hiker, Hokey-Pokey, Hullie-Gullie, Jerk, Limbo-Rock, Mashed-Potato, Monkey, Pachanga, Plena, Pony, Rock-and-Around, Scooter, Slide, Strole, Surfers, Swim, Tumba-Cha, Twist, Twister, and the Watusi; which were all Novelty Fads in vogue in the 1950-60s. Also see Animal-Dances. Also see Balboa Step-Listing.)

Flea-Hop(2):   See Collegiate-Shag, and Arthur-Murray-Shag.

Flick: Only this name for an American **Novelty** or **Fad** of the **1960s** is listed simply as a Dance, Pattern, or Figure in the "*Dance Crazes of the Sixties*."
          (See Novelty-&-Fad Dances-of-the-1960s.) [From *www.sixtiescity.com/Culture/dance*]

Flintstone-Flop: Only this name for an American **Novelty** or **Fad** of the **1960s** is listed simply as a Dance, Pattern, or Figure in the "*Dance Crazes of the Sixties*."
          (See Novelty-&-Fad Dances-of-the-1960s.) [From *www.sixtiescity.com/Culture/dance*]

Flip: Only this name for an American **Novelty** or **Fad** of the **1960s** is listed simply as a Dance, Pattern, or Figure in the "*Dance Crazes of the Sixties*."
          (See Novelty-&-Fad Dances-of-the-1960s.) [From *www.sixtiescity.com/Culture/dance*]

Flip-Flop: Only this name for an American **Novelty** or **Fad** of the **1960s** is listed simply as a Dance, Pattern, or Figure in the "*Dance Crazes of the Sixties*."
          (See Novelty-&-Fad Dances-of-the-1960s.) [From *www.sixtiescity.com/Culture/dance*]

Float: Only this name for an American **Novelty** or **Fad** of the **1960s** is listed simply as a Dance, Pattern, or Figure in the "*Dance Crazes of the Sixties*."
          (See Novelty-&-Fad Dances-of-the-1960s.) [From *www.sixtiescity.com/Culture/dance*]

Florida-Twist: An Unleadable Mexican **Novelty** and **Fad** Singular or Coupledance of the 1960s.

The following is an excerpt from the "***Twist (dance)***" - [http://en.wikipedia.org/wiki/]:

"*In Latin America, the Twist craze was sparked in the 1960-62 period .... by Bill Haley & His Comets. Their recordings of 'The Spanish Twist' and 'Florida Twist' were major successes, particularly in Mexico, and the band were given the credit for starting the dance craze. ....*"

[See Spanish-Twist, Twist(2), and Peppermint-Twist. Also see Novelty-&-Fad Dances-of-the-1960s.]

Fly: The **Fly** was an American, Unstructured and Unleadable, **Novelty Fad** Coupledance of the 1950-60s, danced mainly 1965, that probably Traveled Slightly. The dance Mimicked a **Fly**, and was one of a whole series of 1960s Mimicking dance Patterns, (see Hullie-Gullie.) It was possibly influenced by the timely horror movie, "*The Fly*." Chubby Checker sang its Eponymous song named "*The Fly*". The following are a few excerpted lines from his words to it:

"*You've gotta skake your hands all around and around the sky*
And then you buzz around the floor - you can do it if you really try
We're gonna fly to the sky but you mustn't fly away from me."

Fly, along with other silly Fad-Dances, was banned at Brigham Young University in 1966.

(See the Novelty-&-Fad Dances-of-the-1960s.) [See *www.sixtiescity.com/Culture/dance*]

Fly-Back: An Unleadable **Break-A-Way Novelty Fad** Pattern, usually Performed while dancing the **Carolina-Shag**.

(See Shorty-George, Boogie-Back, Apple-Jacks, Belly-Roll, Flamingo, Belly-Roll, Duck-Walk, Lean, Stutter-Step, and the SugarFoot, for like Patterns. See **Break-A-Way Glossary** for a more complete listing.) [Note: Mechanics of the **Fly-Back** Steps are unknown.]

Foot-Boogie: Of the **Separated-Break-A-Way**(3), these **Foot-Boogie**s are Four Unleadable Spot-Dance Shine-Steps, suitable for **Line-Dances, Country-Western** Fixed-Pattern-Partner-Dances, each as one (one Measure) **Swing-Bal** portion of the **Balboa**, and for other dances. Performed either Singular or as a Couple in Open Position. If as a Couple, Lady dances Same-Feet as Man. One-Measure long, Rhythm Timing is *Slow Slow Slow Slow*.

Supporting-Foot remains Stationary. Weight is on Heel to Swivel Toe, and on Toe to Swivel Heel.

For **Toe-Right-Foot-Boogie**, Man (or person) dances *SwivelToeDiagRight SwivelHeelDiagRight SwivelHeelDiagLeft SwivelToeParallel.*

For **Toe-Left-Foot-Boogie**, Man (or person) dances *swiveltoediagleft swivelheeldiagleft swivelheeldiagright swiveltoeparallel.*

For **Heel-Right-Foot-Boogie**, Man (or person) dances *SwivelHeelDiagRight SwivelToeDiagRight SwivelToeDiagLeft SwivelHeelParallel.*

For **Heel-Left-Foot-Boogie**, Man (or person) dances *swivelheeldiagleft swiveltoediagleft swiveltoediagright swivelheelparallel.*

(See Toe-Movements, Ramble, Double-Foot-Boogie, SugarFoot, Sand-Step, Toe-In, Toe-Out, Toes-Out, Toe-Splits, Toe-Fan, Heel-Fan, Heels-Out, Heel-Splits, Swivet, Chinese-Typewriter, Kid-and-Play, Marchessi, Corta-Jaca, and Celtic-Storm.)

Footsee: Only this name for an American **Novelty** or **Fad** of the **1960s** is listed simply as a Dance, Pattern, or Figure in the "*Dance Crazes of the Sixties.*"
  (See Novelty-&-Fad Dances-of-the-1960s.) [From *www.sixtiescity.com/Culture/dance*]

Foot-Stomping: An American **Fad** dance of 1960. This **Foot-Stomping** had its own Eponymous record, "*Foot Stompin'*" by *The Flares*.
  (See the Novelty-&-Fad Dances-of-the-1960s.)
  [From *Soul*, *www.trinity.unimelb.edu.au*. Also see *www.sixtiescity.com/Culture/dance*]

Forty-Five(1): A **Novelty Fad** Coupledance of 1966. The **Forty-Five** had its own Eponymous record, "*Do The 45*" by *The Sharpees*.
  (See Novelty-&-Fad Dances-of-the-1960s. Also see Eighty-One.)
  [From *Soul*, www.trinity.unimelb.edu.au, and from www.bluejuice.org.au]

Forty-Five(2): A Singular **Country-Line-Dancing**, and **Tap-Dancing** Movement. Executing a **Forty-Five** is as follows: (From http://ourworld.compuserve.com.)
  "*45 -- Feet together, weight on left, Touch Right heel forward at a 45 degree angle and replace together. The term '45' is widely used by Australian Choreographers.*"
  (See Tap Steps-and-Terms-Listing, and Line-Dance Terms.)

Four-Corners: A **Novelty Fad** and early form of **Line-Dance**(1) of the 1970s. How to dance the **Four-Corners** should be found on a VHS Video by Christy Lane (www.centralhome.com).
  The following are excerpts from "*A History of Line Dancing*" by Rick Bowen, (www.dosado.com):
  "*In the 1970s, the form of Line Dance we do today was born. I have no data on specific dates but, when I first got into 'Country Western' style dance, there weren't that many line dances being done. I was told that 'Four Corners' was the second oldest line dance of this style but, no one could ever tell me what was the oldest.*
  "*The 'J.R. Hustle' dating back to 1980 & 'The Traveling Four Corners' were choreographed by a gal from Texas by the name of Jimmie Ruth White. The Traveling Four Corners is (in its original form), a quad dance (square) but choreographed in the general concept of the Line Dance.*"
  There may be Eponymous music: The "*Funky Four Corners*" by Jerry O, and "*Too Busy Thinking About My Baby*" by Marvin Gay, in 1969.
  Note: *"The Hustle"* is the first oldest **Line-Dance**(1).
  See **Line-Dances**(1) for a summary description of **Four-Corners.** Also see the extensive listing of **Line-Dance Terms**. (Also see American-Hustle, Bugg, Bump, Bus-Stop, Locking, Snake, Sprinkler, Tango-Hustle, and the Worm; which were all Novelty Fads in vogue in the 1970s.)

Four-Count or **Four-Count-Hustle** or **Cowboy-Swing** or **Manhattan-Hustle:** A simple, Leadable, **Onestep** Spot-Coupledance. Ideal for dancing to problem music. Best suited for a Marching Rhythm, but usually will suffice where no other Step fits well to the music. Danced on the One-Beat Rhythm-Station. Rhythm Timing is *Slow Slow Slow Slow*. Ideal dance Timing is 120 Steps- or Beats-per-Minute.

Four-Count is danced Circling CW or CCW, with Lady taking long Strides on Opposition-Footwork. Danced varying in Closed Position Lively, in Butterfly Position, or in Varsouvienne Position. Four-Count is excellent for Couple-Rotation in either direction. Arm-Wraps and Pretzel-Wraps are used profusely.

Basic Step is danced in Butterfly Position. Partners Step into each other, Together-and-Apart. Toes overlap upon Stepping Forward:

Man Steps *forward Recover backward Recover*.

Lady Steps *Forward recover Backward recover*.

Note: Slightly similar to the New-York-Hustle and to the Peabody.

See American Onestep Step-Listing. [Also see Minuet, and Four-Count(2). Also see Switch-Dances under Repertoire.]

Fox: Only this name for an American **Novelty** or **Fad** of the **1960s** is listed simply as a Dance, Pattern, or Figure in the "*Dance Crazes of the Sixties*."

(See Novelty-&-Fad Dances-of-the-1960s.) [From *www.sixtiescity.com/Culture/dance*]

Frankenstein-Walk: Only this name for an American **Novelty** or **Fad** of the **1960s** is listed simply as a Dance, Pattern, or Figure in the "*Dance Crazes of the Sixties*."

(See Novelty-&-Fad Dances-of-the-1960s.) [From *www.sixtiescity.com/Culture/dance*]

Freak(1): A **Novelty Fad** dance of 1965. The **Freak** was danced to the record, "*I Second That Emotion*" by *The Miracles*.

(See the Novelty-&-Fad Dances-of-the-1960s.) [From *Soul*, www.trinity.unimelb.edu.au]

Freak(2) or **Le-Freak** or **The-Freak:** A 1977 or 1978 **Urban-Street-Dance;** an American **Novelty Fad**, Stationary Singular-Dance or Coupledance. **The-Freak** became popular with teenage boys in 1977. It was based on its Eponymous hit record "*Freak Out*" by the *Shieks*.

The following is from "*Breakdancing*," [www.wordiq.com]:

"David Toop (1991) describes break dancing as being an adaptation of the Break, a dance popular before being replaced by the Chick's `Le Freak' in 1978, ---."

The following is an exerpt from "*History of Breakdance*," [www.jahsonic.com]:

"Old-style Breaking remained popular until about 1977, when the Freak took over, based on the hit record `Freak Out' by the Shieks."

(See **Breakdown**, and **Good-Foot**. Also see Break-Dancing, Underground Step-Listing, Teen-Dancing, and Open-Step. Also see Ska, Punk-Rock, Grunge, and New-Wave. Also see Hip-Hop, MTV-Style Dancing, Street-Dancer, Lyrical-Dancer, Jazz-Dance, and Urban-Dance. Also see Rock, Hard-Rock, Pop, Rhythm-and-Blues, Motown-Sound, Rap, and Heavy-Metal.)

Freak-Dancing: See Freaking.

Freaking or **Grinding** or **Freak-Dancing** or **Dirty-Dancing**(2) or **The-Freaky** or **The-Grind** or **Booty-Dancing** or **The-Nasty** or **Housing** or **Dubbing** or **Winking** or **Wining-Up** or **Wuking** or **Bubbling** or **Juking**(2): A **Novelty Fad**, sexually explicit **C**oupledance form of dancing and/or Movements, characterized by consensual sexual rubbing in public. This **Freaking** phenomenon began in the 1980s. Basically, **Freaking** is Couples making sexually suggestive **Grinding** Movements of the hips and pelvic areas Together, facilitating the rubbing of genitals on the Partner's thigh through clothing.

How to dance the **Freaking** to the Beat is described as follows in the "*Eighties Dances*," [www.inthe80s.com]:

"Legs apart, knees slightly or deeply bent, thrust hips forward with partner's knee bent between your leg."

The following excerpts are from *freak dancing*; [www.answers.com]:

*"**Grinding** is a slang term for a relatively raunchy dancing style popular in house and hip-hop dance moves. Grinding almost always involves two or more dancers rubbing their bodies against each other in a sexual manner. It is often performed at nightclubs and parties that play house and hip-hop music. Grinding has also gained popularity at high school and middle school dances across America. The meaning is basically the same as the self-describing term 'bump and grind' for party dancing. Elements of 'grinding' may be seen in a 1987 movie 'Dirty Dancing,' and 'grinding' is sometimes referred to by this term as well.*

"Grinding has also been referred to as housing, juking and freak dancing. The Perreo, a Puerto Rican dance associated with reggaeton, is a type of grinding. The word 'perreo' is derived the Spanish word for 'dog'.

"The most common dance techniques involved in grinding are, but not limited to:

"* The partners face the same direction so that the one partner's buttocks are rubbing the other partner's groin. A variation of this technique has one partner supporting her or his weight with one or two hands on the floor (buttocks in the air) while the other partner, holding her or him by the waist, grinds on the buttocks in a manner that simulates the 'doggy style' position. This variation of the dance is referred to in the music genre of reggaeton as perreo.

"* The partners, facing each other, strattle each other's thighs. This may or may not facilitate the rubbing of genitals through their clothing.

"The female commonly does all the work with her hips while the male mainly follows.

"The accompanying dance music may vary but tends to be related tp hip-hop or house, and most often conforms to 808 and 909 drum machine driven tracks; operating within a comparatively narrow tempo range (between 118 and 135 bpm)."

The following is an excerpt from "*Should freak dancing be permitted: NO*"; [http://silverchips.mbhs.edu/inside.php]:

"It's also called 'dirty dancing,' 'the grind,' 'booty dancing,' 'the nasty,' ...."

(Continued)

Freaking: (Continued)

The following are excerpts from *Grinding (dance)*; [http://en.wikipedia.org/wiki]:

"Grinding is a type of close partner dance where two or more dancers rub their bodies against each other in a manner perceived as suggestive. Usually the movement is vertical, as opposed to a horizontal movement usually associated with dry humping. It is popular in the house and hip-hop dance styles. It is often performed at nightclubs and parties that play house and hip-hop music. It has also gained popularity at high school and middle school dances across the United States and Canada, where there have been increasing cases of administrators attempting to ban it.

"Caribbean variation: In the Caribbean 'freak dancing' is much more widely accepted and children as young as 12 engage in it at parties. In these parties, it's referred to as 'dubbing'. In places like Antigua, it is called winking/wining up. In Barbados it is sometimes referred to as wuking. Whatever the caseit is widely accepted as the norm and almost all engage in it during carnival seasons. It is also commonly used in the Virgin Islands such as St. John."

Still continuing to be popular, **Freak-Dancing** is found to be much danced by high school aged Girls in times as late as 2007. **The-Freaky** is the latest way teenagers are driving their parents crazy. Commonly Performed at school dances, this **Freak-Dancing** with your clothes on, on the Dancefloor, is pretty much .... without penetration.

Data in the following paragraph was gleaned from "*Should freak dancing be permitted: NO*"; [http://silverchips.mbhs.edu/inside.php]:

Freaking is famous for its sexual content. Kids, faking sex with each other while the Music plays, refer to it as "*dry sex on the dancefloor*" or "*dry humping a girl you don't know*"; i.e., having sex but keeping your clothes on. Whether in pairs, triplets or long Grind-Trains, Grinding pelvis-to-rear in an orgy of simulated, and sometimes not-so-simulated, sexual activity that is known euphemistically as **Freak-Dancing**. It is a vulgar, degrading, disgusting appeal to prurient interests. **Freak-Dancing** requires virtually no Skill and even fewer inhibitions. It is public, impersonal and often non-consentual. According to a survey taken, 26 percent of students said that strangers had attempted to **Freak-Dance** with them, and only 15 percent said they reciprocated. **Freaking**, unlike all other dance Styles, has no Steps and no Moves. It consists solely of the Grinding of private areas; it is Lap-Dancing set to techno or rap.

Freaking is freaking out school administrators. Many question the appropriateness at a school dance of couples locking legs in order to be able to Grind their hips Together. At times, **Freaking** has gotten so explicit that some parents have complained, saying their children were too uncomfortable to come to the dances, and the parents themselves were too uncomfortable to chaperone. Certain administrations have decided against a detailed description of what constitutes **Freaking**, because it would be less effective than "*just saying no. We decided that there is no sense in splitting hairs about it. Students know what they are not supposed to do.*" The following was posted: "*Dancing and student interactions must be appropriate at all times (no provocative interactions).*"

This **Freaking** is probably the latest form of teen rebellion, since young people will always try to push their boundaries of decency through their dancing, (see Dance-du-Jour). Concerning this sexually suggestive dancing, "*After all,*" some with a liberal views contend, "*it's only dancing, and we have bigger issues to deal with than mere simulated sex.*" Yet some with conservative views are genuinely shocked by these antics as being obscene; they say, "*Sex is not supposed to be flaunted as public recreation.*"

Similar to **Crubbing**, **Lambada**, and **Dirty-Dancing**(1). (See Frottage, Perreo, Grind-Train, and Lap-Dance. Also see Slow-Dancing, Body-Contact, and Bumps-and-Grinds.)

Freddy: **The Freddy** was an Unstructured and Unleadable, **Novelty Fad** American Singular dance or **Coupledance**, that was favored by Gomez in the early "Addams Family" TV Show. Its Eponymous song was *Freddy and the Dreamers'* 1965 hit record, "*Do The Freddy*," soon followed by Chubby Checker's record, "*Let's Do The Freddy*". Following are a few excerpted lines from his words to it:

> "*You flip your wings just like a bird, I know it sound crazy but you gotta take my word*
>
> *It's good to [-] the second hop around,*
> *You wave your hands up to the sky, kick your legs out to the side*
> *Kick your legs up high; gonna do the Freddie.*"

The look of **The Freddy** was one of Rocking Stiffly Side-to-Side in Time with the Music. The Free-Leg was Spread Straight with its Foot some four inches off the Dancefloor, till almost off-Balance. Rocking Arms were Spread Sideways; Hands with Wrist-Back.

The following is from *Dance Crazes of the Sixties* -- [*www.sixtiescity.com/Culture/dance*]:

> "*The Freddy: You simply just stand in one place! Then, in rhythm with the music, first extend the left leg and left arm; then the right leg and right arm (not all at once - you'll fall over!) Repeat until the song's conclusion.*"

Freddy, along with other silly Fad-Dances, was banned at Brigham Young University in 1966.

(See the Novelty-&-Fad Dances-of-the-1960s.)

Freeze(1) or **Still Position:** Terms for a possibly Leadable, General **Coupledance** in-Action. A stop with no Movement; a momentary **Hold** where one's Body is fixed in time with no Movement.

Sometimes synonymous with **Hold, Pause, Balance**(8), and **V-Sit.** [See Position(1), Pausa, Suspension, Hesitation, Hover, Break, Lull, Positura, and Collect. Also see Stage-Fright, Bombed, and Freeze-Reaction. Also see Musical-Rest.]

Freeze(2): A **Novelty Fad** Group-Dance. With a Partner or within the Group, and with strobe lights blinking, each dances along doing their own thing until the music abruptly stops, whereupon every dancer **Freezes**. Each **Freeze** takes in some crazy contorted Position.

Freeze(3): In reference to the **Basic-Moves-for-Break-Dancing**, the **Freeze** greatly helps in defining the character of a certain particular **Break-Dance**.

The following is from "*Definition of Breakdancing*," [www.wordiq.com]:

> "*After performing a 6-step to begin the dance, and then performing a power move, the breakdancer will usually end the dance with a 'freeze' which is when he contorts his body to a strange position and literally freezes, stopping all dance motion. The breakdancer will usually hold the freeze for a second or two. There are nearly infinite variations on freezes, and coming up with new freezes greatly enhances the breakdancers style.*"

(See Six-Step. Also see Underground Step-Listing.)

French Tango: See Cafe Tango.

Fridge: Only this name for an American **Novelty** or **Fad** of the **1960s** is listed simply as a Dance, Pattern, or Figure in the "*Dance Crazes of the Sixties.*"
    (See Novelty-&-Fad Dances-of-the-1960s.) [From *www.sixtiescity.com/Culture/dance*]

Frog: A **Novelty Fad** dance of 1963. The **Frog** had its own Eponymous record, "*The Frog*" by *Sir Guy*.
    (See Novelty-&-Fad Dances-of-the-1960s.) [From *Soul*, www.trinity.unimelb.edu.au]

Frug or **Surf** or **Big-Bea** or **Thunderbird:** An Unstructured and Unleadable, 1960s **Novelty Fad** Singles dance of American origin. The **Frug** was usually danced Apart but Facing Partner. These 1960s dances were free and individualistic. People enmasse, mostly teens with long hair, were dancing by themselves and inventing as they danced.
    In 1962, particular singing records to which the **Frug** was danced, were "*Nobody But Me*" by *The Isley Brothers*, and "*Nobody But Me*" by *The Human Beinz*. [From *Soul*, www.trinity.unimelb.edu.au]
    The **Frug** was derived from The **Chicken**, which had been related to The **Twist**. Later from The **Frug**, In-Place, as dancers Swung hips Side-to-Side, and then with added arm Movements, there were derived The **Swim**, The **Monkey**, The **Dog**, The **Watusi**, The **Waddle**, and The **Jerk** dances. This silly **Frug**, along with other silly Fad-Dances, was banned at Brigham Young University in 1966.
    (See Novelty-&-Fad Dances-of-the-1960s.) [See *www.sixtiescity.com/Culture/dance*]

Fumigate-Funky-Broadway: Only this name for an American **Novelty** or **Fad** of the **1960s** is listed simply as a Dance, Pattern, or Figure in the "*Dance Crazes of the Sixties.*"
    (See Novelty-&-Fad Dances-of-the-1960s.) [From *www.sixtiescity.com/Culture/dance*]

Funky-Alien: An American **Novelty Fad** comical Solo-Dance or Maneuver of the 1980s in Cadence with the Music.
    The following is from "*Eighties Dances*" - [www.inthe80s.com]:
        "*Funky Alien: Put one of your hands under your shirt and pump your fist while pushing out your shirt from underneath simulating the alien being born out of your stomach like the movie. Lower body movements vary from gyrating to writhing in simulated pain.*"
    (See Novelty-&-Fad Dances-of-the-1980s. Also see Pantomime, Mime, and Mimicry-En-Masse.)

Funky-Broadway: An American **Fad** dance of the 1960s. The **Funky-Broadway** had two Eponymous versions of this **Novelty Fad** dance. One was danced in 1966 to the "*Funky Broadway*" Record by *Dyke & The Blazers*. The other was danced in 1969 to the "*Funky Broadway '69*" Record by *Bobby Powell*.
    (See Novelty-&-Fad Dances-of-the-1960s.)
    [From *Soul*, *www.trinity.unimelb.edu.au*. Also see *www.sixtiescity.com/Culture/dance*]

Funky-Bull: Only this name for an American **Novelty** or **Fad** of the **1960s** is listed simply as a Dance, Pattern, or Figure in the "_Dance Crazes of the Sixties_."
        (See Novelty-&-Fad Dances-of-the-1960s.) [From _www.sixtiescity.com/Culture/dance_]

Funky-Butt: **The Funky-Butt** was a **Novelty Fad** Coupledance in vogue in the United States, somewhere in the 1900s-1910s.
        (See Yankee-Tangle, Texas-Rag, Fanny-Bump, Squat, Itch, Flibbertigibbety, Grind, and Mooch.)

Funky-Buzzard: A **Novelty Fad** dance of the 1960s. The **Funky-Buzzard** was danced to the record, "_The Buzzard_" by _Little Oscar_. [From _Soul_, www.trinity.unimelb.edu.au]
        (See Buzzard-Lope. Also see Novelty-&-Fad Dances-of-the-1960s.)

Funky-Chicken: The **Funky-Chicken** was a **Novelty Fad** Singles Dance or Coupledance of 1970, that Identified with Rufus Thomas and his record, "_Do the Funky-Chicken_." An Unstructured and Unleadable One-Step in 4/4 medium Tempo, danced usually to Rock music. The dance Mimicked a **Chicken**, and was one of a whole series of 1960s Mimicking dance Patterns.
        The **Funky-Chicken** Strutted almost In-Place, Deep-Into-Knees with Angular-Elbows Flailing. There were Pecking chin Movements. Weight was upon Balls-of-Feet with Turning and reversing Movements Forward and Rearward. Knees were clapped Together on the Downbeats and Spread on each Upbeat. With Thumbs under armpits, elbows Flapped Up and Down while maintaining Knee Action.
        Almost the same as The **Chicken**. (See Novelty-&-Fad Dances-of-the-1960s.)

Funky-Disposition: A **Novelty Fad** Coupledance of 1969. This had its own Eponymous record, "_Funky Disposition_" by _Dean Francis & the Soul Rockers_.
        (See Novelty-&-Fad Dances-of-the-1960s.) [From www.bluejuice.org.au]

Funky-Donkey: A **Novelty Fad** dance of the 1960s. The **Funky-Donkey** had its own Eponymous record, "_The Funky Donkey_" by _Otis Turner & The Mighty Kingpins_.
        (See Novelty-&-Fad Dances-of-the-1960s.) [From _Soul_, www.trinity.unimelb.edu.au]

Funky-Fat-Man: A **Novelty Fad** dance of the 1960s. The **Funky-Fat-Man** was danced to a record by _Burnett Bynum & The Soul Invaders_.
        (See Novelty-&-Fad Dances-of-the-1960s.) [From _Soul_, www.trinity.unimelb.edu.au]

Funky-Horse: An American **Fad** dance of the 1960s. It's Eponymous Music was "_Funky Funky Horse_" by _Lester Young_.
        (See Novelty-&-Fad Dances-of-the-1960s.)
        [From _www.bluejuice.org.au_. Also see _www.sixtiescity.com/Culture/dance_]

Funky-Hump: A **Novelty Fad** dance of the 1960s. The **Funky-Hump** had its own Eponymous record, *"Funky Hump"* by *LittleJoe Cook & The Thrillers*.
   (See Novelty-&-Fad Dances-of-the-1960s.) [From *Soul*, www.trinity.unimelb.edu.au]

Funky-Jerk: Only this name for an American **Novelty** or **Fad** of the **1960s** is listed simply as a Dance, Pattern, or Figure in the "*Dance Crazes of the Sixties*."
   (See Novelty-&-Fad Dances-of-the-1960s.) [From *www.sixtiescity.com/Culture/dance*]

Funky-Line: A **Novelty Fad** dance of the 1960s. The **Funky-Line** was danced to the record, *"The Funky Donkey"* by the *Fabulous Shalimars*.
   (See Novelty-&-Fad Dances-of-the-1960s.) [From *Soul*, www.trinity.unimelb.edu.au]

Funky-Mississippi: Only this name for an American **Novelty** or **Fad** of the **1960s** is listed simply as a Dance, Pattern, or Figure in the "*Dance Crazes of the Sixties*."
   (See Novelty-&-Fad Dances-of-the-1960s.) [From *www.sixtiescity.com/Culture/dance*]

Funky-Penguin: A **Novelty Fad** dance of 1968. The **Funky-Penguin** had its own Eponymous record, *"Funky Penguin"* by *Rufus Thomas*.
   (See Penguin, and Hullie-Gullie. Also see Novelty-&-Fad Dances-of-the-1960s.) [From *Soul*, www.trinity.unimelb.edu.au]

Funky-Soul-Shake: A **Novelty Fad** dance of the 1960s. The **Funky-Soul-Shake** had its own Eponymous record, *"Funky Soul Shake"* by *E.T. White & The Potential Band*.
   (See Novelty-&-Fad Dances-of-the-1960s.) [From *Soul*, www.trinity.unimelb.edu.au]

Funky-Strut: A **Novelty Fad** dance of the 1960s. The **Funky-Strut** had its own Eponymous record, *"Funky Strut"* by the *Fabulous Soul Eruption*.
   (See Strut. Also see Novelty-&-Fad Dances-of-the-1960s.) [From *Soul*, www.trinity.unimelb.edu.au]

Funky-Twist: A **Novelty Fad** dance of the 1980s. How to dance the **Funky-Twist** should be found on a VHS Video by Christy Lane (www.centralhome.com).
   (See Break-Dancing, Bugg, Cabbage-Patch, Chicken-Dance, Moonwalk, New-Kids-Move, Pac-Man, Popping, Robocop, Roger-Rabbit, Running-Man, Snake, Tickin', Wavin', and the Worm; which were all Novelty Fads in vogue in the 1980s.)

Funky-Walk: An American **Fad** dance of 1969. The **Funky-Walk** had its own Eponymous record, *"Funky Walk"* by *Watson & The Sherlocks*.
   (See Walking-Step. Also see Novelty-&-Fad Dances-of-the-1960s.)
   [From *Soul*, *www.trinity.unimelb.edu.au*. Also see *www.sixtiescity.com/Culture/dance*]

Gaby-Glide: A **Novelty Fad** Coupledance popular in Utah, and possibly in the rest of U.S., about 1915. Principal Performers for this dance were *Gaby Deslys* (for whom the dance was named) and *Harry Pilcer*. The Eponymous sheet Music for this "*The Gaby Glide*" had been copyrighted in 1911and published by *Shapiro Music Pub*. Its Music had been Composed by *Louis A. Hirsch*, with (the same) *Harry Pilcer* as lyricist.

[Note: Mechanics of its Steps are unknown.]

(See the Boston-Dip, Bunny-Hug, Hug-Me-Close, Lame-Duck, Shiver-Dance, and Turkey-Trot; these were all Novelty Fads in vogue at the same time in the 1910s. Also see Saltair Pavilion.)

Gallop: Only this name for an American **Novelty** or **Fad** of the **1960s** is listed simply as a Dance, Pattern, or Figure in the "*Dance Crazes of the Sixties*."

(See Novelty-&-Fad Dances-of-the-1960s.) [From *www.sixtiescity.com/Culture/dance*]

Gamma-Goochie: A **Novelty Fad** Coupledance of the 1960s. This had its own Eponymous record, "*The Gamma Goochie*" by *The Gamma Goochies*.

(See Novelty-&-Fad Dances-of-the-1960s.) [From www.bluejuice.org.au]

Garrett: A 1980s **Novelty Fad** Singular-Dance manipulations. How to dance the **Garrett** was as follows: This crazy dance consists of convulsing the dancer's upper Torso "*in gawky movements*" while one's Feet remain perfectly still. [From the "*Eighties Dances*," www.inthe80s.com]

[See Tilt, Incline, Lean(1), Out-of-Balance, Droop, Arm-Flail, Slumped-Torso, Pelvis-Tucked-Under, and Scratching-for-Fleas.]

Gator(1): Only this name for an American **Novelty** or **Fad** of the 1960s is listed simply as a Dance, Pattern, or Figure in the "*Dance Crazes of the Sixties*."

(See Novelty-&-Fad Dances-of-the-1960s.) [From *www.sixtiescity.com/Culture/dance*]

Gator(2): An American **Novelty Fad** comical Solo-Dance or Maneuver of the 1980s in Cadence with the Music.

The following is from "*Eighties Dances*" - [www.inthe80s.com]:

"***The Gator:*** *You would do this dance to 'Taking Care of Business.' Clap 4 times, then hit your knees 4 times, then hit the floor 4 times, lay on your stomach and hit the floor 4 times. Lay on your right side waving your leg in the air. Lay on your back wave both legs in the air, then lay on your other side and wave that leg in the air. Come up the same way you went down.*"

(See Novelty-&-Fad Dances-of-the-1980s. Also see Animal-Dances.)

Gawk-'n'-Stroll: Only this name for an American **Novelty** or **Fad** of the **1960s** is listed simply as a Dance, Pattern, or Figure in the "*Dance Crazes of the Sixties*."

(See Novelty-&-Fad Dances-of-the-1960s.) [From *www.sixtiescity.com/Culture/dance*]

Gene-Chandler: Only this name for an American **Novelty** or **Fad** of the **1960s** is listed simply as a Dance, Pattern, or Figure in the "*Dance Crazes of the Sixties.*"
(See Novelty-&-Fad Dances-of-the-1960s.) [From *www.sixtiescity.com/Culture/dance*]

Georgia-Grind: An (Unleadable?) 1915 through the 1930s **Novelty Fad** 8-Count **Break-A-Way** Pattern, mostly Performed while dancing the **Big-Apple**. The (Eponymous?) sheet Music for this "*The Georgia Grind*" had been copyrighted in 1915 and published by *Joseph W. Stern & Co.* Its Music had been Composed by *Ford. T. Dabney*.
[Note: Mechanics of its Steps are unknown.]
For the **Big-Apple**, **Georgia-Grind** was one of the **Break-A-Way** Genre. Wiggling their hips, certain **Break-A-Way** Patterns were danced. The original **Suzie-Q, Boogie-Back, Tack-Annie, Georgia-Grind, Praise-Allah!, Truckin', Peckin', Charleston, Shorty-George**, and other Break-A-Ways, were probably originated early by blacks; while **Spank-the-Baby, Rusty-Dusty, Pose-and-a-Peck**, the **Little-Apple**, the **Little-Peach, Mess-Around, Stomp-Off, Apple-Jacks**, and **Fall-Off-the-Log**, and other Break-A-Ways, were probably originated later by whites. Most all of these Patterns seem to have been influenced or derived from the classic **Lindy-Hop** and/or **Big-Apple** dances. See **Break-A-Way Glossary** for a more complete listing.

Georgia-Slop: An American **Fad** dance of 1962. The **Georgia-Slop** had its own Eponymous record, "*Georgia Slop*" by *Big Al Downing*.
(See Novelty-&-Fad Dances-of-the-1960s.)
[From *Soul*, *www.trinity.unimelb.edu.au*. Also see *www.sixtiescity.com/Culture/dance*]

Get-Down: An American **Fad** dance of 1965. **Get-Down** had its own Eponymous record, "*Get Down*" by *Harvey Scales & The Seven Sounds*.
(See Novelty-&-Fad Dances-of-the-1960s.)
[From *Soul*, *www.trinity.unimelb.edu.au*. Also see *www.sixtiescity.com/Culture/dance*]

Get-E-Up: Only this name for an American **Novelty** or **Fad** of the **1960s** is listed simply as a Dance, Pattern, or Figure in the "*Dance Crazes of the Sixties.*"
(See Novelty-&-Fad Dances-of-the-1960s.) [From *www.sixtiescity.com/Culture/dance*]

Get-It: A **Novelty Fad** dance of 1968. **Get-It** had its own Eponymous record, "*The Get It*" by *Bo Dud & Johnny Twist*.
(See Novelty-&-Fad Dances-of-the-1960s.) [From *Soul*, www.trinity.unimelb.edu.au]

Gigolo: An American **Novelty Fad** Solo-Dance or Maneuver of the 1980s in Cadence with the Music.
The following is from "*Eighties Dances*" - [www.inthe80s.com]:
    "*The Gigolo: I thought you kind of spread your legs as wide as your shoulders, hips stationary, and your shoulders did this 'cool' slight sway thing while your head rhythmically bobbed back and forth in a small motion. You would lean back and perform this to the right, then the left...*"
(See Novelty-&-Fad Dances-of-the-1980s.)

Ginza: An American **Fad** dance of the 1960s. It's Eponymous Music was (At The) *"Ginza"* by *The Entertainers.*
    (See Novelty-&-Fad Dances-of-the-1960s.)
    [From *www.bluejuice.org.au.* Also see *www.sixtiescity.com/Culture/dance*]

Girls-Just-Wanna-Have-Fun: An American **Fad** comical Maneuver of the 1980s in Cadence with the Music.
    The following is from *"Eighties Dances"* - [www.inthe80s.com]:
        *"***Girls Just Wanna Have Fun:*** It was shown in Cyndi Lauper's video for 'Girls Just Wanna Have Fun,' where she was seen walking down a sidewalk, kicking one leg and thrusting the opposite arm in one movement."*
    (See Novelty-&-Fad Dances-of-the-1980s.)

Glide: Only this name for an American **Novelty** or **Fad** of the **1960s** is listed simply as a Dance, Pattern, or Figure in the *"Dance Crazes of the Sixties."*
    (See Novelty-&-Fad Dances-of-the-1960s.) [From *www.sixtiescity.com/Culture/dance*]

Glue: A **Novelty Fad** Coupledance of the 1960s. It's Eponymous Music was *"King Louie's Glue"* by the *King Louie's Court.*
    (See Novelty-&-Fad Dances-of-the-1960s.) [From www.bluejuice.org.au]

Goat: Only this name for an American **Novelty** or **Fad** of the **1960s** is listed simply as a Dance, Pattern, or Figure in the *"Dance Crazes of the Sixties."*
    (See Novelty-&-Fad Dances-of-the-1960s.) [From *www.sixtiescity.com/Culture/dance*]

Goblin-Trot: Only this name for an American **Novelty** or **Fad** of the **1960s** is listed simply as a Dance, Pattern, or Figure in the *"Dance Crazes of the Sixties."*
    (See Novelty-&-Fad Dances-of-the-1960s.) [From *www.sixtiescity.com/Culture/dance*]

Go-Go: An American **Fad** dance of the 1960s. It's Eponymous Music was *"Go Go Power"* by *Sugar Pie De Santo.*
    (See Novelty-&-Fad Dances-of-the-1960s.)
    [From *www.bluejuice.org.au.* Also see *www.sixtiescity.com/Culture/dance*]

GoGo-Dancer or **GoGo-Girl:** A Singular-Dance Term of 1960s and 1970s vintage. Referring to a feminine Singular dancer, scantily-clad, perhaps wearing a mini-skirt or hot-pants, Stationary-Dancing the **Pony** and the like with her long hair flying.

The following are excerpts from *Go-Go dancer*; [wwww.answers.com]:

"*Go-Go dancers are scantily-clad erotic dancers who dance on stages in an erotic revue, or on elevated platforms or in bird cages above the crowd in clubs, bars or discotheques to set the tone or increase the energy of a dance floor. They often wear Go-Go boots.*

"*In Thailand and some other Asian countries, go-go bars in the form of erotic revues are popular, and the dancers there are often available to be bar fined by customers.*

"*An example of a Go-Go dancer in the 1960s is Goldie Hawn on the popular TV series Laugh-In. ...*

"*The Oxford English Dictionary lists as etymology of Go-Go the noun go, one meaning of which is 'power of going, energy, vigor'. Another theory has it that the word stems from the name of the nightclub Whisky A Go-Go in West Hollywood, California; this was one of the first night clubs featuring dancers in elevated cages. It was fashioned after an earlier Paris discotheque of the same name; a gogo is a French phrase for 'in abundance, galore'.*"

Similar to the **Cage-Dancer**. (See Disco, and Jacking. Also see Sexercise-Dance, PassaPassa, and Juking.)

GoGo-Girl: See GoGo-Dancer.

Go-Go-Wine: From Kingston, Jamaica, an Underground **Novelty Fad**, Singular- or Group-Dance Movement, associated with dancing **Dancehall/Ragga**, which, in turn, are outgrowths of **Ska/Reggae**. **Go-Go-Wine** was and is danced mainly by youths of color.

The following is from *Ragga Fashions*: [www.bbc.co.uk]

"*Go-Go-Wine - Wine in your own individual style. Go down lower. Continue to wine. Try and go down even lower, continue until you reach your limit.*"

See **Dancehall**(2) for further explanation. (Also see Bogle, Armstrong, Butterfly, Body-Basic-and-Exercise, Tate, and World-Dance. Also see Jerry-Springer, Prang, Heel-and-Toe, Na!Na!Na!, Screechie, Zip-It-Up, Drive-By, Shizzle-Ma-Nizzle, Matrix, and Bin-Laden. Also see Underground Step-Listing.)

Goodfoot: Only this name for an American **Novelty** or **Fad** of the **1960s** is listed simply as a Dance, Pattern, or Figure in the "*Dance Crazes of the Sixties.*"

(See Novelty-&-Fad Dances-of-the-1960s.) [From *www.sixtiescity.com/Culture/dance*]

Good-Times-Stomp: Only this name for an American **Novelty** or **Fad** of the **1960s** is listed simply as a Dance, Pattern, or Figure in the "*Dance Crazes of the Sixties.*"

(See Novelty-&-Fad Dances-of-the-1960s.) [From *www.sixtiescity.com/Culture/dance*]

Goose: Only this name for an American **Novelty** or **Fad** of the **1960s** is listed simply as a Dance, Pattern, or Figure in the "*Dance Crazes of the Sixties.*"

(See Novelty-&-Fad Dances-of-the-1960s.) [From *www.sixtiescity.com/Culture/dance*]

Gorilla: An American **Fad** dance of 1963. The **Gorilla** was danced to a record by _The Ideals_ that may have been named "_Mo Gorilla._"
    (See Novelty-&-Fad Dances-of-the-1960s.)
    [From _Soul, www.trinity.unimelb.edu.au._ Also see _www.sixtiescity.com/Culture/dance_]

Go-Song: An American **Novelty Fad** comical Solo-Dance or Maneuver of the 1980s in Cadence with the Music.
    The following is from "_Eighties Dances_" - [www.inthe80s.com]:
        "_**The 'Go' Song:** Extend one arm then do the same with the other arm as you say 'Stop, Stop!'. Then do the Cabbage Patch dance saying 'Go _____!' (You say any name in place of the blank.)_" [To do the "_Cabbage-Patch,_" Hold your fists closed, bend your elbows, push out and rotate your arms in a circle from your chest out and around!]
    (See Novelty-&-Fad Dances-of-the-1980s. Also see Pantomime, Mime, and Mimicry-En-Masse.)

Gotham-Gobble: An American "_animal dance_", a **Novelty Fad** Coupledance in vogue about 1912 to 1914. Derided by newspapers, magazines, church officials, and even by Pope Pius X, as "such foolish and decadent behavior," over one hundred of these dances were created during this period.
    (See Animal-Dances, Bull-Frog-Hop, Bunny-Hug, Buzzard-Lope, Camel-Walk, Chicken-Reel, Chicken-Scratch, Crab-Step, Fish-Walk, Horse-Trot, Kangaroo-Dip, Kangaroo-Hop, Lame-Duck, Monkey-Glide, Possum-Trot, Snake, and Turkey-Trot; which were all Animal-Dances of 1910-1914.)

Granny: Only this name for an American **Novelty** or **Fad** of the 1960s is listed simply as a Dance, Pattern, or Figure in the "_Dance Crazes of the Sixties._"
    (See Novelty-&-Fad Dances-of-the-1960s.) [From _www.sixtiescity.com/Culture/dance_]

Graple: An American **Novelty Fad** comical Coupledance or Maneuvers of the 1980s in Cadence with the Music.
    The following is from "_Eighties Dances_" - [www.inthe80s.com]:
        "_**The Graple:** It's a rather strange looking 'dance' where you grab someone else, be it by the collar or shoulders, and shake them violently to the music, while they 'graple' onto you and you shake each other. Something you'd see at those old punk shows, and I saw it in a sex pistols video._"
    (See Novelty-&-Fad Dances-of-the-1980s.)

Graveyard-Cha-Cha: A **Novelty Fad** Coupledance of the 1960s. This had its own Eponymous record, the "_Graveyard Cha Cha_" by the _Three D's._
    (See Novelty-&-Fad Dances-of-the-1960s.) [From www.bluejuice.org.au]

Greasy-Chicken: A **Novelty Fad** dance of 1957. The **Greasy-Chicken** had its own Eponymous record, *"The Greasy Chicken"* by *Andre Williams*. [From *Soul*, www.trinity.unimelb.edu.au]

[See Chicken(1), Funky-Chicken, Chicken-Dance, Chicken-Reel, and Chicken-Scratch(1)(2)(3).]

Gremmie: Only this name for an American **Novelty** or **Fad** of the **1960s** is listed simply as a Dance, Pattern, or Figure in the "*Dance Crazes of the Sixties.*"

(See Novelty-&-Fad Dances-of-the-1960s.) [From *www.sixtiescity.com/Culture/dance*]

Grind: The **Grind** was a **Novelty Fad** Coupledance in vogue in the United States, somewhere in the 1900s-1910s. Some say that this **Grind** surfaced again in 1970.

(See Yankee-Tangle, Texas-Rag, Fanny-Bump, Funky-Butt, Squat, Itch, and Mooch.)

Grind-Snake-Novelty-Dance: This **Grind-Snake-Novelty-Dance** that was a **Fad** in vogue in the 1930s, and is known to have been a very sexy **Coupledance**.

[See the Lambada, Dirty-Dancing(1), Crubbing, Freaking, Frottage, Punta y Soka, Perreo, Grind-Train, and Lap-Dance. Also see Grinds, Snake(5), and Snake-Hips.]

Grizzly-Bear: An infamous, **Novelty Fad** Coupledance, very popular in America, beginning in 1889. The sheet Music to its song had directions included by its words, for Steps for this particular dance. This Music, for "*(The Dance of) The Grizzly Bear*", was copyrighted in 1910. This Music was Composed by George Botsford, its words were by Irving Berlin. Its sheet was published by the Ted Snyder Co. Its first Performer was Tim McMahon, and its second Performer was Sophie Tucker.

The following is from *Sonny Watson's Dance History* -- [www.streetswing.com]:

"*1910 - Sophie Tucker was arrested for singing the Grizzly Bear and the Wiggle Worm dance songs in a night club (stage magazine- 1938.)*"

Steps for **Grizzly-Bear** were simple. About 1913, Vernon and Irene Castle's version of the **Grizzly-Bear** brought them fame. The song was called "*Everybody's Doing It*" and it had a repeated phrase, "*It's a bear!*", where the Coupledancers Lurched like a grizzly during the dance, and the Lady would Leap and wrap herself around her Partner in what, at that time, was a most shocking way. Still later, by 1914, Vernon and Irene Castle had much to do with the demise of this Grizzly-Bear.

The following is from *Wikipedia* -- [http://en.wikipedia.org/wiki/Grizzly_Bear]:

"*The **Grizzly Bear** started in San Francisco, along with the Bunny Hug and Texas Tommy and was also done on the Staten Island ferry boats in the 1900's. It has been said that dancers John Jarrott and Louise Gruenning introduced this dance as well as the Turkey Trot at Ray Jones Cafe in Chicago, IL around 1909. The Grizzly Bear was first introduced to Broadway audiences in the Ziegfeld Follies of 1910 by Miss Fanny Brice.*

"*The dance was rough and clumsy. During the dance, the dancers would yell out; 'It's a Bear!' The genuine Grizzly Bear step was in correct imitation of the movements of a dancing bear, moving or dancing to the side. A very heavy step to the side with a decided bending of the upper part of the body from one side to the other, a decidedly ungraceful and undignified movement when performed as a dance.*"

(Continued)

Grizzly-Bear: (Continued)
The following is from _Grizzly Bear Dance History_ -- [www.streetswing.com]:
          "------Sheet Music #1 : -------
          "_I would like to try it, but Mother said I shouldn't dare, to try and do the grizzly_
bear.

          "_Hug up close top your baby, sway me everywhere,_
          "_Show your darlin' beau, how to go to buffalo, doin' the grizzly bear._" (There's
more.)

          "------Sheet Music #2 : -------
          "_Out in San Francisco where the Weather's fair, they have a dance out there,_
          "_They call the Grizzly Bear. All your other lovin' dances can't compare,_
          "_Not so coony, but a little more than Spoon-y. Talk about yo' bears_
          "_that Teddy Roosevelt shot, they couldn't class with what.....Old San Francisco's_
got....

          "_Listen Hone-y, and I will show you the dance of the Grizzly Bear._" (There's
more.)
          Related to **Everybody's-Doin'-It**. [See Castle, Vernon and Irene. Also see the Lanciers,
Money-Musk, and Washington-Post-Twostep; these were all Novelty Fads in vogue in the
1800s. Also see Texas-Tommy, Maxixe, Bunny-Hug, Turkey-Trot, and Ballin'-The-Jack, for
dances of that time, and later, where dance directions were given in their verses. Also see
Animal-Dances (such as Bunny-Hug, and Turkey-Trot), for Coupledances of that time with
some type of animal's name.]

          Guess: An American **Novelty Fad** comical Solo-Dance or Maneuvers of the 1980s in
Cadence with the Music.
          The following is from "_Eighties Dances_" - [www.inthe80s.com]:
          "_**The Guess:** Bend your knees and push them to the left, following the motion_
with your left hand as though you were pushing away an over-eager dog. Stand up straight, then
do the same thing to the right. The idea is to make angular movements with your knees and
hands, resembling the 'Guess' triangle."
          (See Novelty-&-Fad Dances-of-the-1980s. Also see Pantomime, Mime, and Mimicry-
En-Masse.)

          Grunt: A **Novelty Fad** Coupledance of the 1960s. This had its own Eponymous record,
"_The Grunt_" by _Eddie Kirk._
          (See Novelty-&-Fad Dances-of-the-1960s.) [From www.bluejuice.org.au]

Guapacha: A **Novelty Fad, Latin** Coupledance Pattern of the 1950-60's, **Guapacha**(1) **is ChaCha Syncopated with Guapa-Timing. Guapa-Timing** is a Hesitation then a catch-up, holding the first half-of-a-Beat with Feet Spread, almost Freezing but drawing towards closing one's Foot, then a quick quarter-Beat second Step. **Guapa-Timing** is *Hold And Slow Quick Quick Slow.*

  (See Syncopations-in-the-Dance, and Syncopations-in-Music. Also see the Bambuco, Bop, Bunny-Hop, Calypso, Creep, Fish, Flea-Hop, Frug, Hand-Jive, Hitch-Hiker, Hokey-Pokey, Hullie-Gullie, Jerk, Limbo-Rock, Mashed-Potato, Monkey, Pachanga, Plena, Pony, Rock-and-Around, Scooter, Slide, Strole, Surfers, Swim, Tumba-Cha, Twist, Twister, and the Watusi; which were all Novelty Fads in vogue in the 1950-60s. Also see Novelty-&-Fad Dances-of-the-1960s.)

Guitar-Boogie-Stomp: Only this name for an American **Novelty** or **Fad** of the **1960s** is listed simply as a Dance, Pattern, or Figure in the "*Dance Crazes of the Sixties.*"
  (See Novelty-&-Fad Dances-of-the-1960s.) [From *www.sixtiescity.com/Culture/dance*]

Gully: Only this name for an American **Novelty** or **Fad** of the **1960s** is listed simply as a Dance, Pattern, or Figure in the "*Dance Crazes of the Sixties.*"
  (See Novelty-&-Fad Dances-of-the-1960s.) [From *www.sixtiescity.com/Culture/dance*]

Hammer: Only this name for an American **Novelty** or **Fad** of the **1960s** is listed simply as a Dance, Pattern, or Figure in the "*Dance Crazes of the Sixties.*"
  (See Novelty-&-Fad Dances-of-the-1960s.) [From *www.sixtiescity.com/Culture/dance*]

Hammer-Dance: An American **Fad** comical Solo-Dance or Maneuvers of the 1980s in Cadence with the Music.
  The following is from "*Eighties Dances*" - [www.inthe80s.com]:
     "*The Hammer Dance: By M. C. Hammer, he wore those baggy genie pants, keep legs wide apart, slightly bents, shuffle quickly one way, then the other.*"
  (See Novelty-&-Fad Dances-of-the-1980s. Also see Pantomime, Mime, and Mimicry-En-Masse.)

Hand-Jive: An American **Novelty** and **Fad** Group-Dance popular in the late 1950s. This **Hand-Jive** was a flourishing phenomenon in the summer of 1958! There was a 1956 "*Hand Jive*" record by Johnny Otis that might have been Eponymous. In 1958, the Novelty song "*Willie and the Hand Jive*" (Eponymous?) spurred this unusual "dance;" **Hand-Jive** being unusual in that it was danced only with the Hands. This "*Willie and the Hand Jive*" Record was rated in the *"Top Ten"* of popular songs for 16 weeks; - to remain that popular with fickle teens for that long was astounding.

(Continued)

Hand-Jive: (Continued)

The following is an excerpt from "*The Hand Jive*" - [www.jitterbuzz.com/dance50]:

"*The dance consists of various hand movements (slap thighs, cross palms pound fists, touch elbows, hitch-hike). It is incredibly easy to learn, since it is repeated without change over six choruses of the song. No wonder everyone in 1958 could do the Hand Jive!*"

The following is from [http://en.wikipedia.org/wiki/Hand_dancing]:

"***Hand jive*** *is a kind of dance game to Rock and roll and Rhythm and blues music in 1950s. It involves complicated patterns of hand moves and claps at various parts of the body, following and/or imitating the percussion instruments while sitting at the concerts or crowding around jukeboxes. It could also be a highly elaborate version of Pat-a-cake. Hand moves include thigh spalling, cross-wrist slapping, fist pounding, breast slapping and pounding, hand clapping elbow touching, hitch hike moves, etc.*

"*Hand jive was particularly popularized by 1958 Johnny Otis' hit song Willie and the Hand Jive: 'Mama, mama, look at Uncle Joe -- Doing the hand jive with sister Flo...'*

"*It is also featured in the Grease movie: 'Born to hand-jive, baby, Born to hand-jive, baby, - yeah...'* "

How to dance this "*hand dance*" should be found on a VHS Video by Christy Lane (www.centralhome.com). *Atlanticville.gmnews.com* states the following:

"*.... and made their hands move like lightning during the Hand Jive, hitting their fists and throwing a thumb over each shoulder, all while on their knees* "

Similar to **Hitch-Hiker, Churnin'-Butter, Palm-Circles**(1), **Hand-Jive Routine, Belinda, Teen-Wolf, Sprinkler,** and **Tiffany.** [See Stationary-Dancing, Arm-and-Hand Aerobics, Chair-Dancing, Hand, Finger-Flourishes, Free-Hand-Fashioning, and Gestures-Free-Hand.]   (See Bambuco, Bop, Bunny-Hop, Calypso, Creep, Flea-Hop, Guapacha, Hokey-Pokey, Hucklebuck, Pachanga, Plena, Rock-and-Around, Scooter, Stroll, Tumba-Cha, Twist, and the Twister; which were all Novelty Fads in vogue in the 1950s.)

Hand-Jive Routine: This Hand-Jive is an American **Novelty** and **Fad** Group-Dance popular in the 1950s. It is a 4/4 Time Coupledance Pattern, two Measures long, and danced Apart but Facing. The suggested following is only one of many possible **Hand-Jive Routine**s. This Routine is also useful for the *Quick Quick Slow* Timed **Twostep**(1), for the **Twist**(2), and for other dances.

(a) There are Swinging parallel **Side-to-Side Forearm-Movements**, coinciding (or countering) **with Body-Sway.** With Palms Down and Elbows Bent, forearms Held In-Front remain parallel with each other and with the Dancefloor. Fingers might be Snapped during each Swing.

(b) In **Forearm-Circles** while Checking Body-Sway, both of the dancer's Forward-Pointing Hands are vertically rotated from the Elbows in a Circle, parallel and in the same direction CW or CCW, usually with all fingers straight.

While Swaying his Body Side-to-Side, the Man Swings his arms (a) first to his Left then to his Right, and again to his Left whereupon he vertically rotates both his arms (b) in a Circle once CW. Next, while again Swaying his Body Side-to-Side, he Swings his arms (a) first to his Right then to his Left, and again to his Right whereupon he vertically rotates both his arms (b) in a Circle once CCW.

His Lady matches his Movements Mirror-Image Opposite.

(Continued)

Hand-Jive Routine: (Continued)
The (a) Pattern portion called " Swinging parallel Side-to-Side Forearm-Movements" is similar to **Belinda,** and Slightly similar to Palm-Circles(1), Salsa-Arm-Movements, and Teen-Wolf. The (b) Pattern portion called "vertically rotated parallel in Unison CW or CCW" is similar to **Hand-Rolls.**
Note: Pattern may be Cued: *"Sway Left, Sway Right, Circle Hands; Sway Right, Sway Left, Circle Hands."*
(See Stationary-Dancing, Arm-and-Hand Aerobics, Hand-Jive, Hambone, Sway-Side-to-Side, and Arms-and-Hands.)

Handjive-Workout: Only this name for an American **Novelty** or **Fad** of the **1960s** is listed simply as a Dance, Pattern, or Figure in the "*Dance Crazes of the Sixties.*"
(See Novelty-&-Fad Dances-of-the-1960s.) [From *www.sixtiescity.com/Culture/dance*]

Hangin'-Tough: An American **Fad** Solo-Dance or Maneuvers of the 1980s in Cadence with the Music.
The following is from "*Eighties Dances*" - [www.inthe80s.com]:
    *"**Hangin' Tough:** Put your left arm in the air and wave it from side to side."*
(See Novelty-&-Fad Dances-of-the-1980s.)

Hangman: A Leadable **Pure-Balboa** Spot-Coupledance 12-Count Pattern, from the www.2PlySwing.com CD-ROM. Rhythm 4/4 Timing is *Quick Quick Slow* (for 4 Measures,) entirely in Mush Position.
Coupledancing the **Hangman** includes the Partners Stepping the **Heel-Ball-Change** eight times in a row. Two of these **Heel-Ball-Change**s, whose Rhythm Timing is *And Slow And Slow*, are danced; Starting with one Heel Touching Forward, Step Ball with the same Foot and Touch Opposite Heel Forward; Step this Opposite Ball and Touch the original Heel Forward. The Man Leans Back, in line with his leg, as his Left Heel Touches Forward upon the first Count 3:
Man's overall Rhythm Timing is *1slow 2Slow 3andSlow 4Andslow, andSlow Andslow andSlow Andslow, 9andSlow 10Andslow 11ForSlide 12Slow.*
Part of **Pure-Balboa #1.** [See Balboa, and Balboa Step-Listing. Also see Heel-Ball-Change, Heel-Switches, Quick-Points, Switch(3), California-Shuffle, Change-and-Change, and And-Change-And-Change-And.]

Hang-the-Meringue: A **Novelty Fad** Coupledance in vogue in 1959.
(See Merengue, Merengue-Basic-Movement, and Merengue Step-Listing.) [From *Novelty Dances Through the Years* by Pony Moore.]

Hanky-Panky: An Unstructured, American **Novelty Fad** Singular or Coupledance in vogue in the 1960s. In mid-1966, *Tommy James and The Shondells* sang and recorded *The Hanky Panky* as Eponymous Music for this dance, which sang, "*Dance the Hanky-Panky.*" This name stems from erotic activity.
(See the Novelty-&-Fad Dances-of-the-1960s.) [See *www.sixtiescity.com/Culture/dance*]

Happy-Feet: An American **Fad** Solo-Dance or Maneuvers of the 1980s in Cadence with the Music.

The following is from "*Eighties Dances*" - [www.inthe80s.com]:

"*Happy Feet: Kind of like the Hokey Pokey. You hop from your right and left leg while pointing the opposite foot outward.*"

(See Novelty-&-Fad Dances-of-the-1980s. Also see the Hokey-Pokey.)

Harlem-Shuffle: An American **Fad** dance of 1964. The **Harlem-Shuffle** had its own Eponymous record, "*Harlem Shuffle*" by *Bob & Earl*.

(See the **Shuffle** series. Also see Novelty-&-Fad Dances-of-the-1960s.)

[From *Soul*, *www.trinity.unimelb.edu.au*. See *www.sixtiescity.com/Culture/dance*]

Harlem-Tango: Only this name for an American **Novelty** or **Fad** of the **1960s** is listed simply as a Dance, Pattern, or Figure in the "*Dance Crazes of the Sixties.*"

(See Novelty-&-Fad Dances-of-the-1960s.) [From *www.sixtiescity.com/Culture/dance*]

Harvest-Moon Tango: See Contest Tango.

Headache: An American **Fad** comical Solo-Dance or Maneuvers of the 1980s in Cadence with the Music.

The following is from "*Eighties Dances*" - [www.inthe80s.com]:

"***The Headache:*** *It was performed by Janet Jackson in the video where she is in a big dance studio, she is alone and she shows off the 'cabbage patch' as well. You swing your head back to the right then down and back to the other side, then repeat. Bending your arms and swinging them the same way your head is moving.*"

(See Novelty-&-Fad Dances-of-the-1980s. Also see Pantomime, Mime, and Mimicry-En-Masse.)

Heatwave: An American **Fad** dance of 1964. The **Heatwave** had its own Eponymous record, "*Heatwave*" by *Martha Reeves & The Vandellas*.

(See the Novelty-&-Fad Dances-of-the-1960s.)

[From *Soul*, *www.trinity.unimelb.edu.au*. See *www.sixtiescity.com/Culture/dance*]

Heel-and-Toe: From Kingston, Jamaica, an Underground **Novelty Fad**, Singular- or Group-Dance Movement, associated with dancing **Dancehall/Ragga**, which, in turn, are outgrowths of **Ska/Reggae**. **Heel-and-Toe** was and is danced mainly by youths of color.

The following is from *Ragga Fashions*: [www.bbc.co.uk]

"*Heel-and-Toe - This dance can be compared to a stationary moonwalk. Continuously rocking from left to right, shifting the weight from left to right. Add a little flavour to this dance with emphasis on the hand movements.*"

See **Dancehall**(2) for further explanation. (Also see Bogle, Armstrong, Butterfly, Go-Go-Wine, Body-Basic-and-Exercise, Tate, and World-Dance. Also see Jerry-Springer, Prang, Na!Na!Na!, Screechie, Zip-It-Up, Drive-By, Shizzle-Ma-Nizzle, Matrix, and Bin-Laden. Also see Underground Step-Listing. Also see Moon-Walk, SideSlide, and Running-Man.)

Hello-Kitty: An American **Fad** comical Solo-Dance or Maneuvers of the 1980s in Cadence with the Music.

The following is from "*Eighties Dances*" - [www.inthe80s.com]:

"***Hello Kitty:*** *You put your feet together side-by-side and open your legs through your knees. Then you descend lower as you close your knees once, open your knees once, you descend to the ground. Use your hands to push off of your knees and arch your back before coming all the way up (stick your butt out).*"

(See Novelty-&-Fad Dances-of-the-1980s.)

Hip: An American **Fad** dance of the 1960s. This had its own Eponymous record, "*The Hip*" by *The Sparkles*.

(See Novelty-&-Fad Dances-of-the-1960s. Especially see U.T.)

[From *www.bluejuice.org.au*. See *www.sixtiescity.com/Culture/dance*]

Hip-Drop: A **Novelty Fad** Coupledance of 1969 or 70. It's Eponymous Music was "*Hip Drop*" by *The Explosions*.

(See Novelty-&-Fad Dances-of-the-1960s.) [From www.bluejuice.org.au]

HipHop-Lindy: A **Novelty Fad** Coupledance, in vogue beginning in 2005, that is a combination and blending of **Swing** (most often **Lindy**) and **HipHop**. Music is in 4/4 Time and is HipHop, straight or possibly influenced by jazz. **HipHop-Lindy** is probably danced in **16-Count** Patterns. It is said by those that dance **HipHop-Lindy**, "*And it is hard as hell to do.*" HipHopLindy.com says: "*Why is this? Hip Hop Lindy is based from the basic framework of Lindy Hop, but is danced with the style, music, and aggression of Hip Hop. A good knowledge of both dances is a prerequisite, so a tremendous amount of time and energy are going into developing this hybrid form by the dancers who are doing it.*"

With regards to mixing Swing with other dances in 16-Count Patterns in 4/4 Time, there are the three **HipHop-Lindy** "sister-dances", **Swango**, (Swing + Tango,) **Swing-Rueda**, (Salsa-Rueda + Swing,) and **Swalsa**, (Swing + Salsa.)

(See Hip-Hop, Lindy-Hop, and Lindy.)

Hip-Huggin': A **Novelty Fad** Coupledance of the 1960s. It's Eponymous Music was "*Everybody's Hip-Huggin'*" by *Robert Parker*.

(See Novelty-&-Fad Dances-of-the-1960s.) [From www.bluejuice.org.au]

Hippies-Waltz: Only this name for an American **Novelty** or **Fad** of the **1960s** is listed simply as a Dance, Pattern, or Figure in the "*Dance Crazes of the Sixties*." It is probably a Coupledance.

(See Novelty-&-Fad Dances-of-the-1960s.) [From *www.sixtiescity.com/Culture/dance*]

Hippy-Hippy-Shake: An American **Fad** dance of 1959. This had its own Eponymous record, the "*Hippy Hippy Shake*" by *Chad Romero*.

(See Novelty-&-Fad Dances-of-the-1960s.)

[From www.bluejuice.org.au. See *www.sixtiescity.com/Culture/dance*]

    <u>**Hitch-Hike:**</u>   See Hitch-Hiker.

    <u>**Hitch-Hiker**</u> or **Hitch-Hike:** An Unstructured and Unleadable, fun **Novelty Fad** Singular or Coupledance that appeared in the U.S. in the 1960s. In 1963, both _Marvin Gaye_ and _Russell Byrd_ put out the dance record, _The Hitch Hike._ Its Eponymous dance, The **Hitch-Hiker** was a Spot-dance, danced in 4/4 Time to Jazz type Foxtrot music. The dance Mimicked a person **Hitch-Hiking**, and was one of a whole series of 1960s Mimicking dance Patterns, (see Hullie-Gullie.)

    The **Hitch-Hiker** was usually danced Apart but Facing Partner. **Hitch-Hiker** dancing included Thumbing one's Left Thumb to the Left with Head constantly Moving Left with short chin Movements. Mime was keeping Time to Fast Music with Thumb and Knee-Bounce. Dance was usually then repeated Mirror-Image Opposite. This was one of the free and individualistic 1960s dances. People enmasse, mostly teens with long hair, were dancing by themselves and inventing as they danced. This silly **Hitch-Hiker**, along with other silly Fad-Dances, was banned at Brigham Young University in 1966.

    One other of the **Hitch-Hiker** Steps was an Unleadable, Singular, Upper-Body Movement, one Beat long, and Performed by either or both Partners. One or both Thumbs point Rearwards over shoulder(s), usually as one Steps Rearwards. This same Movement was also used in **Country-Western** Line-Dancing.

    The following Basic-Step is from _Crazy Dance Moves!_ by Yana:

    "-- _dancing plays a large role in the Ska subculture. Why? Ska was originally played at clubs and dancehalls in Jamaica. These spaces provided Jamaicans with the opportunity to dance the night away --_

    "_The Hitch-hike_ - _1. Feet slightly apart, very slightly bent knee, arms loose by side, clenched fists with thumb sticking up (thus called the Hitch Hike). 2. Alternate arms over your shoulders and move your hips from side to side quickly. 3. Jump to side remaining in same position. 4. Repeat motions of arms and hips. 5. Then jump so that you are facing front and repeat the same motions._"

    NOTE: While **Skanking** to the **Ska**, the **Hitch-Hiker** is a Variation.

    The following is from _www.sixtiescity.com/Culture/dance_:

    Listed in the "_Dance Crazes of the Sixties_," along with a 12-pictures Sequence (showing Patrick Kerr?) and the following writeup describing this as a Singular-Dance, Pattern, or Figure:

    The Hitch Hike: "_With feet firmly placed, bend knees slightly and shake your hips. Place your hands at your sides and fist them, leaving thumb open and pointing up. Move arms up and down alternately, jerking your fist over your shoulder. Then, occasionally, jerk both fists together over one shoulder and jump to either side._

    "_1. Stand in upright position with feet apart, doing the frug movement._
    "_2. Hitch-hike with right thumb on the counts 1-2-3, to your right side._
    "_3. Clap on the fourth beat on the right side of your body._
    "_4. Hitch-hike with left thumb on the counts 1-2-3, back to the left side._
    "_5. Clap on the fourth beat on the left side of your body. Repeat over and over._"

    Similar to **Hand-Jive**, **Churnin'-Butter**, **Palm-Circles**(1), **Belinda**, **Teen-Wolf**, **Sprinkler**, and **Tiffany**. (Also see the Frug, and the Novelty-&-Fad Dances-of-the-1960s.)

Hitch-It-To-Horse: Only this name for an American **Novelty** or **Fad** of the **1960s** is listed simply as a Dance, Pattern, or Figure in the "*Dance Crazes of the Sixties.*"
(See Novelty-&-Fad Dances-of-the-1960s.) [From *www.sixtiescity.com/Culture/dance*]

Hit-It!: As a spoken signal or Command to the dancers, "**Hit-It!**" is a Term peculiar to the Cuer directing the dancing of the **Madison** Novelty Audience-Participation-Dance. The Cuer Calls-Out "**Hit-It!**" immediately after first having Called-Out some particular Pattern to dance as an interim between several of the **Madison's** Basic-Step; a Pattern such as "the Double-Cross," "the Cleveland-Box," "the Basketball," "the Big-'M'," "the 'T'-Time," "the Jackie-Gleason," "the Birdland," or "the Rifleman." As the Basic-Step for the **Madison** has six Counts; the Cuer always Calls-Out "**Hit-It!**" upon its third Count, (the *DiagBack* Step.)
As a sample **Cuer**, the following are excerpts from "*The Madison*" -- [www.jitterbuzz.com/]:
"*It is danced to the Ray Bryant tune, 'The Madison Time,' with calls for the particular dance sequences provided by Eddie Morrison. Eddie was a Baltimore disc jockey who started calling the steps live on the air. Based on a six count chorus step, The Madison contains several dance sequences which make playful references to 1950s and 1960s Television shows (e.g. The Rifleman) sports stars (e.g. Wilt Chamberlain) and performers (e.g. Jackie Gleason).*
"*In Baltimore, the Madison was done to generic music with the DJ calling the figures. There was one record made which included calls for some of the more common figures on the record.*"
[See Cue(1)&(2), Cuer, Command, Call(1)&(2), and Caller.]

Hitler: Only this name for an American **Novelty** or **Fad** of the 1960s is listed simply as a Dance, Pattern, or Figure in the "*Dance Crazes of the Sixties.*"
(See Novelty-&-Fad Dances-of-the-1960s.) [From *www.sixtiescity.com/Culture/dance*]

Hoe-Down: A General Term for an American Country-Dance that was similar to a Barn-Dance.
The following is from [http://en.wikipedia.org/wiki/Hoedown]:
"*A **hoedown** is a type of American folk dance or square dance in duple meter, and also the musical form associated with it.*
"*In the 19th century the hoedown was mainly associated with African-Americans, and was a dance in quick movement most likely related to the jig, reel or clog dance; however by the early 20th century the term was mainly associated with white Americans, particularly in rural or western parts of the country.*"
The CWDI (Country-Western-Dance-International) calls this Coupledance the "**Hoe-Down**". The following is from their "*97-98 Standard Competition Rules*" "Dance Divisions":
"***Hoe-Down:*** *Any three (3) step, shuffle or polka pattern (1&2,3&4) may be used that has a generally forward progression counterclockwise around the dance floor, however, the dance must incorporate some rendition of a non-progressive step pattern that has a minimum of 8 counts and a maximum of 16 counts of music (10 step, 16 step, etc.). At least four (4) shuffles and not more than 10 shuffles may be performed consecutively without entering the 'Standing Step Pattern', or loss of execution points will result.*"
(See Ten-Step, Cotton-Eyed Joe, Salty-Dog-Rag, and Rocky-Top. Also see Bee, Ceilidh, Country-Dance, Traditional Dancing, Folkdance, International-Folkdance, Assembly, La-La, and Ball.)

Hog: A **Novelty Fad** Coupledance of 1964. This had its own Eponymous record, "*Do The Hog*" by *The WarnerBros*.
          (See Novelty-&-Fad Dances-of-the-1960s.) [From www.bluejuice.org.au]

Hokey-Cokey: See Hokey-Pokey.

Hokey-Pokey or **Hokey-Cokey** or **Okey-Cokey**: Classified herein as in the **Audience-Participation-Dance** Category, and as both a **Novelty** Dance and **Fad** Dance. This American `foot-in-and-out' **Group-Dance** was re-concocted in 1949 and copyrighted in 1950, although it had been danced earlier in 1944 in England as the **Hokey-Cokey** or **Okey-Cokey**. The earlier 1940s English **Hokey-Cokey** or **Okey-Cokey** had had virtually the same lyrics and had similar dance Movements. Becoming a U.S. nation-wide sensation by the mid-1950s and well into the 1960s, this subject **Hokey-Pokey** has its own accompanying Eponymous song; "*Put your left foot in, put your left foot out; do the Hokey-Pokey and then turn yourself about. Etc.*"
          Ray Anthony's Big-Band recorded the **Hokey-Pokey** in the early 1950s.
          Following instructions sounded in the lyrics, this **Hokey-Pokey** is danced with all participants Standing in a large ring Formation. Specific Body-parts are named, sequentially placed into then taken out of the ring. Dancers Wiggle about Slightly inside the ring then Raise Hands Straight Up and Wiggle them. Then each dancer makes a Full-Turn In-Place and begins the next Sequence with a new named Body-part.
          The following is from "*Dance Crazes of the Sixties*." [See www.sixtiescity.com/Culture/dance]:
          "***The Hokey Pokey*** *(or Cokey): The participants stand in a big ring formation during the dance. The dance follows the instructions given in the lyrics of the song, which may be prompted by a bandleader or another danceleader. Specific body parts are named, and these are then sequentially put into the ring, taken out of the ring, and finally wiggled around maniacally inside the ring. After this is done one raises one's hands up to the side of the head, wiggles them, and turns around in place until the next sequence begins, with a new named body part. A sample instruction set would be: You put your left ear in, You put your left ear out, You put your left ear in and you shake it all about. You do the Hokey Pokey and you turn around, That's what it's all about... oi!*"
          As provided by Darrah Chavey, "The following is from the Washington Post Style Invitational contest that asked readers to submit `instructions' for something (anything), but written in the style of a famous person. The winning entry was The *Hokey Pokey* (as written by W. Shakespeare):

> "*O proud left foot, that ventures quick within*
> *Then soon upon a backward journey lithe.*
> *Anon, once more the gesture, then begin:*
> *Command sinistral pedestal to writhe.*
> *Commence thou then the fervid Hokey-Poke,*
> *A mad gyration, hips in wanton swirl.*
> *To Spin! A wilde release from Heavens yoke.*
> *Blessed dervish! Surely canst go, girl.*
> *The Hoke, the poke -- banish now thy doubt*
> *Verily, I say, 'tis what it's all about.*"
> -- by William Shakespeare (Jeff Brechlin, Potomac Falls.)

(Continued)

Hokey-Pokey: (Continued)
(Also see the Bambuco, Bop, Bunny-Hop, Calypso, Creep, Fish, Flea-Hop, Frug, Guapacha, Hand-Jive, Hullie-Gullie, Jerk, Limbo-Rock, Mashed-Potato, Monkey, Pachanga, Plena, Pony, Rock-and-Around, Scooter, Slide, Strole, Surfers, Swim, Tumba-Cha, Twist, Twister, and the Watusi; which were all Novelty Fads in vogue in the 1950-60s. Also see Novelty-&-Fad Dances-of-the-1960s.)

Honey-Dipper: Both an International **Novelty** and **Fad**, and either a Line or Coupledance of the **1960**s. Its Eponymous Music could be "*Does Fort Worth Ever Cross Your Mind*" or "*All My Ex's Live In Texas*," both by George Strait.
The following is from "*Honey Dipper*" -- [*www.arjjazedance.free-online.co.uk/*]:
   "*Choreographed by Ken & Bunny Fargo*
   "*1-2   Swing Rright hip forward twice*
   "*3-4   Swing Left hip back twice*
   "*5-6   Step on Right, Hop as Left kicks front*
   "*7-8   Left steps over Right, Right scuffs forward*
   "*9-10   Touch Right heel to front twice,*
   "*11-12   Touch Right toe back once, Touch Right toe to side*
   "*13-14   Swing Right behind Left leg slap with left hand, Step on right*
   "*Do 2 'Honey Dips' with left foot*
   "*15   Put Left heel (toe up) in front of Right foot 6" from floor. Stomp Left heel to floor quickly. As foot is raised up, hop back on Right*
   "*16   Put Left heel (toe up) in front of Right foot 6" from floor. Stomp Left heel to floor quickly. As foot is raised up, hop back on Right*
   "*17-18   Step to front with Left, Pivot 1/2 turn to right*
   "*19-20   Swivel on Right 1/4 turn to left, landing on Left, Stomp Right as you clap*
   "*21&22 Shuffle back Left, Right, Left*
   "*23&24 Shuffle back Right, Left, Right*
   "*25-26   Put Left out to front, Hook Left over Right leg, Slapping with Right hand*
   "*27-28   Put Left heel to front, Stomp Left*
   "*29-30   Step front with Right, Pivot 1/2 turn to left*
   "*31-32   Step front with Right, Pivot 1/2 turn to left*
   "*Start Again.*"
(See Novelty-&-Fad Dances-of-the-1960s.) [Also see *www.sixtiescity.com/Culture/dance*]

Hoochi-Coochi-Coo: Only this name for an American **Novelty** or **Fad** of the **1960s** is listed simply as a Dance, Pattern, or Figure in the "*Dance Crazes of the Sixties*." In a resurgence, this may have been the same as the 1899s **Hoochy-Koochy** Dance, and/or the ever-popular **Belly-Dance**.
(See Novelty-&-Fad Dances-of-the-1960s.) [From *www.sixtiescity.com/Culture/dance*]

Hoochy-Koochy: An American **Novelty Fad** Coupledance in vogue, at least at the Saltair Pavilion in Utah in 1899. This dance may have been the same dance as the ever-popular **Hootchie-Kootchie**, and/or the **Hoochi-Coochi-Coo** of the 1960s.
(See the **Belly-Dance**. Also see the Cake-Walk, Kickapoo, Rag-Time, and Tiger-Rag; which were all Novelty Fads in vogue in the 1900 to 1910 era.)

Hook: A **Novelty Fad** Coupledance of 1965. It's Eponymous Music was "*The Hook '65*" by *The Naturals.*
    (See Novelty-&-Fad Dances-of-the-1960s.) [From www.bluejuice.org.au]

Hook-and-Boogit: A **Novelty Fad** Coupledance of 1972. This had its own Eponymous record, the "*Hook And Boogit*" by *Abraham & The Casanovas.*
    (See Novelty-&-Fad Dances-of-the-1960s.) [From www.bluejuice.org.au]

Hook-and-Slink or **Hook-and-Sling:** An American **Fad** dance of 1969. It's Eponymous Music was "*Hook Slink*" by *Eddie Bo.*
    (See Novelty-&-Fad Dances-of-the-1960s.)
    [From *www.bluejuice.org.au.* See *www.sixtiescity.com/Culture/dance*]

Hook-Unwind or **HookTurn-Counter-Clockwise** or **HookSwivel-Left** or **HookSpin-Left** or **Backward-Twist-Turn** or **Half-Twist-Turn:** An Unleadable, General, Counter-Clockwise Coupledance Figure, suitable for many different dances. Danced Apart, by either or both Partners. Can be danced to any *Slow Slow Slow,* or *Slow Slow,* or *Slow Quick Quick,* or *Quick Quick Slow* Rhythm. Rhythm Timing is usually *slow Slow.* Hook-Unwind makes a **Half- to Full-Turn** in one Spot.
    One's Left Outer-Ball is Crossed Behind the Supporting-Foot and beyond in CBMP, then one Rotates on the Heel of the Supporting-Foot, ending with Weight on the Left Foot. In other words, one's Left Toe is tucked around and past one's Right Heel, then one Swivels on the Right Heel and Left Ball. Feet re-Cross Opposite with CBM, if upon Full-Turn completion.
    Hook-Unwind is a more explicit version of **Corkscrew.** Similar to the General **Unwind** Figure, which Rotates a **Half-Turn maximum.** Similar to **Hook-Overspin-Left, Hook-Overspin-Right, Cross-Overspin-Left, Cross-Overspin-Right, Toe-Spin-Clockwise,** and **Toe-Spin-Counter-Clockwise,** which Rotate a **Full-Turn minimum.** (See Hook-Wind, Cross-Unwind, Cross-Wind, Twist-Turn(1), Hook, and Cross. Also see Chekessia. Also see Giro, Molinete, and Enrosque.)

Hook-Wind or **HookTurn-Clockwise** or **HookSwivel-Right** or **HookSpin-Right** or **Backward-Twist-Turn** or **Half-Twist-Turn:** An Unleadable, General, Clockwise Coupledance Figure, suitable for many different dances. Danced Apart, by either or both Partners. Can be danced to any *Slow Slow Slow,* or *Slow Slow,* or *Slow Quick Quick,* or *Quick Quick Slow* Rhythm. Rhythm Timing is usually *Slow slow.* Hook-Wind makes a **Half- to Full-Turn** in one Spot.
    One's Right Outer-Ball is Crossed Behind the Supporting-Foot and beyond in CBMP, then one Rotates on the Heel of the Supporting-Foot, ending with Weight on the Right Foot. In other words, one's Right Toe is tucked around and past one's Left Heel, then one Swivels on the Left Heel and Right Ball. Feet re-Cross Opposite with CBM, if upon Full-Turn completion.
    Hook-Wind is a more explicit version of **Corkscrew.** Similar to the General **Unwind** Figure, which Rotates a **Half-Turn maximum.** Similar to **Hook-Overspin-Left, Hook-Overspin-Right, Cross-Overspin-Left, Cross-Overspin-Right, Toe-Spin-Clockwise,** and **Toe-Spin-Counter-Clockwise,** which Rotate a **Full-Turn minimum.** Generally similar to the **About-Face!** military command. (See Turtle-Spin, Hook-Unwind, Cross-Wind, Cross-Unwind, Twist-Turn(1)&(3), Twist-Turn-Tango, Hook, Cross, and Military-Team. Also see Giro, Molinete, and Enrosque.)

Hoopy-Doo: A **Novelty Fad** Coupledance of the 1960s. This had its own Eponymous record, "*Hoopy Doo*" by *Willie Wicher.*
> (See Novelty-&-Fad Dances-of-the-1960s.) [From www.bluejuice.org.au]

Hootch: Only this name for an American **Novelty** or **Fad** of the **1960s** is listed simply as a Dance, Pattern, or Figure in the "*Dance Crazes of the Sixties.*"
> (See Novelty-&-Fad Dances-of-the-1960s.) [From *www.sixtiescity.com/Culture/dance*]

Hootier: An American **Fad** comical Solo-Dance or Maneuvers of the 1980s, in Cadence with the Music.
> The following is from "*Eighties Dances*" - [www.inthe80s.com]:
>> "***Hootier: One hand on forehead and other arm on hip and twist body. Then switch hands until dance is over!!*"**
> (See Novelty-&-Fad Dances-of-the-1980s.)

Hop: An American **Novelty Fad** Coupledance of 1967. The records that the **Hop** was danced to were "*I'll Be Around*" by *The Spinners*, and "*She Used To Be My Girl*" by *The O'Jays*.
> [From *Soul*, www.trinity.unimelb.edu.au. Also see *www.sixtiescity.com/Culture/dance.*]

Hopple-Popple: A **Novelty Fad** Coupledance in vogue in 1966.
> (See Novelty-&-Fad Dances-of-the-1960s.)
> [From *Novelty Dances Through the Years* by Pony Moore.]

Hop-Scotch: Only this name for an American **Novelty** or **Fad** of the **1960s** is listed simply as a Dance, Pattern, or Figure in the "*Dance Crazes of the Sixties.*"
> (See Novelty-&-Fad Dances-of-the-1960s.) [From *www.sixtiescity.com/Culture/dance*]

Hornet: Only this name for an American **Novelty** or **Fad** of the **1960s** is listed simply as a Dance, Pattern, or Figure in the "*Dance Crazes of the Sixties.*"
> (See Novelty-&-Fad Dances-of-the-1960s.) [From *www.sixtiescity.com/Culture/dance*]

Horse: An American **Novelty Fad** Singular or Coupledance in vogue in the 1960s, probably Unstructured. In 1967 or 1968, for the dance, _Cliff Nobles and Company_ sang and recorded a major hit, _The Horse_. Its Eponymous dance, **The Horse**, was a takeoff on **The Camel Walk** Dance. Since it attempts to imitate through Pantomime, some complained that it was difficult to differentiate between the two dances.

The **Horse** Dance in vogue at Brigham Young University, Provo, Utah, had (medium?) 4/4 Timing. Notes given are: 1) _Pull hand toward center on the beat_; 2) _Whip Horse 1 2 3 4 5 6, 7 and up, 8 and spank_; 3) _Travel gallop._

There is a picture labeled and showing a young BYU couple dancing **The Horse**. They are upon Opposing-Feet directly in Tandem with the Lady an arm-stretch Behind, Gripping his belt-loop. Man, as the **Horse**, has his arms Stretched Forward with Wrists-Back.

[See the Gallop(1) Coupledance, and the Novelty-&-Fad Dances-of-the-1960s. Much data from "Rhythm and Dance" by Alma Heaton. Mentioned in _www.sixtiescity.com/Culture/dance_.]

Horse-Trot: A **Novelty Fad** Coupledance in vogue in the United States, probably in the 1910s, and probably danced to Ragtime music.

(See Animal-Dances, Lame-Duck, Grizzley-Bear, Crab-Step, Buzzard-Lope, Turkey-Trot, Kangaroo-Hop, Fish-Walk, and Bunny-Hug.)

Hot-Pastrami: Only this name for an American **Novelty** or **Fad** of the **1960s** is listed simply as a Dance, Pattern, or Figure in the "_Dance Crazes of the Sixties_."

(See Novelty-&-Fad Dances-of-the-1960s.) [From _www.sixtiescity.com/Culture/dance_]

Huckee-Buck: A **Novelty Fad** Coupledance in vogue in 1965.
(See Novelty-&-Fad Dances-of-the-1960s.)
[From _Novelty Dances Through the Years_ by Pony Moore.]

Hucklebuck: An American **Novelty** Coupledance that became a **Fad** again at various times. Quirky and humorous, it was popular in the late 1940s and early 50s at Dance-Parties. In 1961, Chubby Checker released his record version of **_The Hucklebuck_**, which gave the dance new life as a staple for '60s teenagers. Many records then followed by others.

This dance was a dirty boogie, both risque and raunchy, that everybody seemed to know. "_The Hucklebuck_," its Eponymous song, was written by Paul Williams and sung mainly by Chubby Checker. Following are a few excerpted lines from the words to it:

> "_Push ya baby out then you hunch her back_
> _Start a little movement in your sacroilliac_
> _Wiggle like a stick_ [snake] _wobble like a duck_
> _That's what you do when you do the Hucklebuck._"

[See Dirty-Dancing(1). Also see Bambuco, Bop, Bunny-Hop, Calypso, Creep, Flea-Hop, Guapacha, Hand-Jive, Hokey-Pokey, Pachanga, Plena, Rock-and-Around, Scooter, Stroll, Tumba-Cha, Twist, and the Twister; which were all Novelty Fads in vogue in the 1950s. Also see Novelty-&-Fad Dances-of-the-1960s.]

Huddle: Only this name for an American **Novelty** or **Fad** of the **1960s** is listed simply as a Dance, Pattern, or Figure in the "*Dance Crazes of the Sixties*."

(See Novelty-&-Fad Dances-of-the-1960s.) [From *www.sixtiescity.com/Culture/dance*]

Hug-Me-Close: A **Novelty Fad** Coupledance popular in America from about 1912.

(See the Boston-Dip, Bunny-Hug, Gaby-Glide, Lame-Duck, Shiver-Dance, and Turkey-Trot; which were all Novelty Fads in vogue in the 1910s.)

Hula-Dance or **Hula:** The Unleadable, popular State Dance of the Hawaiian Islands, in 4/4 Time. The Hula is also an always-popular **Novelty** Dance.

The following is from "*How to Hula Dance*" -- [www.howtodothings.com]:

"Hula dancing, a form of dancing native to Hawaii, provides entertainment but has its roots in ancient ritual. The purpose of Hula dancing is to convey meaning through movement. Hula dancing intertwines the performers with the spirit of the universe by unifying their existence with nature. Even if you fail to experience a meditative quality while performing the Hula, you can still learn a basic foundation to enjoy this art form."

The following is from "*Learn How To Hula Dance*" -- [www.anytimecostumes.com]:

"Hula is the traditional dance of the Hawaiian Islands. It was once both a religious exercise in honor of the goddess Laka and also their form of entertainment. In traditional hula, poems and stories were interpreted by highly stylized movements of the dancers' arms and hands. Although the angelic dances of old Hawaii have almost disintegrated and bear little resemblance to the modern forms of hula, the modern hula also tells a story. The out spread arms of the dancer represents the swaying of the palm trees gently blown by the wind. To be able to convey the story to the audience the dancer has to coordinate the facial expression and the eye with the graceful movements of the fingers, arms, wrists, hips, knees and feet."

There is a yarn that originally the **Hula** was a sacred dance, supposedly created by the volcano Kala to please his sister-volcano Pele. The **Hula** and grass skirts were banned by the missionaries in the 1800s.

The **Hula** is Spot-Danced Singularly to ukukele Music by bare Footed Hawaiian Ladies, with a soft Swaying of their hips and **Hula** skirts. For their Basic-Step, Ladies Chasse while they Undulate their hips. The Ladies tell stories with their Hands, arms, and Facials. Hawaiian Men dance more violently, with grunts. Tahitian Ladies dance a Faster **Hula**. Beginner dancers seem to tend to avoid bending into their Knees sufficiently.

See **How-to-Hula-Dance**. [Also see Exotic-Dancer(1), Broken-Sways, Hip-Rocks, Hula-Hoops, Washing-Machine, Boogie-Roll(1), Hip-Lift, Side-Lift, Hip-Waves, Side-Rise, Cuban-Hip, Cuban-Motion, Body-Lift, Forward-Roll, Shimmy(1), Knee-Drape, Up-and-Over-the-Top, Arm-Waves, Body-Wave, Body-Ripple, Side-Body-Waves, Figure-Eight, and Side-Stretch.]

Hullabaloo: Only this name for an American **Novelty** or **Fad** of the **1960s** is listed simply as a Dance, Pattern, or Figure in the "*Dance Crazes of the Sixties*." (There was a **Hullabaloo** 1960s television program showing dancing.)

(See Novelty-&-Fad Dances-of-the-1960s.) [From *www.sixtiescity.com/Culture/dance*]

Hullaballoon: Only this name for an American **Novelty** or **Fad** of the **1960s** is listed simply as a Dance, Pattern, or Figure in the "_Dance Crazes of the Sixties_."
(See Novelty-&-Fad Dances-of-the-1960s.) [From _www.sixtiescity.com/Culture/dance_]

Hullie-Gullie or **Hully-Gully:** An Unstructured and Unleadable, American **Novelty Group-Dance Genre** of **Fads** in vogue mostly from about 1963 into 1968. It was actually a game in the early Sixties in the Eastern U.S. The original **Hullie-Gullie** was a kind of endless dance in which someone would Call-Out to everyone some inanimate object, animal or bird, which dancers then attempted to imitate while dancing. The imitated object was danced until someone hollered a change.
The record _"(Baby) Hully Gully"_ by the Olympics was put out in 1959. But the dance started about 1963, when a Florida resort had come up with this novel Mime game, after which it became very popular. As Music played, a certain director there would Call-Out various Actions for the participating dancers to try to Mimic. A few of these Actions that later became Step Patterns were The **Boxer**, **Hitch-Hiker**, **Pony**, and The **Watusi**. Others were probably The **Penguin**, **Swim**, **Washing-Machine**, **Mashed-Potato**, **Typewriter**, **Popcorn**, **Monkey**, **Horse**, and The **Dog**.
The **Hullie-Gullie** dance probably Mimicked all of these subjects and more, which then started the whole series of Mimicking dances, because 1960s recording companies boarded the bandwagon and produced many matching dance records to these objects.
The **Hullie-Gullie** was usually danced Solo, or Apart Facing Partner if there was one. This was one of the free and individualistic 1960s dances. People enmasse, mostly teens with long hair, were dancing by themselves and inventing as they danced. These silly **Hullie-Gullie** Fad-Dances were banned at Brigham Young University in 1966.
(Also see the Novelty-&-Fad Dances-of-the-1960s.)

Hully-Gully: See Hullie-Gullie.

Hully-Gully-Bongo: Only this name for an American **Novelty** or **Fad** of the **1960s** is listed simply as a Dance, Pattern, or Figure in the "_Dance Crazes of the Sixties_."
(See Novelty-&-Fad Dances-of-the-1960s.) [From _www.sixtiescity.com/Culture/dance_]

Hully-Gully-Rock: Only this name for an American **Novelty** or **Fad** of the **1960s** is listed simply as a Dance, Pattern, or Figure in the "_Dance Crazes of the Sixties_."
(See Novelty-&-Fad Dances-of-the-1960s.) [From _www.sixtiescity.com/Culture/dance_]

Hump: A **Novelty Fad** Coupledance of the 1960s. This had its own Eponymous record, _"The Hump"_ by _The Invictas._
(See Novelty-&-Fad Dances-of-the-1960s.) [From www.bluejuice.org.au]

Hump-Back: A **Novelty Fad** Coupledance of 1966. This had its own Eponymous record, the _"Hump Back"_ by _Eldridge Holmes._
(See Novelty-&-Fad Dances-of-the-1960s.) [From www.bluejuice.org.au]

Humphrey-Stomp: Only this name for an American **Novelty** or **Fad** of the 1960s is listed simply as a Dance, Pattern, or Figure in the "_Dance Crazes of the Sixties._"
(See Novelty-&-Fad Dances-of-the-1960s.) [From _www.sixtiescity.com/Culture/dance_]

Humpty-Dance: A **Novelty** or **Fad** dance of an unknown time, listed in "_Novelty and fad dances_" under [http://en.wikipedia.org/wiki].

Hunch: An American **Fad** dance of 1965. The records that the **Hunch** was danced to were "_Selfish One_" by _Jackie Ross_, and "_The Hunch_" by _Gene Taylor_.
(See Novelty-&-Fad Dances-of-the-1960s.)
[From _Soul, www.trinity.unimelb.edu.au._ See _www.sixtiescity.com/Culture/dance._]

Hustle: A popular **Novelty Fad** Singular **Line-Dance** of the early 1970s. It's Eponymous Music was "_Do The Hustle_" by _Van McCoy_.
[See Novelty-&-Fad Dances-of-the-1960s. Also see Line-Dances(1).]
[From www.bluejuice.org.au]

Ickey-Shuffle: An American **Fad** comical Solo-Dance or Maneuvers of the 1980s, in Cadence with the Music.
The following is from "_Eighties Dances_" - [www.inthe80s.com]:
"**_The Ickey Shuffle:_** _Originator Ickey Woods popularized this maneuver as a celebratory touchdown dance during the Cincinnati Bengals 1988 season. Football in right hand, extend right arm, shuffle two steps to right; switch football to left hand, extend left arm, shuffle two steps to left; repeat and repeat._"
(See Novelty-&-Fad Dances-of-the-1980s. Also see Pantomime, Mime, and Mimicry-En-Masse.)

Itch: The **Itch** was a **Novelty Fad** Coupledance in vogue in the United States, somewhere in the 1900s-1910s.
(See Yankee-Tangle, Texas-Rag, Fanny-Bump, Funky-Butt, Flibbertigibbety, Humorous, Laughing, Squat, Grind, and Mooch.)

Itchy-Koo: A **Novelty Fad** Coupledance of the 1960s. This had its own Eponymous record, the "_Itchy Koo_" by _Hank Blackman & The Killers._
(See Novelty-&-Fad Dances-of-the-1960s.) [From www.bluejuice.org.au]

Jackie-Gleason: "And-Away-We-Go!" This **Jackie Gleason** is a Structured but Unleadable, **Novelty** Pattern for a Singular-Dancer; a 2 1/2-Measures Pattern, Mimicking the antics of **Jackie Gleason** as he gleefully danced his two Forward Triples with Bent Elbows. This **Jackie Gleason** Pattern is one of the Qued Steps often Called for while dancing the **Madison** Audience-Participation-Dance.

The following is an excerpt from *Madison Figures* -- [www.sixtiescity.com/Culture/]:
        "*Chasse to the left. Throw R leg out to the front, then swing it back in front of L leg. Launch forward onto RF with arms outstretched (2 beats). 'And awaaaay we go' Step L. Step back R to place.*"

The following are excerpts from *The Madison* -- [www.albertj.btinternet.co.uk/]:
        "*LS, Step forward with left foot, swing right leg and arms back on right side and forward.*

        "*Bring back across left, and with arms bring forward as flying.*
        "*Step back on left, step back on right.*"

[See Double-Cross, Cleveland-Box, Basketball, Big-'M', 'T'-Time, Birdland, and Rifleman. Also see the Novelty-&-Fad Dances-of-the-1960s. Also see **And-Away-We-Go!**, Happy-Feet, Humorous, Laughing, With-Abandon, and Have-to-Dance!]

James-Brown: An Unstructured, American **Novelty Fad** Singular or Coupledance in vogue in 1968. Although having had its own Eponymous song, the dance itself proved to be not very popular and faded soon with its song. This song was *"Cold Sweat"* by *James Brown*.
        (See the Novelty-&-Fad Dances-of-the-1960s.)

James-Brown-Bougelou: A **Novelty Fad** Coupledance of the 1960s. This had its own Eponymous record, "*The James Brown Bougelou*" by *Little Genie Brooks*.
        (See Novelty-&-Fad Dances-of-the-1960s.) [From www.bluejuice.org.au]

Jazz-Box or **Jazz-Square** or **Diamond** or **Dewey-Step** or **Box-Step:** General Shine-Step Figures of the Separated **Break-A-Way**(3) Break-Endings. Danced Left or Right, Mirror-Image Opposite. Usually danced Solo, since these are Unleadable, but are usually Performed Side-by-Side if Coupledanced. These Crossing of the Feet Series of Figures are most suitable for **Tap-Dancing, Clogging, Soft-Shoe, Jazz-Dance, Line-Dancing, CheerLeading**, and the like. **Jazz-boxes** are also useful in the various **Swing Dances**; and, if in 4 Counts, is also suitable for one (one Measure) **Swing-Bal** portion of the **Balboa**.

Each of the following **Jazz-boxes** is one Measure long with various Timings. The **Jazz-Box** Series may begin with a Cross-Step, a Step In-Place, a Forward Step, or a Kick-Step, and may have up to five Changes-of-Weight.

Three even Counts are most common for 3/4 Timing. For the 4/4 Timing, an even Rhythm of *1 2 3 4* is most common, and is most commonly danced: *Step   Cross Foot Over Step Back   Uncross Foot.*

(Continued)

<u>**Jazz-Box:**</u> (Cotinued)
A sample Three-Step, Left Jazz-Box dances *crossinfront Backward close* or *sideward.*
A sample Three-Step, Right Jazz-Box dances *CrossInFront backward Close* or *Sideward.*
A sample Four-Step, Left Jazz-Box dances *crossinfront Backward sideward Close.*
And a Four-Step, Right Jazz-Box dances *CrossInFront backward Sideward close* or *forward.*
Another sample Four-Step, Left Jazz-Box dances *forward CrossInFront backward Sideward.*
(See Break-A-Way Glossary, Shine, Baldosa, Cuadrado, and Abe-Kabbible.)

<u>**Jed:**</u> An Unleadable 1960s American **Novelty Fad** Singular and **Coupledance** Routine that Jumped and Jumped. The following loosely Choreographed Pattern was in vogue at Brigham Young University, Provo, Utah.
Danced at a 4/4 medium Tempo, The **Jed** was danced usually to Rock music, in an open Shine Position, and in Lines Formation or Slightly Facing and Apart. All commenced upon their Right Foot:
Jumping-Jacks: See Jumping-Jacks; except Land with Feet Crossed, In-Front and Behind, instead of Together.
Side-Zap: Jump Sideways onto a single Foot, Touching Free-Heel to Dancefloor, Toe-Up with Free-Leg Straight. Right and Left.
Heel-Springs: Same as Jumping-Jacks except Land upon both Heels and Progress either Forward or Rearward.
Note: As a Heel-Springs Variation, the Man may Squat.
There are three pictures from Brigham Young University, labeled and showing a young couple dancing **The Jed**. They are Apart and partially Facing. There is Forward-Touching of one Heel and Chugging Back-On-Heels. In one picture, the Man is so Deep-Into-Knees that he is Squatting. Arms are swung, and Hands are loosely fisted with Wrists-Back.
Similar to **Outs-and-Ins**. (See Cossak-Dance. Also see the Novelty-&-Fad Dances-of-the-1960s.) [Data mostly from "Rhythm and Dance" by Alma Heaton.]

<u>**Jelly-Belly:**</u> A **Novelty Fad** Coupledance of the 1960s. This had its own Eponymous record, "*Jelly Belly*" by *The Druids.*
(See Novelty-&-Fad Dances-of-the-1960s.) [From www.bluejuice.org.au]

Jerk: A **Novelty Fad** Coupledance Motion in vogue in the U.S. in the late 1960s. In 1965, *The Larks* had recorded its Eponymous music, "*The Jerk.*" More records were "*Nowhere to Run*" by *Martha Reeves & the Vandellas*, "*Do The Jerk*" by *Derrick Harriet*, "*Cool Jerk*" by *The Capitols*, "*Ska Jerk*" by *The Wailers*, and "*Soul Jerk*" by *Bobby Bennet & The Dynamics*. The **Jerk** was usually danced Apart but Facing Partner. These 1960s dances were free and individualistic. People enmasse, mostly teens with long hair, were dancing by themselves and inventing as they danced.

Having been derived from the **Frug**, the **Jerk** was related to the **Swim**, the **Monkey**, the **Dog**, the **Watusi**, and the **Waddle** dance forms. Danced In-Place, dancers Swung hips Side-to-Side, with certain added arm Movements and, obviously, one's Body was constantly **Jerk**ed with a sharp and suddenly abrupt Motion.

The following is from "*Dance Crazes of the Sixties.*" [From *www.sixtiescity.com/Culture/dance*]:

"***The Jerk:*** *This is basically the Monkey but with your arms and hands moving as if you're leading a band -- crossing your wrists in front of your chest, then sweeping out-in time, or at half time, with your body movement, to the count of four. Your hands are up at face level. On count 1, the outward sweep, 'push' your hands out into the outward sweep, giving a jerky motion. For a little more style, snap your fingers on the two outward movements -- the first and third counts of your hand motion.*"

At Brigham Young University, in Provo, Utah, the **Jerk** is recorded to have been **Jerk**ed thusly: With one or both arms Raised at right angles In-Front of chest on Count One, Drop one's chest on Count Two with a **Jerk**. This silly Motion, along with other silly Fad-Dances, was later banned in 1966 at the same University.

(See Monkey, and Frisk. Also see the Novelty-&-Fad Dances-of-the-1960s.)

Jerry-Springer: From Kingston, Jamaica, an Underground **Novelty Fad**, Singular- or Group-Dance Movement, associated with dancing **Dancehall/Ragga**, which, in turn, are outgrowths of **Ska/Reggae**. **Jerry-Springer** was and is danced mainly by youths of color.

The following is from *Ragga Fashions*: [www.bbc.co.uk]

"*Jerry-Springer* - --- *The Jerry Springer show is renowned for the fights and quarrels that break out between guests and in the same vain this dance is supposed to show some sort of upward downward fighting motion. Unfortunately everyone has their own idea of what a Jerry Springer fight looks like, nobody seems to do the dance the same way.*"

See **Dancehall**(2) for further explanation. (Also see Bogle, Armstrong, Butterfly, Go-Go-Wine, Body-Basic-and-Exercise, Tate, and World-Dance. Also see Prang, Heel-and-Toe, Na!Na!Na!, Screechie, Zip-It-Up, Drive-By, Shizzle-Ma-Nizzle, Matrix, and Bin-Laden. Also see Underground Step-Listing.)

Jersey-Bounce: An American **Fad** Coupledance of the 1960s that may have been only a Singular-Dance, Pattern, or Figure. The Music for this may have been the ever-popular "*Jersey Bounce,*" initially played by Benny Goodman's Band, and Composed by Buddy Feyne about 1940.

(See Novelty-&-Fad Dances-of-the-1960s.) [See *www.sixtiescity.com/Culture/dance*]

Jesse-James: A **Novelty Fad** dance of 1967. **Jesse-James** had its own Eponymous record, *"Do The Jesse James"* by *Rosco Gordon*.
(See the Novelty-&-Fad Dances-of-the-1960s.) [From *Soul*, www.trinity.unimelb.edu.au]

Jig-Hop: A **Novelty Fad** dance Performed by Elenor Powell in 1930 in a Broadway play named "*Fine and Dandy*".

Jingle-Bob: A **Novelty Fad** American Coupledance.

Jivin'-Around: Only this name for an American **Novelty** or **Fad** of the 1960s is listed simply as a Dance, Pattern, or Figure in the "*Dance Crazes of the Sixties*."
(See Novelty-&-Fad Dances-of-the-1960s.) [From *www.sixtiescity.com/Culture/dance*]

Joogie-Boogie: Only this name for an American **Novelty** or **Fad** of the 1960s is listed simply as a Dance, Pattern, or Figure in the "*Dance Crazes of the Sixties*."
(See Novelty-&-Fad Dances-of-the-1960s.) [From *www.sixtiescity.com/Culture/dance*]

Jordan-Stomp: Only this name for an American **Novelty** or **Fad** of the 1960s is listed simply as a Dance, Pattern, or Figure in the "*Dance Crazes of the Sixties*."
(See Novelty-&-Fad Dances-of-the-1960s.) [From *www.sixtiescity.com/Culture/dance*]

Joropo *(ho-RO-po)*: An American **Novelty Fad** Coupledance, stemming from a Rustic Latin-American **Folk** Coupledance.
Similar to **Ranchera,** and **Pasillo**.

Jump: Only this name for an American **Novelty** or **Fad** of the 1960s is listed simply as a Dance, Pattern, or Figure in the "*Dance Crazes of the Sixties*."
(See Novelty-&-Fad Dances-of-the-1960s.) [From *www.sixtiescity.com/Culture/dance*]

Jump-and-Hump: Only this name for an American **Novelty** or **Fad** of the 1960s is listed simply as a Dance, Pattern, or Figure in the "*Dance Crazes of the Sixties*."
(See Novelty-&-Fad Dances-of-the-1960s.) [From *www.sixtiescity.com/Culture/dance*]

Jumpen: A **Novelty** or **Fad** dance of an unknown time, listed in "*Novelty and fad dances*" under [http://en.wikipedia.org/wiki].

Junkanoo (or **Junkernoo**?): Being a midnight-to-dawn street parade with **Junkanoo Music**, filled with cowbells, Rake-and-Scrape Music and the distinctive goombay drum, occurring in many towns across the **Bahamas**, **Bermuda**, **Belize**, the **Cayman Islands**, **Turks and Caicos** Islands, Freeport, and the Family Islands, every Boxing Day (December 26) and New Year's Day.   The largest **Junkanoo** happens in Nassau. **Junkanoo**'s origins are obscure. **Junkanoo**'s accompanying Dances have been derived from European forms such as the **Polka** and **Waltz**.

(See Caribbean Dance-Music Amalgamation Listing.) [Most from http://en.wikipedia.org/wiki]

Junkernoo: Only this name for an American **Novelty** or **Fad** of the 1960s is listed simply as a Dance, Pattern, or Figure in the "*Dance Crazes of the Sixties*."

Note: This may be the Caribbean **Junkanoo** Dance, of every December 26 and New Year's Day.

(See Novelty-&-Fad Dances-of-the-1960s.) [From *www.sixtiescity.com/Culture/dance*]

Junk-Man-Rag: A **Onestep**(1) Coupledance of the Novelty-and-Fad Genre, created by **Maurice Mouvet** about 1912, which was then possibly transformed into the **Castle-Walk** by **Vernon and Irene Castle**.

Kangaroo: The **Kangaroo Fad** dance of 1964 in the U.S. is referred to in *www.trinity.unimelb.edu.au/* as follows:

The dance = *"The Kangaroo"*, the Eponymous music = *"Charles Sheffield, The Kangaroo Part 2 - Abraham & Cassanovas 1964."*

This probably includes or consists of a Hopping Action while keeping both Feet Together.

(See Kangaroo-Dip, and Kangaroo-Hop. Also see the Novelty-&-Fad Dances-of-the-1960s.)

[Mentioned in *www.sixtiescity.com/Culture/dance.*]

Kangaroo-Dip: An American "**Animal-Dance**", a **Novelty Fad** Coupledance in vogue about 1912 to 1914. Derided by newspapers, magazines, church officials, and even by Pope Pius X, as "such foolish and decadent behavior," over one hundred of these dances were created during this period.

(See Animal-Dances, Bull-Frog-Hop, Bunny-Hug, Buzzard-Lope, Camel-Walk, Chicken-Reel, Chicken-Scratch, Crab-Step, Fish-Walk, Gotham-Gobble, Horse-Trot, Kangaroo-Hop, Lame-Duck, Monkey-Glide, Possum-Trot, Snake, and Turkey-Trot; which were all **Animal-Dances** of 1910-1914.)

Kangaroo-Hop: A **Novelty Fad** Coupledance written by *Melville Morris*. Music was first copyrighted in 1905, then secondly in 1916. Publisher was *Jerome H. Remick & Co.* for both Music sheet publications. Composer for both publications was *Melville Morris*, but the lyricist for the second publication was *Gus Kahn*.

In 1914 or 1916, its Eponymous sheet Music had again appeared; this time named "*The Kangaroo Hop Fox Trot*",. On its cover, a Facing Couple is shown in a spread Butterfly Position with one set of Clasped Hands Up and the other set Down.

It was in 1914 that the brand new, original **Foxtrot** had caught on fabulously, although then it was vigorous and Jerky. It seems many Foxtrot versions were appearing at that time, including this second **Kangaroo-Hop** version.

[Note: Further Mechanics of its Steps are unknown.]

(See Animal-Dances.)

Kangaroo-Tail-Twist: A **Novelty Fad** Coupledance of 1961. This had its own Eponymous record, the "*Kangaroo Tail Twist*" by *Johnny Devlin.*

(See Novelty-&-Fad Dances-of-the-1960s.) [From www.bluejuice.org.au]

Kangaroo-Twist: An Australian **Fad** Comic Dance of 1965. The brothers Chris and Peter Allen "*did a very funny and well handled Kangaroo Twist, a comic dance on the down under version of our fads -- they're from Sidney, Australia ....*" From Judy Garland Live at the Fontainebleau, 1965, Miami beach, Florida.

(See Novelty-&-Fad Dances-of-the-1960s.)

Karate: A **Novelty Fad** Coupledance of the 1960s. This had its own Eponymous record, the "*Karate*" by *The Emperors.*

(See Novelty-&-Fad Dances-of-the-1960s.) [From www.bluejuice.org.au]

Karate-Boogaloo: A **Novelty Fad** Coupledance of 1967. This had its own Eponymous record, the "*Karate Boogaloo*" by *Jerryo.*

(See Novelty-&-Fad Dances-of-the-1960s.) [From www.bluejuice.org.au]

Karate-Monkey: Only this name for an American **Novelty** or **Fad** of the 1960s is listed simply as a Dance, Pattern, or Figure in the "*Dance Crazes of the Sixties.*"

(See Novelty-&-Fad Dances-of-the-1960s.) [From *www.sixtiescity.com/Culture/dance*]

Ketchup-Song: A **Novelty** or **Fad** dance of an unknown time, listed in "*Novelty and fad dances*" under [http://en.wikipedia.org/wiki].

Kickapoo(1)**:** A **Novelty Fad** Coupledance craze that swept the U.S., beginning in June 1904.

(See the Cake-Walk, Hoochy-Koochy, Rag-Time, and Tiger-Rag; these were all Novelty Fads in vogue in the 1900 to 1910 era.)

Kickapoo(2): A **Novelty Fad** Coupledance of the 1960s. This had its own Eponymous record, the "_Kick-A-Poo_" by _The Kickapoo Kidd & Deputies_.
(See Novelty-&-Fad Dances-of-the-1960s.) [From www.bluejuice.org.au]

Kid-and-Play: Comical 1980s **Novelty Fad** Singular-Dance Foot Movements. How to dance the **Kid-and-Play** to the Beat is described as follows in the "_**Eighties Dances**_," [www.inthe80s.com]:
>"_**The Kid and Play** – You take one ridiculous Indian step forward. Once you have taken this step, immediately twist both feet so that your heels kick out. Take another step with the other foot and do the same process. You could also move back or to the side with the same outward kick._"

Similar to **Heel-Splits**. [See Foot-Boogie, Toe-Splits, Ramble(2), and Chinese-Typewriter.]

Kiddie-A-Go-Go: A **Novelty Fad** Coupledance of 1965. This had its own Eponymous record, the "_Kiddie A Go Go_" by _Pandora & The Males_.
(See Novelty-&-Fad Dances-of-the-1960s.) [From www.bluejuice.org.au]

King-Kong's-Monkey: Only this name for an American **Novelty** or **Fad** of the 1960s is listed simply as a Dance, Pattern, or Figure in the "_Dance Crazes of the Sixties_."
(See Novelty-&-Fad Dances-of-the-1960s.) [From _www.sixtiescity.com/Culture/dance_]

Klak-Stick-Kick: Only this name for an American **Novelty** or **Fad** of the 1960s is listed simply as a Dance, Pattern, or Figure in the "_Dance Crazes of the Sixties_."
(See Novelty-&-Fad Dances-of-the-1960s.) [From _www.sixtiescity.com/Culture/dance_]

Knees-Up-Mother-Brown: A **Novelty Fad** Coupledance in vogue in 1940. It's Eponymous Music was played by at least three bands; (1) _Billy Cotton & his Band_, (2) _Raffi/Rise And Shine Band_, and (3) _The Victor Silvester Orchestra_.
[Some from _Novelty Dances Through the Years_ by Pony Moore.]

Koo-Koo: Only this name for an American **Novelty** or **Fad** of the 1960s is listed simply as a Dance, Pattern, or Figure in the "_Dance Crazes of the Sixties_."
(See Novelty-&-Fad Dances-of-the-1960s.) [From _www.sixtiescity.com/Culture/dance_]

Kosher-Twist: A **Novelty Fad** Coupledance of the 1960s. This had its own Eponymous record, "_The Kosher Twist_" by _Benny Bell & His Pretzel Twisters_.
(See Novelty-&-Fad Dances-of-the-1960s.) [From www.bluejuice.org.au]

Krunch: Only this name for an American **Novelty** or **Fad** of the 1960s is listed simply as a Dance, Pattern, or Figure in the "*Dance Crazes of the Sixties.*"
  (See Novelty-&-Fad Dances-of-the-1960s.) [From *www.sixtiescity.com/Culture/dance*]

Kwella-Stroll: A **Novelty Fad** Coupledance of 1966. This had its own Eponymous record, "*The Kwella Stroll*" by *Lou Berrington.*
  (See Novelty-&-Fad Dances-of-the-1960s.) [From www.bluejuice.org.au]

Lambada: **Lambada** Music in 4/4 Time has a kind of throbbing but lighthearted **Samba** Beat that also relates to the **Rumba**. This Slow, sultry, suggestive and sexy **Lambada** is a **Novelty Fad** Coupledance with a Latin flavor, inspired by the **Salsa**, **Meringue**, **Reggae**, and **Zouk** dances. Some say the **Lambada** name comes from the verb *lambar*, which refers to *Movement of the thighs*. Others say the name comes from a Portuguese verb meaning to *whip* or *flog*, all describe certain Styling of this dance. In addition, there are romantic and beautifully flowing hip Movements where two Bodies dance as one.
  This sensual and exotic **Lambada**'s origins are debateable. Some say the **Lambada**'s original versions came from the natives of a village on the northeast coast of Brazil; some say from Bolivia. Others say **Lambada**'s roots were in Africa, still others say it evolved from many different influences, that the **Lambada** was derived from the **Forro**, while some others say its' origins lie in the **Carimbo**. In any case, the **Lambada** arrived in Brazil in the State of Belem in the 1980s. It caused great excitement with Europeans who were viewing the **Lambada** on their TVs in the late 1980s, since a lighter version of **Lambada** music was developed in Bahia, catching the French record producers' interest in 1988. Then the **Lambada** hit the United States in the early 1990s.
  With a Rhythm similar to that of the **Lambada** but sung in French, the **Lambada** was developed into the **Zouk** dance in both France and Africa. Yet, the **Zouk** is presently danced differently in Brazil, like the **Lambada**, rather than as in other world areas.
  Although originally Partners danced staying Apart, the danced was changed so that they danced together in 2/4 Rhythm Timing, creating the provocative, passionate **Lambada** that has been called "*this sizzling, fiery dance of life.*" With Closeness, waving Shoulders and hip Movements, and broken with Lady's Twirls, the **Lambada** is mostly danced Wrapped in each other's arms in sensual Cuban-Motion. The original together-dance had Steps from Side-to-Side, but with influences from Salsa, Meringue and Rock, steps were improvised and switched to Forward-and-Back. Either dancer might Straddle their Partner's thigh and Bump-and-Grind. Lifted at her waist, the Lady often Straddles her Man's waist by locking her Heels tightly behind him and hanging about his neck as he Slow-Dances. Releasing his neck, she will BackBend herself Around-the-World to where her head hangs up-side-down, where he may Sway her.
  The following is from *Brazilian Music Terminology* [www.slipcue.com/music/brazil]:
    "*Lambada - A dance style whose popularity peaked in the late 1980s, when the group Kaoma had an international hit. Heavily influenced by Caribbean music - particularly the merengue - Lambada [music] is typically more aggressive and hard-driving than samba or pagode.*"

(Continued)

Lambada: (Continued)

The following is from [www.geocities.com/danceinfosa/]:

"LAMBADA is a very sensual Latin American dance known as the 'forbidden dance'. It has been well documented as the most raunchy dance in the world. Originating from the Bahia region of NorthEast Brazil in the mid-1980s, the dance was developed in the sleazy dancehalls known as 'Lambaterias'. This dance is intimately connected with the Salsa, Mambo and Merengue.

"The music borrowed elements from 'Farro' (local folk music based around the accordion), as well as Caribbean and African influences. Lambada gained more widespread popularity in the summer of 1989 when French-African group Kaoma recorded 'Lambada' - it quickly became the latest craze to sweep the dance floors of the world. Normally reserved folk were found dancing tight from Bognor to Budapest, their bodies intertwined as the hip-gyrating movements of this new dance turned Europeans into lusty Latins! All it needs is for you to get some friends together, slip into your best dancing gear and let the rhythm move you. The man holds his partner very tight; right hand low around her waist; left hand almost straight out to his left and his right thigh tightly locked to her left thigh as they sway the hips side to side and 'round and 'round."

The **Lambada** is similar to **Dirty-Dancing**(1), and **Crubbing**. (See Freaking, Frottage, Lap-Dance, Perreo, and Grind-Train. Also see Pagode, RockSteady, Bahia-Carioca, LaBamba, and BossaNova. Also see Swaying-to-the-Music, and Body-Contact. Also see Bomba, Chicken-Dance, Macarena, Punta y Soka, Quebradita, Teen-Dancing, and Urban-Dance; which were all Novelty Fads in vogue in the 1980-90s. Also see Folkdance Genre - Brazilian.)

Lambda-Nu: An American **Novelty Fad** Coupledance.

Lambeth-Walk: From the London Limehouse district, the **Lambeth-Walk** was a British 1930s **Novelty Fad** One-Step, Traveling-Coupledance. It was introduced and popular in the U.S. about 1937. The dance had its accompanying song, named _"Doing the Lambeth Walk"_.

The **Lambeth-Walk** was a pretentious display of Walking with stately pomp and insolent affectation; one would see Couples Strutting Arm-in-Arm and then with arms changing.

(See Bumps-A-Daisy. Also see the Big-Apple, Carioca, and Conga-Line; which were all Novelty Fads in vogue in the 1930s.)

The following is from South Africa in the 2000's [www.geocities.com/danceinfosa/]:

"The Lambeth Walk is a novelty dance which has retained its popularity. It is based on the 'Cockney' walk - a swaggering type of movement peculiar to Cockneys. This is the character of the whole dance. Music played between 38 and 44 bars a minute. Man and lady stand about 3 feet apart, both facing LOD. Man commences with LF Lady with RF Take 8 walks forward. On the 8th step the man turns slightly to R. to face lady (4 bars). Man and lady now link L. arms and strut round in a circle, again taking 8 walks. On the 8th step the man unlinks the arms and offers his R. arm to the lady, who links her L. arm into his R. Finish both facing LOD (4 bars).

(Continued)

Lambada: (Continued)

> *"Man starts with LF and lady RF and continue. Take 3 walks forward counting 1, 2, 3. Transfer weight back to rear foot. (Count `and'). Transfer weight forward to front foot. (Count 4). Repeat the 3 walks and the Rock, the mall commencing with RF and the lady LF 1. 2. 3, and 4 (4 bars). Unlink arms and continue. Man walks 2 steps towards the centre. Lady walks 2 steps towards the wall. (Count 1, 2.). Both man and lady turn to face each other and close the feet together. (Count 3). Slap both hands on the legs, just above the knees and at the same time bend slightly forward. (Count 4) (4 bars). Both man and lady walk two steps towards each other. (Count 1, 2.). Close feet together, facing partner and about 3 feet apart. (Count 3). Raise the R hands about level with the head and give the Cockney salute, shouting `Oi.' (4 bars). Turn to face the LOD and repeat from the start."*

Lame-Duck or **Castle-Lame-Duck:** A **Novelty Fad** Coupledance popular about 1914, certainly in Utah and probably throughout the United States.

Some say more than a hundred new **Coupledances** were invented between 1912 and 1914. **Vernon and Irene Castle** invented many of these, and one was this **Lame-Duck**.

(See Merengue-Basic-Movement. Also see the Castle-Walk, Valse-Classique, Castle-Tango, Last-Waltz, Castle-Combination, and the Maxixe; all written by the Castles. Also see Animal-Dances, the Boston-Dip, Bunny-Hug, Gaby-Glide, Hug-Me-Close, Shiver-Dance, and Turkey-Trot; which were all Novelty Fad dances in vogue in the 1910s.)

Lancers: See Lanciers, and Caledonians-Quadrille.

Lanciers or **Lancers:** A **Novelty Fad** Coupledance popular in Texas in the 1870s. Originally, the **Lanciers** had been a Quadrille Set-Dance, invented by a Paris Dancing-Master about 1836. Then it was fashionable in English polite society for a number of years. Being more intricate and complicated than the plain Quadrille, the **Lanciers** became the most popular of the Quadrille Genre. The old-fashioned music of the **Lanciers** suggested its dance Patterns:

First Pattern: Head Couples advance and retire; advance again, gentlemen Turn Opposite Ladies and retire to places (1st 8 Bars). Cross over, Couple Passing between second (4 Bars). All Balance to Corners, each gentleman Turning his neighbor's Partner on his Left (8 Bars).

Second Pattern: Opposite Couples take Partners by Left Hands; advance and retire; advances again, leaving Lady in the Quadrille Center and retire to his place (1st 8 Bars). Two Cross Chasses, and Turn to places (2nd 8 Bars). Side Couples join, Top and Bottom Couples making a Line of four on each side; advance and retire four Steps, each gentleman Turning Partner to place. Sides repeat.

Third Pattern: Couples Forward and Back (4 Bars); Forward a second time and salute, and return to places (4 Bars). Opposite Couples Right and Left. Sides repeat.

Fourth Pattern: Head Couples visit Couples on their Right, to whom they Bow, Crossing over immediately to the Left Couple and do the same, returning to places. First and Second Couples Right and Left; Turn Partners to places (2nd 8 Bars). Sides repeat.

(Continued)

Lanciers: (Continued)
Fifth Pattern: [_Commences with the music, only one preparatory chord being sounded, so each gentleman should Stand with his Right Hand in that of his Partner ready to Start._] Pattern begins with the _grande chaine_, i.e., each gentleman gives his Right Hand to his Partner, presenting his Left to the next Lady, and so on alternately right around till all have once more reached their places, saluting his Partner each time they meet (16 Bars). First Couple form as if for a **Gallop**, taking one turn around, returning to their places with their backs to their vis-a-vis. Third, fourth and second Couples step in behind them in the order indicated (3rd 8 Bars). All Two Cross Chasses, gentlemen Passing Behind Ladies. First Lady leading off to the Right and gentleman to the Left, each respectively followed by all the Couples, till they reach the Quadrille Bottom, where they Join Hands and Promenade back to places. They then fall back into a Line on each side, four gentlemen and four Ladies Facing each other (4th 8 Bars). Each Line then advances and retreats at the same time. Turn Partners to places (5th 8 Bars). Second Couple and sides repeat.

(See Vintage-Social-Dance, Dance-Programmes-1800s, and Caledonians-Quadrille. Also see the Grizzly-Bear, Money-Musk, and Washington-Post-Twostep; which were all Novelty Fads in vogue in the 1800s.) [Most from www.nzdances.co.nz, also from memory.loc.gov]

L.A.-Stomp: A **Novelty Fad** dance of 1968. The records that the **L.A.-Stomp** was danced to were "_I Want You Back_" by _The Jackson Five_, and "_Thank You_" by _Sly And The Family Stone_.

(See Novelty-&-Fad Dances-of-the-1960s.) [From _Soul_, www.trinity.unimelb.edu.au]

Last-Waltz or **Castle-Last-Waltz:** An American **Novelty Fad** Coupledance in vogue from about 1912 to about 1918. Some say more than a hundred new Coupledances were invented between 1912 and 1914. **Vernon and Irene Castle** invented many of these, and one was this **Last-Waltz.**

(See the Castle-Walk, Lame-Duck, Valse-Classique, Castle-Tango, Castle-Combination, and the Maxixe; all written by the Castles. Also see the Boston-Dip, Bunny-Hug, Gaby-Glide, Hug-Me-Close, Shiver-Dance, and Turkey-Trot; which were all Novelty Fad dances in vogue in the 1910s.)

Latin-Boogaloo: A **Novelty Fad** Coupledance of the 1960s. This had its own Eponymous record, the "_Latin Boogaloo_" by the _Latinaires_.

(See Novelty-&-Fad Dances-of-the-1960s. Especially see Afro-Shingaling.) [From www.bluejuice.org.au]

Latin-Hustle: A Leadable, Six-Count **Disco Novelty Fad** Spot-Coupledance, popular in the U.S. mostly in the late 1970s. Its heavy, pounding Beat Music has a Latin flavor, and this dance is much FUN when danced to its fitting Music. Tempo ranges from 27 to 36 MPM in 4/4 Time, and is played at 108 to 144 BPM. With the dance's multitude of Figures and Patterns in constant change, this Smooth and seductive **Latin-Hustle**'s *Touch, Back-Hitch and Walk-In*, repeated again-and-again, grabs the eye then mesmerizes the on-looker.

Danced on Opposing-Feet, (Feet Mirror-Image Opposite.) Rhythm Timing is *Slow Slow Quick And Slow, Slow Slow;* or *Tap 2 3& 4, 5 6*, with this Footwork kept throughout their dance. Partners *Tap* Sideward or DiagForward on the One-Beat with Opposing Toes. See **Latin-Hustle Basic-Step** and **Latin-Hustle Basic-Walk-In** for more details.

If Skilled, the Man may often Transition and intermix his Footwork between this dance and that of the **Same-Foot-Hustle**. This is handy for special Patterns such as Skaters'-Sways.

See **Hustles-Latin-Same-Foot-and-Couple Step-Listing**. Similar to the **Couple-Hustle**. (See Hustle, Hustles-of-Tap-Genre, and Disco-Era.)

Latin-Hustle Basic-Step: A Leadable, Six-Count, **Novelty Fad** Spot-Coupledance Pattern, unique to the **Latin-Hustle**, 1 1/2-Measures long if in 4/4 Time, (music could also be in 2/4 Time.)

Tap 2 3& 4, 5 6 Rhythm Timing for both Partners for the **Latin-Hustle**, is *tap slow Quick and Slow, slow Slow* for the Man; and, *Tap Slow quick And slow, Slow slow* for the Lady.

Coupledanced with repetition, mostly in Loose-Closed Position. Pattern **does not Travel**. **Basic-Step** may be danced with no Turn or may be Couple-Rotated in either direction.

Partners *Tap* Sideward Bent-Kneed on the One-Beat with Opposing Toes. Next, they both Close their *Tap*ped Foot against their Supporting-Foot and Change-Weight on count 2. For count 3&, they both Slightly Rock-Apart and Together, Ball-Flat for a **Back-Step**. They each Mark-Time Stepping In-Place for counts 4, 5 & 6.

Man Steps *sidetap close *Backward inplace InPlace, inplace InPlace.*
Lady Steps *SideTap Close *backward InPlace inplace, InPlace inplace.*
**Backward* = On Ball with only half one's Weight applied.

Similar to the **Latin-Hustle Basic-Walk-In**, the **Same-Foot-Hustle Basic-Step**, and the **Couple-Hustle Basic-Step**. (See Latin-Hustle, Hustles-of-Tap-Genre, and NewYork-Hustle Basic-Step.)

Latin-Hustle Basic-Walk-In: A Leadable, Six-Count, **Novelty Fad** Spot-Coupledance Pattern, unique to the **Latin-Hustle**, 1 1/2-Measures long if in 4/4 Time, (music could also be in 2/4 Time.)

Tap 2 3& 4, 5 6 Rhythm Timing for both Partners for the **Latin-Hustle**, is *tap slow Quick and Slow, slow Slow* for the Man; and, *Tap Slow quick And slow, Slow slow* for the Lady.

Coupledanced with repetition, mostly in Butterfly Position. Pattern **does not Travel** but **Accordions**. **Basic-Walk-In** may be danced with no Turn or may be Couple-Rotated in either direction.

Partners *Tap* DiagForward on the One-Beat with Opposing Toes. Toes Slightly Pass with Man's Toe Outside. Upon their *Tap*, Man Spreads Lady's Hands Apart, at Chest-Level with Man's Thumbs Up, as Lady often Touches Inside of Man's Left Foot with her Right Toe.

Their first Backward Step is a reaching Step with a Long-Stride for both, while all Forward Steps are short. The third Step *Backward* and Recover is a **Back-Step**.

Man Steps *fortap stridewaybackward *Backward inplace TinyForward, tinyforward TinyForward.*

Lady Steps *ForTap StrideWayBackward *backward InPlace tinyforward, TinyForward tinyforward.*

Backward = On Ball with only half one's Weight applied.

Identical to the **Same-Foot-Hustle Basic-Step** except this is danced with Feet Mirror-Image Opposite. Almost identical to the **Couple-Hustle Basic-Step** except this *Tap* is on the first Beat instead of on the last. (See Latin-Hustle, Hustles-of-Tap-Genre, and NewYork-Hustle Basic-Step.)

Lawn-Mower: In comical Pantomime, a **Novelty Fad** Singular dance Pattern or Routine of the 1980s. How to dance the **Lawnmower** to the Beat is described as follows in the "*Eighties Dances*," [www.inthe80s.com]:

"*You pull the lawn mower cord about three times (to the beat) to get it started – move forward a few steps and pull the cord again. Repeat.*"

You can verbally sound "*Yunnnnnn*" with each Pull.

(See Shopping-Cart, Pedal-the-Bike, and Mime.)

Leg-Kick-Line: An American **Novelty** or **Fad** Group-Dance of the 1980s.

The following is from "*Eighties Dances*" - [www.inthe80s.com]:

"*Leg Kick Line: At a club in Salt Lake City called Confetti's, every time 'Come On Eileen' by 'Dexy's Midnight Runners' came on, we would form a straight line shoulder to shoulder, arms over the person next to you, when the music in the last section slowed down. As the music sped back up, we would do alternating leg kicks on each beat, first knee kick then leg kick, switch legs, knee kick then leg kick, switch legs. As the music gets faster so does the kicking, till, if you were fast enough you could kick all the way through the fast beats, then the group would break up for the end of the song.*"

(See Novelty-&-Fad Dances-of-the-1980s. Also see Rockettes, and Kick-Line.)

LeRoc or **CeRoc** or **Ceroc** or **Modern-Jive** or **French-Jive** or **Mo'jive** or **Swing-Jive** or **Jazz-Jive** or **Swing-Roc** or **Blitz:** Originating in the 1980s, a **Novelty Fad**, current, **French** form of **Swing** Coupledancing that is very popular in England. Except for in Australia and New Zealand, **LeRoc** is easy to dance because Footwork is immaterial or at least minimal. Instead, Single-Stepping with a constant **Jive-Float**, there are very complex Arm-Movements, often to a 6/8 Beat, that appear to some onlookers as being mechanical with a lack of expression. Coupledanced with a Bobbing (Double-Rising) One-Step (Single-Count, no Triples), upon Opposing Feet, **LeRoc** is all contortions of **Spaghettis**, i.e., Turning the Lady by use of her arms. One sample **LeRoc** Pattern is as follows:

This Eight-Count Pattern that Changes-Places is danced in two Measures in 4/4 Time with the Jive-Float, Bobbing *Down Up Down Up, Down Up Down Up.* Starts with a Shake-Hands Pull-Thru, Changing-Places and Turning the Lady CCW, the Man Changes-Hands-Behind-Back (Belt-Turn), then he Leads a Lady's-Right-Underarm-Turn, Turning the Lady CW. Ends in Left-Open-Facing Position.

Notes: 1) For **LeRoc** in Australia and New Zealand, there are Footwork, Jumps, and Drops, in addition to the regular Arm-Movements.

2) **LeRoc** is called **"Blitz"** because this is how current British and French interpret the way American GIs taught Jitterbug, Lindy, Shag, and NewYorker to UK Girls in the early 1940s.

(See DC-Hand-Dancing.)

Letkajenkka or **Letkajenka** or **Letkiss** or **Letka-Enka:** Classified herein as in the **Audience-Participation-Dance** Category, and as both a **Novelty** Dance and **Fad** Dance. This **Letkajenkka** was a Dance-Craze in Europe during the 1960s, and was **Group-Dance**d to a certain Eponymous Traditional Finnish Folkdance song. This **Letkajenkka** can be described as an adaptation of the **Bunny-Hop, Conga-Line,** and the **Madison, Follow-the-Leader Dances** in which the participants form a Chain or File.

(See Novelty-&-Fad Dances-of-the-1960s.) [See LetKiss in *www.sixtiescity.com/Culture/dance.*]

Letkiss: See Letkajenkka.

Letkiss-Trot: Only this name for an American **Novelty** or **Fad** of the 1960s is listed simply as a Dance, Pattern, or Figure in the "*Dance Crazes of the Sixties.*" Perhaps this is a Variation of the **Letkajenkka.**

(See Novelty-&-Fad Dances-of-the-1960s.) [From *www.sixtiescity.com/Culture/dance*]

Letkiss-Walk: Only this name for an American **Novelty** or **Fad** of the 1960s is listed simply as a Dance, Pattern, or Figure in the "*Dance Crazes of the Sixties.*" Perhaps this is a Variation of the **Letkajenkka.**

(See Novelty-&-Fad Dances-of-the-1960s.) [From *www.sixtiescity.com/Culture/dance*]

Limbo-Rock or **Limbo:** An American **Novelty Fad** in vogue in the late 1950s or early 1960s, **Singular dancing under the limbo stick**; a **Gymnastic** sports Competition. **The Limbo** dance had its own accompanying Latin-flavored song, named the "*Limbo Rock*" by *Chubby Checker,* plus other 1962 Eponymous Music, "*Limbo Lucy*" by *The Everglades,* and "*Limbo Girl*" by *The Invaders.*

Along with the other singers, this Eponymous song was sung by *Chubby Checker.* Following are a few excerpted lines from his words to it:

> "*Jack be limbo jack be quick, Jack go under the limbo stick*
> *Limbo lower now, Limbo lower now... how low can you go?*
> *First you spread your limbo feet, then you move to limbo beat*
> *Limbo ankle limbo knee, bend back like a limbo tree*"

As the stick was repositioned progressively Lower, people contorted their Bodies to Balance Lower and Lower, to Slide under the stick without Touching the floor.

The following is from "*Dance Crazes of the Sixties*":

> "**The Limbo:** *Dancers move to a Caribbean rhythm, then lean backwards and 'dance' under a horizontal stick without touching it. Upon touching it, or falling backwards, the dancer is 'out'. When several dancers compete, they travel in single file and the stick is gradually lowered until only one dancer, who has not touched either the stick or the floor, remains.*"

(See the Shout-Dance. Also see the Bambuco, Bop, Bunny-Hop, Calypso, Creep, Fish, Flea-Hop, Frug, Guapacha, Hitch-Hiker, Hokey-Pokey, Hullie-Gullie, Jerk, Mashed-Potato, Monkey, Pachanga, Plena, Pony, Rock-and-Around, Scooter, Slide, Strole, Surfers, Swim, Tumba-Cha, Twist, Twister, and the Watusi; which were all Novelty Fads in vogue in the 1950-60s. Also see Novelty-&-Fad Dances-of-the-1960s.)

[Some from *www.bluejuice.org.au.* and *www.sixtiescity.com/Culture/dance.*]

Little-Apple: A Leadable? 1930s novelty **Fad 8-Count Coupledance Pattern**, usually Performed by two while dancing the **Big-Apple**. The **Little-Apple** was a derivative of the **Big-Apple**.

It is believed that, along with the **Big-Apple**, the **Little-Apple** was born at Fat Sam's Big Apple Club in Columbia, South Carolina.

[Note: Mechanics of the **Little-Apple**'s Steps are unknown.]

For the **Big-Apple**, the **Little-Apple** was one of the **Break-A-Way** Genre. Wiggling their hips, certain **Break-A-Way** Patterns were danced. The original **Suzie-Q, Boogie-Back, Tack-Annie, Georgia-Grind, Praise-Allah!, Truckin', Peckin', Charleston, Shorty-George,** and other Break-A-Ways, were probably originated early by blacks; while **Spank-the-Baby, Rusty-Dusty, Pose-and-a-Peck,** the **Little-Apple,** the **Little-Peach, Mess-Around, Stomp-Off, Apple-Jacks,** and **Fall-Off-the-Log,** and other Break-A-Ways, were probably originated later by whites. Most all of these Patterns seem to have been influenced or derived from the classic **Lindy-Hop** and/or **Big-Apple** dances. See **Break-A-Way Glossary** for a more complete listing.

Little-Peach: An Unleadable? 1930s novelty **Fad** 8-Count Pattern, usually Performed while dancing the **Big-Apple**.

[Note: Mechanics of the **Little-Peach**'s Steps are unknown.]

For the **Big-Apple**, the **Little-Peach** was one of the **Break-A-Way** Genre. Wiggling their hips, certain **Break-A-Way** Patterns were danced. The original **Suzie-Q, Boogie-Back, Tack-Annie, Georgia-Grind, Praise-Allah!, Truckin', Peckin', Charleston, Shorty-George,** and other Break-A-Ways, were probably originated early by blacks; while **Spank-the-Baby, Rusty-Dusty, Pose-and-a-Peck,** the **Little-Apple,** the **Little-Peach, Mess-Around, Stomp-Off, Apple-Jacks,** and **Fall-Off-the-Log,** and other Break-A-Ways, were probably originated later by whites. Most all of these Patterns seem to have been influenced or derived from the classic **Lindy-Hop** and/or **Big-Apple** dances. See **Break-A-Way Glossary** for a more complete listing.

Lock or **Locking** or **Lock-It**: The **Lock** is a **Novelty Fad** and part of the **Electric-Boogie** style of **Break-Dancing**, which, in turn, is one major part of **Hip-Hop**. It is only one of the many **Singular-Dancing, Electric-Boogie** Genre of "Moves". But **Lock** is not a true Mime Move; instead, **Lock** is more like an Abrupt Jazz-Dance Movement. **"Locking"** was created by Don Cambell and his group, *"the Lockers"*, at Crenshaw High School in Los Angeles in the 1990s. This is true, although there is some **"Locking"** claim by *"the Harlem Pop Lockers"* that first formed in 1972. The **Boogaloo**, along with **Popping** and **Locking**, is (or was) actually part of the 1990s **Funk-Style** of dancing, mainly of California.

In the 1990s, while **Uprock** was a favorite of the New York gangs, **Locking** was a favorite of gangs in Los Angeles. Some others say **Locking** had been started by *Lockatron* and *Shabba-Doo*. West Coast *Shabba* was also responsible for introducing New Yorkers to **Popping**, all of which, some say, resulted in the first genuine **Hip-Hop** Dance.

The following is from *"Electric Boogie,"* [www.actor.force9.co.uk/]:

"The Lock or `Locking': Locking is doing some fast moves with the entire body, then freezing in one position. The best way to describe the movement of locking would be thus: You know those little-figured toys that are like inside-out puppets on small plastic circular platforms or pedestals, and if you press the bottom of the platform the figure collapses real fast, then when you let your finger up it goes back into shape? Well that's what locking looks like.

"The Lock came from a comical character called `Rerun', who appeared on a TV show called `What's Happening'. He often did a comic dance that involved moving his arms and legs very fast, and in between each move he would give a brief pause, or lock."

"A Brief History of Breakdancing." [www.angelfire.com], also claims that the **Lock-It** is a dance based on *"the character Rerun from `What's Happening'."*

Some other **Electric-Boogie** Genre of Mime "Moves" are the **Moon-Walk**, the **Pop**(3), the **Wave**(1), the **King-Tut**, the **Tick**, the **Robot**, the **Glides**, **Floating**(2), the **SlowMo**, the **Lean**(4), the **Collapse**, the **Heartbeat**, the **Bicycle**(2), the **Top-Rock**, the **Six-Step**, the **Worm**, and the **Toe/Heel-Walk**.

(See **Locking-and-Popping**, Mime, and Pantomime. Also see Break-Dancing, Underground Step-Listing, Teen-Dancing, and Open-Step. Also see Ska, Punk-Rock, Grunge, and New-Wave. Also see Hip-Hop, MTV-Style Dancing, Street-Dancer, Lyrical-Dancer, Jazz-Dance, and Urban-Dance. Also see Rock, Hard-Rock, Pop, Rhythm-and-Blues, Motown-Sound, Rap, and Heavy-Metal. Also see Underground Step-Listing.)

Loco-Motion: An Unstructured and Unleadable, **Novelty Fad** Coupledance that, at first, never was. The song came first then the dance. Little Eva's hit record, *"The Loco-Motion,"* was popular in the U.S. in 1962, who's song sang, *"Do the Loco-Motion with Me!"* But at first there was no actual dance for it. Little Eva had to work up its dance Movements after many asked, "How does this dance go?" The dance Mimicked a locomotive, and was one of a whole series of 1960s Mimicking dance Patterns, (see Hullie-Gullie.) This silly **Loco-Motion** dance, along with other silly Fad-Dances, was banned at Brigham Young University in 1966.
    (See Locomotor. Also see the Novelty-&-Fad Dances-of-the-1960s.)

Loddy-Lo: An American **Fad** dance of 1962. This had its own Eponymous record, the *"Loddy-Lo"* by *Chubby Checker.*
    [See Novelty-&-Fad Dances-of-the-1960s. Especially see Twist(2).]
    [From *www.bluejuice.org.au,* and *www.sixtiescity.com/Culture/dance.*]

Log: A **Novelty Fad** Coupledance of 1964. This had its own Eponymous record, *"The Log"* by the *Uglies.*
    (See Novelty-&-Fad Dances-of-the-1960s.) [From www.bluejuice.org.au]

Lone-Star-Stomp: Only this name for an American **Novelty** or **Fad** of the 1960s is listed simply as a Dance, Pattern, or Figure in the *"Dance Crazes of the Sixties."*
    (See Novelty-&-Fad Dances-of-the-1960s.) [From *www.sixtiescity.com/Culture/dance*]

Lookey-Dookey: A **Novelty Fad** dance of 1962. The **Lookey-Dookey** had its own Eponymous record, *"Lookey Dookey"* by *King Coleman.*
    (See Novelty-&-Fad Dances-of-the-1960s.) [From *Soul*, www.trinity.unimelb.edu.au]

Loop-De-Loop: An American **Fad** dance of 1964. This had its own Eponymous record, the *"Loop De Loop"* by the *Soul Sisters.*
    (See Novelty-&-Fad Dances-of-the-1960s.)
    [From *www.bluejuice.org.au,* and *www.sixtiescity.com/Culture/dance.*]

Louie-Louie or **Louie-Louie-Swivels:** Two Unleadable, General Coupledance Movements, Left or Right. Used mostly in **Country-Western** Line- or Partner-Dancing, and in **Folkdance.**
    Both Heels Swivel Inward and Outward. Executed with one Foot ahead of the other, with both Knees Softened and with Weight on both Balls-of-Feet.
    The following **Louie-Louie** description is from http://ourworld.compuserve.com:
        "LOUIE LOUIE - With feet 12 inches apart and with your weight on both feet, swivel your heels apart then, with your weight still on the balls of both feet, swivel your left heel to your right and your right heel to your left (your left heel should be slightly in front of your right heel). Bend your knees slightly this step move."
    (See Mashed-Potato, Charleston, Charleston-Crosses, and Quiver.)

Love-Bird: An American **Novelty** or **Fad** comical Solo-Dance or Maneuvers of the 1980s, in Cadence with the Music.

The following is from "*Eighties Dances*" - [www.inthe80s.com]:

"***The Love Bird:*** *Put your hands in front of you and join at the thumbs in the shape of a dove, as if you were doing shadow puppets. Clasp the 'dove' to your chest while turning side on and then release and flap the dove's wings while you push your hands away from your chest.*"

(See Novelty-&-Fad Dances-of-the-1980s. Also see Pantomime, Mime, and Mimicry-En-Masse. Also see Animal-Dances.)

Lowdown-Popcorn: Only this name for an American **Novelty** or **Fad** of the 1960s is listed simply as a Dance, Pattern, or Figure in the "*Dance Crazes of the Sixties*."

(See Novelty-&-Fad Dances-of-the-1960s.) [From *www.sixtiescity.com/Culture/dance*]

Luau: Only this name for an American **Novelty** or **Fad** of the 1960s is listed simply as a Dance, Pattern, or Figure in the "*Dance Crazes of the Sixties*."

(See Novelty-&-Fad Dances-of-the-1960s.) [From *www.sixtiescity.com/Culture/dance*]

Lurch: Only this name for an American **Novelty** or **Fad** of the 1960s is listed simply as a Dance, Pattern, or Figure in the "*Dance Crazes of the Sixties*."

(See Novelty-&-Fad Dances-of-the-1960s.) [From *www.sixtiescity.com/Culture/dance*]

Mac: A Stationary, Bouncing, Unleadable 1960s American **Novelty Fad** Singular dance Routine. The following loosely Choreographed Pattern was in vogue at Brigham Young University, Provo, Utah.

Danced at a 4/4 very Slow Tempo, The **Mac** was danced usually to Rock Music, in an open Shine Position, and Apart in Lines Formation or as a mass of dancers. Arms were swung, and Hands were loosely fisted with Wrists-Back. All commenced upon their Right Foot:

Single-Crosses: *BehindTapbouncetwice SideStepBounceTwice; behindtapBounceTwice sidestepbouncetwice.* Right Hand touches Left Thigh when Right Foot is Behind, and visa-versa.

Double-Bounces: Bounce 4 Counts with legs Spread and with Weight upon Heels, Moving one arm Sideways to Shoulder-Height.

Rocks: (*Slow And Slow And Slow And Slow;* Timing.) *SideStep recover ForStep recover BackStep recover SideStep;* repeat Opposite.

(See the Novelty-&-Fad Dances-of-the-1960s.) [Data mostly from "Rhythm and Dance" by Alma Heaton.]

Macarena (_mah-kuh-RAY-nuh_): Classified herein as in the **Audience-Participation-Dance** Category, and as a **Fad Dance**, the **Macarena** is the name of a **Group-Dance** danced Singularly and fashioned to fit the following particular Eponymous song:

Choreographed by two Latin men singing Los Del Rios. Based on a Samba Rhythm. In vogue the world over and extremely popular in the U.S. in the summer of 1996. Has many hand-gestures In-Place, then Hopping a Quarter-Turn:

1. Extend Right arm, Palm Down 2. Extend Left arm, Palm Down
3. Turn Right Palm Up   4. Turn Left Palm Up
5. Right Hand to Left shoulder   6. Left Hand to Right shoulder
7. Left Hand to Behind Head   8. Right Hand to Behind Head
9. Left Hand to Right hip   10. Right Hand to Left hip
11. Right Hand to Right hip   12. Left Hand to Left hip
13. Rotate hips three times   14. Hop 1/4-Turn Right and repeat.

(See Fila, Time-Warp, YMCA, and Ketchup-Dance, for similar Audience-Participation-Dances. Also see the Bomba, Chicken-Dance, Dirty-Dancing, Lambada, Punta y Soka, Quebradita, Teen-Dancing, and Urban-Dance; these were all Novelty or Fad-Dances in vogue in the 1980-90s.)

Madison: Known as **The-Madison** or **Madison-Time**, this is classified herein as in the **Audience-Participation-Dance** Category, and as both an amusing **Novelty** Dance and **Fad** Dance. Originating in 1957 in Columbus, Chicago or Detroit, this **Madison** is an American **Group-Dance** that was much in vogue in the 1960s, especially in Cleveland and Baltimore. _Ray Bryant Combo_ recorded _Its Madison Time_ as Eponymous Music for this dance. This **Madison** can be seen danced in the 1988 movie "_Hairspray,_" and also in the Broadway musical "_Hairspray._"

Following is from _Some Favorite 50s Dances_ -- [www.loti.com/fifties]:

"_**The Madison**. The Madison first started in the late 1950s and gained popularity in the 1960s. This dance was a little more complicated, and it was done in a group, rather than by a couple. There were several dance sequences with specific steps, and some of the sequences referred to some very popular television shows of the time, like Jackie Gleason._"

Following is from "_Dance Crazes of the Sixties_" -- [www.sixtiescity,com/Culture/]:

"_**The Madison / Madison Time**: ... The tune is in regular 4/4 time._

"_The dance consists of a basic step and a series of figures. Each figure occupies a fixed number of beats, but they are all different. Don't expect the figures to start on the first beat of a bar or at the beginning of a phrase as they go all across the music. The basic step occupies 6 beats or one and a half bars, so the step weaves pleasantly in and out of the tune. Always complete the basic step you're doing, then go straight into the figure, whatever the tune may be doing._

As if a song, picture the Basic-Step as the "_chorus;_" picture the interspersed Patterns as "_verses._"

The Madison's Basic-Step, a Six-Count (1 1/2 Measures) One-Step, repeated over-and-over by all dancers, is danced _1 2 3 4, 5 6._ (or,) _step Close Step tap, tap tap._ (or,) _diagforward....TouchClosedClap....DiagBackward....closetap....diagsidetap....closetap._

A Variation is:
diagforward....TouchClosedClap....DiagBackward....crosstap....diagsidetap....crosstap.

Note: To _Clap_, reach forward with both arms. On the _taps_, spread both Hands at Shoulder-Level and wave them Sideways. Look _Left_ when Stepping _Left_; look _Right_ when Stepping _Right_.   (Continued)

Madison: (Continued)
The following is from "*It's Madison Time!*" -- [*www.columbusmusichistory.com/*]:
      [Originating in Columbus, Ohio,] "*The Madison Dance, purportedly invented by William 'Bubbles' Holloway and the dancers at the LVA Club on Mt. Vernon Avenue in 1957.*
      "*... in the late 50's or early 60's, you know that the Madison is a line dance that was the biggest dance craze of the era, not just in the USA, but around the world. ... you have seen the kids on the dance floor in a long line, much like the Soul Train line of the 70's, doing the Madison.*
      "*The Madison is a basic back-and-forth shuffle done in a line, with a variety of 'call outs' for various steps, such as the Double Cross, the Cleveland Box, The Basketball (with Wilt Chamberlain), the Big 'M', The 'T' Time, The Jackie Gleason and The Birdland.*"
      Cueing this **Madison**, the **Patter from the Cuer** might sound like the following excerpts from *The Madison* -- [*www.albertj.btinternet.co.uk/*]:
      "*Two Up & Two Back with a big strong Turn & Back to the Madison, Hit It! Two Up & Two Back, Double Cross & come out of it with the Rifleman, Hit It! Big strong M, Erase It & back to the Madison, Hit It! It'll be 'T' Time and , Hit It! Big strong Cleveland Box & back to the Madison, , Hit It! Big strong Basketball with the Wilt Chamberlain Hook, , Hit It! Big strong Jackie Gleason & back to the Madison, , Hit It! Bird Land, then Hit It! Two Up & Two Back, Double Cross & Freeze!*"
      (See Double-Cross, Cleveland-Box, Basketball, Big-'M', 'T'-Time, Jackie-Gleason, Birdland, and Rifleman. Also see the Novelty-&-Fad Dances-of-the-1960s.)
      Notes: 1) The two Qued *Slow Slow QuickQuick Slow* Measures of "**Birdland**" could have been danced *forward Backward shake Shake shake...; backward Forward Shake shake Shake....*
      2) This **Madison** is one of the **Follow-the-Leader Dances** that includes the Bunny-Hop, Conga-Line, and the Letkajenkka.

Magoo: Only this name for an American **Novelty** or **Fad** of the 1960s is listed simply as a Dance, Pattern, or Figure in the "*Dance Crazes of the Sixties.*"
      (See Novelty-&-Fad Dances-of-the-1960s.) [From *www.sixtiescity.com/Culture/dance*]

Majestic: Only this name for an American **Novelty** or **Fad** of the 1960s is listed simply as a Dance, Pattern, or Figure in the "*Dance Crazes of the Sixties.*"
      (See Novelty-&-Fad Dances-of-the-1960s.) [From *www.sixtiescity.com/Culture/dance*]

Malibu: Only this name for an American **Novelty** or **Fad** of the 1960s is listed simply as a Dance, Pattern, or Figure in the "*Dance Crazes of the Sixties.*"
      (See Novelty-&-Fad Dances-of-the-1960s.) [From *www.sixtiescity.com/Culture/dance*]

Mambo-Boogie: Only this name for an American **Novelty** or **Fad** of the 1960s is listed simply as a Dance, Pattern, or Figure in the "*Dance Crazes of the Sixties.*"
      (See Novelty-&-Fad Dances-of-the-1960s.) [From *www.sixtiescity.com/Culture/dance*]

Manhattan-Stomp: Only this name for an American **Novelty** or **Fad** of the 1960s is listed simply as a Dance, Pattern, or Figure in the "_Dance Crazes of the Sixties_."
(See Novelty-&-Fad Dances-of-the-1960s.) [From _www.sixtiescity.com/Culture/dance_]

Marathon-Dancing or **Dance-Marathon** or **Non-Stop Dancing:** A Coupledancer's Term for a dated American Fad of the 1930s.

Dance Partners, lured by cash prizes and the possibility of attracting Hollywood talent scouts, participated in these grueling Dance-Marathons of the 1930s. Savvy entrepreneurs took advantage of the popularity of Coupledancing and the escape it offered from the desperate realities of the Great Depression. They would stage these nonstop contests of endurance which often lasted more than 48 hours.

Through days and nights, exhausted Marathon Coupledancers would hang on each other, Competing for the prize money in Marathon Dancehalls. The winners would be **the last Couple** still standing upright on the Dancefloor.

The following is from _Sonny Watson's Dance History_ -- [www.streetswing.com]:
"_1927_ - A _Dance Marathon_ was shut down due to 60 dancers collapsing in a dance marathon after only 20 hours. Los Angeles Herald - 4/22/1927._"

The following are excerpts from _Stepping Into the Past With a Quickstep_ -- [http://query.nytimes.com/gst/fullpage]:

"'_Marathon promoters would hire professional dance teams to get an audience caught up in a new craze,' she continued. 'Many, like the Moochie, where they danced together swiveling their feet -- twist, twist, twist, stop, twist, twist, twist, stop -- were very popular in 1933 but soon disappeared. ...'_

"_Dance marathons reached their frantic height, or perhaps depth, in the early 1930's (in their open-ended form, they were banned in 1937, for safety reasons). In the Depression's atmosphere of desperation, couples danced for days trying to win prize money. Frequently, they would grovel for coins thrown by spectators in interludes that were called 'floor showers'. A marathon would be strung out for weeks, and the survivors, not necessarily the fittest, would gain monetary fame in addition to cash. During the 15-minute rest periods that were permitted after every 45 minutes of dancing (there were also sleep breaks), participants would perform specialty acts, trying to attract radio advertising contracts._"

By the 1980s, Marathon Dancing had returned, but with emphasis more toward philanthropy, rather than Competition. Penn State had its 26th Dance-Marathon in february 1998, in which some 540 students Coupledanced to exhaustion for 48 hours, with no sitting and no sleeping. Proceeds pledged went to treat children with cancer. Their 25th Dance-Marathon had raised $1.5 million for charity in 1997.

(See Moochie.)

    <u>**Marchessi:**</u> A **Break-A-Way**(3) Stationary Shine-Step, this **Marchessi** is Leadable with cooperation. It is two-Measures in length (minimum) in 4/4 Time, Advanced **Coupledance** Pattern, suitable for both **Samba**s, and for the **Cumbia**. It is also suitable for when close-Coupledancing the **Pure-Balboa**, and for other dances. Its even Timing is *Quick Quick, Quick Quick; Quick Quick, Quick Quick; 1&2&3&4&.*

    Danced in a tight Spot with no Float or Rocking. The Man's Right Foot and the Lady's Left Foot remain as the center (Home) point, as Partners *Heel* Forward and *Toe* Rearward. Danced in Loose-Closed Position, or in Mush Position if for Balboa. Man Lowers Lady's Hand below Waist-Level to Lead her Right Foot. The Man's Left with his Lady's Right Feet, and their Joined Hands Move Forward and Backward in Unison, all in the same direction. Weight shifts as they Step **In-Place**.

    Man dances *heel Step toe Step heel Step toe Step.*

    Lady dances the corresponding Opposing Steps, *Toe step Heel step Toe step Heel step.*

    Similar to **Corta-Jaca**, and **Rocking-Chair**. (See SugarFoot, Sand-Step, Electric-Kicks, Rock, and Rocking-Steps.)

    <u>**March-of-the-Mods:**</u> Only this name for an American **Novelty** or **Fad** of the 1960s is listed simply as a Dance, Pattern, or Figure in the "*Dance Crazes of the Sixties*."

    (See Novelty-&-Fad Dances-of-the-1960s.) [From *www.sixtiescity.com/Culture/dance*]

    <u>**Martian-Hop:**</u> Only this name for an American **Novelty** or **Fad** of the 1960s is listed simply as a Dance, Pattern, or Figure in the "*Dance Crazes of the Sixties*."

    (See Novelty-&-Fad Dances-of-the-1960s.) [From *www.sixtiescity.com/Culture/dance*]

    <u>**Marvel:**</u> Only this name for an American **Novelty** or **Fad** of the 1960s is listed simply as a Dance, Pattern, or Figure in the "*Dance Crazes of the Sixties*."

    (See Novelty-&-Fad Dances-of-the-1960s.) [From *www.sixtiescity.com/Culture/dance*]

    <u>**Mash:**</u> Only this name for an American **Novelty** or **Fad** of the 1960s is listed simply as a Dance, Pattern, or Figure in the "*Dance Crazes of the Sixties*."

    (See Novelty-&-Fad Dances-of-the-1960s.) [From *www.sixtiescity.com/Culture/dance*]

    <u>**Mashed-Potato**</u> or **Mash-Potato** or **Mashed-Potatoes:** An Unstructured, partially Leadable, late-1950s or early 60s, **Novelty Fad** Singles and Coupledance of American origin, that Traveled. Eponymous to *DeeDee Sharp's* 1962 song, "*Mashed-Potato Time*," the dance Mimicked the act of **Mashing-Potatoes**, and was one of a whole series of 1960s Mimicking dance Patterns, (see Hullie-Gullie.) Two other 1962 records were "*Mashed Potatoes*" by *Joe Dee & The Starlighters*, and by *Nat Kendricks & Swans*. This silly **Mashed-Potato**, along with other silly Fad-Dances, was banned at Brigham Young University in 1966.

                                               (Continued)

Mashed-Potato: (Continued)

The **Mashed-Potato** was danced to 4/4 Time in moderate Tempo. Rhythm Timing was *AndQuick andquick AndQuick andquick.* Danced Backward and Forward with Softened-Knees, usually in Facing or Open Position; The **Mashed-Potato** involved Pressing the Dancefloor with extreme Swiveling Action on Balls-of-Feet, as if grinding a cigarette butt to extinguish it. This rather difficult Step had Scissors-type Movements with each Foot Swiveling Opposite the other.

Rearward Basic Step Pattern is *BehindSwivel1/4CCW behindswivel1/4CW BehindSwivel1/4CCW behindswivel1/4CW.*

Forward Basic Step Pattern is *infrontswivel1/4CW InFrontSwivel1/4CCW infrontswivel1/4CW InFrontSwivel1/4CCW.*

A Variation Step Pattern is *BehindSwivel1/4CCW behindswivel1/4CW InPlaceSwivelBothHeelsIn swivelbothheelsout*; (This Timing is *AndQuick andquick AndQuick quick.*)

Lady's Step Pattern varied from Identical to Mirror-Image Opposite Man's.

The following **Mashed-Potato** Basic-Steps are from "*Dance Crazes of the Sixties*":

"Right knee bends, right foot lifts off the floor, weight shifts to left foot.

"Pivot on left foot an eighth of a turn clockwise.

"Left foot pivots a quarter turn counterclockwise.

"Right foot steps close to left foot, then right foot pivots a quarter turn clockwise.

"Left knee bends and left foot lifts off the floor.

"Right foot pivots a quarter turn clockwise.

"Left foot steps close to right foot, then left foot pivots quarter turn clockwise.

"Right knee bends and right knee lifts off the floor.

"Left foot pivots quarter turn counterclockwise.

"Right foot steps close to left foot, then right foot pivots quarter turn clockwise.

"Left knee bends and left foot lifts off the floor.

"Right foot pivots quarter turn counterclockwise.

"Repeat."

Note: This **Mashed-Potato** is essentially the same dance as the **Monster-Mash**, but done with added creepy, ghoul-like Arm Movements and Transitions.

(See Charleston, Charleston-Crosses, Louie-Louie, Quiver, Fifth-Position-Break, Traveling-Latin-Crosses, and Twist. Also see Novelty-Dances, Fad-Dances, Novelty-and-Fad Genre, and the Novelty-&-Fad Dances-of-the-1960s. Also see Creamy-Mashed-Potato, Mash, Mashi, Mashed-Potatoes, and Mashed-Taters.)

[See *www.sixtiescity.com/Culture/dance.*]

Mashed-Potatoes: Only this name for an American **Novelty** or **Fad** of the 1960s is listed simply as a Dance, Pattern, or Figure in the "*Dance Crazes of the Sixties.*"

(See Novelty-&-Fad Dances-of-the-1960s.) [From *www.sixtiescity.com/Culture/dance*]

Mashed-Taters: Only this name for an American **Novelty** or **Fad** of the 1960s is listed simply as a Dance, Pattern, or Figure in the "*Dance Crazes of the Sixties.*"

(See Novelty-&-Fad Dances-of-the-1960s.) [From *www.sixtiescity.com/Culture/dance*]

Mashi: Only this name for an American **Novelty** or **Fad** of the 1960s is listed simply as a Dance, Pattern, or Figure in the "*Dance Crazes of the Sixties.*"
   (See Novelty-&-Fad Dances-of-the-1960s.) [From *www.sixtiescity.com/Culture/dance*]

Massacre-Stomp: Only this name for an American **Novelty** or **Fad** of the 1960s is listed simply as a Dance, Pattern, or Figure in the "*Dance Crazes of the Sixties.*"
   (See Novelty-&-Fad Dances-of-the-1960s.) [From *www.sixtiescity.com/Culture/dance*]

Matador: An American **Fad** dance of 1962. The **Matador** had its own Eponymous record, "*The Matador*" by *Major Lance.*
   (See Novelty-&-Fad Dances-of-the-1960s.)
   [From *Soul, www.trinity.unimelb.edu.au.* See *www.sixtiescity.com/Culture/dance.*]

Matrix: From Kingston, Jamaica, an Underground **Novelty Fad**, Singular- or Group-Dance Movement, associated with dancing **Dancehall/Ragga**, which, in turn, are outgrowths of **Ska/Reggae**. **Matrix** was and is danced mainly by youths of color.
   The following is from *Ragga Fashions*: [www.bbc.co.uk]
      "*Matrix - Stand with feet quite wide apart. Bend your back and place your hands in front. Move slowly from left to right, try to bend all the way down to the floor. Only for the very flexible.*"
   See **Dancehall**(2) for further explanation. (See Pike Position, and BackBend Position. Also see Bogle, Armstrong, Butterfly, Go-Go-Wine, Body-Basic-and-Exercise, Tate, and World-Dance. Also see Jerry-Springer, Prang, Heel-and-Toe, Na!Na!Na!, Screechie, Zip-It-Up, Drive-By, Shizzle-Ma-Nizzle, and Bin-Laden. Also see Underground Step-Listing.)

Maxixe pronounced `**Mah she she,**' or **Machich:** An early Brazilian **Coupledance** that became popular as a **Novelty** in the U.S.
   The **Lundu** dance, one of the most important music and dance Genres introduced into Brazil by the black slaves, became the first form of `black' music to be accepted by the aristocracy. Initially considered an erotic, lascivious and indecent dance, it became a solo song (*lundu-cancao*) in the 1700s. At the later part of the 1800s, its fusion with other imported dances, like the Polka, the Cuban Habanera, and lastly the Argentine Tango, gave birth to the first genuinely Brazilian Urban-Dance, the **Maxixe**, about 1880.
   The following is from *The Brazilian Sound* [www.thebraziliansound.com]:
      "*A Musical Melting Pot - Another important song and dance, maxixe, was born in Rio around 1880 from the meeting of lundu with Cuban habanera and polka (with influences from Argentinian tango coming later). Created by Afro-Braxilian musicians who were performing at parties in lower-middle-class-homes, maxixe was the first genuinely Brazilian dance, created from a synthesis of the above forms with additional voluptuous moves performed by the closely dancing couple. Maxixe gave as erotic and scandalous an impression as lundu had one hundred years earlier and lambada would one hundred years later.*"

(Continued)

Maxixe: (Continued)

The **Maxixe** was introduced in Paris in 1912, (some say in 1905,) then was imported into the U.S. by **Maurice Mouvet** in 1913. Mouvet created and/or introduced many new dance Steps for the U.S., including this subject **Maxixe**, but he called it the "**Machich**". The **Maxixe** was later danced to wide acclaim by the Castles. **Vernon and Irene Castle** had toned down the **Samba** of that day into their particular elegant **Maxixe**. Their popular song sheet music had directions, by its words, for Steps for this later particular dance. [Some from http://nfo.net/usa/dance]

Maxixe is played in rapid 2/4 Time, with a Slight Syncopation. The Basic Step is commonly danced in Butterfly Position, **Tilting**. The carriage of one's Head and arm Positioning are important.

Note that the **Machich** name is similar to the **Machichi** name, which is mentioned in the **Carioca** writeup herein.

(See Maxixe-Hold. Also see Pagode, Bahia-Carioca, LaBamba, Street-Samba, BossaNova, and Lambada; all are variations of the **Samba**. Also see Hi-Lo-Sweetheart. Also see Castle-Walk, Valse-Classique, Castle-Tango, Last-Waltz, Castle-Combination, and Lame-Duck; all written by the Castles. Also see Boston-Dip, Gaby-Glide, Hug-Me-Close, and Shiver-Dance; which were all Fad dances in vogue in the 1910s. Also see Texas-Tommy, Bunny-Hug, Grizzly-Bear, Turkey-Trot, and Ballin'-The-Jack, for dances of that time, where dance directions were given in their verses. Also see Folkdance Genre - Brazilian.)

Maxixe-Hold: Two flashy Closed Coupledance Positions, Left and Right; one Grasps Left Hands overhead, the other Grasps Right Hands overhead. The other two arms Grasp around the other's waist. The American **Samba**, or slower **Cumbia**, is most commonly Performed using the Maxixe-Hold in the Left Hands overhead Position.

(See Natural-Roll, Reverse-Barrel-Roll, and Maxixe.)

Melbourne-Shuffle: A **Novelty** or **Fad** dance of an unknown time, listed in "*Novelty and fad dances*" under [http://en.wikipedia.org/wiki].

Mess-Around(1): An Unleadable 1930s **Break-A-Way Novelty Fad** Pattern, usually Performed Stationary while dancing the **Big-Apple,** during a **Tap-Dance,** or as a **Soft-Shoe** Pause. Also suitable for the many **Swing** dances. This Pattern was later worked up again from the 1958 "*Mess Around*" record by *Ray Charles.*

Hands on hips, Feet Apart with Knees Bent, Move hips Circling with a Slight Bounce on Heels. Continue for eight Counts. (See Black-Bottom.)

For the **Big-Apple,** the **Mess-Around** was one of the **Break-A-Way** Genre. Wiggling their hips, certain **Break-A-Way** Patterns were danced. The original **Suzie-Q, Boogie-Back, Tack-Annie, Georgia-Grind, Praise-Allah!, Truckin', Peckin', Charleston, Shorty-George,** and other Break-A-Ways, were probably originated early by blacks; while **Spank-the-Baby, Rusty-Dusty, Pose-and-a-Peck,** the **Little-Apple,** the **Little-Peach, Mess-Around, Stomp-Off, Apple-Jacks,** and **Fall-Off-the-Log,** and other Break-A-Ways, were probably originated later by whites. Most all of these Patterns seem to have been influenced or derived from the classic **Lindy-Hop** and/or **Big-Apple** dances. See **Break-A-Way Glossary** for a more complete listing.

Mess-Around(2): The **Mess-Around** was an Unstructured and Unleadable, 1960s **Novelty Fad C**oupledance; possibly containing a re-invention of, or at least similar to, the earlier 1930s **Mess-Around**(1) gyrating and Lilting Pattern of dancing. At the time, Chubby Checker sang its Eponymous record, *"(Dance the) Mess Around"*. The following are a few excerpted lines from his words to it:

> *"Bout this dance called the Mess Around, baby dig what I'm puttin' down*
> *You can Pony with Tony, Twist with Mr. Lee*
> *But if you're gonna Mess Around, baby Mess Around with me"*

(See the Novelty-&-Fad Dances-of-the-1960s.)

Mexican-Hat-Dance or **LaRaspa** (*lah-rrahs-PAH*): **LaRaspa,** (Spanish for *the ruboff,*) is a Traditional Mexican **Folk** Coupledance of the **Jarabe** Genre. It is also a **Novelty** dance in the United States. **LaRaspa** is from Vera Cruz and has its own special Music. The Mexico City National Dance, **LaRaspa** depicts flirtation and conquest. It has a peculiar Hopping Step of its own, characterized by Blekings and Runs. **LaRaspa** is well known in the U.S. by this other name, the **Mexican-Hat-Dance**, and is an excellent fun dance for Exhibition.

(See Jarana, and LaBamba. Also see Spanish Dance, Quinceanera, Caballito-Blanco, Chiapanecas, Haupango, and Corrido.)

Mexican-Stretch: A **Novelty Fad** Coupledance of the 1960s. This had its own Eponymous record, the *"Mexican Stretch"* by *Tommy Bee & Juareztones.*
(See Novelty-&-Fad Dances-of-the-1960s.) [From www.bluejuice.org.au]

Michael-Jackson-Circles: An American **Novelty** or **Fad** Solo-Dance or Illusionary Maneuvers of the 1980s, in Cadence with the Music.
The following is from "*Eighties Dances*" - [www.inthe80s.com]:

> *"This dance is another one of Michael Jackson's illusionistic dances, but just because it's an illusion dance doesn't mean it doesn't need skill. What you should do is stand up straight and slide your feet in a box shape. When you do this you don't just want to slide them, you want to keep rotating from the balls of your feet to the heel. And because your feet are moving, your body should be moving in the same direction, and when going into the turns, kind of lean and pretend you're getting sucked in that way. And do this repeatedly."*

(See Novelty-&-Fad Dances-of-the-1980s.)

Milking-the-Cow: American **Fad** Solo comical Maneuvers of the 1980s in Cadence with the Music.
The following is from "*Eighties Dances*" - [www.inthe80s.com]:

> *"With your arms at right angles to your body, you pantomime the motion of milking a cow, accentuating the motion in your arms and shoulders."*

(See Novelty-&-Fad Dances-of-the-1980s. Also see Pantomime, Mime, and Mimicry-En-Masse. Also see Animal-Dances.)

Millie: Only this name for an American **Novelty** or **Fad** of the 1960s is listed simply as a Dance, Pattern, or Figure in the "_Dance Crazes of the Sixties._"
 (See Novelty-&-Fad Dances-of-the-1960s.) [From _www.sixtiescity.com/Culture/dance_]

Mint: Only this name for an American **Novelty** or **Fad** of the 1960s is listed simply as a Dance, Pattern, or Figure in the "_Dance Crazes of the Sixties._"
 (See Novelty-&-Fad Dances-of-the-1960s.) [From _www.sixtiescity.com/Culture/dance_]

Miserloo-Folkdance or **Three-Finger-Dance: Miserloo** is a Traditional **Folkdance**, a strung line of dancers. Believed to be of Armenian origin while its Music is possibly an old Greek folk song. It is also a **Novelty** dance in the United States.
 General Movements Throughout All Dancing: All dancers dance throughout in Unison upon Same-Foot. They dance Stretched in a string form throughout. The various Routines are repeated over and over. Comfortably spaced with all mostly Facing the room Center, dancers retain loosely Clasped Hands. Ideally, with no thumbs pressing, Right fingers Hook beneath while Left fingers Hook on top of their neighbor's fingers. The Lead-Dancer, (whether Man or Lady,) decides then indicates to all others which Routine is next to be danced. The Right side of each dancer tends to proceed Counter-Clockwise about the floor, with the Lead-Dancer steering or snaking.
 For the first Step of each Routine throughout the dance, all Stretch by Touching their Left Toe, Crossed Well In-Front, Across their Right Foot which they then Hold for a moment In-Place. For the second Movement of each Routine, all simultaneously Perform an extensively Sweeping Aerial-Ronde (or Floor-Ronde) using their left legs, Flaring Outward and Rearward (usually off) in an Arc from the Dancefloor, while each Right Supporting-Knee remains Bent until Ronde completion, whereupon their Left Toe Steps, Taking-Weight Locked-Behind. Completing this Lock-Behind, each dancer's Shoulders are still Facing Center. But this Locked-Step happens to be the beginning first of four Vine Steps.
 Also beginning at this Locked-Behind instant, the Lead-Dancer starts to signal the next Routine to be danced, by visibly displaying either one, two or three raised fingers of the raised Right Hand.
 Addressing each "_**beginning Routine-Section**_", all Rhythm Timing begins with a _veryslow veryslow quick Slow quick Slow slow_, which all utilizes three Speeds. That Lock-Behind first _quick_ Step Spirals 3/8 CW, the second is a Forward _Slow_ Step, third is a _quick_ Forward-Swivel 3/8 CCW, fourth is a _Slow_ Back-Step. Next comes one _slow_ Back-Step (a Step which Spirals 1/4 or 3/8 CW upon the Two- and Three-Fingers Routines). Neglecting the first two _veryslows_, the remaining _quick Slow quick Slow slow_ equals _spiral3/8CW TinyForward tinydiagforswivel3/8CCW TinyBack tinyback._
 All Routines end with a _Forward close Forward back Close backslowspiral1/4CW Stomp._
Timing for this "_**final Routine-Section**_" is _Quick quick Slow quick Quick veryslow VerySlow._
This section is first and second danced Toward then Away from RLOD. This ends with the Left Foot Spiraling Slowly Toward Facing Center, the Right Foot then Stomps Open Sideways and Holds.
 One-Finger-Routine: Upon displaying a raised Right index finger by the Lead-Dancer, the "_**beginning Routine-Section**_" is danced, immediately followed by dancing the "_**final Routine-Section**_".   (Continued)

Miserloo-Folkdance: (Continued)

Two-Finger-Routine: Upon displaying two raised Right-Hand fingers by the Lead-Dancer, and between the "***beginning Routine-Section***" and the "***final Routine-Section***", two *Slow* Steps are added toward the Center. After the Left Foot has Spiraled 1/4 CW, these are danced *Forward crossforswivel1/4CCW.*

Three-Finger-Routine: Upon displaying Three raised Right-Hand fingers by the Lead-Dancer, and between the "***beginning Routine-Section***" and the "***final Routine-Section***", four Steps are added Down-Line. Their Timing is *quick Slow quick Slow*. These Steps are danced *tinybackspiral3/8CW TinyForward tinydiagforswivel3/8CCW TinyBack.* (Then comes the "*tinyback*" Step then the "***final Routine-Section***".)

[See Same-Foot: Lead-Dancer; Ronde, Aerial; Ronde, Floor; Stomp(1); Spiral; Swivel; Center-of-Hall; CW; CCW; RLOD; and Line-of-Motion.]

Mississippi-Cutback: A **Novelty Fad** dance of 1963. The **Mississippi-Cutback** was danced to the record, "*Jimmy Mack*" by *Martha Reeves & The Vandellas.*

(See FrontCut. Also see Novelty-&-Fad Dances-of-the-1960s.) [From *Soul*, www.trinity.unimelb.edu.au]

Mod: A **Novelty Fad** Coupledance of 1965. This had its own Eponymous record, "*Doin' The Mod*" by *The Flies.*

(See Novelty-&-Fad Dances-of-the-1960s.) [From www.bluejuice.org.au]

Mojo-Workout: Only this name for an American **Novelty** or **Fad** of the 1960s is listed simply as a Dance, Pattern, or Figure in the "*Dance Crazes of the Sixties.*"

(See Novelty-&-Fad Dances-of-the-1960s.) [From *www.sixtiescity.com/Culture/dance*]

Molecule-A-GoGo: Only this name for an American **Novelty** or **Fad** of the 1960s is listed simply as a Dance, Pattern, or Figure in the "*Dance Crazes of the Sixties.*"

(See Novelty-&-Fad Dances-of-the-1960s.) [From *www.sixtiescity.com/Culture/dance*]

Money-Musk: A Vintage American **Novelty Fad Contra-Dance** of the 1840s-1870s.

By Elias Howe in his Vintage **1862** book, "_American Dancing Master, and Ball-Room Prompter_": "MONEY MUSK.

"_First couple join hands and swing once and a half round, go below 2d couple, (the 1st lady goes below 2d gent. on the outside, 1st gent. at the same time goes below and between 2d and 3d ladies), forward and back six, 1st couple swing three quarters round, 1st gent. goes between 2d couple (on the inside), first lady goes between 3d couple inside, forward and back six, 1st couple swing three quarters round to place (below one couple), right and left four._"

By Prof. M.J.Koncen circa **1880** in his "_Quadrille Call Book and Ball Room Guide_": "THE MONEY MUSK.

"_1. The first couple cross right hands and swing once and a half around._

"_2. Then go below one couple, forward and back six._

"_3. Right hand to your partner and swing half around,_

"_4. Forward and back,_

"_5. Swing to your places and right and left four._

"_Repeat and so on._"

(See the Grizzly-Bear, Lanciers, and Washington-Post-Twostep; which were all Novelty Fads in vogue in the 1800s.) [Much from memory.loc.gov]

Monkey: The **Monkey** was an Unstructured and Unleadable, **Novelty Fad** Singles dance in the U.S. in the 1960s. In 1963, it is believed that a _Major Lance_ recorded _Monkey Time._ In 1964, _Jay, Bob and The Hawks_ put out _The Monkey, The Watusi_, and _The Ska_ records. Perhaps they did not originate the songs. Today, the **Monkey** is often danced to **Ska** music.

Having been derived from The **Frug**, The **Monkey** was related to The **Swim**, The **Dog**, The **Watusi**, The **Waddle**, and The **Jerk** dances. These 1960s dances were free and individualistic. People enmasse, mostly teens with long hair, were dancing by themselves and inventing as they danced. The dance Mimicked a **Monkey**, and was one of a whole series of 1960s Mimicking dance Patterns, (see Hullie-Gullie.) This silly **Monkey**, along with other silly Fad-Dances, was banned at Brigham Young University in 1966.

The **Monkey** was danced In-Place Singularly or as a Couple Facing. Danced Deep-Into-Knees and with a Bobbing Head, dancers Swung hips Side-to-Side and sometimes Stepped, with the following added arm Movements: With both fists clenched, dancers would pump their arms Up and Down in Sequence to the Music, with one Up and one Down, as with The **Pony**.

The following is from "_Dance Crazes of the Sixties_" along with a 4-pictures Sequence (showing Patrick Kerr?) and the following writeup. [_www.sixtiescity.com/Culture/dance_]:

"_Taking a fighter's crouch, face your partner and stand with feet apart, knees bent. Bend arms and close fists, thumbs up._

"_Bend forward from waist to the left, raising right arm. As your body bobs, your head also bobs forward on each count. The whole effect is jerky._

"_Straighten up to original position._

"_Bend forward from waist toward your partner, facing centre, switch arms as you do so._

"_Straighten up to original position. Hands and head should give impression of monkey holding two bananas._

"_Bend forward from waist to the right. Straighten up to original position._

"_Bob back to centre, bending at waist and again switching hands._

"_Repeat entire pattern. Counts are double time, hitting every accent in the music._"

(See the Mouse, and the Novelty-&-Fad Dances-of-the-1960s.)

Monkey-Bird: Only this name for an American **Novelty** or **Fad** of the 1960s is listed simply as a Dance, Pattern, or Figure in the "*Dance Crazes of the Sixties*."
 (See Novelty-&-Fad Dances-of-the-1960s.) [From *www.sixtiescity.com/Culture/dance*]

Monkey-Dog: An American **Fad** dance of the 1960s. This had its own Eponymous record, the "*Monkey Dog*" by *O.V.Wright*.
 (See Novelty-&-Fad Dances-of-the-1960s.)
 [From *www.bluejuice.org.au*. See *www.sixtiescity.com/Culture/dance.*]

Monkey-Donkey: Only this name for an American **Novelty** or **Fad** of the **1960s** is listed simply as a Dance, Pattern, or Figure in the "*Dance Crazes of the Sixties*."
 (See Novelty-&-Fad Dances-of-the-1960s.) [From *www.sixtiescity.com/Culture/dance*]

Monkey-Glide: An American "*animal dance*", a **Novelty Fad** Coupledance in vogue about 1912 to 1914. Derided by newspapers, magazines, church officials, and even by Pope Pius X, as "such foolish and decadent behavior," over one hundred of these dances were created during this period.
 (See Animal-Dances, Bull-Frog-Hop, Bunny-Hug, Buzzard-Lope, Camel-Walk, Chicken-Reel, Chicken-Scratch, Crab-Step, Fish-Walk, Gotham-Gobble, Horse-Trot, Kangaroo-Dip, Kangaroo-Hop, Lame-Duck, Possum-Trot, Snake, and Turkey-Trot; which were all Animal-Dances of 1910-1914.)

Monkey-Hop: Only this name for an American **Novelty** or **Fad** of the 1960s is listed simply as a Dance, Pattern, or Figure in the "*Dance Crazes of the Sixties*."
 (See Novelty-&-Fad Dances-of-the-1960s.) [From *www.sixtiescity.com/Culture/dance*]

Monkey-Jerk: Only this name for an American **Novelty** or **Fad** of the 1960s is listed simply as a Dance, Pattern, or Figure in the "*Dance Crazes of the Sixties*."
 (See Novelty-&-Fad Dances-of-the-1960s.) [From *www.sixtiescity.com/Culture/dance*]

Monkey-Jump: Only this name for an American **Novelty** or **Fad** of the 1960s is listed simply as a Dance, Pattern, or Figure in the "*Dance Crazes of the Sixties*."
 (See Novelty-&-Fad Dances-of-the-1960s.) [From *www.sixtiescity.com/Culture/dance*]

Monkey-Shine: Only this name for an American **Novelty** or **Fad** of the 1960s is listed simply as a Dance, Pattern, or Figure in the "*Dance Crazes of the Sixties*."
 (See Novelty-&-Fad Dances-of-the-1960s.) [From *www.sixtiescity.com/Culture/dance*]

Monkey-Ska: A **Novelty Fad** dance of 1963. The **Monkey-Ska** had its own Eponymous record, "*Monkey Ska*" by *Derrick Harriot*.
 (See the Novelty-&-Fad Dances-of-the-1960s.) [From *Soul*, www.trinity.unimelb.edu.au]

Monkey-Stroll: Only this name for an American **Novelty** or **Fad** of the 1960s is listed simply as a Dance, Pattern, or Figure in the "_Dance Crazes of the Sixties._"
(See Novelty-&-Fad Dances-of-the-1960s.) [From _www.sixtiescity.com/Culture/dance_]

Monkey-Walk: Only this name for an American **Novelty** or **Fad** of the 1960s is listed simply as a Dance, Pattern, or Figure in the "_Dance Crazes of the Sixties._"
(See Novelty-&-Fad Dances-of-the-1960s.) [From _www.sixtiescity.com/Culture/dance_]

Monkey-Wobble: Only this name for an American **Novelty** or **Fad** of the 1960s is listed simply as a Dance, Pattern, or Figure in the "_Dance Crazes of the Sixties._"
(See Novelty-&-Fad Dances-of-the-1960s.) [From _www.sixtiescity.com/Culture/dance_]

Monster-Mash: An Unstructured and Unleadable, early 60s, **Novelty Fad** Singles and Coupledance of American origin, that Traveled. Its Eponymous music, "**Monster-Mash,**" was a 1962 hit record by _Bobby Pickett_ and the _Crypt Kickers._
The dance Mimicked the Monster, Frankenstein, and was one of a whole series of 1960s Mimicking dance Patterns, (see Hullie-Gullie.) In a voice like _Boris Karloff's,_ (_Bobby's,_) it's song sang, "_It's The Monster-Mash!_" Dancers Singularly danced the dance of The **Mashed-Potato,** but in addition, each dancer would hold Raised arms in various grotesque, goulish contortions. This silly **Monster-Mash,** along with other silly Fad-Dances, was banned at Brigham Young University in 1966.
See the **Mashed-Potato** for Step details, since this **Monster-Mash** is essentially the same dance as the **Mashed-Potato,** done with creepy, ghoul-like Arm Movements and Transitions.
(See Charleston, Charleston-Crosses, Louie-Louie, Quiver, Fifth-Position-Break, Traveling-Latin-Crosses, and Twist. Also see Novelty-Dances, Fad-Dances, Novelty-and-Fad Genre, and the Novelty-&-Fad Dances-of-the-1960s.) [See _www.sixtiescity.com/Culture/dance._]

Moochie: A **Novelty Fad** Coupledance popular in England from 1930 to 1933.
The following is an excerpt from "_Stepping Into the Past With a Quickstep_" -- [http://query.nytimes.com/gst/fullpage]:
    "'_Marathon promoters would hire professional dance teams to get an audience caught up in a new craze,' she continued. 'Many, like the **Moochie**, where they danced together swiveling their feet -- twist, twist, twist, stop, twist, twist, twist, stop -- were very popular in 1933 but soon disappeared. ...'_"
(See Marathon-Dancing.)

Moon-Step-Twist: A **Novelty Fad** Coupledance of 1965. This had its own Eponymous record, the "_Moon Step Twist_" by _Wane Sherwood._
(See Novelty-&-Fad Dances-of-the-1960s.) [From www.bluejuice.org.au]

Moonstomp: A **Novelty Fad** dance of 1968. The **Moonstomp** had its own Eponymous record, "_Skinhead Moonstomp_" by _Symarip._
(See the Novelty-&-Fad Dances-of-the-1960s.) [From _Soul,_ www.trinity.unimelb.edu.au]

Moon-Walk or Back-Floats or Back-Slide or Walking-Against-the-Wind: A Novelty Fad and one of the Basic-Moves-for-Break-Dancing, this Moon-Walk is part of the Electric-Boogie style of Break-Dancing, which, in turn, is one major part of Hip-Hop. The Moon-Walk is an almost Stationary Singular-Dance Movement, that is also suitable for certain Swings and for still other dances.

Toe-first Rearward Stepping, then the Sliding of the Stepped Foot Forward, that gives the appearance of Forward Motion when the dancer is actually Stepping Backward. The dancer fairly remains in one Spot. The Moon-Walk is the major item of the Glides Moves.

The following is from "*Electric Boogie*," [www.actor.force9.co.uk/]:

"By the time the Harlem Pop Lockers were formed, the Electric Boogie had added the `Float' move. The Back Float or `Moon Walk' was first made commercially popular by James Brown, then Jeffrey Daniels of Shalimar in the early 80's, and most memorably by Michael Jackson."

The following is from "*Definition of Breakdancing*," [www.wordiq.com]:

"Moonwalk: A move where a dancer slides backward while their legs appear to be walking forward."

The following is from the "*Eighties Dances*," [www.inthe80s.com]:

"Moonwalk: ... Leave one foot in place and drag the other back, lifting up the heel. Repeat with the other foot while walking backwards."

Certain people have claimed that this Moon-Walk was born from a Step by Fred Astaire. Moon-Walking has since become a Term for someone claiming to do something but in reality doing nothing.

Some other Electric-Boogie Genre of Mime "Moves" are the Lock(2), the Tick, the King-Tut, the Pop(3), the Wave(1), the Glides, Floating(2), the Robot, the SlowMo, the Lean(4), the Collapse, the Heartbeat, the Bicycle(2), the Toe/Heel-Walk, the Top-Rock, the Six-Step, and the Worm.

Similar to SideSlide. [See Break-Dancing, Electric-Boogie, Cake-Walk, Walkin'-the-Dog, Majorette-Strutting-with-Baton, Praise-You, Running-Man, Step-Scoot, Camel-Walk(3), Stationary-Copas, Heel-and-Toe, Side-Touches, and Syncopated-Splits. Also see Underground Step-Listing.]

Mope: Only this name for an American Novelty or Fad of the 1960s is listed simply as a Dance, Pattern, or Figure in the "*Dance Crazes of the Sixties*."

(See Novelty-&-Fad Dances-of-the-1960s.) [From *www.sixtiescity.com/Culture/dance*]

Moppety-Stomp: Only this name for an American Novelty or Fad of the 1960s is listed simply as a Dance, Pattern, or Figure in the "*Dance Crazes of the Sixties*."

(See Novelty-&-Fad Dances-of-the-1960s.) [From *www.sixtiescity.com/Culture/dance*]

Mother-Goose: Only this name for an American Novelty or Fad of the 1960s is listed simply as a Dance, Pattern, or Figure in the "*Dance Crazes of the Sixties*."

(See Novelty-&-Fad Dances-of-the-1960s.) [From *www.sixtiescity.com/Culture/dance*]

Mother-Popcorn: Only this name for an American Novelty or Fad of the 1960s is listed simply as a Dance, Pattern, or Figure in the "*Dance Crazes of the Sixties*."

(See Novelty-&-Fad Dances-of-the-1960s.) [From *www.sixtiescity.com/Culture/dance*]

Mountain-Stomp: Only this name for an American **Novelty** or **Fad** of the 1960s is listed simply as a Dance, Pattern, or Figure in the "_Dance Crazes of the Sixties_."
(See Novelty-&-Fad Dances-of-the-1960s.) [From _www.sixtiescity.com/Culture/dance_]

Mouse: An American **Fad** Singular-Dance of 1962. This had its own Eponymous record, the "_Mouse_" by _Lou Monte_.
The following is from _Dance Crazes of the Sixties_ -- [From _www.sixtiescity.com/Culture/dance_]
        "**The Mouse** _is another monkey variation. Put your thumbs to your ears, wiggle your fingers, put your upper teeth over your lower lip - and keep the beat with your knees. That's the whole mouse._"
(See Monkey, and Novelty-&-Fad Dances-of-the-1960s.) [Some from _www.bluejuice.org.au_]

Mozart-Stomp: Only this name for an American **Novelty** or **Fad** of the 1960s is listed simply as a Dance, Pattern, or Figure in the "_Dance Crazes of the Sixties_."
(See Novelty-&-Fad Dances-of-the-1960s.) [From _www.sixtiescity.com/Culture/dance_]

Mule: An American **Fad** dance (Coupledance?) of the 1960s. It's Eponymous Music was "_Ride Your Mule_" by _Marvin Holmes_.
(See Novelty-&-Fad Dances-of-the-1960s.)
[From _www.bluejuice.org.au_. See _www.sixtiescity.com/Culture/dance_.]

Mumble-Shing-A-Ling: Only this name for an American **Novelty** or **Fad** of the 1960s is listed simply as a Dance, Pattern, or Figure in the "_Dance Crazes of the Sixties_."
(See Novelty-&-Fad Dances-of-the-1960s.) [From _www.sixtiescity.com/Culture/dance_]

Munch: Only this name for an American **Novelty** or **Fad** of the 1960s is listed simply as a Dance, Pattern, or Figure in the "_Dance Crazes of the Sixties_."
(See Novelty-&-Fad Dances-of-the-1960s.) [From _www.sixtiescity.com/Culture/dance_]

Muppet: American **Fad** Solo comical Maneuvers of the 1980s in Cadence with the Music.
The following is from "_Eighties Dances_" - [www.inthe80s.com]:
        "**The Muppet:** _You make your hands into fists and hold them close together, then move them to one side and shake them twice, then twice on the other side. This is like the way 'the Muppets' on 'Sesame Street' dance._"
(See Novelty-&-Fad Dances-of-the-1980s. Also see Pantomime, Mime, and Mimicry-En-Masse.)

My-Dog: A **Novelty Fad** Coupledance of the 1960s. It's Eponymous Music was "_Oscar's Dog_" by _Oscar Bishop_.
(See Novelty-&-Fad Dances-of-the-1960s.) [From www.bluejuice.org.au]

Na!Na!Na! or **Angel:** From Kingston, Jamaica, an Underground **Novelty Fad**, Singular- or Group-Dance Movement, associated with dancing **Dancehall/Ragga**, which, in turn, are outgrowths of **Ska/Reggae.** **Na!Na!Na!** was and is danced mainly by youths of color.

The following is from *Ragga Fashions*: [www.bbc.co.uk]

"*Na!Na!Na! - Stand with feet apart. Step to the left and step to the right with quick movements. Flick your head in time with your steps, very similar to Body Popping. For originality you can vary the steps taken and the speed.*"

See **Dancehall**(2) for further explanation. (Also see Bogle, Armstrong, Butterfly, Go-Go-Wine, Body-Basic-and-Exercise, Tate, and World-Dance. Also see Jerry-Springer, Prang, Heel-and-Toe, Screechie, Zip-It-Up, Drive-By, Shizzle-Ma-Nizzle, Matrix, and Bin-Laden. Also see Underground Step-Listing.)

Nanigo or **Nanigo-Motion:** A very primitive and savage dance in very Fast 6/8 Time, that was Performed during tribal ceremonies or voodoo rituals. Also, the **Nanigo** is a Latin **Novelty Fad** Coupledance of Afro-Cuban origin, danced at Cuban Carnivals. The **Nanigo** has also been adapted and developed into a Step used in a certain Swing dance. Our deceased world-famous dancing friend, *Laure Haile*, has left notes about this **Nanigo-Motion**. The following are excerpts from these notes:

"*Nanigo motion is a particular styling used in Afro-Cuban dances. It is especially good as an advanced styling in Rumba, Mambo, ChaCha Bossa Nova, etc. Many exhibition dances use Nanigo as a special accent to add spice to various steps.*

"*Nanigo motion is a relaxation of the muscles in the small of the back -- arch your back and a contraction of the hips or pelvic region -- bring the hips forward to a straight posture. Use these two movements alternately. It is not a rib-cage action, it is strictly a hip action, from back to forward, not side to side. Single Nanigo is just one motion per beat. Hips back on count 1, hips forward on count 2. If dancing the rumba box, each quick step gets one motion, the slow step gets 2 motions, from back to forward. Always start with the hips back on the 1st count.*

"*Double Nanigo has 2 motions per beat. The first is back, the 2nd is forward, the forward motion takes the accent. Count could be 'and 1 and 2' etc. Hips would be back on all 'and' counts, and forward on the number counts. Thus, in dancing the box step, the slow counts would take 4 hip motions, 'back-forward-back-forward.' For practice, hum Turkey in the Straw, put your weight on the right foot, and using the left foot in a 'stomping' manner like in real 'hoedown,' keep both knees straight on counts 1 and 3, and bend both knees on counts 2 and 4. The stomping action will be on counts 1 and 3, (the downbeats). The hips will be back when the knees are straight. When the upbeats of 2 and 4 are counted, the knees will be bent, and the hips will move forward. Alternate. When proficient at Turkey in the Straw, try Afro-Cuban Mambos, Rumbas, etc. Lots o' luck!*"

Napoleon: Only this name for an American **Novelty** or **Fad** of the 1960s is listed simply as a Dance, Pattern, or Figure in the "*Dance Crazes of the Sixties*."

(See Novelty-&-Fad Dances-of-the-1960s.) [From *www.sixtiescity.com/Culture/dance*]

Neo-Tango or **New-Tango**(2): A series of Novelty **Fad** Coupledances, in vogue perhaps beginning about 1999 and covering a broad range of experimental Styles. With characteristics that are so Generalized, this Tango sub-Genre has various mini-Styles that have not yet been settled into any definitely defineable Tango dance Style. Still it can be said that all **Neo-Tango**s are of the **Rotary-Tango** type and are Generally part of the **Argentine Tango** Genre.

All of these **Neo-Tango** sub-Genre of Tango spinoffs often riles the Traditional Tango Purist who is normally very resistant to change.   Such Purists often picture all of these hated **Neo-Tango**s as vulgar abominations of that which they love. With blasting Music in 4/4 Time, this **Neo-Tango** sub-Genre includes the **Swango**, so popular in 2005.

See **Swango**. [Also see Tango-Nuevo, Liquid-Tango, Martial-Arts, and Capoeira. Also see Boleo, Gancho, and Sentada. Also see Traditional, Traditional-Dancing, Nuzzle-Dancing, and Tango-Trance. Also see Structured(1), Traditional-Dance-Doctrine, Accepted-Dancing-Mores, Deviating, Innovating-Dancer, and Recalcitrant-Dancer.]

New-Kids-Move: A **Novelty Fad** dance of the 1980s. How to dance the **New-Kids-Move** should be found on a VHS Video by Christy Lane (www.centralhome.com).

The following is from "*New Kids on the Block*" (www.geocities.com):

"*New Kids On The Block or later called **NKOTB** is a group of five, white, clean-cut teens from Boston. It was 1986 when the group was formed by producer Maurice Starr, the man behind New Edition. NKOTB was the very first teen boy band to hit the music industry with a blast. They made tons of followers all over the world. Wherever they go, screamin' fans were there to watch them strut their stuff. These good-looking dudes have good tunes with the right moves.*"

The following is from "***Eighties Dances***" (www.inthe80s.com):

"***The New Kids Dance*** - *You start out with feet at arms length apart kick out your right foot and bring it back to the center, same thing with the left foot and then have both feet in the center.*"

(See Break-Dancing, Bugg, Cabbage-Patch, Chicken-Dance, Funky-Twist, Moonwalk, Pac-Man, Popping, Robocop, Roger-Rabbit, Running-Man, Snake, Tickin', Wavin', and the Worm; which were all Novelty Fads in vogue in the 1980s.)

New-Low-Down: A **Novelty Fad** dance of 1970. The **New-Low-Down** had its own Eponymous record, "*The New Low Down*" by *Bill 'Bojangles' Robinson.*
[From *Soul*, www.trinity.unimelb.edu.au]

Nick-Nack-Hully-Gully: Only this name for an American **Novelty** or **Fad** of the 1960s is listed simply as a Dance, Pattern, or Figure in the "*Dance Crazes of the Sixties.*"
(See Novelty-&-Fad Dances-of-the-1960s.) [From *www.sixtiescity.com/Culture/dance*]

NightClub Tango: See Cafe Tango.

NightLife or **Traveling-Sand-Step** or **Progressive-Sand-Step** or **Toe-Side-Heel-Cross:** A Leadable one-Measure, Sideward-Traveling, Butterfly-Break-A-Way Coupledance Figure and a form of Parallel-Travel. Suitable for Eastern **Swing**, American **Onestep**, and **Four-Count**. When repeated for two Measures in Sequence, **Curls** can be Coupledanced in the **Balboa Swing-Bal** as a Break-A-Way to Butterfly Position. **Curls** can also be cooperatively Coupledanced the Eight-Counts of **Pure-Balboa** entirely in Mush Position, but using the noted Timing.

The name **NightLife** is taken from a popular "*I Love the NightLife*" D'Aloise Routine.

Partners dance Facing in Butterfly Position, Leaning into each other, or resisting each other by Tension in the arms, and then Swiveling their Bodies with CBM. Man usually Faces Wall. Figure Travels Slightly to the Man's Left, normally Toward Line-of-Dance, in *Slow Slow Slow Slow* 4/4 Timing. Lady's part is Mirror-Image Opposite Man's.

Man Steps to Left *toeinSwivelTorso1/8CW SwivelTorso1/4CCW* In-Place *swiveltorso1/4CWHeelTouch* In-Place *swiveltorso1/4CCWCrossInFront*. Lady Follows.

Figure is usually repeated in Sequence many times.

(See Sand-Step, Suzy-Q, and Traveling-SugarFoot. Also see Balboa Step-Listing.)

Night-Stomp: Only this name for an American **Novelty** or **Fad** of the 1960s is listed simply as a Dance, Pattern, or Figure in the "*Dance Crazes of the Sixties*."

(See Novelty-&-Fad Dances-of-the-1960s.) [From *www.sixtiescity.com/Culture/dance*]

Nitty-Gritty: An American **Fad** dance of 1965. The **Nitty-Gritty** had its own Eponymous record, "*Nitty Gritty*" by *Shirley Ellis*.

(See Novelty-&-Fad Dances-of-the-1960s.)

[From *Soul*, *www.trinity.unimelb.edu.au*. See *www.sixtiescity.com/Culture/dance*.]

Okey-Cokey: See Hokey-Pokey.

Olympic-Shuffle: Only this name for an American **Novelty** or **Fad** of the 1960s is listed simply as a Dance, Pattern, or Figure in the "*Dance Crazes of the Sixties*."

(See Novelty-&-Fad Dances-of-the-1960s.) [From *www.sixtiescity.com/Culture/dance*]

Oobie-Doobie: Only this name for an American **Novelty** or **Fad** of the 1960s is listed simply as a Dance, Pattern, or Figure in the "*Dance Crazes of the Sixties*."

(See Novelty-&-Fad Dances-of-the-1960s.) [From *www.sixtiescity.com/Culture/dance*]

Ooh-Poo-Pah-Doo: Only this name for an American **Novelty** or **Fad** of the 1960s is listed simply as a Dance, Pattern, or Figure in the "*Dance Crazes of the Sixties*."

(See Novelty-&-Fad Dances-of-the-1960s.) [From *www.sixtiescity.com/Culture/dance*]

Op: Only this name for an American **Novelty** or **Fad** of the 1960s is listed simply as a Dance, Pattern, or Figure in the "*Dance Crazes of the Sixties.*"
    (See Novelty-&-Fad Dances-of-the-1960s.) [From *www.sixtiescity.com/Culture/dance*]

Ops-and-Ops: Only this name for an American **Novelty** or **Fad** of the 1960s is listed simply as a Dance, Pattern, or Figure in the "*Dance Crazes of the Sixties.*"
    (See Novelty-&-Fad Dances-of-the-1960s.) [From *www.sixtiescity.com/Culture/dance*]

Ostrich: An American **Fad** dance of the 1960s. This had its own Eponymous record, "*The Ostrich*" by the *Primatives.*
    (See Novelty-&-Fad Dances-of-the-1960s.)
    [From *www.bluejuice.org.au.* See *www.sixtiescity.com/Culture/dance.*]

Pachanga (*pah-CHAHN-gah*) or **Pachango:** An authentic Latin **Salsa** Folkdance. One of the many variations of the **Mambo**, the **Pachanga** is a Coupledance that became popular as a **Novelty Fad** for awhile in the U.S. in the late 1950s. **Pachanga**'s Caballo music is generally faster than that for **Rumba** but slower than that for **Mambo**. **Pachanga** is often danced with excessive posterior Twisting.
    The star of **Pachanga** was a Columbian named Eduardo Davidson; he introduced the **Marencumbae** Coupledance to Santiago, Cuba. The original music was named **La Pachanga**, and it had the title, **"Marencumbae"** underneath it. Eduardo made up more Step Patterns for his dance, which was then introduced into the U.S. with new kinds of **ChaCha** Steps. Mistakenly misnamed **"Charanga"** for awhile by a non-English speaker, the name was soon corrected to **Pachanga** in 1956.
    (See Son, Charanga, Salsa-Casino-Rueda, and Clave-Beat. Also see the Bambuco, Boogaloo, Bop, Bunny-Hop, Calypso, Creep, Fish, Flea-Hop, Frug, Guapacha, Hand-Jive, Hitch-Hiker, Hokey-Pokey, Hullie-Gullie, Jerk, Limbo-Rock, Mashed-Potato, Monkey, Plena, Pony, Rock-and-Around, Scooter, Slide, Strole, Surfers, Swim, Tumba-Cha, Twist, Twister, and the Watusi; which were all Novelty Fads in vogue in the 1950-60s. Also see Novelty-&-Fad Dances-of-the-1960s.)

Pac-Man: A **Novelty Fad** dance of the 1980s. How to dance the **Pac-Man** should be found on a VHS Video by Christy Lane (www.centralhome.com).
    Pac-Man, the classic 1980s arcade game, has been voted the greatest video game character of all time. **Pac-Man** is a yellow "C" shaped mouth that is Moved Linearly and eats "monsters."
    (See Break-Dancing, Bugg, Cabbage-Patch, Chicken-Dance, Funky-Twist, Moonwalk, New-Kids-Move, Popping, Robocop, Roger-Rabbit, Running-Man, Snake, Tickin', Wavin', and the Worm; which were all Novelty Fads in vogue in the 1980s.)

Palais-Glide: A **Novelty Fad** Group- or Coupledance in vogue in South Africa in the 1990s and 2000s.

The following is from [www.geocities.com/danceinfosa/]:

"The Palais Glide can hardly be termed a dance; it is reminiscent of the Gallop which has been a feature of Hunt Balls for many years. It has the advantage of creating a very jolly and friendly atmosphere in the ballroom and its popularity has spread rapidly throughout the whole of the country. It can be danced to any Foxtrot tune, although sometimes an old tune such as `John Brown's Body' is used, and it is played at a tempo of about 30 bars a minute.

"Four, six, or even more dancers form a line, all facing the same direction (towards the LOD) and with their arms linked behind them. All dancers do the same sequence of steps. Count 1. LF forward, without the weight on it, and the heel only on the floor. 2. Bring the LF back behind the RF and step back on it - Quick. 3. Bring the RF back and place it slightly to the side of the LF - Quick. 4. LF forward.

"Note: A quarter turn to the R is made throughout steps 1 to 4, turning from a direction diagonally to the centre to one diagonally to the wall. 5 to 8. Repeat, commencing with the RF and turning slightly to the L. Count SQQS. 9 to 12. Repeat, commencing with the LF and turning slightly to the R count SQQS. 13. RF forward, well across the front of the LF count S. 14. LF forward, well across the front of RF count S. 15. RF forward, well across the front of the LF count S. 16. LF forward. Count Q. 17. Swing the RF backwards, off the floor. Count Q. 18. Swing the RF forward, off the floor. Count S. 19. Run forward on to the RF. Count Q. 20. Run forward on to the LF. Count Q. 21. Run forward on to the RF and at the same time bend the body well forward and extend the LF backwards, off the floor. Repeat with the LF from the beginning."

Palais-Stroll: A **Novelty Fad** Coupledance in vogue in 1938. In Paris, France, the Grand Palais is a large glass exhibition hall that was built for the 1900 Paris Exhibition.

[Some from *Novelty Dances Through the Years* by Pony Moore.]

Palm-Tree: American **Fad** Solo comical Maneuvers of the 1980s in Cadence with the Music.

The following is from "*Eighties Dances*" - [www.inthe80s.com]:

*"**The Palm Tree:** With both hands in front of you, you put the left on top of the right and over and over again as if you were climbing a tree. Your hands are not in fists and not touching each other. Move your head left and right as if you were really climbing a tree. Then when you get to the 'top' of the tree, shake ruthlessly for the coconuts to fall down and catch them!"*

(See Novelty-&-Fad Dances-of-the-1980s. Also see Pantomime, Mime, and Mimicry-En-Masse.)

Pancho-Rock: A **Novelty Fad** Coupledance of the 1960s. This had its own Eponymous record, the "*Pancho Rock*" by *Lalo Guerrero*.

(See Novelty-&-Fad Dances-of-the-1960s.) [From www.bluejuice.org.au]

ParaPara: A Japanese **Novelty Fad** Solo-Dance of the 1980s in Cadence with the Music.

The following is from "*Eighties Dances*" - [www.inthe80s.com]:

"*Okey, originating from Japan's disco/eurobeat club culture of the 70's and 80's, this dance is still stronger than ever to this day in Japan! You move your feet in and out one at a time, and that movement stays basically like that all the time. However, the arms are moved in an array of jives and swings. Each song has its own variation of the dance and it is a big teen-hobby.*"

(See Novelty-&-Fad Dances-of-the-1980s.)

Pata-Pata: An American **Fad** dance (Coupledance?) of the 1960s. This had its own Eponymous record, the "*Pata Pata*" by *Miriam Makeba.*

(See Novelty-&-Fad Dances-of-the-1960s.)

[From *www.bluejuice.org.au.* See *www.sixtiescity.com/Culture/dance.*]

Pat-the-Floor: A **Novelty Fad** dance of 1957. **Pat-the-Floor** had its own Eponymous record, "*Pat The Floor*" by *Pee Wee Crayton.*

[From *Soul*, www.trinity.unimelb.edu.au]

Peanut-Butter-Jelly-Time: A **Novelty** or **Fad** dance of an unknown time, listed in "*Novelty and fad dances*" under [http://en.wikipedia.org/wiki].

Peanut-Duck: A **Novelty Fad** Coupledance of the 1960s. This had its own Eponymous record, "*The Peanut Duck*" by *Marsha Gee.*

(See Novelty-&-Fad Dances-of-the-1960s.) [From www.bluejuice.org.au]

Pearl: An Unleadable, General, **Novelty Fad** Singular dance Movement and Pose in vogue in the U.S. in the 1960s.

At Brigham Young University, in Provo, Utah, the **Pearl**, with its Eponymous record *"Pearl Time"* by *Andre Williams* in 1966, is recorded to have been Performed thusly: Step on Count One. On Count Two, Knee-Flick Free-Leg with Toe Down, placing ankle over Supporting-Knee, simultaneously Raising elbow, (corresponding to Supporting-Leg,) Up with a Wrist-Flick.

(See the Novelty-&-Fad Dances-of-the-1960s.) [Data mostly from "*Rhythm and Dance*" by Alma Heaton.]

Peck or **Peckin'** or **Pecking** or **Peckin'-Motion** or **Peckin'-Dance** or **Chicken:** Partially Leadable American **Novelty Fad** Solo series of Actions, normally Singularly Performed in Unison as Partners.

Originated? or at least there was **Peckin'** by African-Americans in the early 1930s. The Chocolateers did a **Peckin'-Motion** Routine at a Night-Club in Los Angeles in 1934. In 1937, the Cotton Club in New York introduced the **Peckin'-Dance**. **Peckin'** became very popular with the Whites in their dancing, late during the Depression. Usually with Feet immobile and In-Place, mostly while dancing the **Lindy-Hop,** or while dancing the **Swing-Bal** portion of the **Balboa**.

One would **Peck with one's face, Forward and Back, like a chicken,** to each Music Beat multiple times, Facing and toward each side of the Partner's Head. One could also **Peck** while Traveling.

For the **Big-Apple, Peckin'** was one of the **Separated-Break-A-Way** Genre. Wiggling their hips, certain **Break-A-Way** Patterns were danced. The original **Suzie-Q, Boogie-Back, Tack-Annie, Georgia-Grind, Praise-Allah!, Truckin', Peckin', Charleston, Shorty-George,** and other Break-A-Ways, were probably originated early by blacks; while **Spank-the-Baby, Rusty-Dusty, Pose-and-a-Peck,** the **Little-Apple,** the **Little-Peach, Mess-Around, Stomp-Off, Apple-Jacks,** and **Fall-Off-the-Log,** and other Break-A-Ways, were probably originated later by whites. Most all of these Patterns seem to have been influenced or derived from the classic **Lindy-Hop** and/or **Big-Apple** dances. See **Break-A-Way Glossary** for a more complete listing.

(Usually associated with Truck. See Shimmy. Also see Tate, Chicken-Dance, and Funky-Chicken.)

Pee-Wee-Herman: Pantomime 1980s **Novelty Fad Singular-Dance** Maneuvers. How to dance the **Pee-Wee-Herman** to the Beat is described as follows in the *"**Eighties Dances**,"* [www.inthe80s.com]:

"As seen in Pee Wee's Big Adventure, you kinda take and wave both hands in the front and then wave them in back of you and then you have to walk on the tips of your toes. Usually in those groovy platform shoes!"

(See Parade-Rest, Toe-Stands, and On-Points.)

Peg-Leg: A **Novelty Fad** Coupledance of 1966. This had its own Eponymous record, *"Peg Leg"* by *Dave Baby Cortez.*

(See Novelty-&-Fad Dances-of-the-1960s. Especially see Shoop.) [From www.bluejuice.org.au]

Pencil: American **Fad** Solo comical Maneuvers of the 1980s in Cadence with the Music. The following is from "*Eighties Dances*" - [www.inthe80s.com]:

*"**The Pencil:** Put both arms high in the air and clasp your hands together as if to make the point of a pencil. While feet are together, shuffle around as if your feet were the eraser. Then continuously shuffle to the beat of the song as if you were erasing something on the floor. (Optional; while dancing say, 'Erase it, Erase it,' continuously.)"*

(See Novelty-&-Fad Dances-of-the-1980s. Also see Pantomime, Mime, and Mimicry-En-Masse. Also see Lapiz.)

Penguin: A funny dance that Traveled, and was one of a whole series of 1960s Mimicking dance Patterns, (see Hullie-Gullie.) An American **Novelty Fad** Singular, loosely Choreographed Routine, in vogue in the 1960s. This Waddling Routine attempted to imitate a **Penguin** through Pantomime and was popular in Utah. This silly **Penguin**, along with other silly Fad-Dances, was banned at Brigham Young University in 1966.

Music was Rock; its Rhythm was *Quick Quick Slow* at 4/4 Tempo. All dancers Waddled every Step they could Waddle. With participants in an open Shine Position enmasse, all commenced initially upon their Left Foot for Waddling with identical Footwork throughout.

Waddles are Charlie-Chaplin Tilting Steps, very short and Flat with Toes pointed Outward. Arms and Hands are Held at sides with Palms-Down. Swaying, the hip Opposite the Stepped Foot protrudes (Side-Stretch) as the Lower-Body Torques with CBM.

The **Penguin**'s Basic Step for each Measure was *Waddle Waddle Waddle Hop*; In-Place, Forward, Backward, or Circling. Assume a Routine of dancing three Measures for each of these directions, ending with Kick-Hops then Cross-Hops with each Foot, 16 Measures total, then repeat.

Same as or similar to **Waddle**, and **Duck**. (See the Novelty-&-Fad Dances-of-the-1960s.) [Much data from "Rhythm and Dance" by Alma Heaton.]

Peppermint-Twist: An American **Novelty** and **Fad** of **1961** is listed as a Dance in the "*Dance Crazes of the Sixties*." Being identical to **The-Twist**, this **Peppermint-Twist** Dance was actually simply the then-popular **Twist** Dance, except, instead of Twisting to *Chubby Checker*'s "*Twist*" record, it was now Twisted to its new Eponymous record, the "*Peppermint Twist (Part 1),*" by *Joey Dee and the Starliters*. *Joey Dee*'s Band played at New York's hot *Peppermint Lounge*.

(See **Twist**, and the Novelty-&-Fad Dances-of-the-1960s.)
[From http://en.wikipedia.org/wiki, and *www.sixtiescity.com/Culture/dance.*]

Peter-Gunn-Twist: An American **Fad** dance of the 1960s. This had its own Eponymous record, the "*Peter Gunn Twist*" by the *Jesters.*

(See Novelty-&-Fad Dances-of-the-1960s.)
[From *www.bluejuice.org.au.* Mentioned in *www.sixtiescity.com/Culture/dance.*]

Philly: Only this name for an American **Novelty** or **Fad** of the 1960s is listed simply as a Dance, Pattern, or Figure in the "*Dance Crazes of the Sixties*."

(See Novelty-&-Fad Dances-of-the-1960s.) [From *www.sixtiescity.com/Culture/dance*]

Philly-Bop(1) or **Bop-Dancing:** An American **Novelty Fad.** Although this **Philly-Bop** is Coupledanced to a mulplicity of **Swing** Dances, it is mostly similar to and is a spin-off from Eastern Swing. **Philly-Bop** is the "*Official Dance of Philadelphia*" (Pennsylvania). **Philly-Bop** is a careless series of Hip-Twisting, Body-Swaying Movements, to (usually) Double-Time (mostly) Eastern Swing Dancing, and danced mostly in Left-Open-Facing Position. Most people consider **Bop** to be a slightly different dance than is Swing or Shag.

    Philly-Bop is danced mostly to Oldies-Music. Besides in Philadelphia, this **Bop-Dancing** happens to also be danced much in Nashville and Memphis Tennessee, Little Rock Arkansas, Cincinnati Ohio, Saint Louis Missouri, Birmingham Alabama, Jacksonville Florida, and many other places.

    Besides the very many **Bop** Clubs, there is the American Bop Association (ABA), and the National Boppers Hall of Fame, (founded in 1990 and incorporated in Florida.) In addition to this **Philly-Bop**, some other Afro-American Social-Dances are the Steppin', Lindy-Hop, Jitterbug, and HipHop.

Philly-Bop(2): See HandDance.

Philly-Dog: An Unstructured, American **Novelty Fad** Singular or Coupledance in vogue in the 1960s. In 1966, *Mar-Keys* recorded "*Philly Dog,*"and *Shorty Long* recorded "*Function At The Junction.*" There were probably Eponymous dance Movements named **The Philly-Dog.** With new dances every week, not all caught on nationally. As songs came out in 1966, so did a corresponding dance in attempts to imitate through Pantomime, and few of either lasted more than a few weeks.
    (See the Novelty-&-Fad Dances-of-the-1960s.)

Philly-Freeze: An American **Fad** dance of 1966. The **Philly-Freeze** had its own Eponymous record, "*The Philly Freeze*" by *Alvin Cash.*
    (See the Novelty-&-Fad Dances-of-the-1960s.)
    [From *Soul, www.trinity.unimelb.edu.au.* See *www.sixtiescity.com/Culture/dance.*]

Philly-Horse: Only this name for an American **Novelty** or **Fad** of the 1960s is listed simply as a Dance, Pattern, or Figure in the "*Dance Crazes of the Sixties.*"
    (See Novelty-&-Fad Dances-of-the-1960s.) [From *www.sixtiescity.com/Culture/dance*]

Philly-Jerk: Only this name for an American **Novelty** or **Fad** of the 1960s is listed simply as a Dance, Pattern, or Figure in the "*Dance Crazes of the Sixties.*"
    (See Novelty-&-Fad Dances-of-the-1960s.) [From *www.sixtiescity.com/Culture/dance*]

Philly-Walk: Only this name for an American **Novelty** or **Fad** of the 1960s is listed simply as a Dance, Pattern, or Figure in the "*Dance Crazes of the Sixties.*"
    (See Novelty-&-Fad Dances-of-the-1960s.) [From *www.sixtiescity.com/Culture/dance*]

Pig: A **Novelty Fad** Coupledance of the 1960s. This had its own Eponymous record, *"Do The Pig"* by *Mercedes & The Blue Notes.*
     (See Novelty-&-Fad Dances-of-the-1960s.) [From www.bluejuice.org.au]

Pigmy-Grind: A **Novelty Fad** Coupledance of the 1960s. This had its own Eponymous record, *"The Pigmy Grind"* by *Sonny Dublin.*
     (See Novelty-&-Fad Dances-of-the-1960s.) [From www.bluejuice.org.au]

Plena: A 1950s **Novelty Fad** Coupledances, developed from the Traditional Puerto Rican Latin, **Plena Folk** Coupledance and songstyle.
     Important to life in the Caribbean, a series of distinctive musical ballads have originated in **Puerto Rico**; among them are the **Plena**s. The **Plena**s are topical ballads similar to the Mexican **Corrido**s. Their lyric content is often about social or political criticisms and/or satire.
     When Coupledanced, **Plena**s resemble Caribbean **Bolero**s and a Variation of the **Merengue.**
     (See Clave-Beat, Soca, Calypso, Conga-Line, and the Bomba. Also see the Bambuco, Bop, Bunny-Hop, Calypso, Creep, Fish, Flea-Hop, Freeze, Frug, Guapacha, Hand-Jive, Hitch-Hiker, Hokey-Pokey, Hucklebuck, Hullie-Gullie, Jerk, Limbo-Rock, Mashed-Potato, Monkey, Pachanga, Pony, Rock-and-Around, Scooter, Slide, Strole, Surfers, Swim, Tumba-Cha, Twist, Twister, and the Watusi; which were all Novelty Fads in vogue in the 1950-60s.)

Pogo: An American Teenage Term for "punks" in the late 1970s, that Performed strange **Novelty Fad** Movements called **The Pogo** at punk music concerts. A precursor of **Slam-Dancing, The Pogo** consisted of Jumping Up and Down to the Beat while Flapping their arms and Lunging Forward with their chins. Contrary to the belief of some, **Pogo** has nothing to do with **Ska**. [Much from "Pit Ettiquette" by Reaz Sacharoff.]   Yet, **Pogo** is described as follows in the *"Eighties Dances"* [www.inthe80s.com]:
     "The Pogo - *Works with ska beat songs, bounce up and down to the beat."*
     (See Underground Step-Listing.)

Polly-Wolly: An American **Fad** dance of 1967. This had its own Eponymous record, *"Polly Wolly"* by *Tony Borders.*
     (See Novelty-&-Fad Dances-of-the-1960s.)
     [From *www.bluejuice.org.au.* See *www.sixtiescity.com/Culture/dance.*]

Pony(2) or **Pony-Swing:** This was an Unstructured and sometimes Unleadable, **Novelty Fad** Singular or **C**oupledance, popular in the U.S. beginning in 1961. *Chubby Checker* sang the **Pony** dance's Eponymous song, it's "*Pony Time*".

For the **Pony**, Partners usually danced Apart, and In-Place or Slightly Forward Traveling, to a 2/4 Time Music Rhythm with medium Counts. The dance Mimicked a pony Stepping or Trotting, and was about the first of a whole series of 1960s Mimicking dance Patterns. The **Pony**, along with the other silly Fad-Dances, was banned at Brigham Young University in 1966.

Pony's Basic two-Measure Pattern was *step bobRise Step Bobrise, step bobRise Step Bobrise.* Another was a four-Measure Pattern, 15 Steps in 8 music Beats; *1&2,&3&4,&5&6,&7&8.*

Raising the Knee, **Bobbing** after Steps *Two, Four,* and *Six,* the dancer would dance *down & down,bob Down & Down,Bob down & down,bob Down & Down.* **The Pony**, at timely intervals, was danced with a mini-Jump that included a Slight Wiggle. Girls that had **Pony** tails would Sweep their Heads in a Circle while dancing, Swishing their **Pony** tails around. With both fists Clenched, both dancers would Pump their arms Up and Down in Sequence with Music, with one Up and one Down, as with The **Monkey**.

The following is from *Dance Crazes of the Sixties* - [From *www.sixtiescity.com/Culture/dance*]:

"*The Pony: The Pony is from Chubby Checker's 'Pony Time'. The beat is 1&2, 3&4, etc, with the feet comfortably together. Various arm and hand motions can be done when Pony-ing, and movement on the dance floor can occur; however, there is no line-of-dance. Couples do not touch, and they are generally facing each other, but turns and chase positions are also possible. Counts are 1 and 2 (right foot pony) 3 and 4 (left foot pony).*
"*1. Stand normally.*
"*2. Jump to the right and land on your right foot leaving the left foot in the air next to your ankle.*
"*3. Step down on your left foot toes lifting up your right foot at the same time.*
"*4. Step down on your right foot lifting up your left foot at the same time.*
"*5. Jump to the left and land on your left foot leaving the right foot in the air next to your ankle.*
"*6. Step down on your right foot toes lifting up your left foot at the same time.*
"*7. Step down on your left foot lifting up your right foot at the same time.*
"*8. Move your arms up when you are ponying on the right foot and move them down on the left foot.*"

The CWDI (Country-Western-Dance-International) calls this **C**oupledance the "**Pony-Swing**". The following is from their "*97-98 Standard Competition Rules*" "Dance Divisions":

"*Pony Swing: Any four (4) or eight (8) count combination of basic pony step patterns may be used that have a generally stationary and circular motion. The swing pattern is counted (&1&2&3&4). The basic dance position is two hand open.*"

This **Pony** was similar to a **Polka** In-Place. (See the Novelty-&-Fad Dances-of-the-1960s, Animal-Dances, Hullie-Gullie, and the Gallop. Also see GoGo-Dancer, Cage-Dancer, and Jacking. Also see Pony-Horse, Pony-Rock, Pony-Swing, Pony-Tail, and Pony-Walk.)

Pony-Horse: Only this name for an American **Novelty** or **Fad** of the 1960s is listed simply as a Dance, Pattern, or Figure in the "*Dance Crazes of the Sixties.*" This must have been a takeoff from **The Pony**.

(See Novelty-&-Fad Dances-of-the-1960s.) [From *www.sixtiescity.com/Culture/dance*]

Pony-Rock: Only this name for an American **Novelty** or **Fad** of the 1960s is listed simply as a Dance, Pattern, or Figure in the "*Dance Crazes of the Sixties.*" This must have been a takeoff from **The Pony**.

  (See Novelty-&-Fad Dances-of-the-1960s.) [From *www.sixtiescity.com/Culture/dance*]

Pony-Swing: A Leadable Coupledance of the **Novelty** or **Fad** variety.

  The CWDI (Country-Western-Dance-International) calls this Coupledance the "**Pony-Swing**". The following is from their "*97-98 Standard Competition Rules*" "Dance Divisions":

  "*Pony Swing: Any four (4) or eight (8) count combination of basic pony step patterns may be used that have a generally stationary and circular motion. The swing pattern is counted (&1&2&3&4). The basic dance position is two hand open.*"

  [See Pony(2) for how to dance this in detail.]

Pony-Tail: Only this name for an American **Novelty** or **Fad** of the 1960s is listed simply as a Dance, Pattern, or Figure in the "*Dance Crazes of the Sixties.*" This must have been a takeoff from **The Pony**.

  (See Novelty-&-Fad Dances-of-the-1960s.) [From *www.sixtiescity.com/Culture/dance*]

Pony-Walk: Only this name for an American **Novelty** or **Fad** of the 1960s is listed simply as a Dance, Pattern, or Figure in the "*Dance Crazes of the Sixties.*" This must have been a takeoff from **The Pony**.

  (See Novelty-&-Fad Dances-of-the-1960s.) [From *www.sixtiescity.com/Culture/dance*]

Pop or **Popping** or **Body-Popping:** This **Pop** is classified as **Novelty Fad** Movements, and is part of the **Electric-Boogie** style of **Break-Dancing**, which, in turn, is one major part of **Hip-Hop**. It is only one of the many **Singular-Dancing, Electric-Boogie** Genre of Mime "Moves". This **Pop** is also a Move of the California `Funk' brand of the **Boogaloo** Genre of Mime "Moves."

  "Popping" is a mechanical type of Movement that originated in Fresno, California. In fact, "*A Brief History of Breakdancing.*" [www.angelfire.com], says that the **Pop** was imported from Southern California. The **Boogaloo**, along with **Popping** and **Locking**, is (or was) actually part of the 1990s **Funk-Style** of dancing, mainly of California.

  In the 1990s, while **Uprock** was a favorite of the New York gangs, **Locking** was a favorite of gangs in Los Angeles. Some others say **Locking** had been started by *Lockatron* and *Shabba-Doo*. West Coast *Shabba* was also responsible for introducing New Yorkers to **Popping**, all of which, some say, resulted in the first genuine **Hip-Hop** Dance. In New York, local Break-Dancers then added **Waves**(1) and Smoother Moves to their **Popping**, resulting Generally in the style that exists today.

  Popping involves creating the illusion of **Robotics** or **Animation**(3). The **Popping** Technique requires fluidic Jerking Movements. **Popping** is tensing some isolated muscle area to the Cadence of the music. Being able to Control a specific area of muscles is the method for good **Popping**.

(Continued)

<u>**Pop:**</u>   (Continued)

The following is from "*Funk Styles*,"   [www.electricboogaloos.com]:

"*Popping was another style created by Sam [Boogaloo Sam of Fresno, California]. People get confused about what this style is. They think it is the name for all the styles that came out of the funk movement (1970s California). It is not. Popping is a style in itself, that involves snapping the legs back, and flexing your muscles continuously to the beat to give a jerky/snapping effect. Popping is a unique style. It's not the universal name for all the funk styles. If you pop, then you're a popper. If you wave, then you're a waver. If you Boogaloo, you're a boogalooer, and so on.*

"*Sam would say the word `pop' (under his breath) every time he flexed while he danced, similar to the way someone might make machine noises when they do the robot, Sam would say the word `pop, pop, pop'. People would always say to him, `Hey do that popping stuff!'*

"*A lot of people ask what <u>Electric Boogaloo style</u> is. Electric Boogaloo style is combining popping and boogaloo style together. The two styles compliment eash other well and is known worldwide as the signature style of the EB's.*"

The following is from "*Electric Boogie - The Moves*."   [www.actor.force9.co.uk/]

"*<u>The Pop</u>: The Pop is a popping movement of different parts of the body, achieved by tensing the muscles. It is very rhythmic, and matches the popping rhythmic style of the music. You can Pop your elbow by sticking it out, or your shoulder by hunching it. The rest of your body remains still.*"

"**Poppin**" is precise and continuous flexing of the muscles to the Beat. The Music for **Poppin** is Funk, and there are certain Body Positions for a Popper to hit on. There are three Types of **Pop**; there are: (1) **Arm-Pops**; (2) **Leg-Pops**; and (3) **Chest-and-Neck-Pops**. Always have Funk Music playing while Practicing your **Pop**. Flex on the Beat and relax off the Beat. Mix all three Styles of **Poppin** during your song.

This **Pop** is similar to the **Tick**. There is no such thing as Pop-Locking, although some are trying to coin this Term (short for Locking-and-Popping). The inventors of **Popping** and **Locking** both admit no link to each other.

The data directly above, and the following exerpts are from "*Dummy's Guide to Popping, Locking, and Bboying*," [www.glowsticking.com]:

"*Popping is also a general term used to describe a whole lot of styles: ticking, strobing, animation, waving, struttin, saccin, filmore, bottin, titting, gliding, boogaloo. Whewwww....*

"*It wasn't always this way. Ticking was ticking, waving was waving, and ---*

"*But then eventually, people who didn't dance --- called everything popping, and eventually it became known that way.*"

Some other **Electric-Boogie** Genre of Mime "Moves" are the **Tick**, the **Moon-Walk**, the **Lock**(2), the **Wave**(1), the **King-Tut**, the **Robot**, the **Glides**, **Floating**(2), the **SlowMo**, the **Lean**(4), the **Collapse**, the **Heartbeat**, the **Bicycle**(2), the **Top-Rock**, the **Six-Step**, the **Worm**, and the **Toe/Heel-Walk**.

(Continued)

Pop: (Concluded)

[For Singular-Dancing, see **Locking-and-Popping**, Mime, and Pantomime. Also see Abrupt, Head-Flick, Jerk(1)&(2), Quick, Staccato, Sharply, Smartly, and Snap(1)&(2). Also see Break-Dancing, Underground Step-Listing, Teen-Dancing, and Open-Step. Also see Ska, Punk-Rock, Grunge, and New-Wave. Also see Hip-Hop, MTV-Style Dancing, Street-Dancer, Lyrical-Dancer, Jazz-Dance, and Urban-Dance. Also see Rock, Hard-Rock, Pop, Rhythm-and-Blues, Motown-Sound, Rap, and Heavy-Metal. The Pop, also being one Move of the California `Funk' brand of the **Boogaloo** Genre of Mime "Moves," others are; Air-Posing, Animation(3), Bop(2), Centipede, Cobra, Crazy-Legs, Dime-Stopping, Filmore, Floating(2), Glides, Hitting, King-Tut, Puppet, Robot, Saccin, Scarecrow, Snake(4), Spiderman, Sticking, Strobing, Strut, Tick, and Wave(1).]

(For Coupledancing, similar to Head-Flick, Head-Fan, and Abrupt. For Coupledancing, see Samba-Tic, Salute, Staccato, Knee-Lead, Flourish, Gesture, and Head-Flick-Link.)

Popcorn(1): Two Unleadable, Singular **Novelty Fad** Spot-Movements, Left and Right Knee. Suitable mostly for **West-Coast-Swing** and **Country-Western** Line-Dancing. Performed by either or both Partners. Each two Beats long, Timing is *Slow Slow*.

Executed Bent-Kneed, with Weight on both Balls-of-Feet, and with Feet some 12 inches apart. Only one Knee is Rolled at a time, and both Balls are kept In-Place. Either Knee is Rolled Forward then Outward in a half circle then returned Home to Center, to Neutral Position.

(See Knee-Pop.)

Popcorn(2): A 1960s American **Novelty Fad**, Stationary Coupledance, Choreographed and perhaps Cued. The **Popcorn** Movements, Mimicking **Popcorn** popping, probably originated from The **Hullie-Gullie** dance Mime game about 1963.

The Popcorn Routine in vogue at Brigham Young University, Provo, Utah, probably was danced In-Place to medium 4/4 Timing, modern pop music. Notes given state: *Lines Formation; Up Down Pulse; Bend Knees on each music Count.*

a) Stretch out arms Left with loose fists then pull arms in, twice. Repeat Right;

b) With Palms Down, Left Hand Straight Down, Right Hand at hip, Left Knee Straight, Right Knee Bent. Repeat Opposite;

c) Clap Hands Behind then again In-Front;

d) Hitch-Hike Right Thumb over Right shoulder twice. Repeat Opposite;

e) Repeat b) and c).

There is a picture labeled and showing a young BYU couple dancing **The Popcorn.** Facing with Feet Together and Deep-Into-Knees, they are Bending to their Left with Spreaded arms Up and Tilted to their Left with loose fists.

In 1969, probably Eponymous for The **Popcorn** dance, *James Brown* sang and recorded *The Popcorn.* Also, there was *Mother Popcorn.* These songs may not have caught on nationally.

(See the Novelty-&-Fad Dances-of-the-1960s.) [Much data from "Rhythm and Dance" by Alma Heaton.]

Popcorn(3): American **Fad** Solo comical Maneuvers of the 1980s.
The following is from "*Eighties Dances*" - [www.inthe80s.com]:
> "***The Popcorn:*** *Ok, kinda hard to explain but basically you are hopping side to side in sync with the music. Little hops with your feet, while moving your hands in the opposite direction of your feet. You look like you are popping off of the ground like popcorn .. Get it?*"
(See Novelty-&-Fad Dances-of-the-1980s. Also see Pantomime, Mime, and Mimicry-En-Masse.)

Popcorn-Boogaloo: A **Novelty Fad** Coupledance of the 1960s. This had its own Eponymous record, the "*Popcorn Boogaloo*" by *Jerryo*.
(See Novelty-&-Fad Dances-of-the-1960s.) [From www.bluejuice.org.au]

Popcorn-Poppin': Only this name for an American **Novelty** or **Fad** of the **1960s** is listed simply as a Dance, Pattern, or Figure in the "*Dance Crazes of the Sixties*."
(See Novelty-&-Fad Dances-of-the-1960s.) [From *www.sixtiescity.com/Culture/dance*]

Popeye: An American **Fad** dance of 1960. The records that the **Popeye** was danced to were "*Now Let's Popeye*" by *Eddie Bo*, and "*Last Night*" by *The Markeys*.
(See Novelty-&-Fad Dances-of-the-1960s.)
[From *Soul*, *www.trinity.unimelb.edu.au*. See *www.sixtiescity.com/Culture/dance.*]

Popeye-Line: Only this name for an American **Novelty** or **Fad** of the 1960s is listed simply as a Dance, Pattern, or Figure in the "*Dance Crazes of the Sixties*."
(See Novelty-&-Fad Dances-of-the-1960s.) [From *www.sixtiescity.com/Culture/dance*]

Popeye-Shimmy: Only this name for an American **Novelty** or **Fad** of the 1960s is listed simply as a Dance, Pattern, or Figure in the "*Dance Crazes of the Sixties*."
(See Novelty-&-Fad Dances-of-the-1960s.) [From *www.sixtiescity.com/Culture/dance*]

Popeye-Stroll: Only this name for an American **Novelty** or **Fad** of the 1960s is listed simply as a Dance, Pattern, or Figure in the "*Dance Crazes of the Sixties*."
(See Novelty-&-Fad Dances-of-the-1960s.) [From *www.sixtiescity.com/Culture/dance*]

Popeye-Waddle: An American **Fad** dance of the 1960s. This had its own Eponymous record, the "*Popeye Waddle*" by *Don Covay*.
(See Novelty-&-Fad Dances-of-the-1960s.)
[From *www.bluejuice.org.au*. See *www.sixtiescity.com/Culture/dance.*]

Pop'n-Loc: American **Novelty Fad** Solo Maneuvers of the 1980s in Cadence with the Music.

    The following is from "_Eighties Dances_" - [www.inthe80s.com]:

        "**Pop'n Loc:** It's in that new car commercial - you just basically wave your arms slowly, locking your joints for a second, and then releasing and moving again. Kinda like a robot, but move both arms in a different direction. It's also in the 'Uptown Girl' video by Billy Joel."

    Same as **Locking-and-Popping**. (See Novelty-&-Fad Dances-of-the-1980s.)

    <u>Note</u>: This **Pop'n-Loc** was actually created in the **1990s**, (not in the 1980s.)

Pose-and-a-Peck: An Unleadable? 1930s novelty **Fad** 8-Count Pattern, usually Performed while dancing the **Big-Apple**.

    [Note: Mechanics of its Steps are unknown.]

    For the **Big-Apple**, **Pose-and-a-Peck** was one of the **Break-A-Way** Genre. Wiggling their hips, certain **Break-A-Way** Patterns were danced. The original **Suzie-Q, Boogie-Back, Tack-Annie, Georgia-Grind, Praise-Allah!, Truckin', Peckin', Charleston, Shorty-George**, and other Break-A-Ways, were probably originated early by blacks; while **Spank-the-Baby, Rusty-Dusty, Pose-and-a-Peck**, the **Little-Apple**, the **Little-Peach, Mess-Around, Stomp-Off, Apple-Jacks**, and **Fall-Off-the-Log**, and other Break-A-Ways, were probably originated later by whites. Most all of these Patterns seem to have been influenced or derived from the classic **Lindy-Hop** and/or **Big-Apple** dances. See **Break-A-Way Glossary** for a more complete listing.

Possum-Trot: An American "_animal dance_", a **Novelty Fad** Coupledance in vogue about 1912 to 1918. Derided by newspapers, magazines, church officials, and even by Pope Pius X, as "such foolish and decadent behavior," over one hundred of these dances were created from 1912 to 1914.

    (See Animal-Dances, Bull-Frog-Hop, Bunny-Hug, Buzzard-Lope, Camel-Walk, Chicken-Reel, Chicken-Scratch, Crab-Step, Fish-Walk, Gotham-Gobble, Horse-Trot, Kangaroo-Dip, Kangaroo-Hop, Lame-Duck, Monkey-Glide, Snake, and Turkey-Trot; which were all Animal-Dances of 1910-1914.)

Potato-Mash: Only this name for an American **Novelty** or **Fad** of the 1960s is listed simply as a Dance, Pattern, or Figure in the "_Dance Crazes of the Sixties_."

    (See Novelty-&-Fad Dances-of-the-1960s.) [From _www.sixtiescity.com/Culture/dance_]

Praise-Allah!: An Unleadable? 1930s novelty **Fad** 8-Count Pattern, usually Performed while dancing the **Big-Apple**.

    [Note: Mechanics of its Steps are unknown.]

    For the **Big-Apple**, **Praise-Allah!** was one of the **Break-A-Way** Genre. Wiggling their hips, certain **Break-A-Way** Patterns were danced. The original **Suzie-Q, Boogie-Back, Tack-Annie, Georgia-Grind, Praise-Allah!, Truckin', Peckin', Charleston, Shorty-George**, and other Break-A-Ways, were probably originated early by blacks; while **Spank-the-Baby, Rusty-Dusty, Pose-and-a-Peck**, the **Little-Apple**, the **Little-Peach, Mess-Around, Stomp-Off, Apple-Jacks**, and **Fall-Off-the-Log**, and other Break-A-Ways, were probably originated later by whites. Most all of these Patterns seem to have been influenced or derived from the classic **Lindy-Hop** and/or **Big-Apple** dances. See **Break-A-Way Glossary** for a more complete listing.

Praise-You: A **Novelty Fad** Group-Dance for a Performance, dated 27 Oct 1999.
The following is from *"Fat boy Slim's 'Praise You'*," (http://members.tripod.com):
        "*Group*: *Start hunched over, back to audience, holding hands. Turn and stand up in sequence.* **Lead**: *Squatting in the middle of the half circle. Roll up, gesture/point to the right half then the left half of the group.*
        "*All*: *Raise arms up, jump like jumping jacks but without arm movements.*
        "*Group*: *Step touch, step touch to the right four times. Arms are jazz hands, air guitar style. Same to the left. Repeat three more times.* **Lead**: *Same, but opposite direction and with own style.*
        "*All*: *Body shake. All step leap front, down to the ground. Step leap back, down to the ground. Repeat* [step leaps] *two and a half times.*
        "*All*: *Form a circle. Front sashay. Fish move back. Fish back again. Step hop backwards. Turn, airplane. Twist to right. B-boys pose with head nodding to the beat.*
        Interruption:
        "*Lead*: *Jump/piggy back the front of the person stopping the music. Tell/assure the audience: 'We got some b-boy moves'*
        Continue:
        "*Group*: *B-boy pose, with head nodding to the beat.* **Lead**: *Uprocking. Six step, front roll, back roll (that turns into a front roll).*
        "*Group*: *Robot starting to the left then facing front then facing right. Repeat. Stand and shake while watching lead.* **Lead**: *Interpretive dance. Two counts of eight. Running man, running man. Step with big arm movements. More ... step with big arm movements.*
        "*All*: *Form a line. Shuffle with right foot. Arm wave with left arm (each person swing their arm in a full circle, one at a time, in sequence.) Again back.*
        "*Lead*: *Moon walk backwards.*
        "*Lead and woman*: *Run and leap, taking turns, ending in Vogue like poses.*
Repeat.
        "*All*: *Form a line, step kicks like crazy. Kind of like the Roger Rabbit but* frontwards.
        "*Lead/All*: *Dancers run into the lead, lead throws each of the dancers into a* leap.
        "*All*: *Run to centre, forming a circle, shake arms upwards. Turn. 80s pound* down. "
        (See Underground Step-Listing. Especially see Jumping-Jacks, Jazz-Hands-Air-Guitar-Style, Air-Guitar, Front-Sashay-Down, Back-Sashay-Down, Front-Sashay, Fish-Back, Airplane-Turn, B-Boy-Pose, Parade-Rest, Arms-Folded, Head-Nods, Piggyback, Uprock, Six-Step, Robot, Interpretative-Dance, Running-Man, Moon-Walk, SideSlide, Roger-Rabbit, and Eighties-Pound-Down.)

Prance: Only this name for an American **Novelty** or **Fad** of the **1960s** is listed simply as a Dance, Pattern, or Figure in the *"Dance Crazes of the Sixties."*
        (See Novelty-&-Fad Dances-of-the-1960s.) [From *www.sixtiescity.com/Culture/dance*]

Prang: From Kingston, Jamaica, an Underground **Novelty Fad**, Singular- or Group-Dance **Hip-Motion**, associated with dancing **Dancehall/Ragga**, which, in turn, are outgrowths of **Ska/Reggae**. **Prang** was and is danced mainly by youths of color.

The following is from *Ragga Fashions*: [www.bbc.co.uk]

"*Prang - This dance involves quite a bit of wriggling and is hard to pick up, but once you've got it you've got it.*

"*Stand with legs apart and knees slightly bent. Create a wave type flowing motion, with the top part of your body (this involves pulling your waist in as you push your chest out and then pushing your waist out as you bring your chest in - creating a wave). Bend your knees and go down in to a crouching position as you continue the wave motion with your top half.*"

This Self-Induced **Prang** Hip-Motion might be intermittent, multiple or continual. This Undulation is one of the **Ripple-Up** Style (or Genre-portion) of the **WaveLike-Contraction-Movements** Genre. **Prang** is similar to **Wave**(1), **Boogie-Roll**(1), and **Body-Ripple**. [See **Dancehall**(2), Body-Wave, Waving(1), Sway-Back-and-Forth, and Sway-To-and-Fro. Also see Bogle, Armstrong, Butterfly, Go-Go-Wine, Body-Basic-and-Exercise, Tate, and World-Dance. Also see Jerry-Springer, Heel-and-Toe, Na!Na!Na!, Screechie, Zip-It-Up, Drive-By, Shizzle-Ma-Nizzle, Matrix, and Bin-Laden. Also see Underground Step-Listing. For Partner-Induced-Hip-Motion, see Double-Resistance or Block-and-Catch-Double, and Double-Bump.]

Prep: American **Novelty** or **Fad** Coupledance of the 1980s in Cadence with the Music. The following is from "*Eighties Dances*" - [www.inthe80s.com]:

"***The Prep:*** *Put your hands in the air and work them back and forth in sync with your neck. Work your neck back and forth as you move your hands through the air.*

"***The Prep:*** *Very big in 1984. You're centered then step to the right with both feet, and hands pointing up with palms flat and fingers together. Then step back to the center pointing both of your hands downwards. Then step to the left with both feet, and hands pointing up with palms flat and fingers together. Then step back again to the center pointing both of your hands downwards.*

"*There are many variations to this dance going opposite of your partner, reaching out like you're mixing dominoes on the table when you're centered, and so on.*"
(See Novelty-&-Fad Dances-of-the-1980s.)

Pretzel: Only this name for an American **Novelty** or **Fad** of the 1960s is listed simply as a Dance, Pattern, or Figure in the "*Dance Crazes of the Sixties.*"
(See Novelty-&-Fad Dances-of-the-1960s.) [From *www.sixtiescity.com/Culture/dance*]

Punta y Soka or **LaPunta y LaSoka:** A Latin Rhythm, fast-Time, one-Step, **Novelty Fad**, Spot-Coupledance. Popular with Latinos in the 1990s, consists of tiny, Quick One-Steps with rump-wiggles, danced close against each other. Partners cycle between dancing on Opposing-Feet and on Same-Feet. Rump-wiggles are achieved by speedy ankle-twisting while retaining Feet fairly parallel. Timing is *Quick Slow Quick Slow Quick Slow Quick Slow*; *Down Up Down Up Down Up Down Up*, (but Float is very Slight.) Man Twirls and Spagettis Lady. At times, they dance rump-to-tummy, although the entire dance is only Slightly sexy. It appears that both Punta and Soka are the same **Coupledance**.

(See the Bomba, Chicken-Dance, Dirty-Dancing, Lambada, Macarena, Quebradita, Teen-Dancing, and Urban-Dance; which were all Novelty Fads in vogue in the 1980-90s.)

Push: Only this name for an American **Novelty** or **Fad** of the 1960s is listed simply as a Dance, Pattern, or Figure in the "*Dance Crazes of the Sixties.*"

(See Novelty-&-Fad Dances-of-the-1960s.) [From *www.sixtiescity.com/Culture/dance*]

Push-and-Pull: An American **Fad** dance of 1968. The **Push-and-Pull** had its own Eponymous record, "*Push And Pull*" by *Rufus Thomas.*

(See Novelty-&-Fad Dances-of-the-1960s.)

[From *Soul, www.trinity.unimelb.edu.au.* See *www.sixtiescity.com/Culture/dance.*]

Push-It: An American **Novelty Fad** Solo-Dance or Maneuver of the 1980s in Cadence with the Music.

The following is from "*Eighties Dances*" - [www.inthe80s.com]:

"*Push-It: This dance was done to the song by Salt & Peppa from which it derived its name. Place your hands next to each other near your belly-button, positioned almost like you are going to loop your thumbs into the waistband of your favorite jordache jeans (but don't or this dance becomes country line dancing). Legs should be slightly bent, feet touching each other. Then you do quick, little shuffling jumps back and forth keeping your feet touching.*"

(See Novelty-&-Fad Dances-of-the-1980s.)

Push-Push: An American **Fad** dance of 1965. The **Push-Push** had its own Eponymous record, "*Push Push*" by *Little Jerry Williams.*

(See Novelty-&-Fad Dances-of-the-1960s.) [From *Soul, www.trinity.unimelb.edu.au.*]

Pyramids-Stomp: Only this name for an American **Novelty** or **Fad** of the **1960s** is listed simply as a Dance, Pattern, or Figure in the "*Dance Crazes of the Sixties.*"

(See Novelty-&-Fad Dances-of-the-1960s.) [From *www.sixtiescity.com/Culture/dance*]

Quebradita or **LaQuebradita:** (Spanish for `*the little breach*'.) A popular Mexican One-Step, **Novelty Fad** Coupledance, originating in 1993 in Mexico City. A cross between the Lambada and the Mexican-Polka, Fast-paced and suggestive, Partners lock themselves in an Embrace, and Prance One-Step to a Salsa oom-pah Beat.

They *Hop hop Hop hop, Hop hop Hop hop* Together on Opposing Feet; the Man *Lifts Lifts Lifts Lifts* her, *Bounce Bounce Bounce Bounc*ing her off her Feet; her legs at times hanging Straight as her Toes *Touch Touch Touch Touch* the Dancefloor, and as her Feet *Flail Flail Flail Flail*.

He Squeezes her tight enough to break her ribs. He rears back to Lift her off the Dancefloor as he Hops. They each *Hop hop Hop hop* Solo at times for about a Measure.

(See the Bomba, Chicken-Dance, Dirty-Dancing, Lambada, Macarena, Punta y Soka, Teen-Dancing, and Urban-Dance; which were all Novelty Fads in vogue in the 1980-90s.)

Q-Tip: An American **Fad** Solo comical shinanigan of the 1980s in Cadence with the Music.

The following is from "*Eighties Dances*" - [www.inthe80s.com]:

"***TheQ-Tip:** Lean your head side to side while putting a hand up to each leaned side. Squeeze your pointer finger and thumb together, up by your ear as if cleaning each ear with a Q-Tip.*"

(See Novelty-&-Fad Dances-of-the-1980s. Also see Pantomime, Mime, and Mimicry-En-Masse.)

Quick-Points: A Leadable In-Place-Coupledance Figure of multiple Changes of the Feet in Sequence; used in **West-Coast-Swing** and in other similar dances.

With no Traveling, one Measure long in 4/4 Time, Rhythm Timing is *1&2&3&4&*. Begins with Man's Left Toe Touching and Extended Slightly Forward. These four Counts can be either **Danced Flat** or Executed **with a Slight Hop**, while almost simultaneously Touching the other Foot Forward.

Man dances *draghomeForTouch DragHomefortouch draghomeForTouch DragHomefortouch.*

Lady, Facing, dances Mirror-Image Opposite.

Similar to **Change-And-Change, And-Change-And-Change-And, Switch**(3), **Side-Switches, Heel-Switches, Hangman,** and **California-Shuffle**. (See Change-Feet-Multiplicity, and Change-Feet.)

Raggedy-Bag: A **Novelty Fad** Coupledance of the 1960s. This had its own Eponymous record, the "*Raggedy Bag*" by the *Reggie Sadler Revue.*

(See Novelty-&-Fad Dances-of-the-1960s.) [From www.bluejuice.org.au]

Rags: A **Novelty Fad** Coupledance of the 1960s. This had its own Eponymous record, "*Rags*" by *T.J.Timber.*

(See Novelty-&-Fad Dances-of-the-1960s.) [From www.bluejuice.org.au]

Rag-Time: A **Novelty Fad** Coupledance popular in Utah about 1906.

(See the Cake-Walk, Hoochy-Koochy, Kickapoo, and Tiger-Rag; which were all Novelty Fads in vogue in the 1900 to 1910 era.)

Ramble or **Swivel:** Two Unleadable Shine-Steps, that are Singular or **Coupledance** Figures or Patterns, Mirror-Image Left or Right. Used mostly in **Country-Western** Line- or Partner-Dancing. Also used cooperatively **Coupledancing** Eight-Counts of Pure-**Balboa**, entirely in a Closed, Mush Position but with Ad-Lib Timing (no Touch Counts). Rhythm Timing is usually *Slow slow Slow slow, Slow slow Slow slow.*

    A form of **Parallel-Travel**, the Body Travels Sideways, by alternating one's Weight, first on one Heel and one Ball, then on the Opposite Heel and Ball, Traveling one direction or visa-versa. Both Feet are Heel-Fanned and Toe-Fanned in the Direction-of-Travel.

    Same as **Toe/Heel-Walk**, and **Traveling-Applejacks**. Similar to **Swivels-Left**, and to **Swivels-Right**. Also similar to **Heel-Shifts-Left**, and to **Heel-Shifts-Right**. [See Toe-Movements, Swivels(1), Heel-Splits, Heels-Out, Toe-Splits, Toe-In, Toe-Out, Toes-Out, Heel-Shifts-Double, Swivet, Squiggle, SugarFoot, Sand-Step, Chinese-Typewriter, Bronco-Twist, Kid-and-Play, Foot-Boogie, Double-Foot-Boogie, Celtic-Storm, and Swivel. Also see Balboa Step-Listing.]

    Rat-Fink: A **Novelty Fad** Coupledance of 1965. This had its own Eponymous records, "*Rat Fink*" by *Lonnie Lord (ron Haydock)*, and "*Doing The Rat Fink*" by the *Kornerstones.* (See Novelty-&-Fad Dances-of-the-1960s.) [From www.bluejuice.org.au]

    Ray-Charles-Ton: Only this name for an American **Novelty** or **Fad** of the 1960s is listed simply as a Dance, Pattern, or Figure in the "*Dance Crazes of the Sixties.*" (See Novelty-&-Fad Dances-of-the-1960s.) [From *www.sixtiescity.com/Culture/dance*]

    Razzle-Dazzle: Only this name for an American **Novelty** or **Fad** of the 1960s is listed simply as a Dance, Pattern, or Figure in the "*Dance Crazes of the Sixties.*" Perhaps this was danced to the Show-Business song, "*Give 'em the old Razzle Dazzle.*" (See Novelty-&-Fad Dances-of-the-1960s.) [From *www.sixtiescity.com/Culture/dance*]

    Rebel-Walk: Only this name for an American **Novelty** or **Fad** of the 1960s is listed simply as a Dance, Pattern, or Figure in the "*Dance Crazes of the Sixties.*" (See Novelty-&-Fad Dances-of-the-1960s.) [From *www.sixtiescity.com/Culture/dance*]

    Red-Indian-Dance: An American **Novelty** or **Fad** Solo-Dance of the 1980s, in Cadence with the Music.

    The following is from "*Eighties Dances*" - [www.inthe80s.com]:

    "*You see this in Michael Jackson's 'Black or White' video when he's dancing with the Native Americans. All you are doing is bending your knees and tipping from the waist while making small but very fast little jumps, lifting your right foot up and down with every jump.*"

    (See Novelty-&-Fad Dances-of-the-1980s.)

    Reel: Only this name for an American **Novelty** or **Fad** of the 1960s is listed simply as a Dance, Pattern, or Figure in the "*Dance Crazes of the Sixties.*" (See Novelty-&-Fad Dances-of-the-1960s.) [From *www.sixtiescity.com/Culture/dance*]

Reggay: A **Novelty Fad** dance of 1968. The **Reggay** had its own Eponymous record, *"Do The Reggay"* by *Toots & The Maytals.*
   (See Novelty-&-Fad Dances-of-the-1960s.) [From *Soul*, www.trinity.unimelb.edu.au]

Rendezvous-Stomp: Only this name for an American **Novelty** or **Fad** of the 1960s is listed simply as a Dance, Pattern, or Figure in the "*Dance Crazes of the Sixties.*"
   (See Novelty-&-Fad Dances-of-the-1960s.) [From *www.sixtiescity.com/Culture/dance*]

Rhumba-Boogie: Only this name for an American **Novelty** or **Fad** of the 1960s is listed simply as a Dance, Pattern, or Figure in the "*Dance Crazes of the Sixties.*"
   (See Novelty-&-Fad Dances-of-the-1960s.) [From *www.sixtiescity.com/Culture/dance*]

Rib: Only this name for an American **Novelty** or **Fad** of the 1960s is listed simply as a Dance, Pattern, or Figure in the "*Dance Crazes of the Sixties.*"
   (See Novelty-&-Fad Dances-of-the-1960s.) [From *www.sixtiescity.com/Culture/dance*]

Rifle: Only this name for an American **Novelty** or **Fad** of the 1960s is listed simply as a Dance, Pattern, or Figure in the "*Dance Crazes of the Sixties.*"
   (See Novelty-&-Fad Dances-of-the-1960s.) [From *www.sixtiescity.com/Culture/dance*]

Rifleman: A Novelty, Singular-Dance two-Measure Pattern, Mimicking the Positioning of a simulated rifle for firing, including pulling the phantom trigger. Such a Position for the Arms is held and retained throughout while the Feet dance their Steps. This **Rifleman** Pattern is one of the Qued Steps often Called for while dancing the **Madison** Audience-Participation-Dance's Basic-Step.
   The following are excerpts from *The Madison*:
      "*X LF in front of RF and squat down.*
      "*Raise up and shoot from the HIP yelling FIRE!*
      "*Step with RF and bring the LF to meet the RF (tap the LF).*"
   [See Double-Cross, Cleveland-Box, Basketball, Big-'M', 'T'-Time, Jackie-Gleason, and Birdland. Also see the Novelty-&-Fad Dances-of-the-1960s.]

Roach: An Unstructured, American **Novelty Fad** Singular or Coupledance in vogue in the 1960s. **The Roach** is believed to have been Choreographed and danced in the movie, *"Hairspray."* "*The Roach*" (Dance) was recorded by *Gene & Wendell* in 1963. **The Roach** Pattern or Routine may have attempted to imitate killing a cockroach through Pantomime.
   Following is an excerpt from *Dance Crazes of the Sixties* [*www.sixtiescity.com/Culture/dance*]:
      "***The Roach:*** *... it starts with a line. There is a stomping, squishing motion with the feet and an arm movement like you are 'fumigating' to kill a roach. The lyrics to the song say 'You stomp, step, skip, 2,3,4,5,6,7, you stomp, step, skip, 2,3,4,5,6,7, you stomp, step, skip, 2,3,4,5,6,7, you stomp, step, skip, 2,3,4,5,6,7, squish, squash, kill that roach.' This suggests that it may have been a box-style dance since there are so many steps. ...*"
   (See the Novelty-&-Fad Dances-of-the-1960s.)

Robbie: Only this name for an American **Novelty** or **Fad** of the **1960s** is listed simply as a Dance, Pattern, or Figure in the "*Dance Crazes of the Sixties*."

(See Novelty-&-Fad Dances-of-the-1960s.) [From *www.sixtiescity.com/Culture/dance*]

Robocop: A **Novelty Fad** dance of the late 1980s. How to dance the **Robocop** should be found on a VHS Video by Christy Lane (www.centralhome.com).

Mimicking a policeman with a gun for "good," and as a machine in human form, these peculiar **Robocop** dance Movements are taken from viewing two films popular with 13-year-olds at that time: "*RoboCop*" (1987), and "*Robocop 2*" (1990).

The following is from "*Eighties Dances*" (www.inthe80s.com):

"There were various ways to do it, but the most common way was to have your right arm up with your fist clinched (like you were giving someone your elbow) and your left arm and fist (like a slot machine). Your left fist would move along with your right fist giving the elbow on the right then to your left and so on..."

(See Robot, Locking-and-Popping, Pantomime, and Mime. Also see Abrupt, Head-Flick, Jerk, Quick, Staccato, Sharply, Smartly, and Snap. Also see Break-Dancing, Bugg, Cabbage-Patch, Chicken-Dance, Funky-Twist, Moonwalk, New-Kids-Move, Popping, Pac-Man, Roger-Rabbit, Running-Man, Snake, Tickin', Wavin', and the Worm; which were all Novelty Fads in vogue in the 1980s.)

Robot or **Mannequin** or **Robotics** or **Bottin**: Being a **Novelty Fad** dance, the **Robot** has a part of the **Electric-Boogie** style of **Break-Dancing**, which, in turn, is one major part of **Hip-Hop**. The **Robot** is also a portion of the California `Funk' brand of the **Boogaloo** Genre of Mime "Moves." The **Robot** could originally have been taken from "*Dancin' Machine*" by *The Jackson Five* in 1974.

Robotics is a series of Movements that was very popular with the Underground in the 1980s. The idea is to make the dancer appear to be a **Robot**. In order to dance these **Robot** Moves, the dancer's joints are kept stiff and Movement is Slow and Jerky. Some dancers voice "*machine-noises*" while "doing the **Robot**."

The following is from "*Electric Boogie*," [www.actor.force9.co.uk/]:

"The Mannequin or Robot (Robotics): This ie a mechanical dance style that goes back a long way - It imitates the movement that a showroom dummy might make if it could come to life. There are two separate parts to the Mannequin style.

"One style is to give a Puppet [a] disjointed rolling movement, as if perhaps the dancer were connected by strings, or being moved by another person. You may have seen mimes do skits on the `Thunderbirds' puppet TV show, using this technique. The classic puppet walk, is to move the same arm and leg forward as you step, rather than the opposite arm and leg, as would normally happen.

"The other style is that of a Robot, often termed `Robotics' in the UK - This involves moving your limbs at constant speed from one position to the other, ending up with a snap or `Tick' of the body, just as a mechanical device would. Usually only one part of your body moves at a time, which makes it look as if you are under the control of a program, and systematically doing the moves."

(Continued)

Robot: (Continued)

The following is from "*A Brief History of Breakdancing.*" [www.angelfire.com]

"*...one which would lead to the development of the Electric Boogie. This dance was called the Robot. People started doing the Robot as early as 1969, but the dance really took off after Michael Jackson danced the Robot while singing `Dancin' Machine' on national TV.*

"*In 1977, a pair of mimes named Shields and Yarnell were discovered performing in San Francisco's Union Square. Soon, the mimes landed a gig on television, where they performed a crazy version of the Robot. The new version was fast -not slow- and the dancers feet seemed to glide across the floor. The mimes only moved one part of their body at a time, and would end each move with a tick or pop. Shields and Yarnell also did comedy skits as a part of their routine.*

"*Shields and Yarnell made many appearances on television, which gave dancers time to study their moves. The new version of the Robot was called the Mannequin. Within a few months, Mannequin battles were being staged at clubs.*"

Some other **Electric-Boogie** Genre of Mime "Moves" are the **Moon-Walk**, the **Lock**(2), the **Tick**, the **King-Tut**, the **Pop**(3), the **Wave**(1), the **Glides**, **Floating**(2), the **SlowMo**, the **Lean**(4), the **Collapse**, the **Heartbeat**, the **Bicycle**(2), the **Top-Rock**, the **Six-Step**, the **Worm**, and the **Toe/Heel-Walk**.

Similar to **Super-Robot**. [See **Locking-and-Popping**, Mime, and Pantomime. Also see Abrupt, Head-Flick, Jerk(1)&(2), Quick, Staccato, Sharply, Smartly, and Snap(1)&(2). Also see Marionette, and Dancing-On-a-String. Also see Break-Dancing, Underground Step-Listing, Teen-Dancing, Praise-You, and Open-Step. Also see Ska, Punk-Rock, Grunge, and New-Wave. Also see Hip-Hop, MTV-Style Dancing, Street-Dancer, Lyrical-Dancer, Jazz-Dance, and Urban-Dance. Also see Rock, Hard-Rock, Pop, Rhythm-and-Blues, Motown-Sound, Rap, and Heavy-Metal. The **Robot**, also being one Move of the California `Funk' brand of the **Boogaloo** Genre of Mime "Moves," others are; Air-Posing, Animation(3), Bop(2), Centipede, Cobra, Crazy-Legs, Dime-Stopping, Filmore, Floating(2), Glides, Hitting, King-Tut, Pop, Puppet, Saccin, Scarecrow, Snake(4), Spiderman, Sticking, Strobing, Strut, Tick, and Wave(1).]

Robotics: See Robot.

Rock-and-Around or **The Rock-and-Around:** A **Novelty Fad** Coupledance that appeared in the U.S. in the 1950s. Derived from Eastern Swing.

(Also see the Bambuco, Bop, Bunny-Hop, Calypso, Creep, Fish, Flea-Hop, Frug, Guapacha, Hand-Jive, Hitch-Hiker, Hokey-Pokey, Hullie-Gullie, Jerk, Limbo-Rock, Mashed-Potato, Monkey, Pachanga, Plena, Pony, Scooter, Slide, Strole, Surfers, Swim, Tumba-Cha, Twist, Twister, and the Watusi; which were all Novelty Fads in vogue in the 1950-60s. Also see Novelty-&-Fad Dances-of-the-1960s.)

Rock-and-Stomp: A **Novelty Fad** dance of 1957. The **Rock-and-Stomp** had its own Eponymous record, "*The Rock and Stomp*" by *J. Mercy Baby.*

[From *Soul*, www.trinity.unimelb.edu.au]

Rocking-Chair: A **Break-A-Way**(3) Stationary Shine-Step, this **Rocking-Chair** is two Leadable, four-Step, two-Measures in length in 4/4 Time, General Singular or Spot-Coupledance Patterns, Left or Right. Rhythm Timing is usually *Slow Slow; Slow Slow.* Dance Positions vary.

Rocking Movements, possibly danced in a Loose-Closed Position, with all Feet in Third-Position-Extended, and with Man's Weight Moving Forward as Lady's Weight Moves Rearward, and visa-versa. Normally no Turning. The Man's Right Foot and the Lady's Left Foot, or visa-versa, remain as the center (Home) point, **In-Place**, as Partners Rock Forward and Rearward. The Home Foot Raises In-Place.

Rocking-Chair-Left is danced as follows:
Man dances *forward RecoverHome backward RecoverHome.*
Lady Follows accordingly.
Rocking-Chair-Right is Mirror-Image Opposite.

Similar to the **Marchessi**, and **Corta-Jaca**. (See Electric-Kicks, Rock, Rocking-Steps, and Rock-the-Boat.)

RockSteady: A loose and relaxed Underground Coupledance, Movements, Pattern or form, associated with **Ska/Reggae**, danced mainly by Jamaican youths of color. In mid-Tempo, this R&B-influenced Style served as crossover from the **Ska** to **Reggae**.

The Eponymous records of 1966 to which the **RockSteady** was danced, were "*Rock Steady*" by *Laurel Aitken*, "*Rock Steady*" by *Alton Ellis*, and "*People Rocksteady*" by *The Uniques*. [From *Soul*, www.trinity.unimelb.edu.au]

The following is from *A Quick Guide To Reggae*: [www.bbc.co.uk]

"*Rocksteady* - *By the mid 60's Ska had slowed itself down, got a bit soulful and transformed itself into Rocksteady, born out of `Rude Boy' culture ---.*"

For dancing to **Ska** music, the following is from *Ska Workshop: Skanking 101*: [ska.about.com]

"*Rocksteady: Steady Rock Easy* - *For the more mellow rocksteady era, you'll want more of a pose, less movement in the arms and legs ('cause it too HOT!) and most of your expression coming from your hips.*"

The following is from *Reggae - Fashion and Dance*: [www.bbc.co.uk]

[In the late 1960s] "*Rock Steady had a more melodic rhythm than the fast pace beats of Ska. In turn, the dances that followed the music were a lot more mellow and laid back, allowing dancers to take it easy and rock steady to the beat. The Rock Steady dance involved a gentle rocking motion, with more emphasis placed on movements from the hips and waist. Songs such as "Do the Rock Steady" by the Bodysnatchers, and "Rock Steady" by Aretha Franklin instructed dancers on the right way to do the dance.*

"*The Rock Steady* - *Stand in one place, keep your arms and legs still and take up a gentle forward and backward rocking motion. Move your hips from side to side gently as you rock. Make sure you keep in time with the beat of the music.*"

Similar to **Crubbing, Slow-Dancing, Dirty-Dancing**, and **Lambada**, except **Partners do not Touch**. A Variation for **Skanking**. (See Underground Step-Listing. Especially see Two-Tone, Third-Wave, Ska-Core, and Skinhead-Stomp. Also see Swaying-to-the-Music, Body-Contact, and Nuzzle-Dancing.)

Rocky-Top: A Folkdance, and a **Novelty** dance in the U.S., **Rocky-Top** is a type of Choreographed **Country-Western** Coupledance. It is danced on Same-Feet as an American Twostep in Varsouvienne Position. Danced first as a Standing-Step Pattern then with Shuffles, repeated and repeated. Only the Shuffle portion is Leadable.

For the first portion, the **Standing-Step**, Rhythm Timing is a _Slow_ **for 14 Counts**, and is Cued; _Heel Together, Rock Step; Brush Cross, Back DiagForward; Brush Cross, Back Side, Cross Kick._

Both dance this **Standing-Step**; _heeltapforward close, bobbackShiftextendforward RockForwardshiftExtendBackward; BrushExtendForward CrossPastInFrontShift, crossbehindshift DiagForwardextendbackward; brushextendforward crosspastinfrontshift, CrossBehindShift sideward, CrossPastInFrontShift kickScootForward._

Then comes the Forward Traveling **Shuffle** portion. Timing is _quick Quick slow, Quick quick Slow;_ four times.

(See Ten-Step, Salty-Dog-Rag, and Cotton-Eyed Joe.)

Roger-Rabbit: A **Novelty Fad** dance of the 1980s. How to dance the **Roger-Rabbit** should be found on a VHS Video by Christy Lane (www.centralhome.com).

The following is from _"**Eighties Dances**"_ (www.inthe80s.com):

"The Roger Rabbit is like the running man but you are doing it backwards.. Your arms are by your sides (or doing some funky move) and you take your right leg and sorta skip backwards once, and then your left leg you do the same thing, and then your right leg does it again but this time when your right leg goes back you sorta rock back and forth (right left right) note that when your right leg goes back your left leg is in front and vice versa!! You have to do it sorta robotically."

(See Break-Dancing, Bugg, Cabbage-Patch, Chicken-Dance, Funky-Twist, Moonwalk, New-Kids-Move, Popping, Pac-Man, Robocop, Running-Man, Snake, Tickin', Wavin', and the Worm; which were all Novelty Fads in vogue in the 1980s. Also see Praise-You.)

Roman: Only this name for an American **Novelty** or **Fad** of the 1960s is listed simply as a Dance, Pattern, or Figure in the "_Dance Crazes of the Sixties._"

(See Novelty-&-Fad Dances-of-the-1960s.) [From _www.sixtiescity.com/Culture/dance_]

Romp: Only this name for an American **Novelty** or **Fad** of the 1960s is listed simply as a Dance, Pattern, or Figure in the "_Dance Crazes of the Sixties._"

(See Novelty-&-Fad Dances-of-the-1960s.) [From _www.sixtiescity.com/Culture/dance_]

Rooster-Walk: Only this name for an American **Novelty** or **Fad** of the 1960s is listed simply as a Dance, Pattern, or Figure in the "_Dance Crazes of the Sixties._"

(See Novelty-&-Fad Dances-of-the-1960s.) [From _www.sixtiescity.com/Culture/dance_]

Rope: A Coupledance Term. Being a type of Salsa, this **Rope** is a Leadable, loosely Choreographed, 1990s American **Novelty** Coupledance Routine.

(See Salsa.)

Rosko: Only this name for an American **Novelty** or **Fad** of the 1960s is listed simply as a Dance, Pattern, or Figure in the "*Dance Crazes of the Sixties.*"
(See Novelty-&-Fad Dances-of-the-1960s.) [From *www.sixtiescity.com/Culture/dance*]

Rosy: Only this name for an American **Novelty** or **Fad** of the 1960s is listed simply as a Dance, Pattern, or Figure in the "*Dance Crazes of the Sixties.*"
(See Novelty-&-Fad Dances-of-the-1960s.) [From *www.sixtiescity.com/Culture/dance*]

Royal-Whirl: Only this name for an American **Novelty** or **Fad** of the 1960s is listed simply as a Dance, Pattern, or Figure in the "*Dance Crazes of the Sixties.*"
(See Novelty-&-Fad Dances-of-the-1960s.) [From *www.sixtiescity.com/Culture/dance*]

Rub: A **Novelty Fad** Coupledance of the 1960s. This had its own Eponymous record, "*The Rub*" by *Joey Charles Drums.*
(See Novelty-&-Fad Dances-of-the-1960s.) [From www.bluejuice.org.au]

Rubber-Knees: Crazy American **Fad** Solo comical Maneuvers of the 1980s, Executed by trading hands on Knees while Crouching, in Cadence with the Music.
The following is from "*Eighties Dances*" - [www.inthe80s.com]:
"*'Rubber Knees' was a popular dance of the eighties in which you stand with feet apart and Knees bent inwards touching each other. You then cross your arms placing hands palm down on each knee. Now open your knees keeping your crossed hands on your knees. Then close them again and this time when you open them, stealthily uncross your hands , leaving the right hand on right knee and left hand on left knee. Continue alternating hands from crossed to uncrossed until the song ends or people stop looking at you.*"
Same as the **Knee-Knock**. [See Novelty-&-Fad Dances-of-the-1980s. Also see Charleston(1)&(3).]

Rubberneck (Rubberneckin'): Only this name for an American **Novelty** or **Fad** of the 1960s is listed simply as a Dance, Pattern, or Figure in the "*Dance Crazes of the Sixties.*"
(See Novelty-&-Fad Dances-of-the-1960s.) [From *www.sixtiescity.com/Culture/dance*]

Running-Man or **Vanilla-Ice**: A Novelty **Fad** dance of the 1980s. How to dance the **Running-Man** should be found on a VHS Video by Christy Lane (www.centralhome.com). The **Running-Man** is Unleadable, two-Measures minimum, usually Singular (rarely Coupledance) Spot-Movements In-Place, danced in two different ways. Popular in the early 1990s, the **Running-Man** Movements are used mainly in **Hip-Hop, Raves, Country Partner-Dances**, and in **Line-Dancing**.

(Continued)

Running-Man: (Continued)

The **Running-Man** is danced in Open, Half-Open, or Semi-Closed Position, and/or in their Mirror-Image Positions. There is no Travel or Turning. The dancer remains stationary at Home, but appears to be Running Forward. Each Movement Timing is _Slow Slow_, or _1 & 2 & 3 & 4 &_, for one-Measure. Left then Right (or vice-versa) Movements are normally Repeated and Repeated.

Each **Running-Man** dance Step consists nominally of a Step with a Rearward Scoot or Slide. In detail, the Man Left-Steps Slightly Forward applying only Partial-Weight while Lifting his Right Knee, and immediately Scoots Backward upon this Left initially Supporting-Foot, onto its Heel at Home. Simultaneously with this Heel arriving Home, his Right Knee Slightly Flexes Forward, then his Right Foot is Stepped Slightly Forward with only Partial-Weight applied while Lifting his Left Knee, and it immediately Scoots Backward. And so-on in Rhythm, repeated as many times as the Count indicates.

Man dances _forward drawbackward_, _Forward DrawBackward_, etc.

Lady dances **Forward DrawBackward, forward drawbackward,** etc.

Or, Running-Man may be danced as follows:

Man dances _pushbehind Forward_, _PushBehind forward_, etc.

Lady dances _PushBehind forward_, _pushbehind Forward_, etc.

The following is from "_Eighties Dances_," (www.inthe80s.com):

"_The Running Man_ - _A mid to late 80's dance that kinda looked like running in place with more arm movements._

"_Also known as The Vanilla Ice, you take a step forward, then slide that foot back, immediately placing the next foot forward. Repeat while moving your bent arms forward and back (together). When done quickly, you'll look as though you're `running'. If you want to get really fancy, you can pivot on one foot so that you're facing in the other direction and do it all over again._"

Very similar to Smoother-danced **Nordic-Tracking.** Also similar to **Step-Scoot,** except the dancer Scoots Backward. [See Copas, Stationary-Copas, Syncopated-Splits, Side-Touches, Moon-Walk, SideSlide, Hitch(1), Camel-Walk(3), Heel-and-Toe, Skanking, Praise-You, Majorette-Strutting-with-Baton, and Cake-Walk.]

Rush-Hour-Stomp: Only this name for an American **Novelty** or **Fad** of the 1960s is listed simply as a Dance, Pattern, or Figure in the "_Dance Crazes of the Sixties._"

(See Novelty-&-Fad Dances-of-the-1960s.) [From _www.sixtiescity.com/Culture/dance_]

Rusty-Dusty or **Dusty** or **Rubber-Legs:** An Unleadable 1930s **Separated-Break-A-Way** Novelty **Fad** Pattern, usually Performed while dancing the **Big-Apple.** Also suitable for Coupledancing the **Swing-Bal** portion of the **Balboa,** and for the many **Swing** dances.

Walk Knock-Kneed holding pants legs with both index and middle fingers Pointing Forward. Walk Forward eight Steps (Counts) then Backward eight Steps.

For the **Big-Apple, Rusty-Dusty** was one of the **Break-A-Way** Genre. Wiggling their hips, certain **Break-A-Way** Patterns were danced. The original **Suzie-Q, Boogie-Back, Tack-Annie, Georgia-Grind, Praise-Allah!, Truckin', Peckin', Charleston, Shorty-George,** and other Break-A-Ways, were probably originated early by blacks; while **Spank-the-Baby, Rusty-Dusty, Pose-and-a-Peck,** the **Little-Apple,** the **Little-Peach, Mess-Around, Stomp-Off, Apple-Jacks,** and **Fall-Off-the-Log,** and other Break-A-Ways, were probably originated later by whites. Most all of these Patterns seem to have been influenced or derived from the classic **Lindy-Hop** and/or **Big-Apple** dances. See **Break-A-Way Glossary** for a more complete listing.

Sailor-Shuffle or **Sailor-Step** or **Cross-Ball-Change** or **Side-Hitches-Behind:** A partially Leadable, two-Measure, Four-Count, Six-Step, Butterfly-Break-A-Way Stationary-Coupledance Shine-Step Pattern with no Turning. Suitable for Eastern **Swing**, West-Coast-Swing and Jive, as a **Swing-Bal** Variation for the **Balboa**, and for the **Peabody**, among other dances.

This **Sailor-Shuffle** is accomplished by Leaning in the opposite direction of the Crossing Foot, wherein the dancer's Weight remains Centered over the original Position of the Foot taking the Initial-Step(1). Normally for the Man, there is a three-Step Left-Half and a three-Step Right-Half; *LeanRightCrossBehind sideslide RecoverHome, leanleftcrossbehind SideSlide recoverhome; Quick and Slow, quick And slow.*

Following is from **Linedance Terminology**, [http://nightmovesdanceclub.aboutpaducah.com]:

"*SAILOR SHUFFLE -- Triple step taking up 2 counts of music. The count is 1 & 2*
  "*Left Sailor Shuffle:*
  "*1. Cross left foot behind right foot & step slightly to right with right foot*
  "*2. Step left foot in place. Lean body to the left during this shuffle*
  "*Right Sailor Shuffle:*
  "*1. Cross right foot behind left foot & step slightly to the left with left foot*
  "*2. Step right foot in place. Lean body to the right during this shuffle.*"

Complete Pattern is usually repeated, and danced Facing Partner Mirror-Image, but Position, direction and Starting-Foot is optional. Figure may be followed by a **Peabody-Recovery** for the Peabody.

Similar to **Sailor-Shuffle-InFront**. Also, similar in feeling to **Fall-Off-the-Log**. [See Scissors(1)&(3), Peabody-Spirals, Traveling-Cross-Chasses, Reverse-Traveling-Cross-Chasses, and Twinkle. Also see Balboa Step-Listing.]

Sailor-Shuffle-InFront or **Side-Hitches-InFront:** A partially Leadable, two-Measure, Four-Count, Six-Step, Butterfly-Break-A-Way Stationary-Coupledance Shine-Step Pattern with no Turning. Suitable for Eastern **Swing**, West-Coast-Swing and Jive, as a **Swing-Bal** Variation for the **Balboa**, and for the **Peabody**, among other dances.

This **Sailor-Shuffle-InFront** is accomplished by Leaning in the opposite direction of the Crossing Foot, wherein the dancer's Weight remains Centered over the original Position of the Foot taking the Initial-Step(1). Normally for the Man, there is a three-Step Left-Half and a three-Step Right-Half; *LeanRightCrossInFront sideslide RecoverHome, leanleftcrossinfront SideSlide recoverhome; Quick and Slow, quick And slow.*

Complete Pattern is usually repeated, and danced Facing Partner Mirror-Image, but Position, direction and Starting-Foot is optional. Figure may be followed by a **Peabody-Recovery** for the Peabody.

Similar to **Sailor-Shuffle**. Also, similar in feeling to **Fall-Off-the-Log**. [See Scissors(1)&(3), Peabody-Spirals, and Twinkle. Also see Balboa Step-Listing.]

Saint-Louis-Hop: A **Novelty Fad** Coupledance of 1926 that was a form of Swing.

Sakkie-Waltz: A current South African **Novelty Fad** Coupledance of European origin. *"The Sakkie Waltz is the South African `Boere Musiek' version of the Viennese Waltz which has a pronounced dipping action on count 1 and an abrupt rise on counts 2, 3."* From *Dancers' Dictionary A-Z and Guide* by *DanceInfo*. [www.geocities.com/danceinfosa/]
(See Sakkie-Sakkie.)

Salsa-Casino-Rueda or **Salsa-Rueda:** (Spanish for *red-hot gambling wheel*, or *saucy circling*.) One of the many variations of the **Mambo, Salsa-Casino** is Miami-Style Salsa, with a combination of Rhythms like Guaracha and Son-Montuno. **Salsa-Casino-Rueda** is a Latin **Salsa Folk** Group-Coupledance originally from Cuba, that made a comeback as a **Novelty Fad** in the U.S. beginning in the late 1990s. **Salsa-Casino-Rueda** is a dance where many Couples (two or more) Circle Together, dancing identical Steps in Unison, as their "*Caller of the Rueda*" (Usually one of the dancers) Calls out the Steps. Hand signals are also used at times. Certain Patterns require Partner Changes.
(See Son, Charanga, Pachanga, and Clave-Beat.)

Salt-'n'-Pepper: A **Novelty Fad** Coupledance of the 1960s. This had its own Eponymous record, "*Salt 'n' Pepper*" by *King Charles & The Counts*.
(See Novelty-&-Fad Dances-of-the-1960s.) [From www.bluejuice.org.au]

Salty-Dog-Rag: A Choreographed **Country** Folkdance. A funky fun thing with a lasting history, the **Salty-Dog-Rag** is an American institution; a **hillbilly** bit of Americana lore, dating perhaps from as early as the 18th Century into the present.
The **Salty-Dog-Rag** is most impressive when watching a company of Cloggers **Clog** this dance. There are fascinating intricacies in the tune as well as in its Flashy Steps.
Salty-Dog-Rag Traditional words sung while dancing were as follows:
"Away down yonder in the state of Arkansas
"Where my great-grandpa met my great-grandma,
"They drink apple cider and they get on a jag
"And they dance all night to the Salty Dog Rag.
"They play an old fiddle like you never heard before.
"They play the only tune that they ever did know;
"It's a ragtime ditty and the rhythm don't drag.
"Now, here's the way you dance to the Salty Dog Rag!"
Chorus:
"One foot front, drag it back,
"Then you start to ball the jack.
"You shake, and you break, and then you sag.
"If your partner zigs, you're supposed to zag.
"Your heart is light, you tap your feet
"In rhythm with that ragtime beat.
"(Just) pack up your troubles in your ol' kit bag
"And dance all night to the Salty Dog Rag!"
(Continued)

<u>Salty-Dog-Rag</u>: (Continued)

"*Away down South `neath the old Southern moon,*
"*The possum's up a tree and the hound's tree'd a coon.*
"*They'll hitch up the buggy to a broken-down nag*
"*And go out dancin' to the Salty Dog Rag.*
"*They tune up the fiddle and they rosin up the bow.*
"*They strike a C chord on the ol' banjo*
"*Then holler, `Hang on, `cause we ain't gonna drag!'*
"*Now, here's the way you dance to the Salty Dog Rag!*"

As for the **Salty-Dog-Rag**'s Flashy Steps, there are four (4) similar yet different renditions elucidated on the Internet:

(1) *www.round-dance.de/html/salty_do.html*;
(2) *www.edb.utexas.edu/coe/depts/kin/Faculty/slacks/crpac/folkdances/*;
(3) *www.arjjazedance.free-online.co.uk/Salty%20Dog%20Rag.htm*; and
(4) *www.mts.net/~jinks/fd/saltydog.htm*.

(See Cotton-Eyed Joe, Rocky-Top, and Ten-Step.)

<u>Sand-Step</u> (*sndstp*) or **SugarFoot-Swivels** or **Toe-Heel-Toe-Swivels:** Two Leadable, Butterfly-Break-A-Way Spot-Coupledance Shine-Step Patterns, Right and Left, Mirror-Image, suitable for **Tap**-Dancing, American **Twostep**, Eastern **Swing**, West-Coast-**Swing**, and a (Sand-Step) Cha version for both **ChaChas**. Also suitable for **Coupledancing** the **Swing-Bal** portion of the **Balboa**.

Rhythm Timing for Twostep and Swing is *Quick Quick Slow*. Timing for ChaCha is *Slow Slow, Quick Quick Slow*. Swing-Bal Timing is *1 2 3 hold, 5 6 7 hold*. Partners dance Facing in Butterfly Position, Leaning into each other, or resisting each other by Tension in the arms, and then Swiveling their Bodies with CBM.

Swivel Supporting-Ball 1/4 Outward then 1/2 Inward, while Rotating one's free ankle Inward then Outward to Touch alternately one's Toe then Heel of the Free-Foot, to the Dancefloor, next to the Instep of one's Supporting Foot, then Crossing the Free-Foot In-Front.

Both Patterns are normally danced in Sequence, Right then Left.

Man dances a Swiveling *toe heel crossinfront* **to his Right**, then *Toe Heel CrossInFront* **to his Left**. In Butterfly Position throughout, with a *Side Cross* added after each *Cross* for ChaCha.

Lady Follows Opposite.

[See SugarFoot, Traveling-SugarFoot, Time-Step(1), NightLife, Suzy-Q, Ramble, Foot-Boogie, Double-Foot-Boogie, Toe-Movements, Toe-In, Toe-Out, Toes-Out, Toe-Fan, Heel-Fan, Heels-Out, Heel-Splits, Toe-Splits, Swivet, Marchessi, Corta-Jaca, and Celtic-Storm. Also see Balboa Step-Listing.]

<u>Saratoga-Drag</u>: An American **Novelty Fad** Coupledance (or possibly just a tune) in vogue in the 1910s or `20s. Other "*drag dances*" of the time were the A-Minor-Drag, Dizzy-Drag, Shoe-Shiner's-Drag, Slow-Drag, Viper's-Drag, and the most famous **Varsity-Drag**.

<u>Saturday-Night</u>: A **Novelty** or **Fad** dance of an unknown time, listed in "*Novelty and fad dances*" under [http://en.wikipedia.org/wiki].

  Scooter or **The Scooter:** A **Novelty Fad** Coupledance that appeared in the U.S. in the 1950s. Derived from Eastern Swing.
  (Also see the Bambuco, Bop, Bunny-Hop, Calypso, Creep, Fish, Flea-Hop, Frug, Guapacha, Hand-Jive, Hitch-Hiker, Hokey-Pokey, Hullie-Gullie, Jerk, Limbo-Rock, Mashed-Potato, Monkey, Pachanga, Plena, Pony, Rock-and-Around, Slide, Strole, Surfers, Swim, Tumba-Cha, Twist, Twister, and the Watusi; which were all Novelty Fads in vogue in the 1950-60s.)

  Scotch: An American **Fad** dance of 1962. The **Scotch** had its own Eponymous record, _"Scotch"_ by _The Olympics._
  (See Novelty-&-Fad Dances-of-the-1960s.)
  [From _Soul, www.trinity.unimelb.edu.au._ See _www.sixtiescity.com/Culture/dance._]

  Scrape: Only this name for an American **Novelty** or **Fad** of the 1960s is listed simply as a Dance, Pattern, or Figure in the _"Dance Crazes of the Sixties."_
  (See Novelty-&-Fad Dances-of-the-1960s.) [From _www.sixtiescity.com/Culture/dance_]

  Scratch: An American **Fad** dance of the 1960s. This **Scratch** had its own Eponymous record, _"The Scratch"_ by _Ty Tyrell._
  (See Novelty-&-Fad Dances-of-the-1960s.)
  [From _www.bluejuice.org.au._ See _www.sixtiescity.com/Culture/dance._]

  Scratchin': Only this name for an American **Novelty** or **Fad** of the 1960s is listed simply as a Dance, Pattern, or Figure in the _"Dance Crazes of the Sixties."_
  (See Novelty-&-Fad Dances-of-the-1960s.) [From _www.sixtiescity.com/Culture/dance._]

  Screechie: From Kingston, Jamaica, an Underground **Novelty Fad**, Singular- or Group-Dance Movement, associated with dancing **Dancehall/Ragga**, which, in turn, are outgrowths of **Ska/Reggae**. **Screechie** was and is danced mainly by youths of color.
  The following is from _Ragga Fashions:_ [www.bbc.co.uk]
    "Screechie - Stand with feet apart. Take one step forward, raise on to the ball of your rear foot and twist your heel inwards. Move your hips with the twist but keep your shoulders straight. Lower foot and repeat with the other foot. Once confident, you can move in different directions and travel."
  See **Dancehall**(2) for further explanation. (Also see Bogle, Armstrong, Butterfly, Go-Go-Wine, Body-Basic-and-Exercise, Tate, and World-Dance. Also see Jerry-Springer, Prang, Heel-and-Toe, Na!Na!Na!, Zip-It-Up, Drive-By, Shizzle-Ma-Nizzle, Matrix, and Bin-Laden. Also see Underground Step-Listing.)

  Screw: An American **Fad** dance of the 1960s. This had its own Eponymous record, _"The Screw"_ by _The Crystals._
  (See Novelty-&-Fad Dances-of-the-1960s.)
  [From _www.bluejuice.org.au._ See _www.sixtiescity.com/Culture/dance._]

Scrogg: Only this name for an American **Novelty** or **Fad** of the 1960s is listed simply as a Dance, Pattern, or Figure in the "*Dance Crazes of the Sixties.*"
(See Novelty-&-Fad Dances-of-the-1960s.) [From *www.sixtiescity.com/Culture/dance*]

Scrubs: Only this name for an American **Novelty** or **Fad** of the 1960s is listed simply as a Dance, Pattern, or Figure in the "*Dance Crazes of the Sixties.*"
(See Novelty-&-Fad Dances-of-the-1960s.) [From *www.sixtiescity.com/Culture/dance*]

Scrumble: Only this name for an American **Novelty** or **Fad** of the 1960s is listed simply as a Dance, Pattern, or Figure in the "*Dance Crazes of the Sixties.*"
(See Novelty-&-Fad Dances-of-the-1960s.) [From *www.sixtiescity.com/Culture/dance*]

Seaside: Only this name for an American **Novelty** or **Fad** of the 1960s is listed simply as a Dance, Pattern, or Figure in the "*Dance Crazes of the Sixties.*"
(See Novelty-&-Fad Dances-of-the-1960s.) [From *www.sixtiescity.com/Culture/dance*]

Seesaw: Only this name for an American **Novelty** or **Fad** of the 1960s is listed simply as a Dance, Pattern, or Figure in the "*Dance Crazes of the Sixties.*"
(See Novelty-&-Fad Dances-of-the-1960s.) [From *www.sixtiescity.com/Culture/dance*]

Sexercise-Dance: Primarily a Singular-Dance Term but possibly also a Coupledance Term.
The following is from *sexercises*; [www.answers.com]:
"*A fusion of erotic dance and aerobics designed by Leda Lim of Newport Beach, California. The dance exercise was designed for women to promote self-expression, grace, sexiness, sensuality, confidence, and eroticism. Derived from exotic dance, the stylized, soft, fluid-like appearance is achieved in a series of progressive moves through training of muscle control using many parts of the body. The body's curves are emphasized by the dance positions, leading the dancer to awareness and appreciation of the uniqueness and beauty of their body.*"
(See Belly-Dance. Also see Exotic-Dancer, Pole-Dance, GoGo-Dancer, Cage-Dancer, PassaPassa, and Juking.)

Shaggy-Dog: Only this name for an American **Novelty** or **Fad** of the **1960s** is listed simply as a Dance, Pattern, or Figure in the "*Dance Crazes of the Sixties.*"
(See Novelty-&-Fad Dances-of-the-1960s.) [From *www.sixtiescity.com/Culture/dance*]

Shake or **The Shake:** A fun **Novelty Fad** Singlular or Coupledance, that was Unstructured and Unleadable. The **Shake** originated in the U.S. in the 1960s. This was an Eponymous dance; there was **Shak**ing in Pantomime to 45rpm records of certain songs then popular. these 1963 records were "_Shake_" by _Sam Cooke_, and "_Shake_" by _Laurel Aitken_. Others were possibly "_Shake, Rattle & Roll_, " "_Shake Your Rump To The Funk_," and/or "_Do It_" _(Let Me See You Shake)._

The following is from _www.sixtiescity.com/Culture/dance_:

Listed in the "_Dance Crazes of the Sixties_," along with a 12-pictures Sequence (showing Patrick Kerr?) and the following writeup describing this as a Singular-Dance, Pattern, or Figure:

The Shake: "_Stand with one foot firmly in front of the other, Stretch your arms out and swing from side to side while nodding your head. Shake your upper body from the hips, occasionally jumping to one side or the other._"
(See the Novelty-&-Fad Dances-of-the-1960s.)

Shake-and-Vibrate: A **Novelty Fad** Coupledance of the 1960s. This had its own Eponymous record, "_Shake and Vibrate_" by _Sir Lattimore Brown_.
(See Novelty-&-Fad Dances-of-the-1960s. Especially see Yak-A-Poo)
[From www.bluejuice.org.au]

Shake-A-Poo-Poo: A **Novelty Fad** Coupledance of the 1960s. This had its own Eponymous record, "_Shake a Poo Poo_" by _Chet Poisen Ivey_.
(See Novelty-&-Fad Dances-of-the-1960s.) [From www.bluejuice.org.au]

Shake-a-Tail-Feather: An American **Fad** dance of 1963. The **Shake-a-Tail-Feather** had its own Eponymous record, "_Shake A Tail Feather_" by the _Five Du-Tones_.
(See the Novelty-&-Fad Dances-of-the-1960s.)
[From _Soul_, _www.trinity.unimelb.edu.au_. See _www.sixtiescity.com/Culture/dance_.]

Shake-and-Shingaling: Only this name for an American **Novelty** or **Fad** of the 1960s is listed simply as a Dance, Pattern, or Figure in the "_Dance Crazes of the Sixties_."
(See Novelty-&-Fad Dances-of-the-1960s.) [From _www.sixtiescity.com/Culture/dance_]

Shake-and-Stomp: Only this name for an American **Novelty** or **Fad** of the 1960s is listed simply as a Dance, Pattern, or Figure in the "_Dance Crazes of the Sixties_."
(See Novelty-&-Fad Dances-of-the-1960s.) [From _www.sixtiescity.com/Culture/dance_]

Shake-Around: Only this name for an American **Novelty** or **Fad** of the 1960s is listed simply as a Dance, Pattern, or Figure in the "_Dance Crazes of the Sixties_."
(See Novelty-&-Fad Dances-of-the-1960s.) [From _www.sixtiescity.com/Culture/dance_]

    Shake-Rattle-Snake: Only this name for an American **Novelty** or **Fad** of the 1960s is listed simply as a Dance, Pattern, or Figure in the "*Dance Crazes of the Sixties.*"
    (See Novelty-&-Fad Dances-of-the-1960s.) [From *www.sixtiescity.com/Culture/dance*]

    Shakey-Bird: Only this name for an American **Novelty** or **Fad** of the 1960s is listed simply as a Dance, Pattern, or Figure in the "*Dance Crazes of the Sixties.*"
    (See Novelty-&-Fad Dances-of-the-1960s.) [From *www.sixtiescity.com/Culture/dance*]

    Shampoo: Only this name for an American **Novelty** or **Fad** of the 1960s is listed simply as a Dance, Pattern, or Figure in the "*Dance Crazes of the Sixties.*"
    (See Novelty-&-Fad Dances-of-the-1960s.) [From *www.sixtiescity.com/Culture/dance*]

    Shelley: An Unleadable, American **Novelty Fad,** Spot-Choreographed Singular or Coupledance, sort of Line-Dance Routine. With a medium-Cadence 4/4 Tempo, the following four-Measures long Pattern was in vogue in the 1960s at the Brigham Young University, in Provo, Utah. It is unknown who Shelley was.
    There is a picture from Brigham Young University, labeled and showing a young couple dancing the **Shelley.** They are Apart Side-by-Side in Shine Position, upon the Same-Feet, Facing the same direction and looking Forward. Their Right Knees are Softened while their Straight-Legged Left Feet are Kicking Forward and Slightly Crossed with Pointed Toes. Their hips Sway Left. Their Right arms are bent and Forward with hands at Waist-Level. Their Left arms are bent and Sideways with hands at Waist-Level; the Man's arm is behind the Lady. All fingers are relaxed.
    Rhythm Timing was all *Slow*s. **Shelley** was danced *sidestep CrossKick StepCrossed close*; *SideStep crosskick stepcrossed Close*; *sidestep TouchClosed TouchSide TouchClosed*; *SideStep touchclosed touchside touchclosed.* Start over.
    (See the Novelty-&-Fad Dances-of-the-1960s.) [Data mostly from "Rhythm and Dance" by Alma Heaton.]

    Shilly-Dilly: Only this name for an American **Novelty** or **Fad** of the 1960s is listed simply as a Dance, Pattern, or Figure in the "*Dance Crazes of the Sixties.*"
    (See Novelty-&-Fad Dances-of-the-1960s.) [From *www.sixtiescity.com/Culture/dance*]

Shimmy(1) (chemise) or **The Shimmy** or **Shimmies** or **Shimmy-Sha-Wabble** or **Shimmy-Shake:** Unleadable, American Ragtime Era, **Novelty Fad** Basic Solo Spot-dance series of Actions, Singularly Performed, suitable for **Jazz** dancing, most **Hustles**, Eastern **Swing**, West-Coast-Swing, Jive, both **ChaChas**, both **Mambos**, and both **Rumbas**, among other dances.

History of Modern Ballroom Dancing [http://linus.socs.uts.edu.au/] describes it as follows:

"The Shimmy was probably derived from a Nigerian dance, the `Shika', taken to America by the black slaves. It was mentioned in the song `The Bullfrog Hop' in 1909 by Perry Bradford. It became very popular in the USA 1910 to 1920, and became a national craze after Gilda Grey introduced it in the Zeigfeld Follies in 1922, and claims the name comes from `chemise', having been asked by a reporter what she shook in the dance. However, Mae West claims to have done it in the show `Sometime' in 1919. It was described by the singer Ethel Waters, saying she put her hands on her hips and worked her body fast without moving the feet (Sadie, 1980, 17/257). Nowadays, the word means to shake the shoulders or hips rapidly, rotating them alternately left and right forward and back about a vertical axis, and is an integral part of Belly Dancing."

The following are excerpts is from Tin Pan Alley - Part 1 [http://www.wrkf.org/tinpan1]:

"The Shimmy was introduced around 1900. Ethel Waters was first a Shimmy dancer before she started singing.

"The 1918 hit `Everybody Shimmies Now' had a picture of Mae West on the sheet music cover. The dance was still going strong when Armond J. Piron wrote `I Wish I Could Shimmy Like My Sister Kate' in 1922."

Others say the **Shimmy** became popular in the U.S. about 1921, as created by Gilda Gray about 1918. **The Shimmy** not only had Shaking of one's shoulders, but especially the hips. This **Shimmy** may have been an offshoot of a **Shimmy** danced by Blacks in the late 1800s. **The Shimmy** also possibly opened the way for the **Charleston** to become the rage.

Ladies in the 1920s and the 1950s-60s, wearing a tasseled dress, would shake their tassels while dancing. With Knees Together and Softened and with attempting to keep one's Lower-Body isolated for no Movement, the Shimmy is Performed seemingly above the waist, although the result is one's entire Body shakes. Shoulders are Rotated flatly in alternately reversing Movements, Clockwise and Counter-Clockwise, either rapidly or slowly, according to the Beat and Rhythm of the music.

The following is from *Line/C&W Dance & Music FAQ* -- [http://ourworld.compuserve.com]:

"*SHIMMY   A left to right or right to left movement of the shoulders and upper body. Essentially a style move. Sometimes referred to as SHIMMIES.*"

The following is from *Sonny Watson's Dance History* -- [www.streetswing.com]:

"*1953 - Actress Sheree North broke her foot doing the Shimmy in the Jitterbug scene in the movie "Living It Up!" with Jerry Lewis.*"

(See Shim-Sham, Peck, and Ahselroten. Also see Shrug, Hip-Motion, Hip-Rocks, Sway, Broken-Sways, Boogie-Roll(1), Snake-Hips, Washing-Machine, Sway-to-and-Fro, Hip-Lift, Side-Lift, Side-Rise, Body-Lift, Hula-Dance, Cuban-Hip, Cuban-Motion, Forward-Roll, Up-and-Over-the-Top, Wag, Waddle, Arm-Waves, Body-Wave, Body-Ripple, Side-Body-Waves, Figure-Eight, and Hip-Waves. Also see the Varsity-Drag, and the Black-Bottom; both Novelty Fads in vogue in the 1920s. Also see Shizzle-Me-Nizzle.)

<u>**Shimmy**</u>(2):   **A Novelty** and **Fad** dance in 1959 and later (and long before). In 1959, there was a profusion of "Shimmy" singing records produced. They were "*Shimmy Like Kate*" by *The Olympics*, "*Shout And Shimmy*" by *James Brown*, "*Shimmy Shimmy*" by *The Orlons*, and "*Let's Shimmy*" by *King Coleman*. [From *Soul*, www.trinity.unimelb.edu.au]

The following is from <u>*Dance Crazes of the Sixties*</u> - [From *www.sixtiescity.com/Culture/dance*]:

"***The Shimmy:*** *The Shimmy is a dance in which the body is held still, except for the shoulders, which are alternated back and forth. When the right shoulder goes back, the left one comes forward. It may help to hold the arms out slightly bent at the elbow and, when the shoulders are moved, keep the hands in the same position.*"

The following rhyme is from *Armand J. Piron* from the 1919 "*Shimmy Like Kate*":

"*I wish I could shimmy like my sister Kate,*
"*She shivers like the jelly on a plate.*"

(See Novelty-&-Fad Dances-of-the-1960s.)

<u>**Shimmy-and-Twist**</u>: A **Novelty Fad** dance of 1960. The **Shimmy-and-Twist** had its own Eponymous record, "*Shimmy & Twist*" by *Neville Esson*. [From *Soul*, www.trinity.unimelb.edu.au]

"*Discourse on virtue and they pass by in droves. Whistle and dance the shimmy, and you've got an audience.*" -- Diogenes

(See the Novelty-&-Fad Dances-of-the-1960s.)

<u>**Shimmy-Shake**</u>:   See Shimmy.

<u>**Shimmy-Sha-Wabble**</u>: See Shimmy.

<u>**Shimmy-Shimmy-Go-Go-Bop**</u>:   A **Novelty Fad** dance Routine in vogue in the United States, probably in the 1960s. In 4/4 Tempo, this Routine probably had its own Eponymous song that described how it was to be danced.

(See Novelty-&-Fad Dances-of-the-1960s.)

<u>**Shimmy-Watusi**</u>: Only this name for an American **Novelty** or **Fad** of the **1960s** is listed simply as a Dance, Pattern, or Figure in the "<u>*Dance Crazes of the Sixties*</u>."

(See Novelty-&-Fad Dances-of-the-1960s.) [From *www.sixtiescity.com/Culture/dance*]

<u>**Shim-Sham**</u>(1) or **Sham** or **Shim-Sham-Shimmy**(2) or **Gofus:** Solo, **Novelty Fad** Coupledance or Group-Dance Terms for a Lazy, **Shuffling Soft-Shoe** Routine. A break-A-Way Shine Step, **Shim-Sham** is a combination of **Tap-Dancing** and Body Movements, and is part of the **Tap-Dance Genre**. Many claim that this **Shim-Sham-Shimmy** to be the "_National Anthem of Tap_."

   Shim-Sham was made famous by the Harlem Cotton Club dancers in the 1920s, and had become a Standard Routine in Show-Business by around 1931. Still earlier in the 1920s, **Shim-Sham** had been a Vaudeville **Tap-Dancing** Routine. It seems that the **Shim-Sham** Step had originally come from **Tap-Jams**, often where the informal circle of Tap-Dancers would mark the ever-increasing Tempo with the following **Time-Step:** _shuf-fle step, shuf-fle step, shuf-fle ball-change, shuf-fle step_, (eight Counts.)

   Shim Sham's beginnings are generally believed to have been invented as an encore Type of Performance in Vaudeville, in which all the Performers knew **Shim Sham**. Everyone from all the different circuits could get together on a moment's notice and perform this `Finale' without any Rehersing.

   Danced Apart, or if as a Group, they sometimes all Faced in the same direction with each person's arms around the next person. The above **Time-Step** would be danced, usually with a more Shuffled Rhythm than with the Lifting of the Feet. **Stop-Times** were included.

   Later in the 1980s-90s, **Shim-Sham** became the name for a Singles Jazz Line Dance.

   This **Shim-Sham,** and other Shine Steps, are most often Executed on the "Back-Beat" or the "And" (also called _anecrusis_ or "Pick-Up"), or on the quarter, eighth or sixteenth division of the Beat. Creating a kind of Poly-Rhythm by dancing on this "Pick-Up", is the Essence and definition of Tap-Dance.

   As with almost all Tap-Dance, this whole **Shim-Sham** Sequence Starts on Count-8, creating what Tap-Dancers and Musicians call Phasing. Tap-Dance Steps are one Beat ahead of its Music Rhythm-Pattern, but remain the same Musical length as those in its Song. Additionally, this **Shim-Sham** shifts as it picks up Accents at the quarter, eighth, and sixteenth of the Beat, while continuing its Phasing Pattern. This is all quite sophisticated for social dancers, but Routine for Tap-Dancers and Musicians.

   The following is from _Vance's Fantastic Tap Dance Dictionary_:

   "_Shim Sham: An early tap combination that endured many years and is still used extensively. Shuffle Step R, Shuffle Step L, Shuffle Ball change R-L, Shuffle Step R. Repeat and Reverse._"

   The following is from _"TAP!"_ by Rusty E. Frank:

   "_SHIM SHAM SHIMMY: A four-step routine created in the 1920s by Leonard Reed and Willie Bryant, originally called Gofus. Shimmying of the shoulders added. (The four steps are: 1. Shim Sham, 2. Push Beat and a cross over, 3. Tack Annie 4. Half Break, and then the Walk Off is tagged on.)_"

   Similar to the **Vaudeville-Time-Step**. [See Tack-Annie, Shimmy, and Swing-Foot. Also see Break-A-Way, Boogie-Woogie(3), and The-Hop.] [Much data from Sonny Watson's StreetSwing.com]

    Shim-Sham(2): **Shim-Sham**(2) **Novelty Fad** Soft-Shoe Routine is a continuation of **Shim-Sham**(1), except this version (complete) was taught by Rhona Mackay (Edinburgh) and Rob Bloom (Sydney):   [Note that all **Shim-Shams** have 4/4 Timing, and begin early on the Pickup(2).]

    The following is from "*The Shim Sham*," [http://golgi.ana.ed.ac.uk]:

        "... the dance consists of two iterations of the first 4 ... blocks ..., followed by two final 32-beat blocks..."

        "... a step-by-step guide to all 320 beats of the dance appears below ... Remember, most figures start on beat 8!"

    1st & 5th blocks, each 32 beats - **Shim-Sham Stomps** - R; L; R; Break:

        "8: Right Stomp #1: R foot extend & drop flat on floor diagonally in front

        "1: drag R foot back

        "2: L foot extend & drop flat on floor diagonally in front

        "3: drag L foot back

        "4: R foot extend & drop flat on floor diagonally in front

        "5: drag R foot back

        "6: R foot extend & drop flat on floor diagonally in front

        "7: drag R foot back

        "8-7: Left Stomp: Mirror-Image of Right Stomp #1.

        "8-7: Right Stomp #2: Repeat Right Stomp #1.

        "8: Full Break: Drop on to R foot in front of you

        "1: Dot L foot behind it

        "2: Step back on to left foot

        "3:

        "&: R knee up

        "4: R foot returns to floor (a little back)

        "&: L knee up

        "5: L foot returns to floor (a little back)

        "6: Slide legs apart

        "7: Bring legs back together.

    [Above Full Break may be replaced by a legs apart stance, R leg diagonally forward of L, with hip swaying and finger clicking on beats 1,3,5,7. For 2nd Full Break, just pause.]

    2nd & 6th blocks, each 32 beats - **Hip-Pushes** - R; L; R; Single-Crosses:

        "8: Right Hip-Push #1: Place R foot diag front right and push hip to it

        "1: (do this facing diag front right)

        "2: Push hip again

        "3:

        "4: Push hip again

        "5: (prepare to lift L foot)

        "6: Cross L foot in front of right and place weight on it

        "7: Pick up R foot and place behind and to right of L foot -

                      this turns your body 90 degrees to face diag front left

        "8-7: Left Hip-Push: Mirror-Image of Right Hip-Push #1.

        "8-7: Right Hip-Push #2: Repeat Right Hip-Push #1.

        "8: Single-Crosses: Place left foot diag forward left (face diag front left)

                (Continued)

<u>**Shim-Sham**</u>(2):   (Continued)
>   *"1:*
>   *"2: Cross R foot in front of L and place weight on it*
>   *"3: Place L foot behind and to left of R foot*
>   *"4: Place R foot diag forward right (face diag front right)*
>   *"5:*
>   *"6: Cross L foot in front or R and place weight on it*
>   *"7: Tap R foot to R of left foot (so you are now facing forward)*

3rd & 7th blocks, each 32 beats - **Tack-Annies** - three times then Break:
>   *"8: Open R leg out, weight shared by both legs.*
>   *"1: Dot R foot behind L (arms swing to L)*
>   *"2: Open R leg out again, weight shared by both legs.*
>   *"3: Dot L foot behind R (arms swing to R)*
>   *"4: Open L leg out again, weight shared by both legs.*
>   *"5: Dot R foot behind L (arms swing to L)*
>   *"6: Open R leg out again, weight shared by both legs.*
>   *"7: Step on L foot behind R (arms swing to R)."*
>   *"8-7: Full Break: Repeat from 1st & 5th blocks.*

4th & 8th blocks, each 32 beats - **Breaks** - 2 Half, 1 Full, 2 Half, 1 Full:
>   *"8: 1st Half Break: Drop weight on R foot in front of you*
>   *"1: Put weight on L foot behind R*
>   *"2: Flick R foot (`shuffle')*
>   *"&3: Ball change R-L*
>   *"4: 2nd Half Break: Drop weight on R foot in front of you*
>   *"5: Put weight on L foot behind R*
>   *"6: Flick R foot (`shuffle')*
>   *"&7: Ball change R-L*
>   *"8-7: Full Break: Repeat from 1st & 5th blocks.*
>   *"8-&3: 1st Half Break: Repeat above*
>   *"4-&7: 2nd Half Break: Repeat above*
>   *"8-7: Full Break: Repeat from 1st & 5th blocks.*

"Now go right back to the top and repeat everything once, with pauses in place of full breaks, then carry on to the 9th & 10th 32-beat blocks below:

9th & 10th 32-beat blocks - **Boogie backs and forwards** (the 1st 4 were done 2x):
>   *"8: 1st Boogie-Back: Flick right foot, Clap*
>   *"&1: ball change (R-L)*
>   *"2: Flick right foot, Clap*
>   *"&3: Ball change R-L*
>   *"4: Flick right foot, Clap*
>   *"&5: Ball change R-L*
>   *"6: Flick right foot, Clap*
>   *"&7: Ball change R-L*
>   *"8: 1st Shorty-George: Flick right foot, then drop to it on `&'*
>   *"1-7: Advance slightly with L,R,L,R,L,R,L foot.*
>   *"8-7: 2nd Boogie-Back: Repeat <u>1st Boogie-Back</u>*
>   *"8-7: 2nd Shorty-George: Repeat <u>1st Shorty-George</u>.*

(See **Boogie-Back-and-Forward-Shorty**, Boogie-Back, and Shorty-George for details. Also see Shim-Sham Break, CrossOvers, Tack-Annie, and Shim-Sham Half-Break. Also see Vaudeville-Time-Step, and Traveling-Time-Step.)   *"And now pair up and dance Lindy Hop!"*

Shim-Sham Break or **Full-Break**: A Solo, **Novelty Fad** Coupledance, or Group-Dance, Soft-Shoe short Routine, and Generally part of the **Shim-Sham** Routine in the **Tap-Dance Genre**. An Unleadable, 8-Count Pattern Sequence Performed several times. See Break(7).

The following is from *"Swing Junction: Routines,"* [http://home.iprimus.com.au]:

"SHIM SHAM BREAK: step R tap L step L tap R step R step L step R step L."

This above 8-Count Pattern Sequence can be found, in detail, in the 1st & 5th, and 4th & 8th, block-portions of the **Shim-Sham**(2) Routine.

Shim-Sham Half-Break: A Solo, **Novelty Fad** Coupledance, or Group-Dance, Soft-Shoe short Routine, and Generally part of the **Shim-Sham** Routine in the **Tap-Dance Genre**. An Unleadable, 8-Count Pattern Sequence Performed twice.

The following is from *"Swing Junction: Routines,"* [http://home.iprimus.com.au]:

"HALF BREAK:

"drop R step L kick-ball-change drop R step L kick-ball-change."

This above Pattern can be found, in detail, in the 4th & 8th block-portions of the **Shim-Sham**(2) Routine.

Shim-Sham-Shimmy: A **Novelty Fad** dance of 1963. The **Shim-Sham-Shimmy** had its own Eponymous record, *"Shim Sham Shimmy"* by *Billy The Kid Emerson*. [From *Soul*, www.trinity.unimelb.edu.au]

Shing-A-Ling(1): An American **Novelty** and **Fad** dance of 1965. The **Shing-A-Ling** had its own Eponymous records, *"Mumble Shing-A-Lingy"* by *The Emperors*, *"The Funky Shing A Ling"* by *Milton Howard*, and *"Shing A Ling"* by *Desmond Dekker & Aces*.

(See Novelty-&-Fad Dances-of-the-1960s.)

[From *Soul*, *www.trinity.unimelb.edu.au*. See *www.sixtiescity.com/Culture/dance*.]

Shing-A-Ling(2): See Boogaloo.

Shing-A-Ling-A-Loo: Only this name for an American **Novelty** or **Fad** of the 1960s is listed simply as a Dance, Pattern, or Figure in the *"Dance Crazes of the Sixties."*

(See Novelty-&-Fad Dances-of-the-1960s.) [From *www.sixtiescity.com/Culture/dance*]

Shing-A-Ling-Stroll: Only this name for an American **Novelty** or **Fad** of the 1960s is listed simply as a Dance, Pattern, or Figure in the *"Dance Crazes of the Sixties."*

(See Novelty-&-Fad Dances-of-the-1960s.) [From *www.sixtiescity.com/Culture/dance*]

Shiver-Dance: A **Novelty Fad** Coupledance popular in America about 1912. One would shake one's shoulders. It appears as if the person is dancing in Jello. **Shiver-Dance** is still danced currently at times.

(See the Boston-Dip, Bunny-Hug, Gaby-Glide, Hug-Me-Close, Lame-Duck, and Turkey-Trot; these were all Novelty Fads in vogue in the 1910s.) [Also see Shake(1).]

Shizzle-Ma-Nizzle: From Kingston, Jamaica, an Underground **Novelty Fad**, Singular- or Group-Dance Movement, associated with dancing **Dancehall/Ragga**, which, in turn, are outgrowths of **Ska/Reggae**. **Shizzle-Ma-Nizzle** was and is danced mainly by youths of color. The following is from _Ragga Fashions_: [www.bbc.co.uk]

"_Shizzle-Ma-Nizzle - Stand with feet apart. Shimmy your shoulders whilst bending your knees. As you bend your knees you pick up one of your legs and kick outwards. Repeat dance with the other leg._"

See **Dancehall**(2) for further explanation. (See Shimmy. Also see Bogle, Armstrong, Butterfly, Go-Go-Wine, Body-Basic-and-Exercise, Tate, and World-Dance. Also see Jerry-Springer, Prang, Heel-and-Toe, Na!Na!Na!, Screechie, Zip-It-Up, Drive-By, Matrix, and Bin-Laden. Also see Underground Step-Listing.)

Shoddy-Shoddy: Only this name for an American **Novelty** or **Fad** of the 1960s is listed simply as a Dance, Pattern, or Figure in the "_Dance Crazes of the Sixties_."

(See Novelty-&-Fad Dances-of-the-1960s.) [From _www.sixtiescity.com/Culture/dance_]

Shoe-Shiner's-Drag: An American **Novelty Fad** Coupledance (or possibly just a tune) in vogue in the 1910s or `20s. Other "_drag dances_" of the time were the A-Minor-Drag, Dizzy-Drag, Saratoga-Drag, Slow-Drag, Viper's-Drag, and the most famous **Varsity-Drag**.

Shoop: A **Novelty Fad** Coupledance of 1966. It's Eponymous Music was "_The Hula Hoop (Shoop Shoop)_" by _Dave Baby Cortez_.

(See Novelty-&-Fad Dances-of-the-1960s. Especially see Peg-Leg.)
[From www.bluejuice.org.au]

Shoot'em-Up-Twist: A **Novelty Fad** Coupledance of the 1960s. This had its own Eponymous record, "_The Shoot'Em Up Twist_" by _Charles LaVerne_.

(See Novelty-&-Fad Dances-of-the-1960s.) [From www.bluejuice.org.au]

Shopping-Cart: In comical Pantomime, a **Novelty Fad** Singular dance Pattern or Routine of the 1980s. How to dance the **Shopping-Cart** to the Beat is described as follows in the "_**Eighties Dances**_," [www.inthe80s.com]:

"_It sorta starts out like the lawnmower. You have your hands in front of you, your fists closed like your holding onto the handle. Then swinging your hips steady and shuffling your feet, you throw one hand out like grasping a can. Placing it back on the cart handle do it again with the other hand. Repeat._"

(See Lawn-Mower, Pedal-the-Bike, and Mime.)

Shorty-George or **Boogie-Walks:** An Unleadable 1930s **Separated-Break-A-Way Novelty Fad** Pattern, originating with the **Cake-Walk**, and usually Performed while dancing the **Big-Apple**, or the **Carolina-Shag**, or a **Swing-Bal** Break from the **Pure-Balboa**. Also suitable for the many **Swing** dances. After separating from one's Partner while dancing the **Lindy-Hop**, one would often **Shorty-George** to return back Together.

The following is an excerpt from "*Wikipedia, the free encyclopedia*":

"***Classic era (1927 to 1935) -*** *This era was inspired by ragtime jazz. Lindy Hop evolved from the combination of Breakaway and Charleston. Dancers, like George Snowden (Shorty George) opened up Breakaway and Charleston. The partners moved closer together and further apart while spinning to make the moves more interesting, eventually creating the swing out.*"

On the Major-Primary-DownBeat, the **Shorty-George** might begin with a Kick-Ball-Change, or a Cucaracha or the like, but the dancer would usually begin with a **Boogie-Back**, which is a **Kick-Ball-Change 4 times for 8 Counts, drifting Rearward, Clapping Hands on Counts 2,4,6,8**. Then the separated Partner `Boogies' from four to six *Slow*, short Steps Forward, with index fingers Pointed Down, as Walks slope Downward.

Free Hip is Raised DiagForward in a Circular Motion and Moved out from one's Supporting-Leg before Free-Foot is Stepped Forward, i.e., one's free Hip-Lifts to Move Circularly in the direction of the Supporting-Foot. Swiveling on Balls, with Knees Together and Well Bent, Hips are Swayed Side-to-Side. One's Right Step rolls from Inner-Edge onto the Outer-Edge of Right Ball-of Foot, as one's Right Hip protrudes Outward and Up. One's Left Step is Opposite.

For the **Big-Apple**, the **Shorty-George**, which is the same as the **Boogie**, was one of the **Break-A-Way** Genre. Wiggling their hips, certain **Break-A-Way** Patterns were danced. The original **Suzie-Q, Boogie-Back, Tack-Annie, Georgia-Grind, Praise-Allah!, Truckin', Peckin', Charleston, Shorty-George**, and other Break-A-Ways, were probably originated early by blacks; while **Spank-the-Baby, Rusty-Dusty, Pose-and-a-Peck**, the **Little-Apple**, the **Little-Peach, Mess-Around, Stomp-Off, Apple-Jacks**, and **Fall-Off-the-Log**, and other Break-A-Ways, were probably originated later by whites. Most all of these Patterns seem to have been influenced or derived from the classic **Lindy-Hop** and/or **Big-Apple** dances. See **Break-A-Way Glossary** for more listing. Also see **Break-Endings** for many additional Break-A-Ways that were derived or influenced by **West-Coast-Swing**. [Also see Shim-Sham(2), Boogie(1), and Boogie-Woogie(3). Also see Point(2).]

Shotgun: An Unstructured, American **Novelty** or **Fad** Singular or Coupledance in vogue in the 1960s. In 1965, *Junior Walker &The Allstars* sang and recorded, "*The Shotgun.*" Its Eponymous dance Movements, which attempted to imitate a **Shotgun** through Pantomime, came into vogue.

(See the Novelty-&-Fad Dances-of-the-1960s.) [See *www.sixtiescity.com/Culture/dance.*]

Shotgun-Boogie: Only this name for an American **Novelty** or **Fad** of the 1960s is listed simply as a Dance, Pattern, or Figure in the "*Dance Crazes of the Sixties.*"

(See Novelty-&-Fad Dances-of-the-1960s.) [From *www.sixtiescity.com/Culture/dance*]

Shotish: Only this name for an American **Novelty** or **Fad** of the 1960s is listed simply as a Dance, Pattern, or Figure in the "_Dance Crazes of the Sixties_."
    (See Novelty-&-Fad Dances-of-the-1960s.) [From _www.sixtiescity.com/Culture/dance_]

Shoulder-Lean: A **Novelty** or **Fad** dance of an unknown time, listed in "_Novelty and fad dances_" under [http://en.wikipedia.org/wiki].

Shout-&-Do-The-Duck: An American **Fad** dance of the 1960s. This had its own Eponymous record, "_Shout & Do The Duck_" by _Larry Hale_.
    (See Duck, Duck-Walk, and Novelty-&-Fad Dances-of-the-1960s.)
    [From _www.bluejuice.org.au_. See _www.sixtiescity.com/Culture/dance_.]

Shout-Dance: A 1980s **Novelty Fad Group-Dance** Routine. How to dance the **Shout-Dance** is described as follows in the "_**Eighties Dances**_," [www.inthe80s.com]:
    "_**The Animal House "Shout" Dance** - There was a song from the Animal House soundtrack that was ALWAYS a hit at EVERY dance I went to as a teen in the 80s: `(You Make Me Wanna) SHOUT'. We would get into a big circle and when it would get to the lyric: `Let's get a little softer now...' we would dance lower and lower to the floor, until `Let's get louder now'._"
    (See Twist-and-Shout, and Limbo-Rock.)

Shovel: Only this name for an American **Novelty** or **Fad** of the 1960s is listed simply as a Dance, Pattern, or Figure in the "_Dance Crazes of the Sixties_."
    (See Novelty-&-Fad Dances-of-the-1960s.) [From _www.sixtiescity.com/Culture/dance_]

Shuffle(1): Only this name for an American **Novelty** or **Fad** of the 1960s is listed simply as a Dance, Pattern, or Figure in the "_Dance Crazes of the Sixties_."
    (See Novelty-&-Fad Dances-of-the-1960s.) [From _www.sixtiescity.com/Culture/dance_]

Shuffle(2): A Coupledance of the 1840s-1870s.

SideSlide or SkyWalk: A **Novelty Fad** Singular dance Pattern or Routine, and one of the **Basic-Moves-for-Break-Dancing**. This **SideSlide** is part of the **Electric-Boogie** style of **Break-Dancing**, which, in turn, is one major part of **Hip-Hop**. This **SideSlide** is danced almost Stationary in Cadence with the Music, and is also suitable for certain **Swing**s and for still other dances.

How to dance the **SideSlide** to the Beat is partially described as follows in the "*Eighties Dances*," [www.inthe80s.com]:

"*Sideslide - Just like a MOONWALK but sideways. Creates an illusion of flitting across the floor. Michael Jackson does this move as well as his moonwalk.*"

A later version of the above "*Eighties Dances*," [www.inthe80s.com] is as follows:

"*Skywalk - This is a Michael Jackson move just like the Moonwalk except it makes you look as if you're floating sideways across the air. Someone listed this move as the SideSlide on here... but the name for it is the Skywalk. Man, Michael Jackson sure is a Master of the Dance, isn't he?*"

See the **Moon-Walk** writeup in this encyclopedia for explicit Moon-Walk instructions. [Also see Novelty-&-Fad Dances-of-the-1980s. Also see Break-Dancing, Electric-Boogie, Cake-Walk, Walkin'-the-Dog, Praise-You, Running-Man, Step-Scoot, Camel-Walk(3), Stationary-Copas, Heel-and-Toe, and Syncopated-Splits. Also see Underground Step-Listing.]

Side-Switches: Two Unleadable, General, In-Place-Coupledance Movements, Left and Right, used in both **Quicksteps**, in **Country-Western** Line- or Partner-Dancing, in **Folkdance**, and in other dances. Generally danced in some Loose-Closed Position. Usually danced in multiples.

Side-Switches are danced by Shifting Weight from one Foot to the other with a rapid Sliding Movement; i.e., bring one Foot **Home with a Hop** while **Extending Straight-Legged Outward Sideways** and Touching the Opposite Instep(4) to the Dancefloor. It is optional for the Instep not to Touch. At Home, Foot Replaces Foot at the identical location. Each Partner looks Toward the side Pointed.

Switches Left then Right are danced *A'slow a'Slow*, (or *And swing and Swing*):

The Man dances *hopHomesidetouch HophomeSideTouch*. The Lady dances Mirror-Image Opposite.

Similar to **Switch**(3), **Change-And-Change**, **And-Change-And-Change-And**, **Heel-Switches**, **Quick-Points**, and **California-Shuffle**. [See Scatter-Chasses, Hop-Scotch(2), Woodpecker, and Woodpecker-Taps, for Quickstep Routines. Also see Change-Feet-Multiplicity, Change-Feet, Replace, and Recover.]

__Side-Touches__ or **Side-Slides:** Two General and Unleadable **Novelty Fad** Spot-Singular or Spot-Coupledance Movements, Left and Right, Mirror-Image Opposite; Closing then Sideways Sliding Movements of one's Feet. At least one set in Sequence is normally danced, Pointing toward one side and then toward the other with Feet. Often used in the **PasoDoble** in conjunction with the Coup-de-Pique. Also frequently used While **Skanking** Singularly to the **Ska** or **Reggae**, in which the **Side-Slides** become a small Variation.

 Side-Touches are Half-a-Measure Movements In-Place in 4/4 Time. With the dancer's Foot Apart Sideways, then that Foot is separately Slid back Together, with a Simultaneous Change-Feet to Stepping Sideways to the Opposite side. Movement is normally repeated Mirror-Image Opposite. Beginning with one Foot Touching to-the-side, Rhythm Timing is either *andSlow, Andslow;* or *Andslow, andSlow.* As a Figure, beginning from one's Left then from one's Right, *slidehome SlideAwayTouch, SlideHome slideawaytouch.* Lady, if Facing, dances Mirror-Image Opposite.

 Similar to **Syncopated-Splits.** [See Slide(3), Skim, and Skid. Also see Underground Step-Listing. Also see Running-Man, Moon-Walk, SideSlide, Step-Scoot, Stationary-Copas, and Cake-Walk.]

__Sightseein':__ Only this name for an American **Novelty** or **Fad** of the 1960s is listed simply as a Dance, Pattern, or Figure in the "*Dance Crazes of the Sixties.*"
 (See Novelty-&-Fad Dances-of-the-1960s.) [From *www.sixtiescity.com/Culture/dance*]

__Simon-Says:__ Only this name for an American **Novelty** or **Fad** of the 1960s is listed simply as a Dance, Pattern, or Figure in the "*Dance Crazes of the Sixties.*"
 (See Novelty-&-Fad Dances-of-the-1960s.) [From *www.sixtiescity.com/Culture/dance*]

__Sissy-Strut__(1): An American **Fad** dance of 1965. The **Sissy-Strut** had its own Eponymous record, "*Cissy Strut*" by *The Meters.*
 (See the Novelty-&-Fad Dances-of-the-1960s.)
 [From *Soul, www.trinity.unimelb.edu.au.* See *www.sixtiescity.com/Culture/dance.*]

__Sissy-Strut__(2): See Sissy-Walk.

__Sissy-Walk__ or **Sissy-Strut**(2): Unleadable, General, **Novelty Fad** Singular dance Forward-Traveling Steps. Usually danced very Slowly with a constant Cadence, the **Sissy-Walk** barely Progresses. Stepped with legs remaining Spread, the dancer diagonally Side-Steps and Swivels each Step, grossly protruding then Forward-Rolling the hip Stepped. Arms hang and Swing. The Head remains vertical throughout.

 The **Sissy-Walk** was danced extensively in the **Chicago-City** novelty Fad dance Routine. Similar to **Boogie**(1), **Camel-Walk**(3), and the **Shorty-George**. (See Cake-Walk, Kiki-Walks, Walkin'-the-Dog, Stroll, Skate, and Skim.)

Sit-Down-Dance: Only this name for an American **Novelty** or **Fad** of the 1960s is listed simply as a Dance, Pattern, or Figure in the "*Dance Crazes of the Sixties.*"
Perhaps similar to (or the same as) the *Sitting-Down-Boogie.*
(See Novelty-&-Fad Dances-of-the-1960s.) [From *www.sixtiescity.com/Culture/dance*]

Sitting-Down-Boogie: A **Novelty Fad** Group-Dance in vogue in 1956.
Possibly similar to Hand-Jive, Hitch-Hiker, Churnin'-Butter, Palm-Circles(1), Belinda, Teen-Wolf, Sprinkler, and Tiffany. (Also see Stationary-Dancing, Arm-and-Hand Aerobics, Chair-Dancing, Finger-Flourishes, Free-Hand-Fashioning, and Gestures-Free-Hand.) [Some from *Novelty Dances Through the Years* by Pony Moore.]

Sizzle: Only this name for an American **Novelty** or **Fad** of the **1960s** is listed simply as a Dance, Pattern, or Figure in the "*Dance Crazes of the Sixties.*"
(See Novelty-&-Fad Dances-of-the-1960s.) [From *www.sixtiescity.com/Culture/dance*]

Ska: An underground Singular- or Group-dance, originating from Jamaica in 1962 and centered in West Kingston in the early 1960s. An extremely danceable precursor of **Reggae** dancing, **Ska** is frenetic, Up-Beat and fun. It is danced to Jamaican **Mento** Rhythm and music, originating with the teen-agers and **Rude-Boy** youths of blacks and people of color. This **Novelty Fad Ska** presently has a dedicated following but has never quite made it into mainstream.
The early 1960s "*first wave*" for the high-energy, raucus **Ska** had its music forming out of both **Mento** Rhythms and American Rhythm-and-Blues, each of which was popular in Jamaica during that time. Jamaican guitarists began emphasizing the Upbeat rather than the Downbeat, and thereby the major characteristic of the new **Ska** sound was developed, combined with heavy jazz soloing and bebop improvisation. **Ska** is considered Jamaica's first commercial music.
By 1963, the following **Ska** records were available: "*Do The Ska*" by *Delroy & Pauline,* "*Ska Jerk*" by *The Wailers,* "*Teach The Ska*" by *Lord Brynner,* "*Jamaica Ska*" by *Byron Lee & Dragonaires,* "*Ska Down Jamaica Way*" by *Ferdie Nelson,* and "*Ska All Over The World*" by *Jimmy Cliff.* [From *Soul,* www.trinity.unimelb.edu.au]
The following is from *www.sixtiescity.com/Culture/dance*:
Listed in the "*Dance Crazes of the Sixties,*" along with a 12-pictures Sequence (showing Patrick Kerr?) and the following writeup describing this as a Singular-Dance, Pattern, or Figure:
The Ska: "*'Milk a cow' with your hands while in a crouched position, swaying from the hips. Keep the rhythm, moving slowly up and down, occasionally lifting one foot up high.*"
Rude-Boys ruled the Jamaican Dance-Halls with the **Skank** dance until the Slow **RockSteady** dancing was born by the mid-1960s, which in turn, influenced the creation of **Reggae**. The **Ska**'s "*first wave*" finally ended about 1968. These were the original Jamaican **Ska** sounds, the swagger and jazz of old school **Ska**. [Much from History of Ska; www.angelfire.com; and www.section3.com]
There had been a conscious effort to soften and de-politicize the new Jamaican music known as **Ska**. **Ska** was modified to make it more appealing to middle-class tastes and political sensibilities. This meant that the music was made "softer", and in terms of the dancing, **Ska** was drastically simplified and de-eroticized. [Ska/Reggae; www.ska.about.com]
(Continued)

Ska: (Continued)

In the U.S. in 1964, *Jay, Bob and The Hawks* had put out *The Ska, The Watusi,* and *The Monkey* 45 rpm records. (Perhaps they did not originate the songs.)

The **Ska** "*second wave*" began in the 1970s from unharmonious racial relations with the many Jamaicans that had immigrated into the U.K. Also, the *punk revolution* was taking form in the 1970s. The following exerpt is from *History of Ska*: [www.angelfire.com]

"*---. Punk music was about treating everyone equal, doing what you want, and not doing what others wanted to force you to do. At the start, however, while there were thousands of punks popping up all over the place [in the U.K.], there were only 3 or 4 actual bands in existance. Needing extra music to fill up space, club owners asked these new Britons [Jamaican Ska musicians] if they would play. They did and the punks loved it. Bands like The Clash would put reggae and ska overtones into their music.*"

There had been a common gangster theme in some **Ska** music lyrics that was attributed to Jamaican **Rude-Boys**. But by the 1970s, **Two-Tone** Records in England had completely revised this **Rude-Boy** image to that of a fun-loving **Ska** fan in a suit and pork-pie hat. White British bands played mainly **Ska** because **Reggae** was more difficult to play. **Two-Tone** Records was formed, and **Ska** bands under this **Two-Tone** label became the heart of the "*second wave.*"

Beginning by the late 1980s, the "*third wave*" of **Ska** has exploded throughout the world, with many variations. **Ska** is still popularly danced by American teen-agers beginning in 1995-96. In fact, **Third-Wave**'s popularity has spread all over the world. Among other countries, youths are **Skanking** to Russian, German, Irish, and Japanese **Ska** bands. The Traditional Jamaican **Ska** sounds have presently been combined with metal, punk, folk, funk, and/or country. [Much from History of Ska; www.angelfire.com; and www.section3.com]

For dancing to **Ska** music, the following is from *Skip's Homepage: Ska and So Much More: How to dance the Ska!* [www.skapages.com]

"*The Basic Jamaican Ska Step - The upper half of the body (waist up) keeps the beat by bowing forward with a straight back and a slight bend in both knees. At the first bow the arms extend to the sides. At the second bow, the arms cross in front. The body straightens up between the change of arms from one position to the other. You continue in this way for the basic ska step done on the spot.*

"*The Basic Ska Step with a Slide - First to the right by moving the right leg on the extension of the arms, then bringing up the left leg on the closing arms, then to the left by moving the left leg on the extension of the arms and by bringing up the right leg on the closing arms. Remember the basic body beat described in the first paragraph is performed during the movements to the right and left.*"

The following is exerpts from *A Quick Guide To Reggae*: [www.bbc.co.uk]

"*Ska - --- to emphasize the offbeat (beats 2 and 4), creating the distinctive `chug' that powered the high speed sound of Ska and its descendants. In 1962 the --- brought Ska to the UK --- by the mid 60's Ska clubs were all over the place --- Ska's upbeat vibe reflected the optimism Jamaican independence had created, its UK revival in 1978 ---.*"

The following Basic-Step is from *Crazy Dance Moves!* by Yana:

"*-- dancing plays a large role in the Ska subculture. Why? Ska was originally played at clubs and dancehalls in Jamaica. These spaces provided Jamaicans with the opportunity to dance the night away --*

"*The Ska - 1. Crouch down low with feet slightly apart with bent knees and bent arms. 2. Move arms as if you were skanking (up and down like robot, but with more feeling than a robot) and raise one knee and one leg. 3. Put leg down, then move arms in skank motion while going lower. 4. Come up with the other leg and knee. 5. Repeat step 2.*"

(Continued)

<u>**Ska:**</u> (Continued)

The following Basic-Step is from *Ska Workshop: Skanking 101*: [ska.about.com]

"*1. <u>Bend Forward</u> - Get that stiffness out of your spine, hang forward, but not too far, and get those arms and knees loose.*

"*2. <u>Bend Knees and Elbows</u> - Bend your elbows and clench your fists if you want to get that real rude attitude. Try to look more like you're getting ready to go sprinting rather than skiing.*

"*3. <u>Claim Your Space</u> - Get those feet shoulder-length apart, move one foot slightly forward, and take up as much of the dance floor as you can while you start your arms cranking back and forth. It might help if you pretend you are shaking some maracas.*

"*4. <u>Start Moving</u> - Feel the beat. Get those arms swinging slightly and feel the bounce as you swing your hips. Move your weight from one foot to the other with each skank. Make sure you coordinate your arms and legs. If your right fist is moving forward, you should also be moving your right knee forward as you shift your weight. Then shift to the left.*

"*5. <u>Skank to the Beat</u> - Now start to vibe with some classic ska sounds. If you're doing a classic skank, your feet should not be moving too much. Rather, you should be bouncing with the upbeats and cranking those elbows. For added style, get a real cool expression and stare somewhere off in the upper corner of the room. Preferably with shades.*"

The above is open to personal Style and Variation. In addition to any Basic-Step, the following Variations could be added: 1. **Two-Tone**; 2. **Third-Wave**; 3. **RockSteady**; 4. **Ska-Core**; 5. **Skinhead-Stomp**; 6. **Dog**; and 7. **Hitch-Hiker**.

[For **Dancehall**(2) and **Ragga** Moves, see Bogle, Armstrong, Butterfly, Go-Go-Wine, Body-Basic-and-Exercise, Tate, World-Dance, Jerry-Springer, Prang, Heel-and-Toe, Na!Na!Na!, Screechie, Zip-It-Up, Drive-By, Shizzle-Ma-Nizzle, Matrix, and BinLaden. See Skanking, Popular Dancing, Teen-Dancing, and Open-Step. Also see Two-Tone, Rock, Punk-Rock, Grunge, and New-Wave. Also see Urban-Dance, Locking-and-Popping, Hip-Hop, Break-Dancing, MTV-Style Dancing, and Street-Dancer. Also see Hard-Rock, Pop, Rhythm-and-Blues, Motown-Sound, Rap, and Heavy-Metal. Also see the Novelty-&-Fad Dances-of-the-1960s. Also see Cumbia-Villera for similarity in Argentina.]

<u>**Ska-Core:**</u> An Underground Singular- or Group-Dance, Movements, Pattern or form, associated with **Ska/Reggae** and danced world-wide, mainly by youths of color.

For dancing to **Ska** music, the following is from *Ska Workshop: Skanking 101*: [ska.about.com]

"*<u>Ska-core: Slam and Mosh</u> - When the skank hits the states, the more hardcore fans take more from the punk/metal moshpit than they do from Kingston style. This is where you really start to see some dance culture clashes on the club floors.*"

A Variation for **Skanking**. (See Underground Step-Listing.)

<u>**Skanking**</u> or **The-Skank** or **Dance-of-the-Rasta** or **Steppa** or **Hotfoot-Skanking** or **Third-Wave-Skanking:** Teen-Age boy's violent, aggressive, and offensive, Singular in a Group-Dance of the early 2000s. A Jog/Strut to the Beat, similar to the Running-Man. Usually **Skank**ed to a live **Ska** music event, in which there is head-butting and the Kicking of Feet out from under other boys. Even some emotionally excited young girls get in and Push. These often hopped-up boys, thoroughly enjoying **Skanking**, are usually 16 to 21 years of age. Besides the "_true punk rockers_", "_skins_" and "_mods_" have also been seen to **Skank**. **Skanking** is not for "_outsiders_", since it is a sub-counter-culture and not necessarily something that a person learns to do.

The History of **Skanking** began to drum beats in Jamaica in the early 1950s with the Nyabinghi **Dance-of-the-Rasta**. Jamaican **Ska** music recorded between 1961 and 1967 increased **Skanking** popularity. The Classic Jamaican **Skank** by West Kingston rudies was really very simple but moving. In the early 1960s, dancers developed a natural Style of Bouncing and Swaying to this hot new Beat in the Dancehalls of Kingston.

Dub, a hybrid form of **Reggae**, was a Teen-Age 1970s music Genre among the English-Caribbeans, and was part of the development of modern **Skanking** as a dance form by the addition of an array of energetic but spontaneous Movements. This led to unofficial Competitions for the champion **Skanker**, for how well the **Skanker** flowed to the **Dub**. Still, **Skanking** was doing "_your own thing_".

Primarily in England **The Skank** seems to have gained most of its U.K. popularity during the 1980s Two-Tone era. Although **Skanking** died out a bit in other places in the 1980s, the **Reggae** music was kept alive. In the 1990s, an Aerobic Exercise and Choreographed dance form called **Hotfoot-Skanking** had been developed, which was a combination of Step Routines and **Skanking**. This outlaw dance form of **Skanking** was shown successfully in September 1998 at the Royal Albert Hall in London, and thereafter was beginning to be accepted and recognized.

For dancing to **Ska** music, the following is from _Learn to Skank Ya Bum!_ [www.angelfire.com]

"--- _Ironically, considering its popularity, it_ [Skanking] _is the most complex to describe. This quality prompts the very common response, `you have to just go to shows and watch everybody else'; that's actually not a bad idea, but not very helpful either. Here's a decent step-by-step how-to: The Basic Skank_:

"_1. Listen to the music carefully. When you can sort out the beats (the constant 1-2-3-4 of the song, easier for some people to catch than for others), you should begin by putting each foot forward and taking it back, forward on the odds and back on the evens. This is similar to a two-step, in ballroom terms._

"_2. Next we add the arms. The elbows stay bent, and the hands are balled into fists; the right hand comes forward when the left foot is out, and the left hand comes forward when the right foot is out. When the hand isn't forward, it ought to come back about as far as the hip. ---._

"_3. To make it look a little smoother, it helps to bob your head along with this movement. If your head goes down on all the ordinary beats (1-2-3-4), it comes up on all the upbeats (the little `ands' in between)._

"_Variations on a Theme_: --- _Elaborating on this takes a little practice. One variation is `bouncing' your fists on the beats. More popular among the skinheads is a variant where the knuckles are pressed together the entire time, and the elbows swing very wide. Sometimes, you can mix in 4 beats of double-time, dancing at twice the speed -- it looks like 4 quick rabbit punches ---. Another move for interludes of double-time is a spurt of running in place with your knees coming way up high, ---._

(Continued)

<u>**Skanking**</u>:   (Continued)

        "*While people usually skank side-by-side in rows facing the stage, --- for two people. One is to simply do the dance facing someone. This looks best if you're NOT a mirror image (i.e., you should each put your right foot in at the same time. Hokey Pokey, anyone?). Another is to do a pinwheel, each person following the other in a circle. Both of these require a bit more coordination than dancing alone, in order to stay in synch. ---.*

        <u>Variations on a Theme</u>:   (Continued)

        "*The amount of variation only increases in today's world where ska mingles with Swing, Latin, and Punk influences. --- sound you could characterize as `Latin ska'. Some songs use rhythms to which you could either do `ska dances' or Latin dances, interchangeably.*"

        As a **novelty Fad,** how to dance **Skanking** to the Music's Beat is partially described as follows in the "***Eighties Dances***," [www.inthe80s.com]:

        "***Skanking*** - *With arms bent at right angles, one in front and one in back, but constantly switching them back and forth as you jerkily hop forward, one foot at a time. Your feet are doing what your arms do, a.k.a. the `ska dance.' Still popular. Head bobbing to rhythm all the while.*"

        Skanking, said by Teens to be a showcase at events and shows, is a favorite as an alternative to conventional Aerobics. A **Ska** show could have the following added Variations (and more): 1. **Two-Tone**; 2. **Third-Wave**; 3. **RockSteady**; 4. **Ska-Core**; 5. **Skinhead-Stomp**; 6. **Dog**; and 7. **Hitch-Hiker**.

        Similar but less popular than **Slam-Dancing** (Moshing). See **Underground Step-Listing**. (Especially see Pogo, and Running-Man.)   [Much from www.caribbeanmixx.com, ska.about.com, and www.geocities.com]

Ska-Punk: An Underground Singular- or Group-Dance, Movements, Pattern or form, associated with **Ska/Reggae** and danced world-wide.

        For dancing to **Third-Wave Ska** music, the following is from *Ska/Reggae*: [ska.about.com]

        "*<u>Ska-Punk</u> - In its evolution through the British punk era, Two Tone and American pop and funk, ska-punk became the most distinctive style of 90s ska. --- mix of fast-paced upbeats with rock rhythms ---. It fostered some of the Third Wave's most reviled efforts, ---.*"

        The following is from *<u>Third Wave Ska - Revival/Ska Punk</u>*: [http://entertainment.msn.com]

        "*Third Wave Ska Revivalists come in two forms- the traditionalists and the moderns. The traditional artists focus more on the '50s Jamaican ska sound, while the moderns fuse punk rock energy with the two-tone ska style.*"

        A Variation for **Skanking**. (See Underground Step-Listing. Especially see Ska-Core, and Skinhead-Stomp.)

Ska-Ride or **Ska-Riding, and Ska-Row** or **Ska-Rowing:** From Kingston, Jamaica, an Underground Singular- or Coupledance Movements, associated with dancing the **Jamaican-Twist**, which, in turn, was an outgrowth of **Ska/Reggae**. These are danced world-wide, mainly by youths of color.

The **Jamaican-Twist** had been introduced with the new Ska music to the American public at the **1964** New York World's Fair. Soon, young Jamaicans had perfected Movements such as **Ska-Rowing, Ska-Riding**, and **Ska-Stomping**, from this **Jamaican-Twist**. [From Reggae - Fashion and Dance, www.bbc.co.uk]

These are two dances that are much more regulated than anything that was done in Kingston.

The following is from *Ska Workshop: Skanking 101*: [ska.about.com]

"In the dancehalls of Kingston, Jamaica, in the early 1960s, dancers developed a natural style of bouncing and swaying to the hot new beat. When the dance and music were introduced to the world at the 1964 World's Fair in New York, however, neither the music, the dancers, nor the dance were completely authentic. Rather than transport genuine West Kingston rudies to Flushing, New York, the Jamaican government chose to present a cleaner, more stylized version to America." Thus, the **Ska-Ride** and **Ska-Row**.

For dancing to **Ska** music, the following is from *Skip's Homepage: Ska and So Much More*: *How to dance the Ska!* [www.skapages.com]

"Ska-ing - This dance step is similar to the action of skiing and is done rapidly to the beat of the guitar. You start out by leaning forward at the waist with the hands in front and straight legs. In the second position, the hands are brought down to the sides and at the same time the knees are bent. Both are repeated simultaneously to the fast ska beat of the guitar.

"Ska-Riding - Ska-Riding is the step usually done immediately after Ska-ing and is similar to the action of riding a horse. --- pretend to be riding a horse giving a pumping action of the hands in front of the body and at the same time behind the knees. The bend of the knees and the push out of the hands are done together on the fast guitar beat. Occasionally, you use one hand to `whip your horse'.

"Rowing - The most energetic of all Ska Steps is the rowing. A similar action to rowing a boat ---. The first step is to reach out with the arms, keeping both back and legs perfectly straight to form an angle at the waist. Then pull back, throwing backwards the upper half of the body (from the knees up). The Ska Beat is maintained first with the forward movement and then with the backward movement. The weight of the body is shifted alternately from the right to the left on each pull back action. If done properly, the heavy ska beat is on the pull back action.

"Rowing Across - Just like `Rowing' only instead, the legs are lifted alternately on the pull back beat, covering ground with each step in order to change your position. This step may also be done on the spot for variation."

Offshoots of **Ska**, and Variations of **Skanking**. (See Underground Step-Listing.)

Skate: An Unleadable, **Novelty Fad**, Singular, loosely Choreographed, Forward-Traveling dance Routine, in vogue in the U.S. in the 1960s. In 4/4 Tempo, the following **Skate** Routine was popular during that time at the Brigham Young University, in Provo, Utah.

In the 1960s, *Lou Courtney* sang and recorded *Skate Now*, a hit song in New York, and the **Skate**'s Eponymous dance, imitating Skating through Pantomime, was popular in clubs in New York for a few months. The Record *"Bernadete"* by *The Four Tops* was "**Skate**d to" in 1967.

See Skate(1) for **Skate** mechanics. Rhythm Timing possibly was *And Slow And Slow And Slow And Slow*; *Slow Slow Slow And Slow*; *Slow Slow Slow And Slow*. **Skate** had **Metronomic-Motion** Side-to-Side, each with a Rise and with a Slight Lifting of the Trailing-Foot. Thumbs would work as with the **Hitch-Hiker**, or Hands would Close and Stretch out as with the **Taffy-Pull**.

Single-Skate was *ForSkateSwivel1/4CW forskateswivel1/4CCW*, repeated.

Double-Skate was *ForStep fortouch ForStep forskateswivel1/4CCW*, repeated.

(See the Novelty-&-Fad Dances-of-the-1960s.)   [Some data from "Rhythm and Dance" by Alma Heaton.]

Skate-Boogaloo: Only this name for an American **Novelty** or **Fad** of the 1960s is listed simply as a Dance, Pattern, or Figure in the "*Dance Crazes of the Sixties*."

(See Novelty-&-Fad Dances-of-the-1960s.) [From *www.sixtiescity.com/Culture/dance*]

Skaters'-Sways: A Leadable, **Novelty Fad** Six-Count Coupledance Pattern, unique to the **Same-Foot-Hustle**, 1 1/2-Measures long if in 4/4 Time. Rhythm Timing for both Partners is *Slow Slow quick And slow, Slow slow*, or *Tap 2 3& 4, 5 6*.

Danced entirely on Same-Feet in Varsouvienne Position. Together, Partners *Sway Left, Sway Right, Sway Left*, during their last three Pattern Steps.

Both Partners dance *ForTap StrideBackward backward Together forrecover, Forward forward*.

Partners **Sway** in Unison with outer thighs retaining contact, especially upon the Forward Steps.

While dancing the similar **Latin-Hustle**, Man may Transition to his Lady's Footwork then intermix back again, perhaps for **Skaters'-Sways** only.

(See Hustle, and Same-Foot-Hustle Basic-Step. Also see Body-Contact.)

Skaters-Waltz: A **Novelty Fad** Coupledance in vogue in 1930. Music for the **Skaters-Waltz** was Composed earlier, in 1882 by *Emil Waldteufel*.

[Some from *Novelty Dances Through the Years* by Pony Moore.]

Skip: Only this name for an American **Novelty** or **Fad** of the 1960s is listed simply as a Dance, Pattern, or Figure in the "*Dance Crazes of the Sixties*."

(See Novelty-&-Fad Dances-of-the-1960s.) [From *www.sixtiescity.com/Culture/dance*]

SkyWalk: See SideSlide.

<u>**Slam-Dancing**</u> or **Moshing** or **Crowd-Dancing:** American Teenage Terms for dangerous, intense **Novelty Fad Crowd-Dancing** with extreme physical contact, at either punk or death metal music concerts, (which are two different kinds of shows.) These often hopped-up boys, thoroughly enjoying **Moshing**, are usually 16 to 21 years of age. Egged on by the "music", **Slam-Dancing** is a writhing pit of excited people, throwing punches and flipping grossly around.

      Slam-Dancing is a 1980s **novelty Fad** Series of offensively rude Movements. How to dance the **Slam** to the Music's Beat is partially described as follows in the "**_Eighties Dances_,**" [www.inthe80s.com]:

      "**_The Slam_** - _Like the pogo, but you slam into other people as you are jumping up and down, and is less rigid. Eventually evolved into moshing, which is a more violent and dangerous form of slam dancing._"

      Probably begun in New York and West Coast punk music clubs. Because of the crowd's desired surge for excitement, the chiropractors' business booms.

      For **Moshing** in the _Mosh-Pit_, "_The entire crowd moves together, bumping each other and bouncing off each other._" The _Mosh-Pit_ is "_the space in front of the stage where fans smash into each other as a band rocks._" "_Stage Diving - literally the act of diving into the crowd from the stage by the fans and/or band members. The idea is for the crowd to catch the individual and body pass them toward the sound board._" "_Crowd Surfing - an individual is horizontally passed overhead, hand by hand by the crowd around the room._" [From http://teenmusic.about.com.]

      Slightly similar but more popular than **Skanking**. (See Pogo, and Underground Step-Listing. Also see Box-In.)

      <u>**Slaussen**</u> or **Slauson:** A possibly Leadable 1960s American **Novelty** or **Fad** Coupledance or Singular dance Pattern. This Pattern was in vogue after 1960, at least at Brigham Young University, in Provo, Utah. Who Slaussen was is unknown.

      The Slaussen was danced to an even 4/4 medium Tempo. Continuous Counts were _1 2 3 4 5 6 7&8._ The two-Measure Basic Pattern was danced _forstep ForPoint BackStep backpoint_; _forstep ForKick BackStep ball Change_; repeated and repeated.

      If Led in Loose-Closed Position, the Lady might have danced _BackStep backpoint forstep ForPoint_; _BackStep backkick forstep Ball change_. The Lady may also have danced Side-by-Side at times, upon the Same-Feet as her Man.

      Similar to **Waltz-Balances-Forward-and-Backward.** (See the Novelty-&-Fad Dances-of-the-1960s.) [Much from "_Rhythm and Dance_" by _Alma Heaton_. See _www.sixtiescity.com/Culture/dance_.]

      <u>**Slauson:**</u> See Slaussen.

      <u>**Slauson-Shuffle:**</u> An American **Fad** Coupledance of 1964. It's Eponymous Music was "_Hitchhike_" by _Marvin Gaye._

      (See Novelty-&-Fad Dances-of-the-1960s.)

      [From _www.bluejuice.org.au_. See _www.sixtiescity.com/Culture/dance_.]

Slide: **The Slide** was an Unleadable American **Novelty Fad** dance Routine, that was in vogue after 1960 and was danced mostly Singularly. These 1960s dances were free and individualistic. People enmasse, mostly teens with long hair, were dancing by themselves and inventing as they danced.

The following loosely Choreographed Pattern, called **The Slide**, was in vogue in the 1960s at Brigham Young University, in Provo, Utah. This Pattern Traveled Forward then returned to the same Home spot. It was danced in an open Shine Position, and in Lines Formation or Slightly Facing and Apart. All commenced upon their Left Foot, Right Foot later:

After initially taking 4 *ForStepCrossBrush*es, dancers would **Slide** by taking a long reaching *Step* Diagonally Rearwards, then they would Slowly **Draw their Free-Foot Closed**, returning Home.

There are two pictures from Brigham Young University, labeled and showing a young couple dancing the **Slide**. They are Apart in both pictures. In the first picture, they are Slightly Facing and shown Drawing their **Opposing** Free-Foot Closed. Arms are at Waist-Level with Hands loosely fisted with Wrists-Back. In the second picture, they are in Shadow Position with the Man Behind. With all arms Stretched straight and banked toward their Free-Feet, they are both Drawing their **Same** Free-Foot Closed.

Note: Scuffing is optional to Brushing.

[See Novelty-Dances, Fad-Dances, Novelty-and-Fad Genre, and the Novelty-&-Fad Dances-of-the-1960s. Also see Aunt-Jemima-Slide, Cha-Cha-Slide, SideSlide, Slip-and-Slide, and Slop-and-Slide. Much data from "Rhythm and Dance" by Alma Heaton. Also see www.sixtiescity.com/Culture/dance.]

Slime: A **Novelty Fad** dance of 1964. The **Slime** had its own Eponymous record, "*The Slime*" by *The Ad Libs*. [From *Soul*, www.trinity.unimelb.edu.au]

The following rhyme by Jerry Leiber:

"*Cheek to Cheek, Toes to Toes*
"*Here's a dance you can do on a dime*
"*Knees to Knees, Nose to Nose*
"*Slowly move, and you're doin' 'The Slime'.*"

(See Stationary-Dancing. Also see Novelty-&-Fad Dances-of-the-1960s. Also see www.sixtiescity.com/Culture/dance.)

Slip-and-Slide: Only this name for an American **Novelty** or **Fad** of the **1960s** is listed simply as a Dance, Pattern, or Figure in the "*Dance Crazes of the Sixties*."

(See Novelty-&-Fad Dances-of-the-1960s.) [From *www.sixtiescity.com/Culture/dance*]

Slop: The **Slop** was an Unstructured and Unleadable, 1960s **Novelty Fad** Singular dance and possibly a **Coupledance**. At the time, in 1962, Chubby Checker sang the words for its Eponymous record, "*The Slop*":

(See Novelty-Dances, Fad-Dances, Novelty-and-Fad Genre, and the Novelty-&-Fad Dances-of-the-1960s. Also see Georgia-Slop, Slop-and-Slide, and Sloppy-Twist.)

Slop-and-Slide: Only this name for an American **Novelty** or **Fad** of the 1960s is listed simply as a Dance, Pattern, or Figure in the "*Dance Crazes of the Sixties*."
      (See Novelty-&-Fad Dances-of-the-1960s.) [From *www.sixtiescity.com/Culture/dance*]

Sloppy-Twist-A-Fish: Only this name for an American **Novelty** or **Fad** of the 1960s is listed simply as a Dance, Pattern, or Figure in the "*Dance Crazes of the Sixties*."
      (See Novelty-&-Fad Dances-of-the-1960s.) [From *www.sixtiescity.com/Culture/dance*]

Slosh: A **Novelty Fad** Coupledance of 1972. This had its own Eponymous record, "*The Slosh*" by *Bernadette.*
      (See Novelty-&-Fad Dances-of-the-1960s. From www.bluejuice.org.au/. Also see www.sixtiescity.com/Culture/dance. Also from *Novelty Dances Through the Years* by Pony Moore.)

Slow-Dance: An American **Novelty** and **Fad** Coupledance of 1966. This **Slow-Dance** had its own Eponymous record, "*You Oughta Slow Dance Baby*" by *The Right Kind.*
      (See Novelty-&-Fad Dances-of-the-1960s.)
      [From *Soul*, *www.trinity.unimelb.edu.au*, and from *www.bluejuice.org.au*, and from *www.sixtiescity.com/Culture/dance.*]

Slow-Drag: An American **Novelty Fad** Coupledance in vogue in the early 1900s.
      The following is from "*Slow Drag*" by *Sonny Watson* [www.streetswing.com/]:
            "*The Slow Drag was first heard of in the 1890's in New Orleans ... and became popular among the college set in the 1900s. It was a variation of the Two-Step. There is some evidence that the pre-tango danza was a strong influence in the original version.*"
      Other "*drag dances*" of the time were the A-Minor-Drag, Dizzy-Drag, Saratoga-Drag, Shoe-Shiner's-Drag, the Viper's-Drag, and the most famous **Varsity-Drag**. In addition, Scott Joplin wrote the songs *Sunflower Slow Drag* in 1899, and *A Real Slow Drag* in 1913.

Slow-Fizz: Only this name for an American **Novelty** or **Fad** of the 1960s is listed simply as a Dance, Pattern, or Figure in the "*Dance Crazes of the Sixties*."
      (See Novelty-&-Fad Dances-of-the-1960s.) [From *www.sixtiescity.com/Culture/dance*]

Slow-Jerk: Only this name for an American **Novelty** or **Fad** of the 1960s is listed simply as a Dance, Pattern, or Figure in the "*Dance Crazes of the Sixties*."
      (See Novelty-&-Fad Dances-of-the-1960s.) [From *www.sixtiescity.com/Culture/dance*]

Slow-Locomotion: Only this name for an American **Novelty** or **Fad** of the 1960s is listed simply as a Dance, Pattern, or Figure in the "*Dance Crazes of the Sixties*."
      (See Novelty-&-Fad Dances-of-the-1960s.) [From *www.sixtiescity.com/Culture/dance*]

<u>**Slurp:**</u> Only this name for an American **Novelty** or **Fad** of the 1960s is listed simply as a Dance, Pattern, or Figure in the "*Dance Crazes of the Sixties.*"
  (See Novelty-&-Fad Dances-of-the-1960s.) [From *www.sixtiescity.com/Culture/dance*]

<u>**Smashed-Potato:**</u> Only this name for an American **Novelty** or **Fad** of the 1960s is listed simply as a Dance, Pattern, or Figure in the "*Dance Crazes of the Sixties.*"
  (See Novelty-&-Fad Dances-of-the-1960s.) [From *www.sixtiescity.com/Culture/dance*]

<u>**Smock:**</u> Only this name for an American **Novelty** or **Fad** of the 1960s is listed simply as a Dance, Pattern, or Figure in the "*Dance Crazes of the Sixties.*"
  (See Novelty-&-Fad Dances-of-the-1960s.) [From *www.sixtiescity.com/Culture/dance*]

<u>**Smurf:**</u> An American **Novelty** or **Fad** Solo Maneuver of the early 1980s in Cadence with the Music. These **Smurf** Movements generally fuse with smoothed out elements of **Break-Dancing**. Their name comes from the '**Smurf**' *bluebuddies* cartoon figures popular in the United States in 1982. These blue colored Smurfs and Smurfettes had a corresponding theme song, plus at least 12 other Smurf songs.
  The following is from "*Eighties Dances*" - [www.inthe80s.com]:
    "***The Smurf:*** *Kind of complicated. Right toe down, right heel up and left heel down, left toe up at the same time then switch your feet to right heel down, right toe up and left toe down, left toe up - repeat.*"
  (See Novelty-&-Fad Dances-of-the-1980s. Also see Genre of both Heel and Toe-Movements.)

<u>**Snacky-Poo:**</u> An American **Fad** dance of the 1960s. This had its own Eponymous record, "*The Snacky Poo*" by the *Del-Mars*.
  (See Novelty-&-Fad Dances-of-the-1960s.)
  [From www.bluejuice.org.au. See *www.sixtiescity.com/Culture/dance.*]

<u>**Snake**</u>(1): Entertaining Partners Perform this Figure or Pattern, perhaps in a **Cabaret-**Style Coupledance or while **CheerLeading**.
  The Lady, after an Aerial or having been Lifted across the Man's shoulders, **Snakes her way Down his Body** Feet first, ending with a Slide between her Partner's Spread legs.
  Similar to **Head-Long-Slide**. (See Cabaret Performers, and Belt-Buckle-Floor-Sweep.)

Snake(2) or **Neck-Wrap** or **Double-Cross** or **Double-Shoulder-Drape:** Two Leadable, Basic Coupledance Spaghetti Figures, Snake or Left-Snake, suitable for American and Country-**Twosteps**, **Four-Count**, **Polka**, the **Discos** and **Hustles**, **PasoDoble**, **Cajun-Jittergug**, and other dances.

Both the Lady and Man may be Snaked; the means for **Right-Snak**ing follows, the **Left-Snake** being Mirror-Image Opposite:

Begins by Facing each other, Grasping Opposing-Hands and being Offset to their Right. Raising and retaining all Hands, they slip into the **Snake Position** by each Head-Looping with their Left Hand, then Lowering their Partner's Right Hand onto the back of their necks.

(See Snake-Out, and Buddy-Buddy. Also see Reverse-Right Position, and Reverse-Left Position.)

Snake(3): An American "*animal dance*", a **Novelty Fad** Coupledance in vogue about 1912 to 1914. Derided by newspapers, magazines, church officials, and even by Pope Pius X, as "such foolish and decadent behavior," over one hundred of these dances were created during this period.

See **Snake**(2), which could be the same or similar Movements. (Also see Animal-Dances, Bull-Frog-Hop, Bunny-Hug, Buzzard-Lope, Camel-Walk, Chicken-Reel, Chicken-Scratch, Crab-Step, Fish-Walk, Gotham-Gobble, Horse-Trot, Kangaroo-Dip, Kangaroo-Hop, Lame-Duck, Monkey-Glide, Possum-Trot, and Turkey-Trot; which were all Animal-Dances of 1910-1914.)

Snake(4): A **Novelty Fad** Movement, this **Snake** is one small Move of the California `Funk' brand of the **Boogaloo** Genre of Mime "Moves," which seems to be part of the **Electric-Boogie** Style of **Break-Dancing**, which, in turn, is part of **Hip-Hop**.

This **Snake** may be the same as **Snake**(5). [See Air-Posing, Animation(3), Bop(2), Centipede, Cobra, Crazy-Legs, Dime-Stopping, Filmore, Floating(2), Glides, Hitting, King-Tut, Lean(4), Pop(3), Puppet, Robot, Saccin, Scarecrow, Spiderman, Sticking, Strobing, Strut, Tick, and Wave(1); for other related Moves. Also see Underground Step-Listing.]

Snake(5): A **Novelty Fad** dance of the 1970s and 1980s. How to dance the **Snake** should be found on a VHS Video by *Coach Coz and the Kid Crew* (www.centralhome.com).

There is mention of a 1980s **Snake** Pantomime **novelty Fad Singular-Dance** Movement, described as follows in the "*Eighties Dances*," [www.inthe80s.com]:

"*The Snake - Pretend you're having to duck under a bar that is next to you. Then let that motion travel all the way down to your foot. Then do it again, the other way...*"

May be the same as **Snake**(4). (See the Centipede, and the Dolphin. Also see American-Hustle, Bugg, Bump, Bus-Stop, Four-Corners, Locking, Sprinkler, Tango-Hustle, and the Worm; which were all Novelty Fads in vogue in the 1970s.)

Snake(6): Only this name for an American **Novelty** or **Fad** of the 1960s is listed simply as a Dance, Pattern, or Figure in the "*Dance Crazes of the Sixties*."

(See Novelty-&-Fad Dances-of-the-1960s.) [From *www.sixtiescity.com/Culture/dance*]

      Snake-Hips: Only this name for an American **Novelty** or **Fad** of the 1960s is listed simply as a Dance, Pattern, or Figure in the "*Dance Crazes of the Sixties.*"
      (See Novelty-&-Fad Dances-of-the-1960s.) [From *www.sixtiescity.com/Culture/dance*]

      Snake-Walk: Only this name for an American **Novelty** or **Fad** of the 1960s is listed simply as a Dance, Pattern, or Figure in the "*Dance Crazes of the Sixties.*"
      (See Novelty-&-Fad Dances-of-the-1960s.) [From *www.sixtiescity.com/Culture/dance*]

      Snatch(1) or **The-Snatch!:** A Coupledance Aerial Pattern suitable for the **Lindy-Hop**. In the 1929?-1932? era, certain **Lindy-Hop** dancers, calling these "**Air-Steps**", created and developed the **The-Snatch!**, the **Over-Head**, and the **Back-Flip**, among others, as attention-getters.
      (See Jitterbug or Lindy-Hop Step-Listing, and Lindy-Hoppers.)

      Snatch(2): A **Novelty Fad** dance of 1965. The **Snatch** had its own Eponymous record, "*Do The Snatch*" by *The Lancers.*
      (See Novelty-&-Fad Dances-of-the-1960s.) [From *Soul*, www.trinity.unimelb.edu.au]

      Sno-Cone: A **Novelty Fad** Coupledance of the 1960s. This had its own Eponymous record, "*The Sno-Cone*" by *Lloyd Hendricks.*
      (See Novelty-&-Fad Dances-of-the-1960s.) [From www.bluejuice.org.au]

      Snoopy: An Unleadable, American **Novelty Fad**, Choreographed Singular or Coupledance, sort of Line-Dance Routine. With a medium-Cadence 4/4 Tempo, the following four-Measures long Pattern was in vogue in the 1960s at the Brigham Young University, in Provo, Utah. The dance was probably supposed to Mime the dance of the comic-strip dog, *Snoopy.*
      There is a picture from Brigham Young University, labeled and showing a young couple dancing the **Snoopy**. They are Apart in a Shine Position, upon the Same-Feet, only partially Facing but looking at each other. But for most of their Routine, they probably both Face the same direction. All Knees are shown Softened. Their hips Sway Left. Weight is Forward upon their Left Feet while their Right Feet Trail Diagonally. Arms are Spread, all with fists and bent elbows.
      Rhythm Timing was *Slow Slow Slow Slow*; *Slow Slow Quick Quick Quick Hold*; *Slow Slow Slow Slow*; *Quick Quick Slow Slow Hold*: **Snoopy** was danced *sidepoint close SidePoint Close*; *sidepoint close Flick Ball flat hold*; *ForStep cutstep BackStep backstep*; *Flick Ball flat ForStepSwivel1/4CW Hold*. Start over in new direction.
      (See the Novelty-&-Fad Dances-of-the-1960s.) [Data mostly from "Rhythm and Dance" by Alma Heaton.]

Soca: A Variation of the **Merengue**, the **Soca** is a **Novelty Fad** and Latin **Folk** Coupledance.

How to **Coupledance** the **Soca** to the Music's Beat is partially described as follows in the _**Eighties Dances**_," [www.inthe80s.com]:

"_**Soca Dance** - A couple, Man behind, Woman in front, Man's hands on woman's waist. Man leans on woman's back. It seemed to be a very sexual figure!!_"

(See Clave-Beat, Calypso, Conga-Line, Bomba, and the Plena. Also see Chutney.)

Soch: Only this name for an American **Novelty** or **Fad** of the 1960s is listed simply as a Dance, Pattern, or Figure in the "_Dance Crazes of the Sixties_."

(See Novelty-&-Fad Dances-of-the-1960s.) [From _www.sixtiescity.com/Culture/dance_]

Sookie: A **Novelty Fad** Coupledance of the 1960s. This had its own Eponymous record, "_Sookie_" by _Mel Williams._

(See Novelty-&-Fad Dances-of-the-1960s.) [From www.bluejuice.org.au]

Soul-Clap: Only this name for an American **Novelty** or **Fad** of the 1960s is listed simply as a Dance, Pattern, or Figure in the "_Dance Crazes of the Sixties_."

(See Novelty-&-Fad Dances-of-the-1960s.) [From _www.sixtiescity.com/Culture/dance_]

Soulful-Jerk: Only this name for an American **Novelty** or **Fad** of the 1960s is listed simply as a Dance, Pattern, or Figure in the "_Dance Crazes of the Sixties_."

(See Novelty-&-Fad Dances-of-the-1960s.) [From _www.sixtiescity.com/Culture/dance_]

Soulful-Stomp: A **Novelty Fad** dance of the 1960s. The record that the **Soulful-Stomp** was danced to was "_Burnin' Spear_" by _The Soulful Strings._

(See the Novelty-&-Fad Dances-of-the-1960s.) [From _Soul_, www.trinity.unimelb.edu.au]

Soulja-Boy: A **Novelty** or **Fad** dance of an unknown time, listed in "_Novelty and fad dances_" under [http://en.wikipedia.org/wiki].

Soul-Stomp: Only this name for an American **Novelty** or **Fad** of the 1960s is listed simply as a Dance, Pattern, or Figure in the "_Dance Crazes of the Sixties_."

(See Novelty-&-Fad Dances-of-the-1960s.) [From _www.sixtiescity.com/Culture/dance_]

Soul-Struttin': A **Novelty Fad** Coupledance of the 1960s. This had its own Eponymous record, "_Soul Struttin'_" by _Jamie Lyons._

(See Novelty-&-Fad Dances-of-the-1960s.) [From www.bluejuice.org.au]

Soul-Train: A **Novelty Fad** Coupledance of 1969. This had its own Eponymous record, "*Soul Train*" by *Bo Diddley*, and "*Soul Train*" by *Little Richard.*
     (See Novelty-&-Fad Dances-of-the-1960s.) [From www.bluejuice.org.au]

Soul-Twine: Only this name for an American **Novelty** or **Fad** of the 1960s is listed simply as a Dance, Pattern, or Figure in the "*Dance Crazes of the Sixties.*"
     (See Novelty-&-Fad Dances-of-the-1960s.) [From *www.sixtiescity.com/Culture/dance*]

Soupy-Shuffle-Stomp: A **Novelty Fad** Coupledance of 1962. This had its own Eponymous record, "*Soupy Shuffle Stomp*" by *Bruce Johnson.*
     (See Novelty-&-Fad Dances-of-the-1960s.) [From www.bluejuice.org.au]

Spanish-Strut: Only this name for an American **Novelty** or **Fad** of the 1960s is listed simply as a Dance, Pattern, or Figure in the "*Dance Crazes of the Sixties.*"
     (See Novelty-&-Fad Dances-of-the-1960s.) [From *www.sixtiescity.com/Culture/dance*]

Spanish-Twist: An Unleadable Mexican **Novelty** and **Fad** Singular or Coupledance of the 1960s.
     The following is an excerpt from the "*Twist (dance)*" - [http://en.wikipedia.org/wiki/]:
          "*In Latin America, the Twist craze was sparked in the 1960-62 period .... by Bill Haley & His Comets. Their recordings of 'The Spanish Twist' and 'Florida Twist' were major successes, particularly in Mexico, and the band were given the credit for starting the dance craze. ....*"
     [See Florida-Twist, Twist(2), and Peppermint-Twist. Also see Novelty-&-Fad Dances-of-the-1960s.]

Spank-the-Baby: An Unleadable 1930s **Separated-Break-A-Way** Novelty **Fad** Pattern, usually Performed while dancing the **Big-Apple**. Also suitable for the many **Swing** dances. After separating from one's Partner while dancing the **Lindy-Hop**, or the **Swing-Bal** portion of the **Balboa**, one would often **Spank-the-Baby** to return back Together.
     While one Hand is held Upward, the other hand Spanks one's hip on Counts 2,4,6,8. Stomp one Foot Forward then Drag the other Foot Closed Together. Continue for eight Counts while Moving Diagonally.
     For the **Big-Apple**, **Spank-the-Baby** was one of the **Break-A-Way** Genre. Wiggling their hips, certain **Break-A-Way** Patterns were danced. The original **Suzie-Q, Boogie-Back, Tack-Annie, Georgia-Grind, Praise-Allah!, Truckin', Peckin', Charleston, Shorty-George**, and other Break-A-Ways, were probably originated early by blacks; while **Spank-the-Baby, Rusty-Dusty, Pose-and-a-Peck**, the **Little-Apple**, the **Little-Peach, Mess-Around, Stomp-Off, Apple-Jacks**, and **Fall-Off-the-Log,** and other Break-A-Ways, were probably originated later by whites. Most all of these Patterns seem to have been influenced or derived from the classic **Lindy-Hop** and/or **Big-Apple** dances. See **Break-A-Way Glossary** for a more complete listing.

Spanns-Stomp: Only this name for an American **Novelty** or **Fad** of the 1960s is listed simply as a Dance, Pattern, or Figure in the "*Dance Crazes of the Sixties.*"
          (See Novelty-&-Fad Dances-of-the-1960s.) [From *www.sixtiescity.com/Culture/dance*]

Speed-Lindy: A possibly rare but current **Novelty Fad** Coupledance, mentioned only under *Name That Dance!* [www.outdancing.com], and possibly developed by 2000 by Ronnen Levinson. This **Speed-Lindy** is actually a Half-Timing variant of the **Lindy**, (4 Steps in 8 Beats,) danced to Music with a very Fast Beat.
          Let us assume that its 4/4 **Music** is played nominally at 200 Beats-per-Minute (50 MPM). An excerpt from *Name That Dance!* states that this **Speed-Lindy** has "*fewer steps per eight count basic*" than does the **Lindy**. Another of its excerpts gives this 50 MPM **Speed-Lindy** 100 Steps-per-Minute at two Steps-per-Measure. A **Lindy** Pattern is two Music Measures long, therefore this **Speed-Lindy** takes four Steps per Pattern (Basic-Step), or half as many as for the **Lindy**. As for the **Lindy**, let us assume that there is Clockwise Couple-Rotation with Momentum ensuing for its Basic-Step, (but with a more extra-tight Spinning); Lively in Butterfly or in Loose-Closed Position, **C**oupledanced Flat and Low with Softened Knees, and that the Man commences each Pattern with his Left Foot and the Lady with her Right.
          The latter excerpt also gives the two-Measure Rhythm Timing as "*(1 2 3) (4 5) 6 (7 8)*".
          Translating, for the Man, (4 Steps for 360 degrees Couple-Rotation,); *veryslow Slow quick Slow.*
          Man dances *sideward   DiagCrossInFronTurn3/8CW   diagforturn1/2CW LockBehind3/8CW.*
          Lady dances *LockBehind1/8CW   sideturn1/4CW   CrossInFronTurn3/8CW diagforturn1/4CW.*
          [See **Lindy**. Also see **Eastern Swing and Jive Step-Listing**. Also see Break-A-Way(3), and Break-A-Way Glossary for a listing of possible Challenge-Steps for this **Speed-Lindy**. Also see Swing(1), Swing-Derivation, Lindy-Timing, Eight-Count, and Eight-Count-Swing.]

Spider-Walk: Only this name for an American **Novelty** or **Fad** of the 1960s is listed simply as a Dance, Pattern, or Figure in the "*Dance Crazes of the Sixties.*"
          (See Novelty-&-Fad Dances-of-the-1960s.) [From *www.sixtiescity.com/Culture/dance*]

Spin: Only this name for an American **Novelty** or **Fad** of the 1960s is listed simply as a Dance, Pattern, or Figure in the "*Dance Crazes of the Sixties.*"
          (See Novelty-&-Fad Dances-of-the-1960s.) [From *www.sixtiescity.com/Culture/dance*]

Split: Only this name for an American **Novelty** or **Fad** of the 1960s is listed simply as a Dance, Pattern, or Figure in the "*Dance Crazes of the Sixties.*"
          (See Novelty-&-Fad Dances-of-the-1960s.) [From *www.sixtiescity.com/Culture/dance*]

Spongebob: A **Novelty** or **Fad** dance of an unknown time, listed in "*Novelty and fad dances*" under [http://en.wikipedia.org/wiki].

Sprinkler: A comical Pantomime **Novelty Fad Singular-Dance** Hand Maneuver of the 1970s and 1980s, simulating the Actions of a lawn sprinkler in Cadence with the Music. How to dance the **Sprinkler** to the Music's Beat is described as follows in the *"Eighties Dances,"* [www.inthe80s.com]:

"The Sprnkler - Stand there with your right arm (or left) in front of you with a fist, pull back 3 times as you move your arm to the left, and then swing right arm back to the right."

A later version of the above *"Eighties Dances,"* [www.inthe80s.com] adds another way to Perform this **Sprinkler** as follows:

"Put one hand straight out in front of you with a closed fist and rotate to the beat one direction moving your arm up and down. When you reach the other side of your body, pull your arm straight back over to the other side (without any beats)."

Also, how to dance the **Sprinkler** should be found on a VHS Video by *Coach Coz and the Kid Crew* (www.centralhome.com).

Similar to **Churnin'-Butter, Teen-Wolf, Hand-Jive, Hitch-Hiker, Palm-Circles**(1), **Belinda**, and **Tiffany**. (See Chair-Dancing. Also see YMCA, and Fila,. Also see Finger-Flourishes, Arms-and-Hands, Free-Hand-Fashioning, and Gestures-Free-Hand. Also see American-Hustle, Bugg, Bump, Bus-Stop, Four-Corners, Locking, Snake, Tango-Hustle, and the Worm; which were all Novelty Fads in vogue in the 1970s. Also see Novelty-&-Fad Dances-of-the-1980s.)

Spunky-Onions: A **Novelty Fad** Coupledance of the 1960s. This had its own Eponymous record, *"Spunky Onions"* by *Johnny Adams.*

(See Novelty-&-Fad Dances-of-the-1960s.) [From www.bluejuice.org.au]

Squat(1): **The Squat** was a **Novelty Fad** Coupledance in vogue in the United States, somewhere in the 1900s-1910s.

(See Yankee-Tangle, Texas-Rag, Fanny-Bump, Funky-Butt, Itch, Grind, and Mooch. Also see Squat Position, Squat-Charleston, and Cossack-Squat-Kick-Dance.)

Squat(2): A **Novelty Fad** dance of 1960. The Squat had its own Eponymous record, *"Du De Squat"* by the *T-Bird Party.*

(See Novelty-&-Fad Dances-of-the-1960s.) [From *Soul*, www.trinity.unimelb.edu.au]

Squat-Charleston: One of the many Figures of the 1920s overall **Charleston** Dance Genre. A crazy, difficult and uncomfortable Singular Figure Executed Squatting Low while dancing the **Charleston**. Rhythm with 4/4 Timing is *quick and Slow* Quick And *slow*.

Begins Balanced upon both Balls-of-Feet while Squatting with Knees Together on one's haunches. The dancer Bobs in order to Slide the Right leg Straight Forward. After Quickly again Balancing upon both Balls-of-Feet, the dancer Bobs again in order to Slide the Left leg Straight Rearward.

Elbows might be held Outward, or arms could be folded. The Figure may be repeated.

Similar to the **Cossack-Squat-Kick-Dance**. [See Squat(1)&(2), and Squat Position. Also see Charleston(1)&(3). Also see Pot-Stir, Leg-Up-Pot-Stir, Dip-Stand, Coffee-Grinder, and Around-the-World(2).]

Squat-Dance: See Cossack-Squat-Kick-Dance.

Stereo-Freeze: An American **Fad** dance of 1963. The **Stereo-Freeze** had its own Eponymous record, *"Stereo Freeze"* by *The Stereos.*
    (See Novelty-&-Fad Dances-of-the-1960s.)
    [From *Soul, www.trinity.unimelb.edu.au.* See *www.sixtiescity.com/Culture/dance.*]

Steve-Martin: A **Novelty** or **Fad** dance of an unknown time, listed in *"Novelty and fad dances"* under [http://en.wikipedia.org/wiki].

Stewardess: Of the 1980s, comical Pantomime **Novelty Fad Singular-Dance** Movements and Hand Maneuvers in Cadence with the Music, simulating the Actions of an airline **Stewardess** giving her speel.
    The following is from *"Eighties Dances"* - [www.inthe80s.com]:
        "This is a very complex move with 3 individual steps, giving the total effect of those lessons the stewardesses give you regarding airline safety.
        "The first set of motions involves acting like you're putting on the seat belt. You can really move your hips on this one.
        "The second set of motions involves pointing with both hands, using two fingers on each hand, to show people where the exit doors are. Make sure to turn around and show them where the doors are behind them.
        "For the big ending, you pantomime putting on the mask. Step 1: Grab the mask from up above. Step 2: Grab the rubber band and pull it behind your head while holding the breathing cup in front of you. Step 3: Gently release the cup and the rubber band to secure the breathing apparatus to your head."
    (See Novelty-&-Fad Dances-of-the-1980s. Also see Pantomime, Mime, and Mimicry-En-Masse.)

Stomp: A **Novelty Fad** Singular dance Routine in vogue in the U.S. in the 1960s. A sort of Line-Dance in 4/4 Tempo, this **Stomp** Routine was popular at the Brigham Young University, in Provo, Utah.
    Two "**Stomp**" singing 45rpm dance records were available in 1963; they were *"Let's Stomp"* by *Bobby Comstock,* and the *"Bristol Stomp"* by *The Dovells.* [From *Soul,* www.trinity.unimelb.edu.au]
    This **Stomp**'s one-Measure Basic Figure, with *Slow Slow Slow Slow* Rhythm, was *sidetouch closestomp SideTouch CloseStomp*; probably repeated. A two-Measure Pattern with all *Slows* followed, which was *sidetouch backtouch sidetouch closestomp; SideTouch BackTouch SideTouch CloseStomp.* Then a two-Measure Pattern was danced, with *Slow Slow Quick Quick Slow* Rhythm: *forstep BackStep sidestomp SideStomp Hold; backstep BackTouch SideStomp sidestomp ForStep.* All was probably repeated and repeated. [Data mostly from "Rhythm and Dance" by Alma Heaton.]
                                                (Continued)

Stomp: (Continued)

Similar to **Stomp-Off**. [See Novelty-Dances, Fad-Dances, Novelty-and-Fad Genre, and the Novelty-&-Fad Dances-of-the-1960s. Also see Alligator-Stomp, Beatle-Stomp, Black-Stomp, Bristol-Stomp, Bull-Nose-Stomp, Cheater-Stomp, Dartell-Stomp, Drum-Stomp, Foot-Stomping, Good-Times-Stomp, Guitar-Boogie-Stomp, Humphrey-Stomp, Jordan-Stomp, L.A.-Stomp, Lone-Star-Stomp, Manhattan-Stomp, Massacre-Stomp, Moonstomp, Moppety-Stomp, Mountain-Stomp, Mozart-Stomp, Night-Stomp, Pyramids-Stomp, Rendezvous-Stomp, Rock-and-Stomp, Rush-Hour-Stomp, Shake-and-Stomp, Soulful-Stomp, Soul-Stomp, Soupy-Shuffle-Stomp, Spanns-Stomp, Surfer-Stomp, Train-Stomp, Ubangi-Stomp, Wild-Stomp, and Zombie-Stomp.]

Stomp-Off: An Unleadable 1930s **Separated-Break-A-Way Novelty Fad** Pattern, usually Performed while dancing the **Big-Apple**. Also suitable for the many **Swing** dances. After separating from one's Partner while dancing the **Lindy-Hop**, or the **Swing-Bal** portion of the **Balboa**, one would often **Stomp-Off** to return back Together.

With one Hand Up and the other on stomach, <u>Stomp</u> one Foot Forward then Drag the other Foot Closed Together. Continue for eight Counts.

For the **Big-Apple**, the **Stomp-Off** was one of the **Break-A-Way** Genre. Wiggling their hips, certain **Break-A-Way** Patterns were danced. The original **Suzie-Q**, **Boogie-Back**, **Tack-Annie**, **Georgia-Grind**, **Praise-Allah!**, **Truckin'**, **Peckin'**, **Charleston**, **Shorty-George**, and other Break-A-Ways, were probably originated early by blacks; while **Spank-the-Baby**, **Rusty-Dusty**, **Pose-and-a-Peck**, the **Little-Apple**, the **Little-Peach**, **Mess-Around**, **Stomp-Off**, **Apple-Jacks**, and **Fall-Off-the-Log**, and other Break-A-Ways, were probably originated later by whites. Most all of these Patterns seem to have been influenced or derived from the classic **Lindy-Hop** and/or **Big-Apple** dances.

Similar to **Stamp**(2). [See **Break-A-Way Glossary** for a more complete listing. Also see Novelty-Dances, Fad-Dances, Novelty-and-Fad Genre, and the Novelty-&-Fad Dances-of-the-1960s. Also see Alligator-Stomp, Beatle-Stomp, Black-Stomp, Bristol-Stomp, Bull-Nose-Stomp, Cheater-Stomp, Dartell-Stomp, Drum-Stomp, Foot-Stomping, Good-Times-Stomp, Guitar-Boogie-Stomp, Humphrey-Stomp, Jordan-Stomp, L.A.-Stomp, Lone-Star-Stomp, Manhattan-Stomp, Massacre-Stomp, Moonstomp, Moppety-Stomp, Mountain-Stomp, Mozart-Stomp, Night-Stomp, Pyramids-Stomp, Rendezvous-Stomp, Rock-and-Stomp, Rush-Hour-Stomp, Shake-and-Stomp, Soulful-Stomp, Soul-Stomp, Soupy-Shuffle-Stomp, Spanns-Stomp, Surfer-Stomp, Train-Stomp, Ubangi-Stomp, Wild-Stomp, and Zombie-Stomp.]

Stop: Only this name for an American **Novelty** or **Fad** of the 1960s is listed simply as a Dance, Pattern, or Figure in the "*Dance Crazes of the Sixties*."

(See Novelty-&-Fad Dances-of-the-1960s.) [From *www.sixtiescity.com/Culture/dance*]

Stop-Touch: Only this name for an American **Novelty** or **Fad** of the 1960s is listed simply as a Dance, Pattern, or Figure in the "*Dance Crazes of the Sixties*."

(See Novelty-&-Fad Dances-of-the-1960s.) [From *www.sixtiescity.com/Culture/dance*]

Strand: An American **Fad** dance of (1962?). The **Strand** had its own Eponymous record, *"The Strand"* by *Chubby Checker*.

(See the Novelty-&-Fad Dances-of-the-1960s.)

[From *Soul, www.trinity.unimelb.edu.au*. See *www.sixtiescity.com/Culture/dance*.]

Stretch: Only this name for an American **Novelty** or **Fad** of the 1960s is listed simply as a Dance, Pattern, or Figure in the "*Dance Crazes of the Sixties*."

(See Novelty-&-Fad Dances-of-the-1960s.) [From *www.sixtiescity.com/Culture/dance*]

Strobing: **Novelty Fad** Singular Movements, **Strobing** is one small Move of the California `Funk' brand of the **Boogaloo** Genre of Mime "Moves," which seems to be part of the **Electric-Boogie** Style of **Break-Dancing**, which, in turn, is part of **Hip-Hop**.

Strobing is Moving in ways that give the illusion of being under a strobe light.

The name **Strobing** comes from the lighting use of a strob-o-scope which makes moving objects appear stationary by intermittent illumination or observation. Such an instrument renders a body visible only at intervals or at certain points of its path.

The following is from "*Move Lessons*," [www.mrwiggleshiphop.net]:

"Strobing is based on exactly what the word means. It is based on short stop motion type movements and is done generally with out a pop, but more of a subtle stop between each movement. Imitating the illusions of movements under a strobe light. What your doing is basic movements that you would see in a night club, movements like walking, looking at your watch, pointing, taking off your hat, dancing, drinking. You can also imitate things like waking up, yawning, etc. To accomplish this style:

"1- Choose an action or style of movement, lets say for example combing your hair.

"2- Now without applying the strobe technique just practice a motion that you would use to comb your hair, and try going from taking a comb out of your front shirt pocket and then combing your hair a few times and putting the comb back.

"3- Now lets apply the technique of creating a strobe light illusion to this motion. Use short `stop and go' type movements. Keep it very sharp and staccato like. No popping or heavy jerking. The simpler you keep your movement and effect, the better the illusion. Now do the same hair combing movements that you just practice and apply strobing to it."

Ticking is also dancing in ways that give the illusion of being under a strobe light. Consequently, **Strobing** and **Ticking** are commonly confused with each other.

Similar to the **Tick**. See **Mime**, and **Pantomime**. [Also see Air-Posing, Animation(3), Bop(2), Centipede, Cobra, Crazy-Legs, Dime-Stopping, Filmore, Floating(2), Glides, Hitting, King-Tut, Lean(4), Pop(3), Puppet, Robot, Saccin, Scarecrow, Snake(4), Spiderman, Sticking, Strut, and Wave(1); for other related Moves. Also see Underground Step-Listing.]

Stroke: An American **Fad** dance of 1966. The **Stroke** had its own Eponymous record, *"The Stroke"* by *Andre Williams*.

(See the Novelty-&-Fad Dances-of-the-1960s.) [From *Soul*, www.trinity.unimelb.edu.au]

Strokin':   A 1980s **Novelty Fad** Group-Dance Pattern or Routine.

How to dance the **Strokin'** to the Music's Beat is described as follows in the *"Eighties Dances,"* [www.inthe80s.com]:

　　　　*"**Strokin** - Done to the song by Clarence Carter, `Strokin.' Drag left foot to the left and the right foot to the right then pivot half around and do it again. Usually done at big dances as a line dance. Once you watch someone it is easy."*

　　　　[See Skate(1), Skid, Skim, Sweep(1), Sway-Side-to-Side, Slither, Side-Rise, Scoop, Swoop, and Level-Progression. Also see Novelty-Dances, Fad-Dances, Novelty-and-Fad Genre, and the Novelty-&-Fad Dances-of-the-1960s. Also see Stroke, and Donkey-Stroke.]

Stroll: The Stroll was an American **Novelty Fad** and classic **Line-Dance** in vogue about 1956-57. Later, John Travolta danced **The Stroll** in the movie, *"Grease."* It is Performed to Slow Swing or Rhythm-and-Blues Music. In 1962, two "**Stroll**" singing 45rpm Eponymous records were available for dancing **The Stroll**. They were *"The Stroll"* by *The Diamonds*, and *"C.C. Rider"* by *Chuck Willis*.

This **Stroll** is danced in two parallel lines, with Men on one side and Facing their Ladies across the divide. A simple Basic Step-Pattern is Executed in such a fashion that the line advances one Pace with each Pattern worked. Individuals at the Head end pair up and Perform a **'Shine'** Routine as they proceed down the line with all eyes on them, which at the end they separate and rejoin their lines. Then the next couple pairs up and makes their way down the line. Meanwhile, everyone Moves In-Place to the Music.

Following is from *Some Favorite 50s Dances* - [www.loti.com/fifties]:

　　　　*"**The Stroll**. The Stroll was often done only by girls, but that isn't a 'rule' in this classic 50s dance. The Stroll is basically two lines of dancers with a large space in the middle. Lead dancers are on one side, their partners on the other. Dancers do a step pattern to advance the line, and leaders do a solo routine through the line, joining it at the end. The dance continues this way through the music. The Stroll was one of the most popular dances of the 50s, and many nostalgic 50s movies feature a scene featuring The Stroll."*

　　　　[See Cake-Walk, and Line-Dances(1). Also see Novelty-Dances, Fad-Dances, Novelty-and-Fad Genre, and the Novelty-&-Fad Dances-of-the-1960s. Also see the Bambuco, Bop, Bunny-Hop, Calypso, Creep, Fish, Flea-Hop, Frug, Guapacha, Hand-Jive, Hitch-Hiker, Hokey-Pokey, Hullie-Gullie, Jerk, Limbo-Rock, Mashed-Potato, Mess-Around(2), Monkey, Pachanga, Plena, Pony, Rock-and-Around, Scooter, Slide, Surfers, Swim, Tumba-Cha, Twist, Twister, and the Watusi; which were all Novelty Fads in vogue in the 1950-60s. Also see Blackout-Stroll, Cleopatra-Stroll, Camel-Walk-Stroll, Gawk-'n'-Stroll, Kwella-Stroll, Monkey-Stroll, Palais-Stroll, Popeye-Stroll, and Shing-A-Ling-Stroll.]

Strut: Only this name for an American **Novelty** or **Fad** of the **1960s** is listed simply as a Dance, Pattern, or Figure in the *"Dance Crazes of the Sixties."*

　　　　(See Novelty-Dances, Fad-Dances, Novelty-and-Fad Genre, and Novelty-&-Fad Dances-of-the-1960s. Also see African-Strut, Funky-Strut, Sissy-Strut, Soul-Struttin', Spanish-Strut, and Struttin'.) [From *www.sixtiescity.com/Culture/dance*]

Struttin':   Only this name for an American **Novelty** or **Fad** of the **1960s** is listed simply as a Dance, Pattern, or Figure in the *"Dance Crazes of the Sixties."*

　　　　(See Novelty-&-Fad Dances-of-the-1960s.) [From *www.sixtiescity.com/Culture/dance*]

Stupidity: Only this name for an American **Novelty** or **Fad** of the **1960s** is listed simply as a Dance, Pattern, or Figure in the "_Dance Crazes of the Sixties._"
(See Novelty-&-Fad Dances-of-the-1960s.) [From _www.sixtiescity.com/Culture/dance_]

Stutter-Step: An Unleadable **Break-A-Way** novelty **Fad** Pattern, usually Performed while dancing the **Carolina-Shag**.
(See Shorty-George, Boogie-Back, Apple-Jacks, Belly-Roll, Flamingo, Belly-Roll, Duck-Walk, Fly-Back, Lean, and the SugarFoot, for like Patterns. See **Break-A-Way Glossary** for a more complete listing.) [Note: Mechanics of its Steps are unknown.]

SugarFoot(1) or **Heel-and-Toe Footwork** or **Sugars:** Two possibly Leadable, **Break-A-Way** Novelty **Fad**, Spot-Coupledance Movements, Figure or Pattern, Left and Right, Mirror-Image. Suitable for **Charleston**, American **Twostep**, Eastern **Swing**, West-Coast-Swing, **Country-Western**, **Balboa**, **Carolina-Shag**, and for other dances. While dancing the **Lindy-Hop**, or the **Swing-Bal** portion of the **Balboa**, in Butterfly Position throughout, or after separating from one's Partner, one would often dance this **SugarFoot** to return back Together.
The following is from _Line/C&W Dance & Music FAQ_ -- [http://ourworld.compuserve.com]:
"_SUGAR FOOT -- A two count pattern of touching the toe of the right foot to the instep of the left foot then touching the heel of the right foot to the instep of the left foot, or touching the left toe and heel to the right_ instep."
Alternately Swiveling Feet in the direction of the Supporting-Foot; i.e., Swivel Supporting-Ball 1/4 Inward then 1/2 Outward, while Rotating one's free ankle Inward then Outward to Touch alternately one's Toe then Heel of the Free-Foot, to the Dancefloor, next to the Instep of one's Supporting-Foot. Usually continued for eight Counts. **SugarFoot** is normally danced In-Place, but could also Travel either Forward or Rearward.
This **SugarFoot**(1) was danced in the 1930s early days of **Swing**(1) as the precursor Stylized means of developing the **SugarPush**.
(See Traveling-SugarFoot, Swivel-Walks, Toe-Movements, Sand-Step, Swivel, Ramble, Foot-Boogie, Double-Foot-Boogie, Toe-In, Toe-Out, Toes-Out, Toe-Splits, Toe-Fan, Heel-Fan, Heels-Out, Heel-Splits, Swivet, Marchessi, Corta-Jaca, and Celtic-Storm. Also see Shorty-George, Boogie-Back, Apple-Jacks, Belly-Roll, Flamingo, Belly-Roll, Duck-Walk, Fly-Back, Lean, and the Stutter-Step, for like Patterns for the Carolina-Shag. See **Break-A-Way Glossary** for a more complete listing. Also see Balboa Step-Listing.)

Sugartime-Twist: A **Novelty Fad** Coupledance of 1961. This had its own Eponymous record, "_Sugartime Twist_" by the _McGuire Sisters_.
(See Novelty-&-Fad Dances-of-the-1960s.) [From www.bluejuice.org.au]

Super-Robot: Pantomime 1980s **Novelty Fad Singular-Dance** Maneuvers. How to dance the **Super-Robot** to the Beat is described as follows in the "_Eighties Dances_," [www.inthe80s.com]:
"**_Robot or Super Robot_** - _Robot: Kinda like the poplock except you keep all your body parts straight. Super Robot: Kind of between the robot and poplock with legs and arms even neck and stomach._"
(See Mime, Robot, and Locking-and-Popping.)

Surf: Only this name for an American **Novelty** or **Fad** of the **1960s** is listed simply as a Dance, Pattern, or Figure in the "*Dance Crazes of the Sixties*."

This **Surf** dance may have been the **Surfers**. (See Novelty-&-Fad Dances-of-the-1960s.) [From *www.sixtiescity.com/Culture/dance*]

Surfer-Boogie: Only this name for an American **Novelty** or **Fad** of the **1960s** is listed simply as a Dance, Pattern, or Figure in the "*Dance Crazes of the Sixties*."

(See Novelty-&-Fad Dances-of-the-1960s.) [From *www.sixtiescity.com/Culture/dance*]

Surfers: A 1960s **Novelty Fad** Singles dance, originating in the U.S. This **Surfers** dance may have been the **Surf**, which in turn was actually the **Frug**. These 1960s dances were free and individualistic. People enmasse, mostly teens with long hair, were dancing by themselves and inventing as they danced.

(See Novelty-Dances, Fad-Dances, Novelty-and-Fad Genre, and Novelty-&-Fad Dances-of-the-1960s. Also see the Bambuco, Bop, Bunny-Hop, Calypso, Creep, Fish, Flea-Hop, Guapacha, Hitch-Hiker, Hokey-Pokey, Hullie-Gullie, Jerk, Limbo-Rock, Mashed-Potato, Monkey, Pachanga, Plena, Pony, Rock-and-Around, Scooter, Slide, Strole, Swim, Tumba-Cha, Twist, Twister, and the Watusi; which were all Novelty Fads in vogue in the 1950-60s. Also see Surf, Surfer-Stomp, Surfin'-Bird, Surfink, and Surfer-Boogie.)

Surfer-Stomp: A Leadable **Novelty Fad**, Sideward-Traveling dance Step or Routine, in vogue in the United States in the 1960s. A sort of co-ed Line-Dance in 4/4 Time, this **Surfer-Stomp** was the dance 15-year-old Buddy Schwimmer joined in with in about 1965.

The following is an excerpt from "*Nightclub Two Step (NC2S),*" *www.lovemusiclovedance.com*:

> "**Nightclub Two Step History**
>
> [Philip] "*Seyer: Is it true that you developed it more than 30 years ago?*
>
> [Buddy] "*Schwimmer: Yep. I was 15 years old. I was doing a line dance called Surfer Stomp, where the guys stand on one side and the girls on the other. You do Side, Cross, Side, Stomp. Side, Cross, Side, Stomp. We'd join hands and push `em up in the air on the stomp. The count was: one, two, three, touch four; one, two, three, touch four. We'd do that to the faster music and it worked fine. But when a slow piece would come on, we still wanted to dance, but the footwork was too slow. We'd be going: o---n---e….…., t---w---o….….. So we double timed it and the count became One & Two & Three & Four. We thought of taking two steps with the left foot then two steps with the right foot like this (leader's part):*
>
> "*Left & Left – Right & Right. Or 1 & 2 – 3 & 4 – "*

[The girls Followed the boy's Steps by Mirroring them.]

(See See Novelty-Dances, Fad-Dances, Novelty-and-Fad Genre, and Novelty-&-Fad Dances-of-the-1960s.)

Surfin'-Bird: Only this name for an American **Novelty** or **Fad** of the **1960s** is listed simply as a Dance, Pattern, or Figure in the "*Dance Crazes of the Sixties*."

(See Novelty-&-Fad Dances-of-the-1960s.) [From *www.sixtiescity.com/Culture/dance*]

Surfing-Monkey: A **Novelty Fad** Coupledance of the 1960s. This had its own Eponymous record, the "*Surfing Monkey*" by the *Spinners*.

(See Novelty-&-Fad Dances-of-the-1960s. Especially see Swing-Out.)

[From www.bluejuice.org.au]

Surfink: Only this name for an American **Novelty** or **Fad** of the 1960s is listed simply as a Dance, Pattern, or Figure in the "*Dance Crazes of the Sixties*."

(See Novelty-&-Fad Dances-of-the-1960s.) [From *www.sixtiescity.com/Culture/dance*]

Suzie: Only this name for an American **Novelty** or **Fad** of the 1960s is listed simply as a Dance, Pattern, or Figure in the "*Dance Crazes of the Sixties*."

(See Novelty-&-Fad Dances-of-the-1960s.) [From *www.sixtiescity.com/Culture/dance*]

Suzie-Q or **Susie-Q** or **Suzy-Q** or **Suzi-Q** or **Heel-Twist**(2) or **Grind-Walk:** Two Leadable, two-Measure, eight-Count, six-Step Coupledance Patterns, Left and Right; i.e., (unless to Travel laterally,) each **Suzie-Q** Measure is usually followed by a Mirror-Image Opposite **Suzie-Q** Measure.

The various **Suzie-Q** Patterns are all suitable for **Country-Western**, American **Twostep**, the **Big-Apple**, the **Swing-Bal** portion of the **Balboa**, and for other dancing. Partners normally Coupledance Mirror-Image Opposite, Facing in Butterfly Position throughout. For the **Big-Apple**, several different ways to **Suzie-Q** were some of the **Break-A-Way** Genre; Wiggling their hips, certain **Break-A-Way** Patterns were danced. For the **Balboa**, the **Suzie-Q** Pattern is danced in Butterfly Position throughout, or after separating from one's Partner, one will often dance the Solo version in "**Suzie-Q Position**", then will return back Together for the **Pure-Balboa**.

Rhythm with 4/4 Timing may be *Quick Quick Slow, Quick Quick Slow;* or *Slow Quick Quick, Slow Quick Quick;* or, for the **Balboa**, Swing-Bal Timing is *1 2 3 4, 5 6 7 8*.

One method to **Suzie-Q**: Partners dance Cross Swivel Steps Toward one Side, Fan Thru, then dance Cross Swivel Steps Toward Opposite Side, and Swivel to Face. This is followed by a **Suzie-Q** in Mirror-Image. For the **Right-Suzie-Q**, to the Man's Right, the Man dances *Swivel1/4CW shortforswivel1/4CCW ShortSideSwivel1/4CW shortforswivelFanThru1/2CCW, ShortForSwivel1/4CW shortsideswivel1/4CCW ShortForSwivel1/4CW* to Face. His Lady Follows Mirror-Image if Facing. **Left-Suzie-Q** is Mirror-Image Opposite.

Another method to **Suzie-Q** to the Left follows: The Right Heel is Extended Forward Across the Left Foot with the Right Toe Pointed Outward. With Weight kept on Right Heel, the Right Toe is Rotated CW a Quarter-Turn as Left Foot Steps Sideward, then Weight is again transferred to Right Foot, etc.

For the **Balboa**, Swing-Bal Timing, the Man dances the **Suzie-Q** to the Right then Left as follows:

SwivelIn swivelout SwivelIn crossinfront, swivelin SwivelOut swivelin CrossInFront.

For the Parallel-Traveling **Suzie-Q** as a General Singular-Dance Figure or Pattern, this one has been danced for Vaudville shows, Solo dance demos, and the like. This **Suzie-Q** version was popularized by dancers at the Harlem Cotton Club in the 1920s-30s. Danced in "**Suzie-Q Position**" in which both Hands are Clasped In-Front of the Body at Knee-Level, with one's fingers interlaced, and with one's Body Poised Forward from the waist. Knee-Bend is Deep-Into-Knees.

(Continued)

Suzie-Q: (Continued)

Beginning in this **Suzie-Q Position**, one dances Sideways, Traveling Left in a series of **Cross-Swivel**s with one's bent elbows Swinging in counter balance Opposition. In *and One And two* Rhythm Timing, one dances *swivel1/8CCW CrossHeelInFront Swivel1/8CW sideward,* etc. Elbows Swing Clockwise on Count *One* and Counter-Clockwise on Count *And*.

The following "*Suzi-Q*" is from *Vance's Fantastic Tap Dance Dictionary*:

"Dance craze of 1937: Clasp the hands and hold them extended in front of the body; slide one foot across in front of the other and step to the side with the opposite foot. The arms move to the R on the cross movement and to the L as you step on the L foot to the L side."

The original **Suzie-Q, Boogie-Back, Tack-Annie, Georgia-Grind, Praise-Allah!, Truckin', Peckin', Charleston, Shorty-George**, and other Break-A-Ways, were probably originated early by blacks; while **Spank-the-Baby, Rusty-Dusty, Pose-and-a-Peck**, the **Little-Apple**, the **Little-Peach, Mess-Around, Stomp-Off, Apple-Jacks**, and **Fall-Off-the-Log**, and other Break-A-Ways, were probably originated later by whites. Most all of these Patterns seem to have been influenced or derived from the classic **Lindy-Hop** and/or **Big-Apple** dances. See **Break-A-Way Glossary** for a more complete listing.

(See Sand-Step, Traveling-SugarFoot, and NightLife. Also see Butterfly-Break-A-Ways, Separated-Break-A-Ways, and Balboa Step-Listing.)

Swalsa: A **Novelty Fad C**oupledance, invented probably in 1997 and in vogue beginning in 2005, that is a combination and blending of **Swing** (most often **Lindy**) and **Salsa**. Music in 4/4 Time is usually Salsa, but can possibly be jazz or certain Swing Music.

Swing influenced by Salsa is not difficult to reconcile, since both are on eight Counts. **Swalsa** is probably danced in **16-Count** Patterns. It is said by those that dance **Swalsa**, that *"most of the moves transfer over relatively painlesssly."* HipHopLindy.com says: *"There are differences in the steps and styling, of course, but the upper body work is largely the same. Salsa and Latin dances in general have a very different feel, with different breaks, variations, and Cuban (hip) motion. All of these things can be transferred back into swing."* HipHopLindy.com says **Swalsa** is **Swing** with **Salsa** Figures added in. Salsa Figures are adjusted so as to fit into Swing vocabulary. Salsa's Turns, Changes-of-Direction, and Footwork adjust Well.

While continually CW Couple-Rotating in the Wrapped-Lindy Position (with Lady's **Right** arm on top), it is nice to **dance the Lindy Basic-Pattern then switch to Salsa Timing**. Another **Swalsa** Pattern often used is as follows: Starting in Cradled Position (with Lady's **Left** arm on top), Man's Left Hand is Lifted overhead while retaining both Hands, the Lady is brought Behind and to the Man's Left as the Man Wraps himself with his Right arm on top. The Man then Tunnels Back and Rotates Lady to UnCross arms.

With regards to mixing Swing with other dances in 16-Count Patterns in 4/4 Time, there are the three **Swalsa** "sister-dances", **Swango,** (Swing + Tango,) **Swing-Rueda,** (Salsa-Rueda + Swing,) and **HipHop-Lindy,** (Swing + HipHop.)

(See Lindy-Hop, and Lindy.)

Swango: A **Novelty Fad C**oupledance of the **Neo-Tango** sub-Genre, in vogue beginning in 2005, that is a combination and blending of **Swing** (most often **West-Coast-Swing**) and the **Argentine-Tango**. Music is in 4/4 Time and is a Steady-Beat Slow Tango, or possibly Slow Swing Music.

The **Basic-Step** seems to be a **16-Count** Pattern: This **Swango** Step begins with one Basic Sugar-Push for the first six Counts then uses two Counts to blend to Loose-Closed Position.   With both Partners next Swivel-Stepping for Four Counts upon Same-Feet, both Step Left Feet to Sidecar, Swivel then Step Right Feet to Banjo, then repeat same. Next the Man Freezes as his Lady dances two Forward-Ochos for two Counts (still in Loose-Closed Position). Lastly, both use two Counts to blend to Butterfly preparing for a Sugar-Push again.

The following are **Swango** excerpts from www.hiphoplindy.com:

"*Swango is a developing dance form that is an intoxicating and challenging mix of Swing (Lindy, West Coast, East Coast, Carolina Shag, whatever your thing is) and Argentine Tango.*

"*Danced to mellow Swing music. It is great for dancers ... At first glance you might think Swing and Argentine Tango appear totally different, well you'd be right, they are. However, their very differences make the transitions possible and it turns out they have surprising things in common! If you know some Argentine Tango take one of your favourite (mellow) swing tunes and just dance tango to it and see what happens. ...*"

The following are **Swango** excerpts from www.swangoseattle.com:

"*Dancing is our passion. And our skills in both West Coast Swing and Argentine Tango have allowed us to create a method to accelerate the process of learning to dance Swango. ...*

"*The exotic nuevo tango music is perfect for Swango. But Swango can also be done to much of the popular West Coast Swing music.*"

The following is a **Swango** excerpt from www.time2dance.com:

"*rob and sheila: West Coast Classes & SWANGO dance at The Atrium on Wednesdays!!*"

The following are **Swango** excerpts from www.usaswingnet.com:

"***Swango dancing is hot!***

"*If you love the sexiness of Swing and the passion of Tango, 'Swango' may be a great new experience for you. It offers the best of both dance worlds.*"

The following are reviews of the Stage presentation, "**SWANGO**" [www.mainstage-mgmt.com]:

"*'SWANGO' is hot! The music will have you groovin' in your seat, and a new script by Rupert Holmes kicks it up a notch. 'SWANGO' combines the passion of the tango with the sexy sizzle of swing in a new dance show that will leave you wanting to head for the ballroom or the bedroom!* " -- The Scarsdale Inquirer

"*As the title implies, the result is a magical synthesis. The dancers of both traditions are thrilling. Sensuous moves, beautiful spins and amazing lifts come one after another. Tango alternates with swing, couples switch with multiple pairs, and men and women have their times alone. It's all mesmerizing.*" -- The Journal News

With regards to mixing Swing with other dances in 16-Count Patterns in 4/4 Time, there are the three **Swango** "sister-dances", **Swalsa**, (Swing + Salsa,) **Swing-Rueda**, (Salsa-Rueda + Swing,) and **HipHop-Lindy**, (Swing + HipHop.) In addition, see the **Neo-Tango** sub-Genre, to which this **Swango** belongs.

(See the full series of Sugar-Pushes.)

Sway: An American **Fad** dance of the 1960s. This had its own Eponymous record, *"The Sway"* by *The Virgos*.
> (See Novelty-&-Fad Dances-of-the-1960s.)
> [From *www.bluejuice.org.au*. See *www.sixtiescity.com/Culture/dance*.]

Swim: A fun **Novelty Fad** Singlular or Coupledance, that was Unstructured and Unleadable. The **Swim** originated in the U.S. about 1963, (some say in 1961,) and was very popular about 1964 to 1968. In 1963 or 1964, for this dance, *Robert Ward* sang and recorded *"The Swim,"* while *Bobby Freeman* sang and recorded *"C'mon And Swim."* Its Eponymous dance attempted to imitate human **Swim**ming Motions through Pantomime. In addition, *Chubby Checker* sang and recorded *She Wants T'Swim*. The **Swim** was a Spot-Dance, danced in 4/4 Time to Jazz type Foxtrot Music. The dance Mimicked **Swim**ming, and was one of a whole series of 1960s Mimicking dance Patterns, (see Hullie-Gullie.) This silly **Swim**, along with other silly Fad-Dances, was banned at Brigham Young University in 1966.
> The following is from *Dance Crazes of the Sixties* -
> [*www.sixtiescity.com/Culture/dance*]:
>> *"**The Swim:** You do **The Twist** with your hips and legs and do all sorts of swimming (or diving) motions with your hands."*
> The **Swim**, having been derived from The **Frug**, was usually danced Apart but Facing Partner, and was often danced in conjunction with The **Fish**. The **Swim**'s primary, Unleadable Movement was, with one's arms Pointed Forward and horizontal, and with Body Undulations, the dancer weaved Hands, wrists and elbows to the Music, as if **Swim**ming. Movements included simulating the *back stroke*.
> The **Swim** was related to The **Twist**, The **Monkey**, The **Dog**, The **Watusi**, The **Waddle**, and The **Jerk** dances. (Also see the Novelty-&-Fad Dances-of-the-1960s.)

Swing: Only this name for an American **Novelty** or **Fad** of the **1960s** is listed simply as a Dance, Pattern, or Figure in the *"Dance Crazes of the Sixties."* But this might be the same dance as the **Swing-Out**.
> (See Novelty-&-Fad Dances-of-the-1960s.) [From *www.sixtiescity.com/Culture/dance*]

Swing-Out (or Swing?): An American **Fad** dance of 1968. **Swinging-Out** was danced to the record of *"I'll Be Around"* by *The Spinners*.
> (See Novelty-&-Fad Dances-of-the-1960s. Especially see Surfing-Monkey.)
> [From *Soul, www.trinity.unimelb.edu.au*; and *www.bluejuice.org.au*. Also see *.sixtiescity.com/Culture/dance*.]

Swing-Rueda: A Novelty **Fad** Group-Coupledance, in vogue beginning probably in 2005, that is a combination and blending of **Swing** (most often **Lindy**) and **Salsa**. Music in 4/4 Time is usually Salsa, but can possibly be jazz or certain Swing Music.

Swing influenced by Salsa is not difficult to reconcile since both are on eight Counts. As with the **Salsa-Casino-Rueda**, this offshoot **Swing-Rueda** is a dance where many Couples (two or more) Circle Together, dancing identical Steps in Unison, as their *"Caller of the Rueda"* (Usually one of the dancers) Calls out the Steps. Hand signals are also used at times. Certain Patterns require Partner Changes.

Some of the special **Swing-Rueda** Calls are as follows (from www.swingrueda.com): *Open Break, Swing Out, Dame, Outside Turn, Inside Turn, Sushi, Texas Tommy, Stop Texas, Mini-Dip, Dame Dos, Circle Down, Amoeba, Chalupa, Chalupa Dame, Treble Clef, Right Foot Stomp, Turn Her In, Turn Him In,* and *Tranke.*

With regards to mixing Swing with other dances in 16-Count Patterns in 4/4 Time, there are the three **Swing-Rueda** "sister-dances", **Swalsa**, (Swing + Salsa,) **Swango**, (Swing + Tango,) and **HipHop-Lindy**, (Swing + HipHop.)

(See Salsa-Casino-Rueda, Lindy-Hop, and Lindy.)

Swish-Fish: Only this name for an American **Novelty** or **Fad** of the 1960s is listed simply as a Dance, Pattern, or Figure in the *"Dance Crazes of the Sixties."*

(See Novelty-&-Fad Dances-of-the-1960s.) [From *www.sixtiescity.com/Culture/dance*]

Switch: An American **Fad** dance of the 1960s. This **Switch** had its own Eponymous record, *"The Switch"* by *Race Marbles.*

(See Novelty-&-Fad Dances-of-the-1960s.)

[From *www.bluejuice.org.au.* See *www.sixtiescity.com/Culture/dance.*]

Switch-A-Roo: An American **Fad** dance of the 1960s. This **Switch-A-Roo** had its own Eponymous record, *"The Switch-A-Roo"* by the *Five Royales.*

(See Novelty-&-Fad Dances-of-the-1960s.) [From *Soul,* www.trinity.unimelb.edu.au]

Switchy-Walk: Only this name for an American **Novelty** or **Fad** of the 1960s is listed simply as a Dance, Pattern, or Figure in the *"Dance Crazes of the Sixties."*

(See Novelty-&-Fad Dances-of-the-1960s.) [From *www.sixtiescity.com/Culture/dance*]

Syncopated-Splits: Two General and Unleadable **Novelty Fad** Spot-Singular or Spot-Coupledance Figures, Left or Right, Mirror-Image Opposite. At least one set in Sequence is normally danced. With Feet Together, beginning with a tiny Hop, Feet are Quickly Split Apart separately, to Side-by-Side Shoulder-Width with Weight upon both Feet. Then with another tiny Hop, Feet are Quickly brought back Together again. Rhythm Timing is either *Andslow, andSlow;* or, *andSlow, Andslow.* Both Arms are Spread upon the Apart.

Left **Syncopated-Splits** are danced *HopsideSide, HopcloseClose.* The similar Right **Syncopated-Splits** are danced *hopSideside, hopCloseclose.*

Similar to **Side-Touches.** (See Running-Man, Moon-Walk, SideSlide, Step-Scoot, Stationary-Copas, Cake-Walk, and Splits. Also see Underground Step-Listing.)

Syrtaki: See Zorba's-Dance.

Tack-Annie or **Tacky-Annie:** A 1920s-30s **Novelty Fad**, Unleadable, Solo, Coupledance or Group-Dance, 8-Count Pattern Sequence Performed several times. Being Generally of the **Tap-Dance Genre**, the Shimmying **Tack-Annie** is one part of the extensive **Shim-Sham** Soft-Shoe Routine. **Tack-Annie** is also a part of the **Swing** Genre. In the 1930s the **Tack-Annie** was usually Performed while dancing the **Big-Apple**.

The following is *Tacky Annie* from *Shim Sham History*, [www.jitterbuzz.com]:

"Debra Sternberg's story (and she's sticking to it) is that Tacky Annie was a stripper. She used to do that little step (while shimmying, of course!) in her altogether.

"... some insight on the origin of the Tacky Annie move in the Shim Sham. Apparently Annie was a rather large Irish woman who ran a bar or a house of ill-repute (maybe somewhere in New York, not sure.) Anyway, when the police came in trying to close her down, Annie grabbed the officer with both hands and hit him with her belly. That's what's happening every time you step back during the Tacky Annie. ..."

The following is from an unknown source:

"... the Tack Annie step ... derived its name from a former chorus line dancer. The dancer's name was Annie. She was the last dancer in the line to exit the stage at the end of the performance. To add pizzazz to her exit she created this step. The name Tack Annie was given to the step in a tribute to her.

"... We jumped open so that our feet were about shoulder width apart. Tack Annies are a series of toe touches behind the opposite foot. We completed a series of 4 tack annies, each new series begins on the count of, and eight (and8,1,2,3,4,5,6,7). At the completion of the fourth tack annie we performed a half break."

Note that all **Tack Annies** have 4/4 Timing, and begin early on the Pickup(2).

The following is for (three) *Tack Annies* from the *The Shim Sham*; [http://golgi.ana.ed.ac.uk]:

"8: Open R leg out, weight shared by both legs.

"1: Dot R foot behind L (arms swing to L)

"2: Open R leg out again, weight shared by both legs.

"3: Dot L foot behind R (arms swing to R)

"4: Open L leg out again, weight shared by both legs.

"5: Dot R foot behind L (arms swing to L)

"6: Open R leg out again, weight shared by both legs.

"7: Step on L foot behind R (arms swing to R)."

The following is from *Shim Sham Shimmy* - Peter Renzland [http://dancing.org]:

"TACK ANNIES: (7: step Lb, &: step R, 8: step L)

On 8 pick up knees and let body drop! Arms swing loosely with tap foot.

STEP L   tap Rb   STEP R   tap Lb   STEP L   tap Rb   STEP R   STEP STEP

STEP L   tap Rb   STEP R   tap Lb   STEP L   tap Rb   STEP R   STEP STEP

STEP L   tap Rb   STEP R   tap Lb   STEP L   tap Rb   STEP R   STEP L."

The following is from *Jo's Tap Routines 4*, [http://tapdancing.tripod.com]:

"... jump feet apart... 3x Tack Annie (pick-up R, ball dig RNL, step R to side, pick-up L, ball dig LNR, step L to side, pick-up R, ball dig RNL, step R to side, pick-up R, ball dig RNL, step R to side - +12+34+56+7+8) ... 2 jumps with feet apart..."

(Continued)

Tack-Annie: (Continued)
For the **Big-Apple**, **Tack-Annie** was one of the **Break-A-Way** Genre. Wiggling their hips, certain **Break-A-Way** Patterns were danced. The original **Suzie-Q**, **Boogie-Back**, **Tack-Annie**, **Georgia-Grind**, **Praise-Allah!**, **Truckin'**, **Peckin'**, **Charleston**, **Shorty-George**, and other Break-A-Ways, were probably originated early by blacks; while **Spank-the-Baby**, **Rusty-Dusty**, **Pose-and-a-Peck**, the **Little-Apple**, the **Little-Peach**, **Mess-Around**, **Stomp-Off**, **Apple-Jacks**, and **Fall-Off-the-Log**, and other Break-A-Ways, were probably originated later by whites. Most all of these Patterns seem to have been influenced or derived from the classic **Lindy-Hop** and/or **Big-Apple** dances. See **Break-A-Way Glossary** for a more complete listing.

[For **Tack-Annie**, see 3rd & 7th blocks of the Shim-Sham(2) Routine.]

Tango-Hustle: A **Novelty Fad** Coupledance to the heavy Hustle Beat of the late 1970s in the U.S., especially in Los Angeles. A Hustle with an American Tango flavor, the **Tango-Hustle** was probably one of the Hustles-of-Tap-Genre, all of which were Six-Count. Its 4/4 constant Timing was probably either *1 2& 3 4, 5 Tap*, or *1 2 3& 4, 5 Tap*. From the writer's memory, its Basic-Step Started in a Tango Promenade Position; there may have been a Back-Hitch then a Pickup with a Tango-Close Tap. Opening again to Promenade, perhaps the Lady did an Outside Underarm-Turn or Spin followed by the Tango-Close. The **Tango-Hustle** must have had many additional Patterns.
(See Disco-Era.)

Tango-Twist: An American **Fad** Coupledance of 1963. This had its own Eponymous record, "*The Tango Twist*" by *Paul Wayne*.
(See Novelty-&-Fad Dances-of-the-1960s.)
[From *www.bluejuice.org.au*. See *www.sixtiescity.com/Culture/dance*.]

Tantrum: An American **Fad** dance of the 1960s. This had its own Eponymous record, "*Temper Tantrum*" by the *Warlocks*.
(See Novelty-&-Fad Dances-of-the-1960s.)
[From *www.bluejuice.org.au*. See *www.sixtiescity.com/Culture/dance*.]

Tarzan's-Monkey: Only this name for an American **Novelty** or **Fad** of the 1960s is listed simply as a Dance, Pattern, or Figure in the "*Dance Crazes of the Sixties*."
(See Novelty-&-Fad Dances-of-the-1960s.) [From *www.sixtiescity.com/Culture/dance*]

Tate: From Kingston, Jamaica, an Underground **Novelty Fad**, Singular- or Group-Dance Movement, associated with dancing **Dancehall/Ragga**, which, in turn, are outgrowths of **Ska/Reggae**. **Tate** was and is danced mainly by youths of color.

    The following is from *Ragga Fashions*: [www.bbc.co.uk]

       "*Tate - Arms are bent and legs are close together. Flap arms in time with the music (as if impersonating a chicken). Legs move from right to left simultaneously. For extra effect you can raise your clothing (shirt, jacket) as if looking for something.*"

    See **Dancehall**(2) for further explanation. [Also see Bogle, Armstrong, Butterfly, Go-Go-Wine, Body-Basic-and-Exercise, and World-Dance. Also see Jerry-Springer, Prang, Heel-and-Toe, Na!Na!Na!, Screechie, Zip-It-Up, Drive-By, Shizzle-Ma-Nizzle, Matrix, and Bin-Laden. Also see Underground Step-Listing. Also see Chicken(1), Peck, Funky-Chicken, and Chicken-Dance.]

Teenagers-Waltz: Only this name for an American **Novelty** or **Fad** of the 1960s is listed simply as a Dance, Pattern, or Figure in the "*Dance Crazes of the Sixties.*"

    (See Novelty-&-Fad Dances-of-the-1960s.) [From *www.sixtiescity.com/Culture/dance*]

Teen-Dancing: A Genre of modern dances popular with teenagers in the 1990s and 2000s are:

    1) **Ska**; 2) **Two-Tone**; 3) **Rock**; 4) **Punk-Rock**; 5) **Grunge**; 6) **New-Wave**; and 7) **Reggae**, (see **Street-Samba**.)

    See **Underground Step-Listing**. (Also see Popular Dancing, Locking-and-Popping, Hip-Hop, Break-Dancing, MTV-Style Dancing, and Street-Dancer. Also see Hard-Rock, Pop, Rhythm-and-Blues, Motown-Sound, Rap, and Heavy-Metal.) [For **Dancehall**(2) and **Ragga** Moves, see Bogle, Armstrong, Butterfly, Go-Go-Wine, Body-Basic-and-Exercise, Tate, World-Dance, Jerry-Springer, Prang, Heel-and-Toe, Na!Na!Na!, Screechie, Zip-It-Up, Drive-By, Shizzle-Ma-Nizzle, Matrix, and BinLaden.] (Also see Teamdance, Drill-Team, Military-Team, Jazz-Dance, Dance-Sneaker, and Open-Step. Also see LaBomba, Chicken-Dance, Dirty-Dancing, Lambada, Macarena, Punta y Soka, Quebradita, and Urban-Dance; which were all Novelty Fads in vogue in the 1980-90s.)

Teen-Wolf: Pantomime 1980s **Novelty Fad Singular-Dance** Hand Maneuvers, simulating dog-like Actions. How to dance the **Teen-Wolf** to the Beat is described as follows in the "*Eighties Dances*," [www.inthe80s.com]:

       "*The Teen Wolf - Place hands in a position like a dog begging in front of you above your waist like* [as if] *you are going to claw someone. Now move your arms up to the left then down and slightly bend over towards the floor then do the other side. This dance can be seen in both 'Teen Wolf' and Michael Jackson's 'Thriller'.*"

    Similar to **Churnin'-Butter, Tiffany,** and **Sprinkler**. [See Chair-Dancing. Also see Hand-Jive, Hand-Jive Routine, Hitch-Hiker, Palm-Circles(1), and Belinda. Also see YMCA, and Fila.]

Temptation-Walk: An American **Novelty Fad** dance of the late 1960s. How to dance the **Temptation-Walk** should be found on a VHS Video by Christy Lane (www.centralhome.com). This dance is mentioned in the "*Dance Crazes of the Sixties*."

Temptation-Walk had its own Eponymous song by Jackie Lee in 1968 named *Temptation Walk*.

(See Novelty-&-Fad Dances-of-the-1960s. Also see *www.sixtiescity.com/Culture/dance*]

Ten-Step: A Folkdance and **Novelty** dance popular in the U.S., this **Ten-Step** is a type of Choreographed **Country-Western** Coupledance. Danced on Same-Feet as an American Twostep in Varsouvienne Position. Danced first as a Standing-Step Pattern then with Traveling Shuffles, repeated and repeated. Only the Shuffle portion is Leadable.

For the first portion, Rhythm Timing is a *Slow* **for 10 Counts**. Both dance this **Standing-Step**; *heeltapforward closeshift, ToeTapBehind ToeTapClose, HeelTapForward LiftKneePastInFront, HeelTapForward CloseShift, heeltapforward liftkneepastinfront.*

Then comes the Forward Traveling **Shuffle** portion. Timing is *quick Quick slow, Quick quick Slow*; four times.

Note: This **Ten-Step** (first portion) Standing-Step Pattern is often incorporated repeatedly while dancing the **Polka**, (in place of the Traveling Shuffles.)

(See Ten-Count, Rocky-Top, Salty-Dog-Rag, Hook-Combination, Lindy-Charleston, and Cotton-Eyed Joe. Also see Boot-Hook, and Crooss.)

Texas-Hop: A **Novelty Fad** dance of 1966. The **Texas-Hop** was danced to the record of *"I Wish It Would Rain"* by *The Temptations*.

(See Novelty-&-Fad Dances-of-the-1960s.) [From *Soul*, www.trinity.unimelb.edu.au]

Texas-Rag: The **Texas-Rag** was a **Novelty Fad** Coupledance in vogue in the United States, somewhere in the 1900s-1910s.

(See Yankee-Tangle, Fanny-Bump, Funky-Butt, Squat, Itch, Grind, and Mooch.)

    Texas-Tommy: A **Novelty** American **C**oupledance that was popular in the 1910s. "Tommy" was slang for "prostitute" in the 19th Century.

    Texas-Tommy is believed to have begun in San Francisco about 1909, where a Johnny Peters would Perform it with Ethel Williams regularly at the Fairmont Hotel. This same Fairmont Hotel supposedly also gave birth to the "Bunny-Hug," "Turkey-Trot," and the "Grizzly-Bear." In 1913, Ethel Williams, with Partners, again Performed the **Texas-Tommy**. This time it was in *The Darktown Follies* Broadway Musical at the Lafayette Theater in Harlem.

    The **Texas-Tommy** had changed names by some to the **Mooch-and-Sugar** in 1916. By 1919, this dance was called by some the **Break-A-Way**.

    A Schottische-style dance with all Steps even Timing. Its 4/4 Time music had an Eight-Count Swing Rhythm. The four Measures long **Texas-Tommy Basic-Step**, all in a Closed Position, was a Curved Glide to the side with a Kick followed by three Curving Hops, then repeated Mirror-Image Opposite but Curved in the **same** direction. This was followed by two Glide-Hops and four short Steps. *glidesideturnRaiseRearKick hopturn HopTurn* hopturn; GlideSideTurnraiserearkick HopTurn hopturn* HopTurn. glideside hop GlideSide Hop; forward Forward forward Forward.* Each of the eight Turns in series was an Eighth-Turn or more, all Clockwise or all Counter-Clockwise, and each Eight-Count Turning series total Couple-Rotation was one Full-Turn minimum. All Hops were Slight.

    <u>Notes</u>:   1) *All three Hops could have been, at times, upon the same Foot for the Man.

           2) **Swing-Out**s and **Apache-Whip**s were probably Executed only during their **Clockwise** series of Turning. (See **Dale's-Top** with Man's *Hops* instead of *LockBehind*s.)

    This **Basic-Step** often included or was followed by a Break-Apart, with some **Break-A-Way** Pattern for one or two Measures, ending with some back together Steps, then all was repeated except all was now Turned in the **Opposite** direction.

    Many composers of that day would write Music with directions by the words of its song to its dance. The **Texas-Tommy** had its own music, *"The Original Texas Tommy Dance"*, (piano solo music by King Chanticleer,) and this sheet music possibly had directions, by the words of its song, for Steps for this particular dance.

    Texas-Tommy is said by some to have been **the Dance-Step that started Swing-Dancing**, or at least it started the **Lindy-Hop**. In the 1910s, all Coupledances were usually executed in some Closed Position, while the **Texas-Tommy** continually Broke-Apart to various Open-Facing Positions, either momentarily or for eight Counts for a **Break-A-Way**. See **Break-A-Way Glossary** for a listing of **Break-A-Way**s up to modern.

    Vernon and Irene Castle's version of the **Texas-Tommy** brought them fame.

    See **Swing-Out** for it's most characteristic Movement. Also see **Apache Dance**. (Also see Castle, Vernon and Irene. Also see Ballin'-The-Jack, Maxixe, Bunny-Hug, Grizzly-Bear, and Turkey-Trot, for dances of that time where dance directions were given in their verses.) [Much data from Sonny Watson's StreetSwing.com]

    Thang: A **Novelty Fad C**oupledance of the 1960s. It's Eponymous Music was *"We're Doin' It (The Thang)"* by *Eddie Bo*.

    (See Novelty-&-Fad Dances-of-the-1960s.) [From www.bluejuice.org.au]

    Thaxton: Only this name for an American **Novelty** or **Fad** of the 1960s is listed simply as a Dance, Pattern, or Figure in the *"Dance Crazes of the Sixties."*

    (See Novelty-&-Fad Dances-of-the-1960s.) [From *www.sixtiescity.com/Culture/dance*]

Thing: Only this name for an American **Novelty** or **Fad** of the 1960s is listed simply as a Dance, Pattern, or Figure in the "*Dance Crazes of the Sixties*."
        (See Novelty-&-Fad Dances-of-the-1960s.) [From *www.sixtiescity.com/Culture/dance*]

Thriller: A **Novelty** or **Fad** dance of an unknown time, listed in "*Novelty and fad dances*" under [http://en.wikipedia.org/wiki].

Tiffany: **Novelty Fad Singular-Dance** Head and arm Maneuvers. How to dance the **Tiffany** to the Beat is described as follows in the "***Eighties Dances***," [www.inthe80s.com]:
        "***The "Tiffany"*** - *That classic Tiffany dance where the body remained motionless while the head was bobbing forward and backward to the beat and her hand would sort of make a frame around her face by moving it horizontally and vertically next to her head and chin. I saw it mostly performed by the `mall girls' of the eighties.*"
        Similar to **Churnin'-Butter**, **Teen-Wolf** , and **Sprinkler**. (See Chair-Dancing. Also see Hand-Jive, Hitch-Hiker, Palm-Circles(1), and Belinda. Also see YMCA, and Fila.)

Tiger: Only this name for an American **Novelty** or **Fad** of the 1960s is listed simply as a Dance, Pattern, or Figure in the "*Dance Crazes of the Sixties*."
        (See Novelty-&-Fad Dances-of-the-1960s.) [From *www.sixtiescity.com/Culture/dance*]

Tiger-Rag: A **Novelty Fad** Coupledance popular in Utah about 1906.
        (See the Cake-Walk, Hoochy-Koochy, Kickapoo, and Rag-Time; which were all Novelty Fads in vogue in the 1900 to 1910 era.)

Tiger-Walk: Only this name for an American **Novelty** or **Fad** of the 1960s is listed simply as a Dance, Pattern, or Figure in the "*Dance Crazes of the Sixties*."
        (See Novelty-&-Fad Dances-of-the-1960s.) [From *www.sixtiescity.com/Culture/dance*]

Tighten-Up: An Unstructured, American **Fad** Singular or Coupledance that hardly ever came in vogue. In 1968, as Music for this dance, *Archie Bell and the Drells* sang and recorded a major hit, *Tighten Up*. It is believed that its Eponymous dance never caught on.
        (See the Novelty-&-Fad Dances-of-the-1960s.)

  <u>Time-Warp:</u> A 1980s **Novelty Fad** Group-Dance Routine.
  The following are excerpts from **"Time Warp,"** [http://en.wikipedia.org]:
        *"**The Time Warp** is a dance featured in the cult film `The Rocky Horror Picture Show,' performed during the chorus of the song of the same name. The song is both an example and a parody of the dance song genre in which much of the content of the song is given over to dance step instructions. Participation in the dance is one of the major audience-participation activities during screenings of the film. It has become a popular song beyond the reaches of the cult film, and is often played at dances and weddings. ... .*
        "The basic dance step is described in the chorus of the song:
              "It's just a jump to the left.
              And then a step to the right.
              With your hands on your hips.
              You bring your knees in tight.
              But it's the pelvic thrust   (three pelvic thrusts forward)
              That really drives you insane.
              Let's do the time-warp again.
        "After which the dancers turn around and repeat the same motions."
  How to dance the **Time-Warp** to the Music's Beat is described as follows in the **"Eighties Dances,"** [www.inthe80s.com]:
        *"**The Time Warp** - I don't know if this was nationwide, but at my college in Massachusetts we did it at*
  practically every big dance or dorm party. We were Rocky Horror freaks. Basically, you form a group and just follow the music: It's just a jump to the left, and then a step to the right. (Touch toe to the right a couple times to the music.) With you're hands on your hips, you bring your knees in tight. (Without moving your feet, lock your knees together.) But it's the pelvic thrust, (move your hips back and forth to the beat of the above words,) that really drives you insa-a-a-ane. (Move your shoulders in a circle to the beat.) Let's do the time-warp again...."
  (See Macarena, and YMCA.)

  <u>Tip-Toe:</u> Only this name for an American **Novelty** or **Fad** of the 1960s is listed simply as a Dance, Pattern, or Figure in the "*Dance Crazes of the Sixties.*"
  (See Novelty-&-Fad Dances-of-the-1960s.) [From *www.sixtiescity.com/Culture/dance*]

  <u>Toe/Heel-Walk:</u> This **Toe/Heel-Walk** is part of the **Electric-Boogie** style of **Break-Dancing**, which, in turn, is one major part of **Hip-Hop,** and is also a form of **Parallel-Travel.**
  The following is from "*Electric Boogie*," [www.actor.force9.co.uk/], which was from the book, "*Breakdancing - You can do it*":
        "This move is always done with the Mannequin dance style and is another great way of travelling around the dance floor. It involves moving sideways by spinning on the toes of one foot, and the heel of the other, and then transferring your weight onto the opposite heel and toe, and continuing. It is best done very smoothly, and makes it look like you are gliding sideways across the floor."
  Some other **Electric-Boogie** Genre of Mime "Moves" are the **Moon-Walk,** the **Lock**(2), the **Tick,** the **King-Tut,** the **Pop**(3), the **Wave**(1), the **Glides, Floating**(2), the **SlowMo,** the **Lean**(4), the **Collapse,** the **Heartbeat,** the **Bicycle**(2), the **Top-Rock,** the **Six-Step,** the **Worm,** and the **Robot.**

(Continued)

Toe/Heel-Walk: (Continued)
   Same as the **Ramble**(2), and **Traveling-Applejacks**. [See Locking-and-Popping, Mime, and Pantomime. Also see Abrupt, Head-Flick, Jerk(1)&(2), Quick, Staccato, Sharply, Smartly, Squiggle, and Snap(1)&(2). Also see Break-Dancing, Underground Step-Listing, Teen-Dancing, and Open-Step. Also see Ska, Punk-Rock, Grunge, and New-Wave. Also see Hip-Hop, MTV-Style Dancing, Street-Dancer, Lyrical-Dancer, Jazz-Dance, and Urban-Dance. Also see Rock, Hard-Rock, Pop, Rhythm-and-Blues, Motown-Sound, Rap, and Heavy-Metal.]

   Toe-Splits or **Toe-Spreads** or **Splits** or **Buttermilks** or **Click-Toes** or **Toe-Click:** An Unleadable, General In-Place-Coupledance Figure, most suitable for **Tap-**, **Line-**, and **Country-Western** dancing. Timing is either *Slow Slow* or *And Quick*. Begins with Feet Together and Weight Back on both Heels; both Toes are Rotated Outward then returned Home to Close with a Click sound.
   Similar to **Strike**(2). [See Toe-Movements, Toes-Out, Toe-Fan, Toe-Out, Chinese-Typewriter, Kid-and-Play, Bronco-Twist, Corkscrew(2), Swivet, SugarFoot, Sand-Step, Toe-Tap, and Ramble(2). Also see Tap-Dance Genre.]

   Toe-Stands or **Toe-Walk:** Unleadable General Singular, Coupledance, or Group-Dance **Movements**, mostly related to the **Tap-Dance Genre**. Done In-Time-with-the-Music.
   "TOE STANDS: A movement of the old school of tap wherein the dancer is on the points of both feet. Can also be done on one foot at a time -- Toe Stand." [From *"TAP!"* by *Rusty E. Frank*]
   The following is from *"Eighties Dances"* - [www.inthe80s.com]:
   *"**Toe-stand:** A Michael Jackson move done immediately at the end of either the moonwalk or spin. Simply stand on the very tips of your toes and bend your knees so it looks like you are sitting in air. Can be done by standing up straight, standing on the inner-front part of your feet."*
   Similar to **On-Points**, and **In-Releve Position**. (See On-Pointe, Demi-Pointes, Releve, Monter, Toe-Dancing, Pique, and Foot-Positions-on-Floor. Also see Ballet, Tip-Toe, Pee-Wee-Herman, Done-in-Toe, and Pointe-Shoes. Also see Novelty-&-Fad Dances-of-the-1980s.)

   Tootsie-Roll: A **Novelty Fad** dance of 1960. The **Tootsie-Roll** had its own Eponymous record, *"Tootsie Roll"* by *Bobby Martin*.
   (See the Novelty-&-Fad Dances-of-the-1960s.) [From *Soul*, www.trinity.unimelb.edu.au]

   Train: A **Novelty Fad** dance of the 1960s. The **Train** had its own Eponymous record, *"Do the Train"* by *Little Joe Cook & The Thrillers*.
   (See the Novelty-&-Fad Dances-of-the-1960s.) [From *Soul*, www.trinity.unimelb.edu.au]

   Train-Stomp: Only this name for an American **Novelty** or **Fad** of the 1960s is listed simply as a Dance, Pattern, or Figure in the *"Dance Crazes of the Sixties."*
   (See Novelty-&-Fad Dances-of-the-1960s.) [From *www.sixtiescity.com/Culture/dance*]

Trance: A **Novelty Fad** **C**oupledance of the 1960s. It's Eponymous Music was "*The Trance*" by *Count Drac (Bobby Saver)*, and "*The Trance*" by *Gary Shelton.*
(See Novelty-&-Fad Dances-of-the-1960s.) [From www.bluejuice.org.au]

Traveling-SugarFoot or **Cross-and-Swivel** or **Sugar:** Two possibly Leadable Coupledance Figures that Travel Sideways, Left or Right Mirror-Image. Suitable for the **Charleston**, both **Quickstep**s, and the **Swing-Bal** portion of the **Balboa**, among other dances. One of the forms of **Parallel-Travel**.
Danced in Loose-Closed Position or in Butterfly Position; Heels-In, Heels-Out, Heels-In, Heels-Out. Timing is *Slow Slow Slow Slow*. To dance **Traveling-SugarFoot** to Man's **Right**:
Man dances *crossbehindlower SideSwivelFoot1/4CCWRise crossbehindSwivelFoot1/4CWlower SideSwivelFoot1/4CCWRise.*
Lady dances *CrossBehindLower sideswivelfoot1/4CCWrise CrossBehindswivelfoot1/4CWLower sideswivelfoot1/4CCWrise.*
(See SugarFoot, Charleston-Kick, Side-Kick, Knee-Knock, and Arm-Flail. Also see Sand-Step, NightLife, and Suzy-Q. Also see Balboa Step-Listing.)

Trot: Only this name for an American **Novelty** or **Fad** of the 1960s is listed simply as a Dance, Pattern, or Figure in the "*Dance Crazes of the Sixties.*"
(See Novelty-&-Fad Dances-of-the-1960s.) [From *www.sixtiescity.com/Culture/dance*]

Truck or **Truckin':** An Unleadable, American **Novelty Fad** way of Stepping, Solo or as a Couple, perhaps originating with minstrel shows of the 1830s. There was **Truckin'** by African-Americans in the early 1930s, and **Truckin'** became very popular with the Whites in 1937. After separating from one's Partner while dancing the **Lindy-Hop** or **Balboa**, one will often **Truck** to return back Together.
Singularly Performing particular Actions or Movements, with delayed type Walks Traveling Forward for eight Steps. One would **Shuffle along while shaking their Right index finger Raised High**. Facials were made while Stepping Slightly Pigeon-Toed with an 8-Count Shuffling gait, and one's shoulders would Rise-and-Fall. One's finger that Points Up would be wiggled like a windshield wiper. One dances *forstepswivel1/8CCW ForStepSwivel1/8CW*, etc.
For the **Big-Apple**, **Truckin'** was one of the **Break-A-Way** Genre. Wiggling their hips, certain **Separated-Break-A-Way** Patterns were danced. The original **Suzie-Q, Boogie-Back, Tack-Annie, Georgia-Grind, Praise-Allah!, Truckin', Peckin', Charleston, Shorty-George,** and other Break-A-Ways, were probably originated early by blacks; while **Spank-the-Baby, Rusty-Dusty, Pose-and-a-Peck**, the **Little-Apple**, the **Little-Peach, Mess-Around, Stomp-Off, Apple-Jacks,** and **Fall-Off-the-Log**, and other Break-A-Ways, were probably originated later by whites. Most all of these Patterns seem to have been influenced or derived from the classic **Lindy-Hop** and/or **Big-Apple** dances. See **Break-A-Way Glossary** for a more complete listing.
(Usually associated with Peck.)

Truckin': See Truck.

'T'-Time: A Structured but Unleadable, **Novelty** Pattern for a Singular-Dancer; a 2 1/2-Measures Pattern. This **'T'-Time** Pattern is one of the Qued Steps often Called for while dancing the **Madison** Audience-Participation-Dance's Basic-Step.

The following is an excerpt from *Madison Figures* -- [www.sixtiescity.com/Culture/]:
"*Chasse to the left and close with RF. Star jump to arms outstretched (T) position. Jump back to normal arms down position. Chasse to place, extending arms on each step R.*"

The following are excerpts from *The Madison* -- [www.albertj.btinternet.co.uk/]:
"*LS, LS, stand feet together and do a star jump, take two steps backwards starting with the right foot.*"

The following is an excerpt from *The Madison* -- [www. rossmernyk.com/swing]:
"*T Time: 2 Up 4 Counts, do a jumping jack Q Q, 2 Back 4 Counts.*"

(See Double-Cross, Cleveland-Box, Basketball, Big-'M', Jackie-Gleason, Birdland, and Rifleman. Also see the Novelty-&-Fad Dances-of-the-1960s.)

Tumba-Cha: A **Novelty Fad**, 1950s Latin Rhythm Coupledance.

(Also see the Bambuco, Bop, Bunny-Hop, Calypso, Creep, Fish, Flea-Hop, Frug, Guapacha, Hand-Jive, Hokey-Pokey, Hullie-Gullie, Jerk, Limbo-Rock, Mashed-Potato, Monkey, Pachanga, Plena, Pony, Rock-and-Around, Scooter, Slide, Strole, Surfers, Swim, Twist, Twister, and the Watusi; which were all Novelty Fads in vogue in the 1950-60s.)

Turkey-Neck-Stretch: A **Novelty Fad** Coupledance of the 1960s. This had its own Eponymous record, the "*Turkey Neck Stretch*" by *Gradie O'Neal*.

(See Novelty-&-Fad Dances-of-the-1960s.) [From www.bluejuice.org.au]

Turkey-Trot(1): A Fast, **Novelty Fad** Coupledance, popular in America from about 1903 to 1910. But others say it originated from a 1912 New York musical show named "*Over the River*". There is a report dated February 1912 of the **Turkey-Trot** being banned in Annapolis.

The following is from *Sonny Watson's Dance History* -- [www.streetswing.com]:
"*1910s - A Patterson, New Jersey court imposed a fifty day prison sentence on a young woman for dancing the Turkey-Trot.*"

Some say that the **Turkey-Trot** had its own music, and that its sheet music had directions, by the words of its song, for Steps for this particular dance.

The **Turkey-Trot** was danced to a Fast and Syncopated 4/4 Ragtime Beat with an `oom-pah' bass, such as Scott Joplin's "*Maple Leaf Rag*".

The **Turkey-Trot** achieved its popularity mainly as a result of its being denounced by the Vatican. With rears protruding, it was danced in a Closed Position with all arms wrapped tightly around each other, the Man's above, which was thought to be scandalously licentious at the time, and denounced as "lingering close contact".

The **Turkey-Trot** Basic Step was four Hopping Steps Sideways, first on one leg then on the other. Embellished with Scissor-like Foot Flicks, the dance was a One-Step Fast **Trot**ting Promenade with shoulder and waist Wriggles, and with abrupt stops. Arms would be Pumped at their sides, with occasional arm-Flapping, hense the name "**Turkey**".

(Continued)

Turkey-Trot(1):   (Continued)
[See the Boston-Dip, Gaby-Glide, Hug-Me-Close, Lame-Duck, and Shiver-Dance; which were all novelty Fads in vogue in the 1910s. Also see Texas-Tommy, Maxixe, Bunny-Hug, Grizzly-Bear, and Ballin'-The-Jack, for dances of that time where dance directions were given in their verses. Also see Animal-Dances (such as Bunny-Hug, and Grizzly-Bear), for Coupledances of that time with some type of animal's name. Also see Flap(3).]

Turkey-Trot(2):   This same Fast, **Novelty Fad** Coupledance was resurrected in 1963. In 1963, the singing 45rpm record of "*Let's Turkey Trot*" by *Little Eva* was available for dancing.
    (See Novelty-&-Fad Dances-of-the-1960s.) [From *Soul*, www.trinity.unimelb.edu.au]

Twirl: Only this name for an American **Novelty** or **Fad** of the 1960s is listed simply as a Dance, Pattern, or Figure in the "*Dance Crazes of the Sixties.*"
    (See Novelty-&-Fad Dances-of-the-1960s.) [From *www.sixtiescity.com/Culture/dance*]

Twine: An Unstructured, American **Novelty Fad** Singular or Coupledance in vogue in the 1960s. In 1965, *Alvin Cash and The Crawlers* recorded *Twine Time*. There were probably Eponymous dance Movements named **The Twine**. With new dances every week, not all caught on nationally. As songs came out in 1965, so did a corresponding dance, and few of either lasted more than a few weeks.
    (See the Novelty-&-Fad Dances-of-the-1960s.)

Twist or **The Twist:** A 1958-60 **Novelty Fad** Singles Dance or a Coupledance. The **Twist** was danced Apart, Unstructured and Unleadable, Facing each other, to 4/4 Time in moderate Tempo. Rhythm Timing was *Slow Slow Slow Slow*.
    The **Twist**'s Basic look was a Swiveling Action of the hips alone, Clockwise and Counter-Clockwise, with shoulders Torqued in the opposite Rotation; pelvic Gyrations in which Torso and hips are Twisted with counter-action. Basic Step is similar to vigorously toweling one's tush, while Lowering Well Into-the-Knees and Stepping to one side and then to the other, with Body-Swaying Side-to-Side dancing the Hand-Jive Routine.
    Of American origin, The **Twist** was written by a black musician in Georgia in 1958. He and some of his band members made up particular Twisting Movements for his musicians to do while playing The **Twist** music, then *Chubby Checker* made his **Twist** record called "*Let's Do The Twist!* " in 1960. The **Twist** was an innovation by the male stage dancers for the black R&B artist, *Hank Ballard*, who first recorded the song "*The Twist.*" *Chubby Checker* made an exact copy in 1960, and *Chubby* made this dance, The **Twist**, a hit in Philadelphia. The craze started by *Chubby Checker*'s appearance on American Bandstand singing its Eponymous song. The following are a few excerpted lines from his words to it:
            "*You should see my little sis,*
            She knows how to rock and she knows how to twist
            Ee oh twist, baby, baby, twist [round and round and a round and a]
            Just, just like this [round and a round] *come on little miss and do the twist.*"
                                        (Continued)

Twist: (Continued)

The **Twist** went to New York, New Jersey, then to the rest of the U.S. and to most world countries. There is a report dated October 1961 of The **Twist** traveling up the social ladder. There was the movie, "*Twist Around the Clock*," featuring *Chubby Checker*. In addition to *Chubby Checker*'s 1960 record, "*Let's Do The Twist!* ", there was also, in 1962 for this **Twist** dance, *Joey Dee*'s "*Peppermint Twist*," and the *Isley Brother*'s "*Twist And Shout*." Also in 45rpm singing records during that time, there were "*Let's Twist Again*" by *Chubby Checker*, "*C.C. Twist*" by *C.C. & The Vagabonds*, "*Soul Twist*" by *King Curtis*, and "*Twistin' The Night Away*" by *Sam Cooke*.

The **Twist** was banned in Buffalo, New York, on 26 January 1962. **Twist**, along with other silly Fad-Dances, was banned at Brigham Young University in 1966.

"*It changed forever the way we dance. Arriving at the dawn of that decade of liberation, the swinging '60s, the Twist not only emancipated dancers from their partners, and from a host of social conventions into the bargain, but put an end to the awful tyranny of ability: It took almost no time or talent to learn the basics. `Put out a cigarette with both feet, wiping off your bottom with a towel,' instructed Checker. It was the dance everyone could do, and - so it would seem - everyone did.*

"----. *But wherever revellers of a certain age gather to dance to the hits of their youth, you'll see it again, the step everyone remembers and anyone can do.*" -- [From www.geocities.com/danceinfosa.]

"*The Twist was a guided missle, launched from the ghetto into the very heart of suberbia. The Twist succeeded , as politics, religion, and law could never do, in writing in the heart and soul what the Supreme Court could only write on the books.*" -- Eldridge Cleaver

"*And we love to dance -- especially that new one called Civil War Twist. The Northern part of you stands still while the Southern part tries to secede.*" -- Dick Gregory

The **Twist** was wildly popular but only for a brief time, yet the **Twist** fostered many similar U.S. Novelty dances. The **Frug** was derived from The **Chicken**, which had been related to The **Twist**. Later from The **Frug**, there were derived The **Swim**, The **Monkey**, The **Dog**, The **Watusi**, The **Waddle**, and The **Jerk** dances. The dancers' Body attitudes seemed to express "doing your own thing."

[See Body-Rotation, Twisted-Waist, Scalene-Muscles, Mashed-Potato, Louie-Louie, Quiver, Belinda, Charleston, and Charleston-Crosses. Also see Novelty-Dances, Fad-Dances, Novelty-and-Fad Genre, and the Novelty-&-Fad Dances-of-the-1960s. Also see Afro-Twist, Chicken-Back-Twist, Corrido-Twist, Florida-Twist, Funky-Twist, Jamaican-Twist, Kangaroo-Twist, Kangaroo-Tail-Twist, Kosher-Twist, Moon-Step-Twist, Peppermint-Twist, Peter-Gunn-Twist, Shimmy-and-Twist, Shoot'em-Up-Twist, Sloppy-Twist, Spanish-Twist, Sugartime-Twist, Tango-Twist, Twist-and-Freeze, Twist-and-Limbo, Twist-and-Shout, Twister, and Wombat-Twist. Some data is from Dan VanArsdale, www.eijkhout.net, and www.hankster.hypermart.net.]

Twist-and-Freeze: An American **Fad** Coupledance of the 1960s that must have been a takeoff of **The Twist**. Still, this had its own Eponymous record, the "*Philadelphia Twist & Freeze*" by *Orlie & the Saints*.

(See Novelty-&-Fad Dances-of-the-1960s.)

[From *www.bluejuice.org.au*. See *www.sixtiescity.com/Culture/dance*.]

Twist-and-Limbo: Only this name for an American **Fad** of the 1960s is listed simply as a Dance, Pattern, or Figure in the "*Dance Crazes of the Sixties*." This must have been a takeoff of **The Twist**.

 (See Novelty-&-Fad Dances-of-the-1960s.) [From *www.sixtiescity.com/Culture/dance*]

Twist-and-Shout: An American **Fad** dance of 1960 that must have been a takeoff of **The Twist**. Still, this **Twist-and-Shout** had its own Eponymous record, "*Twist And Shout*" by *The Isley Brothers*.

 (See Shout-Dance. Also see Novelty-&-Fad Dances-of-the-1960s.)
 [From *Soul*, www.trinity.unimelb.edu.au]

Twister or **The Twister:** A **Novelty Fad** Coupledance that appeared in the U.S. in the 1950s. Derived from Eastern Swing, and not related to the Twist.

 (Also see the Bambuco, Bop, Bunny-Hop, Calypso, Creep, Fish, Flea-Hop, Frug, Guapacha, Hand-Jive, Hitch-Hiker, Hokey-Pokey, Hullie-Gullie, Jerk, Limbo-Rock, Mashed-Potato, Monkey, Pachanga, Plena, Pony, Rock-and-Around, Scooter, Slide, Strole, Surfers, Swim, Tumba-Cha, Twist, Twister, and the Watusi; which were all Novelty Fads in vogue in the 1950-60s. Also see Novelty-&-Fad Dances-of-the-1960s.)

Twitch: An American **Novelty** or **Fad** dance of 1963. The **Twitch** had its own Eponymous record, "*The Twitch*" by *Danny White*.

 (See Novelty-&-Fad Dances-of-the-1960s.) [From *Soul*, www.trinity.unimelb.edu.au]

Twostep: An American **Novelty** or **Fad** Coupledance of 1970. It's usual Music was "*Me And Mrs. Jones*" by *The Dramatics*. This particular "**Twostep**" might have been a takeoff from the Traditional **Twostep**(1) or of the newly emerging **Country-Twostep**.

 [See Twostep(1)-and-Country-Twostep Differences, and Novelty-&-Fad Dances-of-the-1960s.]

 [From *www.bluejuice.org.au*. See *www.sixtiescity.com/Culture/dance*.]

Typewriter: In comical Pantomime, an Unleadable 1960s American **Novelty** Singular dance Routine that Traveled Forward. The ten-Measure dance Mimicked a **Typewriter**, and was one of a whole series of 1960s Mimicking dance Patterns. The following **Typewriter** Movements probably originated from The **Hullie-Gullie** dance Mime game about 1963. Mimicking The **Typewriter** in operation, the following Pattern was in vogue at Brigham Young University, Provo, Utah. This silly **Typewriter**, along with other silly Fad-Dances, was later banned in 1966 at the same University.

Danced at a 4/4 medium Tempo with *Slow Slow Quick Quick Slow* Rhythm as for ChaCha. The **Typewriter** was danced usually to Rock music, in Lines Formation and in an open Shine Position. All commenced upon their Left Foot:

Danced *fortouch ripple Close inplace InPlace*; *ForTouch Ripple close InPlace inplace*; (Repeat.) *ForStep MoveCarriage Stomp stomp Stomp.* (Repeat all.)

See **Ripple** for how to Ripple.

Move-the-Carriage as follows: With Weight upon Right Foot Forward, push Head Turned Left by four Right fingertips at Right side of nose.

The **Typewriter** re-emerged **in the 1980s**, again as a **Novelty** Singular dance Routine. The following is from "*Eighties Dances*" - [www.inthe80s.com]:

"*Typewriter: Seen in Kool Moe Dee's video, 'Wild Wild West.' Motion yourself sideways, move one whole leg, and motion the other in the typewriter mode.*"

(See Chinese-Typewriter, Pantomime, Mime, and Mimicry-En-Masse. Also see Novelty-&-Fad Dances-of-the-1980s.) [Data mostly from "Rhythm and Dance" by Alma Heaton.]

Ubangi-Stomp: Only this name for an American **Novelty** or **Fad** of the 1960s is listed simply as a Dance, Pattern, or Figure in the "*Dance Crazes of the Sixties.*"

(See Novelty-&-Fad Dances-of-the-1960s.) [From *www.sixtiescity.com/Culture/dance*]

Uncle-Willie: An American **Novelty** or **Fad** dance of the 1960s. This had its own Eponymous record, "*Uncle Willie*" by *Plookie McLine*.

(See Novelty-&-Fad Dances-of-the-1960s.)

[From *www.bluejuice.org.au.* See *www.sixtiescity.com/Culture/dance.*]

Underdog-Back-Street: An American **Novelty** or **Fad** dance of 1968. This **Underdog-Back-Street** had its own Eponymous record, "*Underdog Back Street*" by *Warren Lee*.

(See Novelty-&-Fad Dances-of-the-1960s.) [From *Soul*, www.trinity.unimelb.edu.au]

Underwater: Only this name for an American **Novelty** or **Fad** of the 1960s is listed simply as a Dance, Pattern, or Figure in the "*Dance Crazes of the Sixties.*"

(See Novelty-&-Fad Dances-of-the-1960s.) [From *www.sixtiescity.com/Culture/dance*]

Unwind-Twine: Only this name for an American **Novelty** or **Fad** of the 1960s is listed simply as a Dance, Pattern, or Figure in the "*Dance Crazes of the Sixties.*"

(See Novelty-&-Fad Dances-of-the-1960s.) [From *www.sixtiescity.com/Culture/dance*]

Urban-Dance: An American underground, **Novelty Fad**, Singles-Dance form, associated with **Hip-Hop** and **Rap**; similar to the more aggressive New York style **Break-Dancing** or Rocking.   Involves **Locking-and-Popping**.   In vogue in 1997, (see MTV-Style Dancing, and Break-Dancing.)   Certain **Urban-Dance** Styles predate **Hip-Hop**.

(See Teen-Dancing, and Open-Step.   Also see Ska, Punk-Rock, Grunge, and New-Wave. Also see Street-Dancer, Lyrical-Dancer, and Jazz-Dance.   Also see Rock, Hard-Rock, Pop, Rhythm-and-Blues, Motown-Sound, Rap, and Heavy-Metal.   Also see LaBomba, Chicken-Dance, Dirty-Dancing, Lambada, Macarena, Punta y Soka, Quebradita, and Teen-Dancing; which were all Novelty Fads in vogue in the 1980-90s.)

Urban-Street-Dancing: See Hip-Hop, and Street-Dancing.

Urkel or **Do-The-Urkel** or **Steve-Urkel-Dance:**   A very funny **Novelty Fad** dance developed from the 1990s TV sitcom *'Family Matters.'*

The following are excerpts from *the Urkel*; [www.answers.com]:

"... *portrayed as an archtypical nerd, with large, thick eyeglasses, 'high-water' pants held up by suspenders, and a high-pitched voice with a snorting laugh. Highly intelligent, he was also quite accident-prone and socially awkward. ...*

"*In the 1991 episode 'Life of the Party,' Urkel creates a dance called 'The Urkel' to help win friends at school. ...* :

"*Now if you want to do the Steve Urkel Dance, All you have to do is hitch up your pants*

Bend your knees and stick up your pelvis, I'm tellin you baby, it's better than Elvis

Do it   Do it   Everybody Do the Urkel Dance.
Now point your fingers up to the sky, And talk through your nose way up high
Spin and dip and jump and cavort, And finish it off with a laugh and snort
Heh Heh Heh [Snort]   Heh Heh Heh [Snort], Heh Heh Heh Heh Heh Heh Ohhhhh

Do it   Do it   Everybody Do the Urkel Dance."

U.T.:   A **Novelty Fad** Coupledance of 1962.   This had its own Eponymous record, *"The U.T."* by *The Sparkles.*

(See Novelty-&-Fad Dances-of-the-1960s.   Especially see Hip.)   [From www.bluejuice.org.au]

Valentino Tango: An American Tango Style of Coupledance, ideally suited for beginners. The dreamy **Valentino Tango** is danced to a Slower Tempo, 30 MPM or less, in Syncopated 2/4 Cut-Time.

    The **Valentino Tango** is danced with Rocks, Swivels, and Fan Movements. Its Basic-Step is common with that for the American Tango, and it is Patterned upon the Man taking the Five-Step-Basic-Tango, (three Forward Walking Steps, a Right Sideward-Step, a Tango-Draw then a Tango-Close.) Basic-Step Rhythm Timing is _slow Slow, slow Quick Hold, slow Hold._ The Tango-Close finish without Weight can have several Foot Stylings, (see Brush-Tap.) This subject Basic-Step is danced Starting in Closed, Banjo, or in Promenade Positions; the Lady is Picked-Up from being in these last two Positions.

    A simple version of the **American Tango**. [See Basic-Step(4), and Contest Tango.]

Valse-Classique or **Castle-Valse-Classique:** A **Novelty Fad** Coupledance in vogue from about 1912 to about 1918. Some say more than a hundred new Coupledances were invented between 1912 and 1914. **Vernon and Irene Castle** invented many of these, and one was this **Valse-Classique**.

    (See the Castle-Walk, Lame-Duck, Castle-Tango, Last-Waltz, Castle-Combination, and the Maxixe; all written by the Castles. Also see the Boston-Dip, Bunny-Hug, Gaby-Glide, Hug-Me-Close, Shiver-Dance, and Turkey-Trot; which were all Novelty Fad dances in vogue in the 1910s.)

Varsity-Drag: A wild, **Novelty Fad** Coupledance in vogue for a short while in the late 1920s and was credited to Donald Tomkins. Its song made it the most famous of all the "_drag dances._" The **Varsity-Drag** was probably first introduced as a Charleston-style dance number in the hit 1927 stage show "_Good News._" Later in the movie "_Good News_" in 1947, Donald Tomkins danced it with Ruth Mayon.

    One of at least two dances inspired by the Charleston, this naughty-and-nice dance suited the time. Nevertheless, this **Varsity-Drag** "_show dance_" that was popularized didn't last long, although its song by that name is still around. "_Do The Varsity Drag!_" song was composed by Ray Henderson with lyrics by Buddy DeSylva and Lew Brown. Its song's words are as follows:

        "_This is the drag, see how it goes;_
        Down on your heels and up on your toes;
        That's the way to do the Varsity Drag."

    Varsity-Drag's most memorable Pattern was with Partners Coupledancing in Shadow Position, at times not touching; instead, with arms wide and elevated, both would stretch in Sequence, Bending from Side-to-Side while dancing Charleston-Kicks.

    Other "_drag dances_" of the time were the A-Minor-Drag, Dizzy-Drag, Saratoga-Drag, Shoe-Shiner's-Drag, Slow-Drag, and the Viper's-Drag. (Also see Black-Bottom, and the Shimmy; both Fads in vogue in the 1920s.) [Much from www.streetswing.com/ & www.musicals101.com/]

    Veleta: A **Novelty** Coupledance popular in England in 1900 through at least 1912. **Veleta** was also a Sequence-Dance, a Sequence-Waltz Choreographed by Arthur Morris. Dancing-Masters had created a Choreographed Sequence-Dance movement by 1900 for the working class in the outskirts of London, England, through which hundreds of dancers would memorize this **Velveta** Waltz among other Coupledances, which were then at times called "Saunters."

    The following is an excerpt from "*Bush Dance & Music Club of Bendigo Inc.*" from [http://home.vicnet.net.au/]:

       "*... quite significantly the **Veleta Waltz**, the first perceived choreographed sequence dance, was entered in 1899 but it didn't win a place. The music publishers 'Francis, Day & Hunter' noted its potential and with the cooperation of the arranger Arthur Morris, it was re-vamped and introduced as a new dance in 1900. The **Veleta** was not really the first of the competition dances. ...*"

    The following is an excerpt from "*Centenary of Federation Ball Programme*" from [http://www.users. bigpond.net.au/]:

       "***Veleta Waltz** -- Choreographed by Arthur Morris in England in 1900, is a credited with being the first sequence dance of that style that led to an influx of English sequence dances, later to be known as 'Old Time' and 'New Vogue' in a modernise form in Australia. The **Veleta Waltz** also qualifies as a Colonial dance, just making it at the close of the 19th century and Victorian Era. Charlie Reardon recalled it arriving at Nariel about 1912. It was popular on programs for many years.*"

    (See Boston-Dip, Gaby-Glide, Hug-Me-Close, and Shiver-Dance; which were all Novelty Fads in vogue in the 1910s. Also see Texas-Tommy, Maxixe, and Ballin'-The-Jack, for dances of that time, where dance directions were given in their Eponymous verses. Also see Animal-Dances, Bunny-Hug, Lame-Duck, Grizzly-Bear, and Turkey-Trot, for Coupledances of that time with some type of animal's name. Also see Sauter-Dance.)

    Viper's-Drag: An American **Novelty Fad** Coupledance (or possibly just a tune) in vogue in the 1910s or `20s. Other "*drag dances*" of the time were the A-Minor-Drag, Dizzy-Drag, Saratoga-Drag, Shoe-Shiner's-Drag, Slow-Drag, and the most famous **Varsity-Drag**.
    (See Animal-Dances.)

    Voodoo-Mash: A **Novelty Fad** Coupledance of the 1960s. This had its own Eponymous record, "*Voodoo Mash*" by *Shalimar & His Friends*.
    (See Novelty-&-Fad Dances-of-the-1960s.) [From www.bluejuice.org.au]

Waddle or **Wabble:** An Unstructured and Unleadable, 1960s **Novelty** or **Fad** American Singular Traveling dance. The dance Mimicked a person **Waddl**ing, and was one of a whole series of 1960s Mimicking dance Patterns, (see Hullie-Gullie.) Having been at least partially derived from the **Frug**, the **Waddle** was related to the **Swim**, the **Monkey**, the **Dog**, the **Watusi**, and the **Jerk** dances. Danced In-Place, dancers **Waddle**d and Swung hips Side-to-Side, with certain added arm Movements. This silly **Waddle**, along with other silly Fad-Dances, was banned at Brigham Young University in 1966.

Waddles are Charlie-Chaplin Tilting Steps, very short and Flat with Toes pointed Outward. Arms and Hands are Held at sides with Palms-Down. Swaying, the hip Opposite the Stepped Foot protrudes (Side-Stretch) as the Lower-Body Torques with CBM.

The following is from *Dance Crazes of the Sixties* - [From *www.sixtiescity.com/Culture/dance*]:

"*The Waddle: 1. Shake the water off your back. 2. Strut your stuff. 3. Get up, get loose. 4. Walk choppy like a long-neck goose.*"

Same as or similar to **Penguin**, and **Duck**. (See the Novelty-&-Fad Dances-of-the-1960s.)

Wah-Watusi: Only this name for an American **Novelty** or **Fad** of the 1960s is listed simply as a Dance, Pattern, or Figure in the "*Dance Crazes of the Sixties*." This must have been a takeoff from **The Watusi**.

(See Watusi, and Novelty-&-Fad Dances-of-the-1960s.)

[From *www.sixtiescity.com/Culture/dance*]

Wak-A-Cha: Only this name for an American **Novelty** or **Fad** of the 1960s is listed simply as a Dance, Pattern, or Figure in the "*Dance Crazes of the Sixties*."

(See Novelty-&-Fad Dances-of-the-1960s.) [From *www.sixtiescity.com/Culture/dance*]

Walk: An American **Fad** dance of 1958. The **Walk** had its own Eponymous record, "*The Walk*" by *Jimmy Mccracklin*.

(See Novelty-&-Fad Dances-of-the-1960s.)

[From *Soul, www.trinity.unimelb.edu.au.* See *www.sixtiescity.com/Culture/dance.*]

Walkin'-the-Dog(1): A **Novelty Fad** Singular-Dance (and at times Coupledance) of 1916 and later. Without lyrics, this Music was Composed by ***Sheldon Brooks***, (see Darktown-Strutters'-Ball for further data.)

The following is an excerpt from *www.cstone.net/*:

"--- [Sheldon] *Brooks wrote some instrumental numbers and sometimes performed as a trap drummer. His 1916 instrumental number, which he named 'Walkin' the Dog' inspired a dance of the same name in Manhattan that soon spread to the rest of the country* [United States]."

This **Walkin'-the-Dog**(1) was resurrected almost 50 years later. [See **Walkin'-the-Dog**(2).]

[Also see Cake-Walk, Shorty-George, and High-Stepping.]

Walkin'-the-Dog(2) or **Walk-the-Dog:** A **Novelty Fad** Singular-Dance of 1964. Probably danced similar to **Walkin'-the-Dog**(1), this **Walk-the-Dog** had continuous small Forward Tripling Steps accompanied by Slight Forward Bows, while Traveling.

      Walk-the-Dog had its own Eponymous record, "*Walkin' The Dog*" by Rufus Thomas. [From "*Soul*," www.trinity.unimelb.edu.au]

      Similar to a minutely-Stepped **Cake-Walk**. [See Majorette-Strutting-with-Baton, Moon-Walk, SideSlide, Camel-Walk(3), Boogie, and Sissy-Walk. Also see Novelty-&-Fad Dances-of-the-1960s.]

Wallop: An American **Fad** dance of 1962. The **Wallop** had its own Eponymous record, "*The Wallop*" by *The Tabs*.

      (See Novelty-&-Fad Dances-of-the-1960s.)

      [From *Soul*, www.trinity.unimelb.edu.au. See www.sixtiescity.com/Culture/dance.]

Wamboo: An American **Fad** dance of 1962. This had its own Eponymous record, "*The Wamboo*" by *Del Shannon*.

      (See Novelty-&-Fad Dances-of-the-1960s.) [From *www.bluejuice.org.au*.]

War-Canoe: Only this name for an American **Novelty** or **Fad** of the 1960s is listed simply as a Dance, Pattern, or Figure in the "*Dance Crazes of the Sixties*."

      (See Novelty-&-Fad Dances-of-the-1960s.) [From *www.sixtiescity.com/Culture/dance*]

Warm-Up: An American **Fad** dance of the 1960s. This had its own Eponymous record, "*The Warm Up*" by *Clifton White*.

      (See Novelty-&-Fad Dances-of-the-1960s.) [From *www.bluejuice.org.au*.]

Washboard-Rub: An Unleadable, Singular, General, Purposeful Body-Language **Novelty** Gesture, Movement, or Flourish in Pantomime. **Washboard-Rub** Gestures, a part of the Line-Dance "*Dirty Laundry*," are Executed as follows while dancing around: With Clenched-Fists Held Together In-Front of the dancer's Body, fingers-Down and with Slightly bent elbows, both Fists are continually Bobbed Up-and-Down Together in Time with the Music. Movement is as if the dancer was scrubbing clothes upon an old washboard. (This pretended "*Washboard*" is a non-existent object.)

      (See Arms-and-Hands, Gestures-Free-Hand, and Free-Hand-Fashioning. Also see Chair-Dancing.)

Washing-Machine(1): A 1990s American **Novelty Fad**. Four Singular Figures or Patterns, two for the **Right-Hip-Washing-Machine**, and two for the **Left-Hip-Washing-Machine**, Mirror-Image Opposite. The **Washing-Machine** is for General **C**oupledancing but was originally for **Salsa**, as danced in the movie "*Salena*". This descriptive name comes from that movie, and was named by and Performed by the original *Salina*:

(1) **Positioning:** One's Weight is Balanced over a *Side-Step* Flat on the first Beat with legs Spread 16 inches. With Side-Stretching the hip of one's Supporting-Leg, the Free-Toe is Pointed.

(2) **Start:** With Feet remaining In-Place and with one's initially **Supporting-Foot remaining Flat throughout**, Weight is Transferred Sideways onto one's Free Ball-of-Foot with Softened Knee to Start Rotation. Ball-of-Foot **remains on same Ball-of-Foot** throughout **Washing-Machin**ing.

(3) **Washing-Machine:** One's Weight is fully Transferred from Side-to-Side with each **Full Circle Hip-Action**, actively **Rotating** either Clockwise or Counter-Clockwise to the music.

(4) **Recovering:** Finally, after the specified number of hip Rotations, one *Recovers Flat-Footed* from Ball-of-Foot with Softened-Knee.

Similar to **Hip-Rocks**, **Boogie-Roll**(1), and **Broken-Sways**. (See Hip-Motion, Hip-Bumps, Snake-Hips, Hip-Lift, Side-Lift, Sway, Switch-Sway, Bumps-and Grinds, Metronomic-Motion, Pendulum-Motion, Hip-Waves, Side-Rise, Body-Lift, Cuban-Motion, Figure-Eight, Forward-Roll, Shimmy, Side-Body-Waves, Sensuous, Sinuous, and Grinds. Also see Knee-Drape, Up-and-Over-the-Top, Arm-Waves, Body-Wave, and Body-Ripple. Also see Exotic-Dancer, Belly-Dance, Hula-Dance, Sexercise-Dance, GoGo-Dancer, Cage-Dancer, Perreo, Juking, and PassaPassa. Also see Burlesque with its Strip-Tease.)

Washing-Machine(2): A 1960s American **Novelty Fad** Coupledance Swiveling Routine that was partially Leadable. The dance Mimicked a **Washing-Machine**, and was one of a whole series of 1960s Mimicking dance Patterns. The following **Washing-Machine** Movements probably originated from The **Hullie-Gullie** dance Mime game about 1963. The following Pattern was in vogue at Brigham Young University, Provo, Utah. This silly **Washing-Machine**, along with other silly Fad-Dances, was later banned in 1966 at the same University.

With 4/4 Rhythm Rock music at medium Tempo, the **Washing-Machine** was a 16 Measures long Routine that Mimicked one in operation. It was danced entirely in Butterfly Position and upon Opposite Footwork. Solidly Toned arms were maintained to help each other Swivel and keep Balanced.

Swivel-and-Kick: With Free Foot In-Back of Supporting Foot, Swivel back and forth upon Balls-of-Feet Toward side of Supporting-Foot seven Counts. Forward-Kick then repeat Opposite-Feet. Repeat all 4 times.

Kick-Step: Upon Forward-Kicking, Hop Back upon Supporting-Foot.

Toe-Toe: During Swiveling, Lower Deep-Into-Knees.

(See the Novelty-&-Fad Dances-of-the-1960s.) [Data mostly from "Rhythm and Dance" by Alma Heaton.]

Washington-Post-Twostep: An American **Novelty Twostep** Coupledanced to its own particular Music. John Philip Sousa composed the *Washington Post March* in 1889 or 1891, to which this Quick 5/8 Meter Twostep was danced, with a Skip in each Step. It became popular for a short period when brought to England in 1894.

[See the **Twostep**(1)**-and-Country-Twostep Differences.** Also see the Twostep(1), and Saltair Pavilion. Also see the Grizzly-Bear, Lanciers, and Money-Musk; which were all Novelty Fads in vogue in the late 1800s.]

Wash-Wash or **Wash:** An American **Fad** dance of 1963. The **Wash-Wash** had its own Eponymous record, "*Wash Wash*" by *Prince Buster*.

(See the Novelty-&-Fad Dances-of-the-1960s.)

[From *Soul*, www.trinity.unimelb.edu.au. See www.sixtiescity.com/Culture/dance.]

Watusi: An Unstructured and Unleadable, 1960s **Novelty Fad**, Singles dance of American origin. In 1964, *Jay, Bob and The Hawks* put out "*The Watusi*," "*The Ska*," and "*The Monkey*" records. Perhaps they did not originate the songs. Also for music, *Orlons* is mentioned and "*The Wah-Watusi.* " Also, there was "*The Watusi*" records by both *The Vibrations* and *Richard Berry*.

The **Watusi** was one of a whole series of 1960s Mimicking dance Patterns, (see Hullie-Gullie.) The **Watusi** originally had Smooth but small Leaping Movements, some with a Slight Ripple. It is believed that The **Watusi** Dance, itself, was first inspired by the fabulous black dancers in a scene from the movie, "*Treasure of King Solomon's Mines*," in which their dancing Traveled considerably with much Float and Head Sweeps. Others say The **Watusi** was derived from The **Frug**, because, viewing later dancers, one could see that The **Watusi** was influenced by The **Swim**, The **Monkey**, The **Dog**, The **Waddle**, and The **Jerk** dances. Danced In-Place, dancers did Hip-Lifts and often Swung hips Side-to-Side, with certain added arm Movements, some as if Throwing spears while others were The **Swim** Motions. This silly **Watusi**, along with other silly Fad-Dances, was banned at Brigham Young University in 1966.

The following is from *Dance Crazes of the Sixties* - [From www.sixtiescity.com/Culture/dance]:

"***The Watusi*** *(Dance to moderate tempo)*

"*Stance: Stand with your feet about 12 inches apart. Keep both knees bent at all times. Pretend you are going to take a golf swing.*

"*Hip Movement: On the count of one, shift weight to right foot, making right hip move out to the right. On the count of two, shift weight to left foot, making left hip move out to the left. Move from side to side with hips swinging right to left to a 1-2, 1-2 rhythm.*

"*Arm Movement: Hold arms out in front of you as if you were holding a golf club. Swing hands to your right, then down in a semi-circular motion to your left, back to right, then to left, counting 1-2, 1-2.*

"*Putting Them Together: Now do the hand and hip movements simultaneously from right to left on a count of 1-2.*"

(See Wah-Watusi, Watusi-Boogaloo, and Watusi-Wussi'-'Wo, and Werewolf-Watusi. Also see the Novelty-&-Fad Dances-of-the-1960s.)

Watusi-Boogaloo: An American **Fad** dance of the 1960s. This had its own Eponymous record, "*Watusi Boogaloo*" by *Willie Rosario*. This must have been a takeoff from **The Watusi**.
(See Novelty-&-Fad Dances-of-the-1960s.) [From www.bluejuice.org.au]

Watusi-Wussi'-'Wo: Only this name for an American **Novelty** or **Fad** of the 1960s is listed simply as a Dance, Pattern, or Figure in the "*Dance Crazes of the Sixties*." This must have been a takeoff from **The Watusi**.
(See Novelty-&-Fad Dances-of-the-1960s.) [From *www.sixtiescity.com/Culture/dance*]

Wa-Wabble: Only this name for an American **Novelty** or **Fad** of the 1960s is listed simply as a Dance, Pattern, or Figure in the "*Dance Crazes of the Sixties*."
(See Novelty-&-Fad Dances-of-the-1960s.) [From *www.sixtiescity.com/Culture/dance*]

Weasel: An American **Fad** dance of the 1960s. This had its own Eponymous record, "*The Weasel*" by *Little Eddie.*
(See Novelty-&-Fad Dances-of-the-1960s.)
[From *www.bluejuice.org.au.* See *www.sixtiescity.com/Culture/dance.*]

Wedge: Only this name for an American **Novelty** or **Fad** of the 1960s is listed simply as a Dance, Pattern, or Figure in the "*Dance Crazes of the Sixties*."
(See Novelty-&-Fad Dances-of-the-1960s.) [From *www.sixtiescity.com/Culture/dance*]

Werewolf-Watusi: Only this name for an American **Novelty** or **Fad** of the 1960s is listed simply as a Dance, Pattern, or Figure in the "*Dance Crazes of the Sixties*." This must have been a takeoff from **The Watusi**.
(See Novelty-&-Fad Dances-of-the-1960s.) [From *www.sixtiescity.com/Culture/dance*]

Whammy: Only this name for an American **Novelty** or **Fad** of the 1960s is listed simply as a Dance, Pattern, or Figure in the "*Dance Crazes of the Sixties*."
(See Novelty-&-Fad Dances-of-the-1960s.) [From *www.sixtiescity.com/Culture/dance*]

Whatchama-Call-It: Only this name for an American **Novelty** or **Fad** of the 1960s is listed simply as a Dance, Pattern, or Figure in the "*Dance Crazes of the Sixties*."
(See Novelty-&-Fad Dances-of-the-1960s.) [From *www.sixtiescity.com/Culture/dance*]

Wheel: Only this name for an American **Novelty** or **Fad** of the 1960s is listed simply as a Dance, Pattern, or Figure in the "*Dance Crazes of the Sixties*."
(See Novelty-&-Fad Dances-of-the-1960s.) [From *www.sixtiescity.com/Culture/dance*]

Whip: There were two Eponymous versions of this **Fad** dance.   One was danced in 1964 to *"The Whip Part 1"* U.S.A. Record by *Billy The Kid Emerson.* The other was danced in 1968 to *"The Whip"* Jamaican Record by *The Ethiopians.*
> (See Novelty-&-Fad Dances-of-the-1960s.)
> [From *Soul, www.trinity.unimelb.edu.au.* See *www.sixtiescity.com/Culture/dance.*]

Whiplash: An American **Fad** dance of 1964. The **Whiplash** had its own Eponymous record, *"The Whiplash"* by *The Shells.*
> (See Novelty-&-Fad Dances-of-the-1960s.)
> [From *Soul, www.trinity.unimelb.edu.au.* See *www.sixtiescity.com/Culture/dance.*]

Whirl: Only this name for an American **Novelty** or **Fad** of the 1960s is listed simply as a Dance, Pattern, or Figure in the *"Dance Crazes of the Sixties."*
> (See Novelty-&-Fad Dances-of-the-1960s.) [From *www.sixtiescity.com/Culture/dance*]

Whirlwind-Waltz: A **Novelty Fad** Coupledance. Created in 1907, the **Whirlwind-Waltz** was said to have similarities with the **Apache Dance**, in that in one part, each Partner would alternately swing the other by the arms in a Circle to Waltz Time. It was Performed in the "Passing Show of 1912".

Whisk: Only this name for an American **Novelty** or **Fad** of the 1960s is listed simply as a Dance, Pattern, or Figure in the *"Dance Crazes of the Sixties."*
> (See Novelty-&-Fad Dances-of-the-1960s.) [From *www.sixtiescity.com/Culture/dance*]

Whoopee: Only this name for an American **Novelty** or **Fad** of the 1960s is listed simply as a Dance, Pattern, or Figure in the *"Dance Crazes of the Sixties."*
> (See Novelty-&-Fad Dances-of-the-1960s.) [From *www.sixtiescity.com/Culture/dance*]

Wibble: Only this name for an American **Novelty** or **Fad** of the 1960s is listed simply as a Dance, Pattern, or Figure in the *"Dance Crazes of the Sixties."*
> (See Novelty-&-Fad Dances-of-the-1960s.) [From *www.sixtiescity.com/Culture/dance*]

Wiggle: A **Novelty Fad** Coupledance of 1962. This had its own Eponymous record, *"The Wiggle"* by *Jack Hammer.*
> (See Novelty-&-Fad Dances-of-the-1960s.) [From www.bluejuice.org.au]

Wiggle-Wobble: Only this name for an American **Novelty** or **Fad** of the 1960s is listed simply as a Dance, Pattern, or Figure in the *"Dance Crazes of the Sixties."*
> (See Novelty-&-Fad Dances-of-the-1960s.) [From *www.sixtiescity.com/Culture/dance*]

Wiggle-Worm: An infamous, **Novelty Fad** Coupledance, that was in vogue in America circa 1910.

The following is from *Sonny Watson's Dance History* -- [www.streetswing.com]:

"*1910 - Sophie Tucker was arrested for singing the Grizzly Bear and the Wiggle Worm dance songs in a night club (stage magazine- 1938.)*"

[See Animal-Dances (such as Bunny-Hug, and Turkey-Trot), for Coupledances of that time with some type of animal's name.]

Wild-Stomp: Only this name for an American **Novelty** or **Fad** of the 1960s is listed simply as a Dance, Pattern, or Figure in the "*Dance Crazes of the Sixties.*"

(See Novelty-&-Fad Dances-of-the-1960s.) [From *www.sixtiescity.com/Culture/dance*]

Wild-Weekend: Only this name for an American **Novelty** or **Fad** of the 1960s is listed simply as a Dance, Pattern, or Figure in the "*Dance Crazes of the Sixties.*"

(See Novelty-&-Fad Dances-of-the-1960s.) [From *www.sixtiescity.com/Culture/dance*]

Willy-Nilly: A **Novelty Fad** dance of 1965. The **Willy-Nilly** had its own Eponymous record, "*Willy Nilly*" by *Rufus Thomas*.

(See Novelty-&-Fad Dances-of-the-1960s.) [From *Soul*, www.trinity.unimelb.edu.au]

Wobble: An American **Fad** dance of 1964. The **Wobble** had its own Eponymous record, "*The Wobble*" by *L.C. Cooke*.

(See Novelty-&-Fad Dances-of-the-1960s.)

[From *Soul, www.trinity.unimelb.edu.au.* See *www.sixtiescity.com/Culture/dance.*]

Wobble-Cha: An American **Fad** dance of the 1960s. This had its own Eponymous record, the "*Wobble Cha*" by *Cool Benny*. This must have been a takeoff from the **ChaCha**.

(See Novelty-&-Fad Dances-of-the-1960s.) [From *www.bluejuice.org.au*]

Wobble-Drum: Only this name for an American **Novelty** or **Fad** of the 1960s is listed simply as a Dance, Pattern, or Figure in the "*Dance Crazes of the Sixties.*"

(See Novelty-&-Fad Dances-of-the-1960s.) [From *www.sixtiescity.com/Culture/dance*]

Wobble-Lou: An American **Fad** dance of the 1960s. This had its own Eponymous record, the "*Wobble Lou*" by *Hector & The Eastmen.*

(See Novelty-&-Fad Dances-of-the-1960s.) [From www.bluejuice.org.au]

Wombat-Twist: A **Novelty Fad** Coupledance of the 1960s. This had its own Eponymous record, the "*Wombat Twist*" by *Glenn & Christy.*

(See Novelty-&-Fad Dances-of-the-1960s.) [From www.bluejuice.org.au]

Woodpecker or **Charleston**: An Unleadable Coupledance Pattern, suitable for both **Quickstep**s. Rhythm with 4/4, Eight-Count-Timing is *Slow Slow Slow Quick Quick, Slow Slow Slow Quick Quick.*

Danced in Loose-Closed Position. Each Slow is a **Hop-Tap**, (*And Quick.*) Lady dances Mirror-Image to Man.

Man dances *hopTapBehind hopChangetapbehind HopchangeTapBehind TapBehind TapBehind*, then Mirror-Image Opposite, *Hoptapbehind HopchangeTapBehind hopChangetapbehind tapbehind tapbehind.*

Lady dances *Hoptapbehind HopchangeTapBehind hopChangetapbehind tapbehind tapbehind*, then Mirror-Image Opposite, *hopTapBehind hopChangetapbehind HopchangeTapBehind TapBehind TapBehind.*

Note: These In-Place **Woodpecker**s are most often accompanied by **Side-Switches**, and preceded by the swiftly flowing **Scatter-Chasses**.

[See Woodpecker-Taps, Hop-Scotch(2), and Side-Switches.]

Woodpecker-Taps or **Hop-Taps**: An Unleadable Coupledance Movement, suitable for both **Quickstep**s. Any number of tiny Hops or Rises on one Foot, simultaneously Tapping Toe of Opposite Foot Behind one's Supporting-Foot and beyond. Timing is *And Quick* for each **Woodpecker-Tap**.

Similar to **Dot**. [See Woodpecker, Hop-Scotch(2), and Side-Switches. Also see Scatter-Chasses, and Floating-Chasse.]

World-Dance: From Kingston, Jamaica, an Underground **Novelty Fad**, Singular- or Group-Dance Movement, associated with dancing **Dancehall/Ragga**, which, in turn, are outgrowths of **Ska/Reggae**. **World-Dance** was and is danced mainly by youths of color.

The following is from *Ragga Fashions*: [www.bbc.co.uk]

"*World-Dance - Stand with legs apart, arms hanging down. Flick left foot forward and outwards keeping the leg fairly rigid. As you kick swing the opposite shoulder forward with a jerk, allowing the arm to swing round loosely. Repeat movement with opposite leg and shoulder.*"

See **Dancehall**(2) for further explanation. (Also see Bogle, Armstrong, Butterfly, Go-Go-Wine, Body-Basic-and-Exercise, and Tate. Also see Jerry-Springer, Prang, Heel-and-Toe, Na!Na!Na!, Screechie, Zip-It-Up, Drive-By, Shizzle-Ma-Nizzle, Matrix, and Bin-Laden. Also see Underground Step-Listing.)

Worm: A comical **Novelty** and **Break-Dancing** Rippling Move in Layout; i.e., one of the **Basic-Moves-for-Break-Dancing**. The **Worm** is a Movement Performed during Floor-Work, (`Floor-Rock' or `Down-Rock' dancing.)

In 1968, *Lloyd Robinson* put out the Eponymous 45rpm singing record, "*The Worm.*" [From *Soul*, www.trinity.unimelb.edu.au]

The following is from "*Definition of Breakdancing*," [www.wordiq.com]:

"*The Worm: A move in which a dancer lies on the ground and form a rippling motion through his body. This can be done in one of two ways, either forward or backwards, either shifting your weight from the upper body to the lower body (backwards) or vice-versa for forwards. Sophie Tucker is recognized as the creator of this move, which goes back to the 1920's.*"   (Continued)

<u>**Worm**</u>:   (Continued)

The **Worm** re-emerged **in the 1980s**, again as a **Novelty** Singular Movement. The following is from "*Eighties Dances*" - [www.inthe80s.com]:

"*You lay down flat on your stomach and kind of push your body up and down* [to the Beat] *as you go forward. It was big with break dancers.*"

Similar to the **Centipede**, and the **Caterpillar**. [See Six-Step, and Layout(1) face Down with arms Forward. Also see Ripple, Body-Wave, Side-Body-Waves, Continuous-Body-Waves, and Shimmy. Also see other listed Basic-Moves-for-Break-Dancing; the Top-Rock, the Moon-Walk, and the Six-Step. Also see Underground Step-Listing. Also see Novelty-&-Fad Dances-of-the-1980s.]

<u>**Wrangler-Stretch:**</u>   Only this name for an American **Novelty** or **Fad** of the 1960s is listed simply as a Dance, Pattern, or Figure in the "*Dance Crazes of the Sixties*."

(See Novelty-&-Fad Dances-of-the-1960s.) [From *www.sixtiescity.com/Culture/dance*]

<u>**Yak-A-Poo:**</u>   A **Novelty Fad** Coupledance of the 1960s. This had its own Eponymous record, the "*Yak-A-Poo*" by *Lattimore Brown*.

(See Novelty-&-Fad Dances-of-the-1960s. Especially see Shake-and-Vibrate.) [From www.bluejuice.org.au]

<u>**Yale-Blues-SugarStep:**</u>   A **Novelty Fad** Coupledance popular in England in 1929.

<u>**Yankee Doodle:**</u>   An old American Folk Country-Dance.

<u>**Yankee-Tangle:**</u>   **The Yankee-Tangle** was a **Novelty Fad** Coupledance in vogue in the United States, somewhere in the 1900s-1910s.

(See Texas-Rag, Fanny-Bump, Funky-Butt, Squat, Itch, Grind, and Mooch.)

<u>**YMCA**</u>:   Classified herein as in the **Audience-Participation-Dance** Category, and as both a **Novelty** Dance and **Fad** Dance, **YMCA** is the name of a **Group-Dance** fashioned to fit a particular Eponymous song:

This **YMCA Group-Dance** is a repeating Pattern danced Quickly in sequence, almost entirely by arm-Positioning forming letters: "**Y**" is formed by Straight legs Together at "attention", and with Straight **arms Raised forming a "V"**. "**M**" is formed, with Straight legs Together at "*attention*", by **elbows Raised High and forearms Drooping**. "**C**" is formed, with Straight legs Together and Waist Arched protruding Left, by **Curved Left arm High and Curved Right arm Low**. "**A**" is formed by **Straight legs Astride with Straight arms Down at the sides**.

The **YMCA** Eponymous song has a Marching Disco Beat. This funny 1978 song by *The Village People* keeps hollering "**YMCA**"! It's lyrics carry a hidden homosexual message.

The **YMCA** organization has numerous facilities where men, when in town, can stay overnight and usually swim.

The **YMCA** initials stand for **Young Men's Christian Association**.

(See Fila. Also see Macarena, and Time-Warp.)

<u>Yolk</u>: A **Novelty Fad** Coupledance of the late 1960s. This had its own Eponymous record, "*The Yolk*" by *Harvey Scales*.
(See Novelty-&-Fad Dances-of-the-1960s.) [From www.bluejuice.org.au]

<u>Yo-Yo</u>: Only this name for an American **Novelty** or **Fad** of the 1960s is listed simply as a Dance, Pattern, or Figure in the "*Dance Crazes of the Sixties*."
(See Novelty-&-Fad Dances-of-the-1960s.) [From *www.sixtiescity.com/Culture/dance*]

<u>Yuletide-Jerk</u>: Only this name for an American **Novelty** or **Fad** of the 1960s is listed simply as a Dance, Pattern, or Figure in the "*Dance Crazes of the Sixties*."
(See Novelty-&-Fad Dances-of-the-1960s.) [From *www.sixtiescity.com/Culture/dance*]

<u>Zig-Zag</u>: Only this name for an American **Novelty** or **Fad** of the 1960s is listed simply as a Dance, Pattern, or Figure in the "*Dance Crazes of the Sixties*."
(See Novelty-&-Fad Dances-of-the-1960s.) [From *www.sixtiescity.com/Culture/dance*]

<u>Zip-It-Up</u>: From Kingston, Jamaica, an Underground **Novelty Fad**, Singular- or Group-Dance Movement, associated with dancing **Dancehall/Ragga**, which, in turn, are outgrowths of **Ska/Reggae**. **Zip-It-Up** was and is danced mainly by youths of color.
The following is from *Ragga Fashions*: [www.bbc.co.uk]
"*Zip-It-Up - Stand with feet close together. Rotate the knee of one leg in a full circle forwards and outwards, raising the foot in the movement. Follow through the knee movement with a slight rotation to the hips. Repeat with the other leg.*"
See **Dancehall**(2) for further explanation. Same as **Knee-Drape**. (Also see Bogle, Armstrong, Butterfly, Go-Go-Wine, Body-Basic-and-Exercise, Tate, and World-Dance. Also see Jerry-Springer, Prang, Heel-and-Toe, Na!Na!Na!, Screechie, Drive-By, Shizzle-Ma-Nizzle, Matrix, and Bin-Laden. Also see Underground Step-Listing.)

<u>Zizzle</u>: Only this name for an American **Novelty** or **Fad** of the 1960s is listed simply as a Dance, Pattern, or Figure in the "*Dance Crazes of the Sixties*."
(See Novelty-&-Fad Dances-of-the-1960s.) [From *www.sixtiescity.com/Culture/dance*]

<u>Zombie-Stomp</u>: A **Novelty Fad** Coupledance of the 1960s. This had its own Eponymous record, "*The Zombie Stomp*" by *Danny Ware*.
(See Novelty-&-Fad Dances-of-the-1960s.) [From www.bluejuice.org.au]

<u>Zonk</u>: Only this name for an American **Novelty** or **Fad** of the 1960s is listed simply as a Dance, Pattern, or Figure in the "*Dance Crazes of the Sixties*."
(See Novelty-&-Fad Dances-of-the-1960s.) [From *www.sixtiescity.com/Culture/dance*]

Zorba's-Dance or **Syrtaki:** A **Novelty Fad** Coupledance in vogue in 1965.
(See Novelty-&-Fad Dances-of-the-1960s, and the Miserloo-Folkdance.)
[Some from *Novelty Dances Through the Years* by Pony Moore.]